Dylan Jones is Group Editor of *Arena* and *Arena Homme Plus*. Formerly a senior editor at the *Observer* and the *Sunday Times*, he has also worked for the *Independent*, the *Guardian* and *Mojo*, and has a long association with *The Face*. Between 1989 and 1992 he was Editor of *Arena*, for which he won Magazine Editor of the Year in 1992. He has written various books on pop culture including the international best-selling biography *Jim Morrison: Dark Star; Easy! The Lexicon of Lounge; Sex, Power and Travel: Ten Years of Arena*; and a recent portrait of Paul Smith, *True Brit*. He is 36 years old and lives in London.

SCEPTRE

Meaty Beaty Big & Bouncy!

Classic Rock and Pop Writing from Elvis to Oasis

Edited by DYLAN JONES

SCEPTRE

First published in 1996 by Hodder and Stoughton
First published in paperback in 1997 by Hodder and Stoughton
A division of Hodder Headline PLC
A Sceptre Paperback

10 9 8 7 6 5 4 3 2 1

British Library Cataloguing in Publication Data

Meaty beaty big & bouncy! classic rock
and pop writing from Elvis to Oasis
1. Rock music in literature
2. Rock music – Literary collections
I. Jones, Dylan
808.8'49357

ISBN 0 340 67434 2

Printed and bound in Great Britain by
Mackays of Chatham PLC, Chatham, Kent

Hodder and Stoughton
A division of Hodder Headline PLC
338 Euston Road
London NW1 3BH

For Sarah, of course

'Journalists are a species of foul vermin. I mean, I wouldn't hire people like you to guard my sewer.'

— Lou Reed

ACKNOWLEDGEMENTS

As well as thanking all the authors for allowing their work to be included here, I would also like to acknowledge the help of Mel Agace, Simon Prosser, Tony Peake, Peter Blake, Robin Derrick, Simon Kelner, Robin Morgan, Kathryn Flett, Gordon Burn, Tony Elliott, Helen Gallacher, Simon Reynolds, Nick Logan, Art Collins, Jane Krupp, Georgina Knight, Alyson Schenck, Jann Wenner, Tom Wolfe, Neil Spencer, Terry Jones, Paul Du Noyer and The New York City Library. Also a very special thank you to Adrian Deevoy, Robert Sandall, Sean O'Hagan and Tony Parsons, as well as to Pete Townshend, obviously.

CONTENTS

INTRODUCTION

The Devil Still Has All The Best Tunes

In the interests of expediency, both financial and creative, origins have often been the work of journalists. The expression 'rock'n'roll' was not invented by a journalist, strangely, but by a DJ, the legendary Alan Freed, who coined the term in the early Fifties having stolen it from a 1922 blues lyric ('My baby rocks me with a steady roll') revived in 1952 by Big Joe Turner. But as a catalyst he might as well have been a journalist, helping shape the way that 'rock'n'race' became the modern soundtrack of young America. It was self-aggrandisement as much as anything, and Freed's pitch for youth power and money was reflected in everything he said and played on the air. 'Hey kids,' he'd cry to listeners on WINS and WABC, New York, 'they can't do that to us!' And he'd emphasise it by playing Jackie Wilson's latest, 'I'll Be Satisfied' or the Isley Brothers' 'Shout' all night long.

Music journalism has come a long way in the last 40 years, from cod-sociological scare mongering in the national press and cod-sycophantic adulation in teen magazines, to a thriving industry which supports hundreds and thousands of newspapers, magazines and fanzines; and has multi-media exposure through radio, TV, video and the Internet — and of course local bookshops, which are now full of the collected writings of everyone from Tom Wolfe, Philip Norman, Tony Palmer, Nik Cohn and Joan Didion to Charles Shaar Murray, Lester Bangs, Ian

Penman and Simon Reynolds. Decoding pop is now an industry of gigantic proportions, and the arcane delights of Rock'n'Roll Past can today be accessed from your local W.H. Smith, Waterstones or Helter Skelter.

Back in the Sixties, when rock journalism was in its infancy, great pieces of writing stood head and shoulders above the rest. These days the rest is pretty much as good as the best. Music journalism has become so commonplace, so everyday, that true opinion, true experience and true style have become difficult to find, not to mention difficult to trust. Reading a lot of rock writing nowadays you start to wonder why the people involved picked up a pen in the first place.

These days the lingua franca of the rock'n'roll lifestyle has become a cliché, an all-too-easily drawn litany. In fact the *ur*-myth of Beatledom (a lifetime squeezed into ten short years) is now so well known, so much a part of modern British history that it can be emulated (at least in theory) by fledgling pop stars from places as far apart as Leningrad and Auckland. When Rod Stewart wanted to be a pop star he was more or less escaping the drudgery of the production line; these days his job comes with a pension plan. It's not surprising that pop journalism has become a cliché too.

It wasn't always this way.

In the beginning there was sex, drugs and rock'n'roll, though there was always room along the way for a little pathos, despair and the occasional accidental overdose. Great rock stars have always been larger than life, figures with a grand sense of tragedy and spectacle – boys and girls, men and women incandescent with self-belief. This was once true of rock journalists, too. Whereas once they were seen as a glorified extension of the public relations business, during the late Sixties and early Seventies they became stars in their own right, solitary young men (mainly) who somehow – usually through a mixture of tenacity, belligerence, luck and an impressive capacity for drugs – managed to worm their way into the eye of the storm while still able to capture the euphoria, the madness, the sadness, and the arbitrary nature of the rock star's lot. 'Loud music made by self-destructive white boys was what I wanted to write about,' says Nick Kent. 'The Stones, the Stooges, the New York Dolls. I wasn't interested in temperance, I was devoured by rock'n'roll. I wasn't interested in Lord Byron, as I was hanging out with the Byron of the Seventies, Keith Richards. I wanted to speak up for the counter-culture – this was life in the extreme.'

As is all rock journalism, good rock journalism, that is: writing which doesn't just grapple with rock'n'roll's own Heart of Darkness and Hollow Soul, but that which enlightens and uplifts us, that entertains us and makes us laugh. The music business is an absurd, salacious, unwieldy monster, and the only way to do it justice is to treat it as such. The true spirit of rock has less to do with sociology and rather more to do with excess, indulgence and the gratification of intense, wanton desires (and that's just the roadies).

As we all know, a lot of rock stars are just big, bad-tempered babies ('You have to be a bastard to make it, and that's a fact,' said John Lennon many moons ago, 'And the Beatles are the biggest bastards on earth'); they have bigger egos than politicians, tougher lawyers than movie producers or mobsters, and libidos not seen (or felt) since the last days of Rome. Charlie Watts, whilst watching Margaret Trudeau pose for pictures with the Stones sometime in 1977, said, to no one in particular, 'I wouldn't want *my* wife associating with us.'

For many bands over the years, trashing your accommodation, abusing the help, and misbehaving generally became *de rigueur*. This organised mayhem can be traced back through Led Zeppelin, the Rolling Stones and others, but mostly the blame lies firmly with Keith Moon. As Robert Chalmers writes in 'King of Wreck'n'Roll', 'Moon, more than any other artist, provided what truth there was in the definition of "Rock Stars" tirelessly fostered by the tabloid press: musicians whose immense wealth and capacity for drink and drugs allowed them to indulge their seemingly insatiable appetite for hotel-wrecking free from fear of the Wrath of God or the Test and County Cricket Board . . . Wrecking of all kinds became increasingly acceptable: there were even reports that one hotel manager (Edgewater Hotel, Seattle,

1972) who had just watched Led Zeppelin toss a number of televisions into the sea, expressed a desire to join in, and accepted Peter Grant's invitation to "have one on us".

'It was, above all, Moon's 21st birthday party – celebrated, with typical impetuousness, a year early, at the Holiday Inn, Flint, Michigan (23/8/67: Ruined suite/Piano/Six cars required respraying/Lincoln Continental in Pool) – that set the standard for the next decade and helped to establish the main events (television out of window/car treated as amphibious vehicle etc) at which Moon turned out to be a gifted and enthusiastic all-rounder.'

There were journalists who did this sort of thing, too, those who involved themselves in Warp Factor hedonism just for the heck of it. Journalists who turned it all the way up to eleven. Others were less indulgent, but just as cavalier. 'Not having been to a place never stopped me from describing it. Any more than not meeting someone stopped me talking about my interview with them,' says Nik Cohn, author of *Awopbopaloobop Alopbamboom*! – one of the first and most enduring books on pop. There are many stories concerning Cohn's embellishment – on a press trip to the Caribbean, he apparently fabricated a mugging in order to jazz up his copy – though his most famous attempt at decoration involves the feature he wrote for *New York* magazine in 1976; 'Tribal Rites Of The New Saturday Night' focused on a nightclub in the New York suburb of Bay Ridge, called Odyssey 2001, where disco had firmly taken root. This essay was the basis for Robert Stigwood's mirrorball behemoth *Saturday Night Fever*, although a lot of it was pure fiction: unable to infiltrate Odyssey's tightly knit groups of dance disciples, and believing that 'nasty pieces of work aged 19 are the same in any country, any generation', Cohn decided to base his characters on the Mods he had known in Shepherd's Bush ten years previously. Remarkably, no one noticed.

Towards the end of the Eighties I became embroiled in a biography of Jim Morrison and over the course of six months travelled to Paris and New York, meeting Morrison's wife and many of his friends and associates. But one key figure proved elusive: Danny Sugerman, who co-wrote the notorious Doors biography *No One Here Gets Out Alive*. Having created his own little industry from posthumous Doors-related material, he didn't appear inclined to help any rival biographers.

I persisted, as there were certain questions about Morrison that I thought only Sugerman could answer. Having tried unsuccessfully to get through to him, I asked a friend to help. This he did by drafting a letter to Sugerman, a letter that began: 'Dear Danny, You might remember me. I once OD'd in your bathroom with Iggy Pop in 1974 . . .' Only Nick Kent could have written a letter like that.

One of the foremost music journalists of his generation, Kent made his name as a writer on the *NME* in the early Seventies, alongside Charles Shaar Murray, Ian MacDonald, Tony Tyler, Mick Farren and the late Pete Erskine – young men plucked from the underground press who wielded their pens like machetes. Frank Zappa once said that 'rock journalism is people who can't write, preparing stories based on interviews with people who can't talk, in order to amuse people who can't read'. This is churlish in the extreme, though Kent – like many of his peers – was never just a music journalist. Like Hunter Thompson, Nik Cohn and Lester Bangs before him, there exists around Kent an almost mythic glow. Degenerate poseur, celebrity drug addict and genius wordsmith, he is a man who has lived rock'n'roll to the full. 'I could tell you stories about Nick Kent that would uncurl the hair in your afro,' said Morrissey in 1990.

Predictably, this culture of ego and spite became a trap of sorts, establishing a role for the music journalist as uberhack, the gonzo journo as superstar. Being a drugged-up, shook-up, Biro-toting longhair became a fully-fledged career. Free records, concert tickets, meals, drink, drugs, sex and trips to America – these were the pop writer's lot, a giddy cocktail of abuse, corruption and damn good fun. But as Jon Savage writes in the introduction to his own anthology, *Time Travel*, 'The [pop] weeklies were, and remain, pure pop with rock window-dressing: great for learning in public, but you burn out quickly.' Just look at Nick Kent, a superstar scribe who took to drugs like ducks do to water, or Rolls-Royces take to swimming pools. Equanimity, you see, was never really his thing.

During the Seventies Kent was as famous for his drug intake as he was for his journalism, and from 1974 to 1988 was addicted to heroin, cocaine, methadone and various tranquillisers. 'At the age of 19 I started smoking hashish in earnest,' he says, 'and then moved on to speed and cocaine. Finally I was offered some heroin, and that was it for me. It was like being in heaven, it was ecstasy. I thought: this is worth getting lost for. I was on a death trip – I was into smack, cocaine, valium, all kinds of things. If I hadn't got myself off I would be into crack by now. I should be insane, or dead.'

Kent wasn't alone in his quest for the 'total experience': Hunter Thompson's gonzo reporting is well documented, while Lester Bangs was a one-man orgy of abandon and excess; when a doctor told him he was courting death by living on a diet of cough syrup and belladonna, he switched to shooting speed. Even Tom Wolfe was a maverick in his own way, spending months on Ken Kesey's magic bus researching *The Electric Kool-Aid Acid Test,* his white seersucker suit and button-down shirts totally at odds with the Merry Pranksters around him.

'Any record company launch in the Seventies was a complete scrum,' says *The Observer* critic, and ex-*NME* man Neil Spencer. 'You saw the most appalling things; every music critic in London seemed to take it for granted that they had to behave as disreputably as possible, as often as possible.' Journalists would regularly pick fights with each other, steal each other's drugs, and abuse any rock star who came within spitting distance. And the abuse took many forms: one female journalist only agreed to interview Iggy Pop on the condition that he make a pass at her (he did); while another asked to see a famous rock guitarist's cock, only to be shown his gun. 'It was a totally mental time,' says Spencer. 'It reminds me of something Charles Shaar Murray once said: "Rock'n'roll is full of stupid people pretending to be intelligent, and intelligent people trying to look stupid." It's still quite difficult to tell them apart.'

In the early Seventies sex and drugs came with the territory, as they still do to a certain extent (standing in a toilet cubicle with a girl in one hand and a rolled up £10 note in the other). When Kent kicked into gear, rock journalism was going through one of its golden periods. Due largely to *NME* editor Nick Logan, during the Seventies the paper became legendary in Britain for its acerbic, cynical and occasionally puerile attitude towards the music industry in general and rock stars (*any* rock star) in particular.

Because of its irreverent nature, it was remarkably easy for the paper to cope with the onslaught of punk, hiring another batch of angry young men and women who liked nothing better than by-turns championing and rubbishing their heroes, often in the space of a few days (why annihilate Genesis and Barclay James Harvest when you could have a pop at Joey Ramone or the Stranglers?). Tony Parsons, Julie Burchill, Danny Baker, Paul Morley, Angus MacKinnon and Ian Penman were among the more notorious punk and post-punk *NME* writers, later alumni including Sean O'Hagan, Mat Snow, Stuart Cosgrove, Alan Jackson, James Brown, Barney Hoskyns, Andy Gill, Andrew Collins, Cynthia Rose, Danny Kelly and Steve Sutherland.

The paper couldn't ride the Zeitgeist forever though, and at various times in the Eighties became a home for recalcitrant pseuds – young men with handshakes like fish whispers who would act all meek and mild during interviews and then turn into vitriolic traffic wardens as soon as they sat down at their typewriters. Young writers dissecting a culture of margins surrounding a collapsed centre, they were destined for obscurity. Shrill voices in the dark? You had to hear them to believe it.

The tempo was elsewhere. As the influence of the traditional British music press – *NME, Melody Maker, Sounds, Record Mirror* etc – began to wane, new agendas were being set by EMAP in one camp, and by the style press in another. East Midlands Allied Press began their move into music magazine publishing with the launch of *Smash Hits* in 1978 (an idea conceived for them by Nick Logan); from there they branched out with *Q* (initiated by Mark Ellen), *Seleet* (bought from a rival publisher when it began to look shaky) and then *Mojo*, well targeted magazines which celebrated the power of pop with humour, a librarian's attention to detail and, perhaps crucially, the common touch. The style press – a pejorative term if ever there was one – also drew up their own charter (*i-D, Blitz* and *The Face* all launched at the decade's dawn), becoming the cultural barometer the inkies had been just ten years before. Music had to fight harder to warrant space in magazines which also featured film directors, fashion designers and footballers, and tended to shout a little louder when it won.

In the Eighties, Fleet Street started poking its nose in, using Culture Club, Frankie Goes To Hollywood and Duran Duran to create various 'pop wars'. British pop then was more successful abroad than at any time since the mid-Sixties, and this global interest, the flamboyant nature of Boy George, Annie Lennox et al, and the brazen – almost compliant – way in which the new groups made themselves available to the dailies, made for a great media spectacle. After 30 years, in Britain at least, pop had become a front page tabloid staple.

In America, the market had for years been dominated by the rock bible *Rolling Stone,* a talismanic tip-sheet which didn't inspire any serious competition until the launch of *Spin,* in the mid-Eighties. There was *Creem* and *Crawdaddy* and what have you, but nothing which infected the mainstream. Now there are *Vibe, Details, Raygun* and a dozen other titles devoted to the thoughts and theories of pop stars and music journalists, and, much like Britain, you are as likely to find the definitive portrait of Oasis, Alanis Morissette or Radiohead in a Sunday supplement or a men's glossy as you are in the music press. These days the *NME* has to fight for its ground, and while it does it pretty well, the counterculture hardly has time to gestate properly anymore. In the Nineties, great pieces of rock journalism are not always where you expect them to be.

Today, everyone is a rock critic, even cartoon characters. Beavis and Butt-Head, the pre-teen Siskel and Ebert of the MTV generation, have taken 'dumbing' to new, unexplored levels. Banal, cretinous, their monosyllabic retorts nevertheless have the ring of finality. Who can argue with Butt-Head, when, watching

Björk run around as if in some primary school dance class – 'Be a tree!' – he spits, 'Some of these weird chicks make *lots* of money'?

As ever, good rock journalism should highlight the power, the glory and the depravity of rock music, not just the theory. It should concentrate on the flavour of rock, not just the aftertaste. It's all very well getting in a tizzy over the 'validity' of David Bowie's *Station To Station*, but what kind of drugs was he taking when he recorded it? And whose drugs?

It goes without saying that not all rock stars take too kindly to this type of speculation, increasingly viewing it as some kind of gross intrusion, incompatible with their own POV. But if journalism doesn't offer to say the unsaid (if not always the unspeakable), then it is little but PR. And as for Lou Reed, well, to hell with him. Compared to Reed, Nick Kent was always more fascinating, and certainly better company.

Kent is, when all is said and done, the definitive rock'n'roller. Towards the end of 1986, Nick was dining with his friends David Bowie and Iggy Pop in a little Chinese restaurant in Gerard Street, in Soho. Confronted with a triumvirate of pop icons, the confused, if star-struck waitress approached the man who most looked like a rock star for his autograph. Bowie and Iggy were shocked. Nick was flattered.

* * * *

'Show me a hero and I'll write you a tragedy.' Or a farce. This anthology brings together some of the most forthright examples of rock journalism, from the dawn of pop to the present day, reflecting the fun, the absurdity and above all the sheer visceral thrill of rock'n'roll. These stories of orgiastic excess and glamorised wish-fulfilment are telegrams from the front line of indulgence. Some put me in mind of the infamous Hollywood producer Don Simpson: just hours before his death early in 1996, he had taken a call from his writer-director friend James Toback who described to Simpson a new film he was considering, called *Harvard Man*. When Toback explained that it was all about sexual obsession, drugs, madness and death, Simpson replied enthusiastically, 'This is a movie about everything that's the centre of my life.'

Anthologies of rock and pop writing are often such monolithic creatures that they seem like encyclopaedias. Not this one. This collection, like others, is obviously – sometimes fiercely – subjective, though I hope I haven't been as blinkered as one editor, who, in the introduction to his own anthology, wrote that, 'A scan of all the issues of *Q* to date and an entire Eighties wad of *Rolling Stone* yielded exactly no usable features.' That's right, and the Beatles were rubbish. Some of these books try and reinforce the idea that both rock music and rock journalism were somehow better back in the Fifties, Sixties and Seventies, a ludicrous conceit which I've tried to challenge by including many more pieces from the last 20 years. Because of this, and restrictions of space, there are some great pieces missing – Gram Parsons by Judson Klinger and Greg Mitchell say, or the Runaways by Charles M. Young, both from a 1976 issue of *Crawdaddy* – though a lot of these can be found elsewhere. Many celebrated writers have also been anthologised themselves, and though there are some pieces here which have already appeared in book form, most have not.

The anthology begins, as everything must, with Elvis, and with Samuel Charters' wry take on the young singer's ability to cope with his early fame, *Elvis Presley Calls His Mother After The Ed Sullivan Show*. Now that every aspect of Elvis' life has been exhumed and scrupulously examined, listening to his records has become a strangely religious experience, though exactly *what* religion, no one's yet exactly sure.

The Beatles were a religion from the word go, and Michael Braun's *'Love Me Do!'* – one of the first feature-length portraits of the band – attempts to scratch away at a surface which had already been far too well polished; Tom Wolfe's famous profile of Phil Spector, meanwhile, *The First Tycoon Of Teen*, published in 1965, was a hint that 'pop' culture was perhaps going to be more important, or at least more pervasive, than many at first thought.

Jim Morrison, the Rolling Stones and Led Zeppelin all hit their stride in the Sixties, and the pieces here (by Joan Didion, Stanley Booth and Stephen Davis) detail their seamless shift into a world of debauchery, drink and drugs – even, on one particularly awful occasion, death. A murder like the one at Altamont could have put paid to a lot of artists' careers, but with the Stones it only seemed to enhance their satanic, nihilistic image. Jagger was unstoppable after that. As the legendary promoter Bill Graham said, 'That cunt is a great entertainer.'

There are many tales of excess here – Nick Kent on Sid Vicious (surely one of the greatest pieces ever written on punk), Jerry Hopkins on Keith Moon, Richard Ben Cramer on Jerry Lee Lewis, David Ritz on Marvin Gaye, Georgina Howell on Axl Rose, and Steven Dougherty, Johnny Dodd, Bill Donahue and Craig Tomashoff on Kurt Cobain to name just a few – but perhaps the two which fascinate and appall the most are the stories concerning Chuck Berry and David Crosby. Berry was arrested and charged with invasion of privacy for the ritualistic way in which he videotaped hundreds of women using the toilets in his various clubs, restaurants and homes. It is such an astonishing litany of abuse that 'My Ding-A-Ling' now acquires new, deeper connotations. The most revealing chapter of David Crosby's autobiography *Long Time Gone* highlights his ability to drive a car and freebase at the same time. Well, as Stephen Stills, Crosby's one-time partner-in-crime put it: 'You can only apologise for so much.'

Rock'n'roll is often an absurd comedy of errors, a self-contained world where a drug overdose will be rewarded with a blow job, a temper tantrum or radical haircut with a new recording contract. Danny Baker understood this Faustian bargain when he went to Los Angeles to interview the Jacksons in 1981, the resulting 7500-word article being one of the funniest, most incisive pieces the *NME* ever ran. Equally ridiculous is the infamous Troggs Tape, a transcript of an abortive attempt by the group in 1970 to record a much-needed smash-hit single. 'Fuckin' drummer? Oi shit 'im . . .'

Casting is crucial in these matters, as it is in all others: included here are Fiona Russell Powell on Simon Lebon, Sam Shepard on Bob Dylan, Alix Sharkey on Malcolm McLaren, Charles Shaar Murray on David Bowie, Sean O'Hagan on U2, Peter York on the Sex Pistols' boat trip and Iggy Pop on himself

('So I just take her in the bathroom and lay her down on the floor, you know, and just fuck her'). Some are obvious choices, others not, but all are successful in their own way. Unfortunately, by the time Michael Lydon caught up with Carl Perkins, for *Rolling Stone* in 1968, his moment of glory was over, and the man with a small beginning was looking forward only to a small ending.

Any music journalist worth his salt will have mastered the art of obituary. I commissioned Albert Goldman to write an exhaustive essay on his theory of Elvis' apparent 'suicide' after reading a similar piece he had written for *Life* in 1990. Goldman on the phone seemed a world away from the obsessive character he appeared to be in print: quiet, clipped and rather pissy, he was totally professional, eager to spread the word. In his biography *Elvis,* a damning indictment of the man and a demolition of the myth, Goldman not only trashed the music, he claimed Presley was a paranoid gun fetishist, a pervert and a junkie. Now he went further. As a picture of the King during his 'In The Gateaux' period, Goldman's piece is fascinating, and maybe all the more poignant in the light of Goldman's own untimely death, just a few years ago.

Perhaps predictably, futurism was never going to look good with hindsight, and it always seemed destined to rank alongside the second coming of Mod or the first coming of Oi! as a socio-economic cult too far. Subtitled 'Those Glory Days of Aural Pretension', Adair Nye and David Quantick's *When We Were Glass* is a beautifully drawn take on the whole Proto-Romo business, leaving Gary Numan, David Sylvian and Ultravox stranded on the shores of Pseudonia with nothing but a shiny red plastic cube for company.

Julie Burchill's hand-grenade of a love letter to Annie Lennox caused such a rumpus when it was published in *Time Out* in 1985 that RCA – Lennox's record company – were reportedly under pressure from the singer to pull all their advertising from the magazine. Why? It might have had something to do with Burchill stating that, 'When I saw a shooting star, my wish was invariably a simple one – "Please, let the Eurythmics die painlessly in a plane crash." ' Ian Penman's scathing attack on

Frank Zappa also elicited a strong response when it was published in *The Wire* in 1995, drawing the largest amount of hate mail the magazine had ever seen. Frank Owen's report on Morrissey, which appeared in the *Melody Maker* in 1986, caused a huge fuss, too. Furious at Owen's innuendo, he has not talked to him since. Conversely, Tony Parsons' interview with Robert Palmer is an old-fashioned face-to-face hatchet job, a rare thing these days. Parsons disliked the ageing smoothie intensely, and he does his best – his very best – to tell us why. 'He deserved it,' says Tony.

Mick Brown, John Sweeney and Robert Sandall write here about media overexposure, tabloid culture and litigation – Sweeney cataloguing Elton John's appalling treatment by *The Sun*, Sandall dissecting George Michael's protracted beef with Sony, and Brown charting Boy George's monumental fall from grace. None of these stories are really about music, as such, they're about fame.

Tom Hibbert's *Who The Hell Does Ringo Starr Think He is?*, published in *Q* in 1992, is a shocking portrait of a man who has spent the last 30 years living down a rather unfortunate reputation. 'Poor old Ringo,' it was whispered, as the bejewelled sticksman walked through the hallowed corridors of London's swankiest nightclubs. 'He's not the best drummer in the world.' 'You know what?' the reply would come, 'He's not even the best drummer in the Beatles.'

Adrian Deevoy, James Brown, Jessica Berens and Miranda Sawyer all profile seminal British lads, purveyors of seriously bad behaviour and lairy rock music. Deevoy's Q&A with Rod Stewart personifies both journalist and star, two impulsively funny men prepared to make their encounter as enjoyable as possible, both for themselves and the reader. As for those who have come in Stewart's wake, Damon Albarn is prodded and teased by Berens, Shaun Ryder is craftily deified by Brown, while Sawyer presents the bawling, brawling Gallagher brothers in all their fame-fuelled glory, soliciting from Noel his by-now famous wish that Damon Albarn and Blur bassist Alex James catch Aids (something he later retracted).

We end, unmistakably, with Ike Turner, the man who helped invent rock'n'roll when he recorded 'Rocket 88' with his first group the Kings of Rhythm in 1951 (the 'leerics' of which went, 'You women have heard of jalopies, you've heard the noise they make/Well let me intro-dooce my new Rocket 88!'). Robert Chalmers' piece, published in *The Observer* in 1995, is not just a pin-sharp picture of a rather black-hearted 20th Century figure, it is also a reflection of pop's flip side, a parable of doomed ambition, tainted love and a battered chord that just won't quit. Piss stains and pathos, fellatio and firearms – they're all here, through a glass darkly.

ELVIS PRESLEY CALLS HIS MOTHER AFTER THE ED SULLIVAN SHOW

The King by Samuel Charters

I got to see if I can find something more to eat. I told them to send downstairs for some more cheeseburgers. You got something there to eat yourself? Don't worry about what it's going to cost me to talk to you. The RCA people take care of everything like that. All I have to do is tell Colonel Parker and he gets it taken off the bill. Anyway, Momma, I don't look at the bills anymore. I got somebody else to take care of all that. I know this rock and roll won't go on for long, but I don't worry. If it loses out I can always do some other kind of singing. I don't worry about anything. Would you, Momma, if it was you doing the singing and everything was going so good?

You know I just come by the room where those writers were sitting a while ago and they're still all there and I don't think any of them have smiled about anything. They're talking to one of the guys that's working with us, and he's heard me interviewed so many times he's giving them all my answers. All that stuff about the coloured people doing the same kind of show only nobody noticed it until some white cat come along and started doing it their way. I stood outside listening to them, keeping myself out of the way so they wouldn't notice, and this guy even stood up and started to show them about the dancing I do, showing them how I goosed up what the coloured people had been doing and that's why everybody's noticing it now.

I don't want to talk about those writers so much, but they did say some pretty mean things about me in the papers and the magazines. I think another thing they got wrong is trying to use words to tell about what I'm doing. They think I have everything all decided and I've worked out what I'm doing and when I go out on the stage I have some kind of plan to show people what I'm thinking. That isn't the way it goes with my kind of music. I just go out there and go crazy. If there were any words for what I was doing, I'd just stand there like Mr Como and sing the words. But even if I could think up any words they wouldn't let me sing them on the stage anyway. That's what gets those writers all mixed up. They're trying to use words to describe something that there isn't words to describe. That doesn't work when they're writing about anybody, and I think that's the cause of so much writing being so bad when it applies to me, or when it applies to anything when it comes out of someplace except your head. I'm just using a new way to show something, and they're still trying to write about in the same old way.

Just a minute, Momma. Why don't you go get yourself a Coke and put a little something in it and then you come on back.

Man, what you doing in here? I'm pleased to meet you lady, but what did you bring her in here for? Man, no, you got to be crazy. You can't do it right there in the bed. I'm talking on the telephone to my mother and what would she say if she heard you grunting in the background there. Lady, I think you've had too much to drink. I think both of you have had too much to drink. Lady, don't you have anything on under that blanket? No, you sure don't. What did you do, get started in the other room and you got chased out? Come on, get up off the bed. I told you it has to be someplace else. I don't care if somebody's getting something in every bed in the place. Lady, you dropped all those things you were carrying and I don't want them lying there on my floor. I have a very nice young lady coming back to visit me and she wouldn't want to see things messed up.

What's that thing in your hand? It's one of those little rubber girdles? I don't know why you girls put on those things when you come to party. You know you just going to take them off. Come on, get up off the bed, stop doing that. Man, if you so ready to get it off just find a place on the floor somewhere. I know the floor isn't all filled up. But just get out of here. I got my mother on the phone and she's going to be back in a minute. Take that girdle with you. Come on now, baby, nobody's saying anything against a little rocking and rolling. You just got to find yourselves someplace else to do it in. And if you see that girl who was here with me, tell her I'll be off the telephone soon and then she and I can get to know each other a little better. And when you talking to her try to keep yourself covered up. I don't want her to get any wrong ideas about the kind of parties we have here.

Momma, did you get yourself something to drink? I know. I know. It's getting late and they going to get me up just like always to do some crazy interview first thing in the morning, but you know I don't sleep the way I should. I do a show like that and it really wears me out so that I have to eat a little, and that gets me all waked up and then I have to start again to get ready to sleep. Somebody looked at me tonight and said, man, you got it made, doing what you want anytime you get ready, but I really feel like a yo-yo, just going up and down. I get all wound up with some sleep and some rest when I'm traveling, then I let it all out when I'm singing and I got to come back up the string, a little bit at a time, and sometimes I can feel my arms getting tired when I pull myself up.

I was telling you about how the lights get so bright up there on the stage I sometimes can't see so good out in the theater. There was one time, Momma, before Colonel Parker started taking care of business for me, when Bill and Scotty and me got hired to play for a private party. I think it was down in Alabama someplace. We were going to play one of those shows in Louisiana – you know that Hay Ride Show we did – and we thought we could swing past this little town and do the job and get a little extra money.

It was one of those kind of places with lots of bright lights shining right in our eyes and we couldn't make out anything except that everybody seemed to have some kind of costume on. Okay, we said, it's going to be a costume party, and we can go out and do our show, just like always. We didn't let the crowd bother us none in those kind of places. Even with all the lights shining I could see people kind of crowding to get close when we started and I thought everything was going to be alright. But they didn't make much noise, even when I shook it up a little for them, and I figured, well, they got those costumes on and that must keep them dampered down a little. But when we finished the number and I went into my bow, there wasn't any kind of sound out of them. Everything was so quiet you couldn't tell they were breathing. Finally somebody said something in a loud voice right down in front. What he said was, 'Boy, can't you do nothing but that nigger shit?'

Now the fellow that had hired us, he was standing off on the side of the stage, and when he heard that he jumped out there and he started in on the guy that said it: 'You told me to get you something really hot, somthing that's really happening, and this is the boy out of Memphis who's got those records playing everywhere you go. This is Elvis Presley.' And the other guy, who's still standing out there in the dark and we can't really get a look at him, he says, 'What kind of name is Elvis?' Then the fellow on the stage with us got up and he started saying things and he was getting more and more answers from down in front, and finally, to calm everybody down, some of the public crawled up on the stage to get between them. We were still standing there, holding our instruments, and Bill had taken a couple of steps back so he could start running if the trouble got any worse, and then we got a look at their costumes. They were wearing sheets, and they had hoods that they'd pushed back so they couldn't talk. They were white sheets they had on them. It was the Ku Klux Klan. That crazy guy had hired us to play a party for the Ku Klux Klan!

When we saw that, we started to go off the stage, but then the crowd started shouting and whistling. They'd paid their money to see the show and we were the only show they had. The guy down in front was a little quieter and the fellow that had hired us kind of backed up across the stage, coming toward us. He was smiling and waving his arm for everybody to be quiet, but when he got back close to us we could see him shaking. In that part of the country you don't mess around with the Klan. He stood there beside me waving his arms and he whispered out of the side of his mouth, 'You know any other kind of numbers?'

We were just about as scared as he was, but when he said that we started in to some hillbilly number. I can't remember what it was. Something you and Daddy Vernon used to sing, and it was so simple we didn't have to rehearse it. This got everybody quieted down and we sang them every hillbilly number we could think of, but I could see we weren't going over. You know how I feel when I can't move around while I'm singing, and I didn't dare do anything that might get them started on us again. Finally I looked over at the guy at the edge of the stage and he gave us the sign that we'd been out there singing long enough to get our money.

Now you know I still didn't know what to expect when we did a show in those days, and I thought the way to end it was to try to get everybody on my side. What I did was start singing 'The Star-Spangled Banner.' I figured this would show them that we were good people, even if we did make a mistake with our first number. But right in the middle of it the noise started in again and I could see some of those boys in those white sheets starting to climb up on the stage again. Bill had more experience with this kind of show then I did, and when I stopped playing my guitar and turned round to ask the guys what I should do, Bill all of a sudden dragged his bass up to the microphone and started singing 'Dixie' as loud as he could. When they heard this the boys climbing up on the stage started walking up and down like it was some kind of parade and we played 'Dixie' over and over for them until we could get out of there.

That isn't the kind of thing that happens to me now, but I still don't know who's out there in the dark half of the time when I'm singing.

Just a minute, Momma. There's somebody who's just come in that I have to say hello to.

* * * *

Where did you go off to, baby? When I told those girls to get out I wasn't thinking of you. I could tell by looking at them they weren't nice girls. You're different. You just sit down on the bed again and I'll be through talking to my mother and you and me will have all the time we want. Where do you go to school? You don't go to school anymore? You got some kind of job? You sell jewellery at Woolworth's? Woolworth's is a good place to be. One of those big companies you know they won't go out of business on you. Before I was doing this I had a job driving a truck. If nobody likes my movie and people get tired of rock and roll, I can always get my old job back.

I bet you have every one of my records. Well, if you don't have all the new ones you don't need to buy them. Before you leave I'll have one of the boys find all he can for you. But you're not thinking of leaving now. I wouldn't want to think about you going away just before we getting started. I can see you got on a fancy petticoat under that skirt you're wearing. I see the little edge of it there, and it gets me wondering what you got on under that petticoat.

But you stay over on the bed there. I'll just lie back and look at you while I finish talking.

No, Momma, we didn't get cut off. I had my hand over the phone so you wouldn't have to listen to all those business things we have to talk about. No, you don't need to hang up. I can keep talking. I know you're just like me. It's as hard for you to get to sleep as it is for me. You taking your pill? I don't like to take too many pills. Oh, I take them if I have to sleep real bad. I hate it when I lie there and I don't feel like sleeping and I'm too tired to get out of bed and do something else. When I stay up so late it isn't so bad. If it gets to be nine or ten o'clock in the morning then I can sleep.

I had to use the pills when I was out in Hollywood. I had to get up early so I could go to work on the picture. That was the way they did it out there. If I was going to get up and not look like I was a hundred years old, then I had to get to sleep on time. But I don't like to use them. You take yours now, and I'll keep talking until you feel like you want to lie down. It isn't my place to ever say anything about how God made the world, but

sometimes I wish He'd made it just a little bit easier to sleep.
Just a minute, Momma.

Miss, if you like everybody else around this crazy place you probably feeling tired. You're not? Honey, I know why that is. You're thinking about what's coming next. You just keep lying there and let me look at those pretty legs of yours.

No, Momma, we didn't get cut off this time either. I just had something to discuss with the boys. You know, like you told me to do, I always have Gene or Junior sleeping in the room with me in case I start to walking around in my sleep, and I had to tell them to wait a little. I wouldn't let them cut off the connection while you still are waiting to get to sleep. Anyway, I know I won't walk off anywhere in my sleep tonight. After all that dancing they had me do in those rehearsals – and then after I got all ready they didn't show it anyway! You know how those people are. I'm telling you the truth, just like the preacher tells the congregation when he wants to let them know they're hearing the word. Listen to this, Momma, what you are hearing is the truth, it's God's truth, it's the one hundred and ten percent truth – and the truth is, when I get into my bed tonight, I'm going to stay right in it and not get up for one minute. And you know I mean every word I'm saying.

Who am I talking to? I'm just talking to you, Momma. And one of the boys – he's still here. Somebody's always watching me so I don't get in any trouble.

THE BEATLES IN YORK & LONDON

Mop Tops by Michael Braun

York

That evening in the dressing-room of the cinema at York two girls came in and asked to interview them. They said they wanted the interview so they could make a tape of it for a third girl who was ill in hospital. John sat in a corner away from the group. 'It's probably just an excuse to get into our dressing-room,' he says. 'Anyway women should be obscene and not heard.'

'Switch it on now,' says Paul conducting the interview for the bewildered girls. 'What's your name?' he asks Ringo. 'John', says Ringo. He then asks the girls their names. 'How did you like Germany when you were there?' asks the girl whose name is Eileen. 'We liked it fine,' says Paul. 'It was hard work,' says Ringo. 'Yeah,' says George.

All during the interview they sign autograph books that had been sent to their dressing-room, and when they aren't actually answering a question they read letters from fans.

The girls walk over to John. 'How do you write the songs?' says the girl whose name is Daphne. John doesn't answer. Paul shouts across the room in a voice you use to an errant child, 'Tell us about the songs, John, tell us about the songs.'

'Sometimes we write them together,' says John. 'Sometimes not. Some of them take four hours; some twenty minutes. Others have been known to take as long as three weeks.'

'What's your favourite song that you've written?'

'I think "Glad All Over",' says Paul, opening his eyes even wide. 'No, I'm kidding. I think at the moment it's our new record "I want to hold your hand". Is that all right?'

'Yes, that's fine,' says Eileen. 'Thank you very much indeed.'

'Oh dear,' says Daphne. 'It doesn't seem to have been recording. Sorry about that.'

Two hours before the first show in York the crowd was queueing beneath the theatre marquee that read 'Bingo every night (except Thursday)'. Fifteen minutes before the performance the doors were opened. In the lobby was a case lined with gold foil. On the foil were Beatle aprons and belts at 9s 6d. The aprons were red and blue striped and were trimmed with a beetle playing a guitar and the words 'From me to You'. Decorating the case was a spray of plastic roses.

Inside, the compere is asking: 'Do you want to see John?' (Screams.) 'George?' (Screams.) 'Paul?' (Screams.) 'Ringo?' (Pandemonium.) They appear, and all during their act a man in a dinner jacket stands in front of the stage looking bewildered. The girls wave, hold up pictures, and scream. The man continues to look bewildered. After 'Twist and Shout' the screaming rises, then stops dead for 'The Queen'; but as soon as this dies out the screaming starts again.

Paul runs off stage shouting, 'Oh my God, my ulcer. Nell, do you have a ciggy?' Neil Aspinall alternately hands him a cigarette and leads him towards the stage door where their car is waiting to take them to the hotel.

Immediately after the Austin comes a Jaguar driven by the tour promoter, Arthur Howes. He is a short, intense man with a crew-cut. He is wearing a coat made of snakeskin. Two girls who work for *Boyfriend*, a teenage fan magazine, are also in the car. The photographer is a tall rangy girl called Fiona Adams, the reporter a redhead called Maureen Grady. Miss Grady is explaining to Howes why she doesn't take notes when interviewing the Beatles. 'It's really that I know them so well I know just what they're going to say anyway so I just try to listen to the way they say it.'

At the hotel, the two girls and Howes are joined by several other people at a table in the lobby where they are having a drink. 'I wish I was back in London,' says Howes, 'there's nothing more boring than an English hotel lounge; but I want the boys to know that I care; that I'm more than just someone who pays their wages.'

The Beatles are in their hotel bedrooms finishing their dinners. George feels tired and goes to sleep. John, wearing a T-shirt and an old pair of trousers, wanders down the hallway past the guard, into the room shared by Paul and Ringo. The table filled with the empty dinner dishes is at the foot of Ringo's bed. Ringo, dressed in pyjamas, is sitting up in bed. Paul, also in pyjamas, is talking about a film, *The Trial*, which he has just seen in London. He is describing a scene in which there is a misunderstanding about a word, when the telephone rings.

'Hello, helloho,' says Paul in a falsetto and then, realizing it is a friend, says Hello seriously. The radio on the bedside night table is playing 'Our Love Is Here to Stay'. Paul asks what days they have off the following week. Ringo starts to tell him, and John tries to confuse them by mentioning other days. The radio plays 'Old Devil Moon'. Paul continues to talk on the phone. 'That was "That Old Devil Moon" in a magnificent interpretation by the MacGuire Sisters,' says the radio. 'Now straight from the moon to the stars.' The radio plays 'Swinging on a Star'.

They start talking about their forthcoming appearance in America and decide they will not be successful. 'After all,' says John, 'Cliff went there and he died. He was fourteenth on a bill with Frankie Avalon, and George said that *Summer Holiday* was second feature at a drive-in in St Louis.'

The radio played 'You'll Always Be Mine', and Paul returned from the telephone to announce 'We've been invited to a masque, what's that?' John tells him it means a masked ball. 'It sounds like a rave,' says Paul and returns to the phone.

'Wonderful singing by Mark Wynter,' says the radio. 'Only you would say that,' says Paul. 'Sure Trader Vic's is great . . . first the friends come, then the relatives of the friends . . . I mean the friends are bad enough.'

Paul finishes his telephone conversation and resumes talking about films. 'What I liked best in *The Trial*,' he says, 'was when they walked quietly through the concentration camp. It was so dead quiet, just like another world and Elsa Martinelli in the background just necking like mad.'

'Now the Shadows sing to you,' said the radio and I asked Paul whether he had seen *8½*. 'Oh, Peter told me to see that,' he said. 'But I don't know. I have this friend and every time he tells me to see something it turns out to be a drag for an evening's entertainment. He told me to go see *Next Time I'll Sing to You* and it was a dead bore. Then he suggested *A Severed Head* – it was the crappiest thing I'd seen for years. It's all this bit outside, "Well worth crossing the Atlantic for." Eccch, you can have it – crap.'

He turned to John. 'Stupid things like getting up in bed – no clothes on – fucking soft – they could have just had her herself without him getting into bed. I was getting bored and I spent most of the time watching this woman putting this scarf on and off and thinking that's not with it, tying it that way.'

He starts to joke with John and Ringo over just what is the right way to tie a scarf. After this he says, 'When I see an ordinary film – you know, one made without tricks – I know it sounds crap calling them tricks, but anyway, you get the idea . . . and then it cuts into a whole new action. When you're used to that it's hard to get used to the new kind like *The Trial* and *8½* I suppose. It sort of foxes me. I'm used to when they cut it's always a new thing happening.'

During the discussion about *A Severed Head* Ringo has turned the radio off. Now he turns it back on. 'Du-ah-du-ah . . .'

'Uh, I need another drink, baby,' says John.

Paul goes to the phone. 'Hello? Yeah, send us six single Scotches – No, make it doubles, yeah, doubles.'

'Du-ah-du-ah . . . And now a number from Xavier Cugat,' says the radio.

'Uh, no, thank you,' says John, 'I always thought he was a

kind of saint until I saw a photograph of his wife Abbie Lane. You know, St Francis Xavier with the cows.'

'No, he was somebody else,' says Paul. 'Assisi, with the cows or birds or something.'

The radio plays 'I'm in Love'.

John: 'Nothing better than British country and western.'

Paul: 'Ringo likes this.'

Ringo: 'What? I can't hear.'

Paul: 'Ringo has trouble with his ears.' (To Ringo): *'I say you love this song.'*

Ringo: 'I love the words.'

Paul (in heavy Liverpool accent): 'He loves the words. Have they brought your grapes then?'

Ringo: 'No, they didn't bother today.'

Paul: 'We brought you a couple of eggs.'

Ringo: 'Put them in here and the nurse will take them and do them for me.'

Paul: 'Have you got your potty?'

Ringo: 'It's in there in the bath-tub. You've changed your hair since you last came to see me.'

Paul: 'Well, keep a fresh mind about all things.'

There is a moment of silence. Then Paul says that people from the Dingle in Liverpool have a basic fear of hospitals and always seem to bring people eggs.

'You see,' says John, 'psychologically they still regard the egg as something precious from the harder years. The egg is a sort of symbol of fertility and wealth.'

John notices that the radio has been turned off and asks who did it. Both Ringo and Paul deny it and John says he saw Ringo do it.

Paul: 'Tension is mounting.'

John: 'Tension all shipping.'

Paul: 'I once knew a fellow on the Dingle who had two dads. He used to call them number one dad and number two dad. Now apparently number one dad wasn't nice. He used to throw the boy on the fire – which can develop a lot of complexes in a young lad.'

Ringo: 'I remember my uncle putting the red-hot poker on me, and that's no lie. He was trying to frighten me.'

Paul: 'Tell me, Ringo, do all your relatives go around applying red hot pokers to you?'

John: 'It's the only way they can identify them.'

Paul: 'You see, Ringo comes from a depressed area.'

John: 'Some people call it the slums.'

Ringo: 'No, the slums are farther.'

The drinks arrive and they begin discussing the derivation of American names like Melvin, Clyde, and Dusty. They say that most of the slang that they have picked up is American Negro slang.

'Except that we get it late,' says John. 'For instance, we say "with it", which went out in America two years ago. And also, we sing "Yeah, Yeah", that went out a couple of years ago although it's still featured by American coloured groups.'

They start to talk about fads and how they get started. 'For instance,' says Paul, 'it's taken a long time for the papers to realize that we've caught on. We knew a year ago that we were catching on. But it's taken until this Command performance for the papers to say, "What is this thing?" I mean when Maureen Cleave wrote her first thing in the *Evening Standard* we thought it was just a piece of old hat.'

'The thing is,' says John, 'British journalists refused to accept that we were nothing more than ordinary in the pop world and they just weren't interested, you see.'

'A fella called Dick Fontaine from Granada TV in Manchester came to the Cavern to see us,' said Paul. 'He was raving. He kept saying, "I must do a film with you fellas." Nobody wanted to know. They actually made the film and of course they show it now.'

Another thing they say hurt them was being from Liverpool. Paul recalls that their manager Brian Epstein was told, 'You'll never make it, from the provinces. Move down to London and you'll really get moving.' 'Our publicity man had trouble getting things in the paper because as soon as people heard Liverpool they thought we were all from the docks with sideboards. And the name. Practically everybody who knew told us to change it. "Beatles?" they'd say. "What does that mean?" '

They talked about Dick Rowe, an A. and R. man at Decca Records who had turned them down when they first sent in demonstration tapes.

'He must be kicking himself now,' says Paul.

'I hope he kicks himself to death,' says John.

'I don't blame him for turning us down,' says Paul.

They started discussing the feelings of adults towards pop music. 'We're definitely fighting a prejudice,' says John.

'That's why I'm interested in John getting this book out,' says Paul. 'I mean, I haven't got a cut or anything. It's just that one of us would be doing something to make people notice. I mean, it's the same as if one of us wrote a musical. People would get rid of their prejudice and stop thinking that pop people can only sing or go into a dance routine.'

'Which is what the normal pop artist does,' says John. 'He learns to tap-dance. We don't want to learn to dance or take elocution lessons.'

'People keep asking us whether we're going to broaden our scope,' says Paul. 'I don't know whether we will or not. One of the things about us is that we intrigue people. We seem a little bit different. If you read about Cliff Richard you know the things that he says; you've read about them before. But us . . . it's like when Maureen Cleave interviewed us – she asked us what we were doing culturally. I had read about *The Representative* and said I wanted to see it. She was reading *The Naked Lunch* and I said I was reading *The Packed Lunch* by Greedy Blighter. It's also like when people ask why they like the Beatles. Quite a few people mention the word genuine . . .'

'Which we're not,' interrupted John.

'. . . because they feel that's the impression we give. I remember thinking, about two years ago, "What have the people who have made it – I mean really made it – got?" It seems it's a sort of awareness of what's going on. I mean, I can imagine Sinatra to be, you know, not thick. I also thought, "What about the people who made it and then just sort of went?" I mean, look at Marty Wilde. I remember seeing him and being very impressed. Then when he started falling off I wondered what happened? Then we met him; and then we understood.'

They started to talk about idols and whether they have to have sex appeal. John said that Bill Haley was the first person to sing rock'n'roll but that he was too old to appeal to the girls that Elvis appealed to. 'After all,' said Paul, 'a young girl just couldn't see herself married to Bill Haley.'

John said that they have been told that girls masturbate when they are on stage.

'We're still at the masturbating stage ourselves,' interrupted Paul. 'You just can't get any on stage. I'm joking, of course. Seriously, anybody that gets as much publicity as we are and who are idols, I hate saying that because we don't feel like idols particularly but obviously we must be by now . . .'

John starts to laugh, and Paul protests.

'No, I really don't feel like one . . . I really don't . . . that is I don't feel like I imagine an idol is supposed to feel; however, anybody who gets this amount of publicity is in ordinary people's eyes a fantastic being; he always was in my eyes, anyway – y'know, Presley . . . Well, anyway, today this woman came up to the car; she'd never go up to just anybody in the street and kiss them; I mean, she was about forty; she was just sort of talking to me and she suddenly grabbed hold of me and kissed me. I mean, I was definitely embarrassed. What is it that with anybody who has had this amount of publicity . . . ? It creates some sort of reaction which doesn't have to do with sex or anything. They just say, "Look, there's that person we've been reading about in our good-as-the-Bible *Daily Express* every day." It's like the royal family. You have to like them because you've read so much about them.'

'Why?' says John. 'I didn't like *them* even when I was little. I disliked having to stand, which sometimes I didn't.'

'Another thing,' says Paul, 'we get letters saying, "You probably won't get this letter; it probably will never reach you", and before they have started out on the letter they're sure it will never reach you anyway. Letters that start out, "If you read this letter please read it to the end". I mean, there's no hope of us reading it as far as they're concerned.'

'Then there's people like my cousin Stanley,' says John, 'who I admired as a boy because he had a car and a Meccano set; and, uh, now that I have, uh, made it he treats me as if I was royalty or something. It unnerves me; I mean, he's thirty and I'm young and it's, uh, rather embarrassing from my boyhood hero.'

'But maybe it's only human,' says Paul. 'I mean, I know that if one of us had gone up and shaken Cliff's hand only two years ago we would have leapt home to the fellas – "I've met him! I've met him, there you go!" – and we would have been like that . . .'

John: 'Even though we never bought any of his records.'

Paul says, 'I remember the first time we did meet him. We were in the business and Cliff and the Shadows invited us to this great kind of party. I mean all I could say was "Oh, wait till I tell the girls back home." Mind you, I knew it was a soft thing to say . . .'

'Yeah, you're supposed to make up things like, uh, "What a great job you're doing in the industry",' said John.

Paul: 'Because we've never been fans of Cliff's.'

John: 'We've always *hated* him. He was everything we hated in pop. But when we met him we didn't mind him at all. He was very nice. Now when people ask us if he's a bit soft we say no. We still hate his records but he's really very nice.'

'I really don't think there is anything sad about idol-worshipping,' says Paul. 'I mean it's the same as when you haven't got religion, you can say "Isn't it sad that all the Catholics believe that there's a God and they go to mass every morning and get up early and those poor buggers have the priest as their god." I used to think they're having a rough time, until you think about it again and think they're the blokes who're having a great time, 'cause in actual fact they believe.

'I mean, we think a lot of people lead dull lives but they don't really. Like the woman who comes to clean our house and make meals. If I actually analysed it, all she does it get up in the morning, see her sons off to work, comes to our house, does the meals for us, goes home, watches telly and goes to bed and the same next day. Compared to us it's dull but for her it's not dull. She comes to our house, y'know, the great stars' house . . .'

John: 'You're a great star, eh?'

Paul: 'Huh? Oh, yeah, yeah . . . this is all purely fictional . . .'

John: 'What it is is that people will go to see the original instead of a copy. Like I took a look at the original mouldy Mona Lisa in Paris – eccch, crap!'

Paul: 'I mean, it's like the Eddie Cochrane show. We all used to think he was fantastic. I remember thinking before the show that I was actually there. I mean, it's the same thing as when you go to people's houses, mates, or people you used to know, sort of thing . . .'

John: 'Notice he said *used* to?'

Paul: 'And they have all your records – there's always one of them who will say "Give us a song". They want to see you, even though it will sound terrible. It's like why people want to see the film of Picasso drawing . . .'

John: 'Uh, he saw it at school. Uh, we all did.'

Paul (laughing): 'You see the film of Picasso actually creating . . .'

We started to talk about the reaction of fans. Paul said he thought that a lot of the reaction now came from what people believed they ought to do. I mentioned reading about the violent reception in Liverpool of *Rock Around the Clock*.

'I went to see it,' said John, 'and I was most surprised. Nobody was screaming and nobody was dancing. I mean, I had read that everybody danced in the aisles. It must have all been done before I went. I was all set to tear up the seats too but nobody joined in.'

'I know if I went to see our show,' said Paul, 'I wouldn't scream no matter how great I thought it was. I remember seeing the Eddie Cochrane show and there was this coloured fellow. Well, he walked to the front of the stage and did one of those great big actions, y'know, and everyone just laughed at him.'

We got on to the subject of the importance of fans and the press. Paul said there were so many people who claimed to have 'made' the Beatles in a short year that 'I sometimes wonder just who actually did make us.'

'You remember after that big spate of publicity we got in the national papers,' says John, 'which was uncalled for by our office. We were news at the time, and it only just happened we clicked in fourteen editors' minds at the same time. One day Paul was ill and I believe one of the papers wanted a picture of him. Nell told them they couldn't have it, and the photographer said: "You mean, after all the publicity we gave them – we *made* them." I'd like to meet this fella who said it.'

Paul explained that they never talk to the teenage magazines. 'They just make it up. I think they prefer it that way. Also photographers . . . We work much harder with someone like Robert Freeman or Parkinson than with the nationals who only want a cheesy grin. Of course, you have to start somewhere. What happens is that you get magazines like *Boyfriend* or *Valentine* first, then the *New Record* and *Show Mirror*. They will do an article even if you're not known. Then you get to the *New Musical Express*, and *Melody Maker*, which, though it's not the top-selling one, has a jazz influence, and you can talk sense to them. Then you really have to be very well known to be in *Time* or the *Observer* or the *Sunday Times*. I mean, the *Sunday Times* – a lot of the old codgers who read that just never know what's happening.

'But really your tastes change in everything. I remember when we first got a photographer in Britain. We got this fella Dezo Hoffmann. It sounded good – Dezo Hoffmann – when he came to the studio we did all our good poses. He's all right for a pop photographer. But I remember at the beginning of this year we thought Dezo was the greatest photographer in the world.'

I mentioned Avedon and Cartier-Bresson. They had never heard of either.

'What makes Cartier-Bresson so great?' asked Paul.

We talked about him for a moment and then Paul said that Parkinson was doing a book on the Beatles. 'As far as photos are concerned and techniques of photography it may all be very good. Some of the things looked a bit contrived. For instance he had over-exposed film and film that was so obviously wrong that they *had* to be great.'

'Uh, Robert Freeman thinks it's old, out-dated,' says John, 'but I suppose some think a lot of the things Robert Freeman does are out-dated also.'

'Parkinson's big thing with us,' said Paul, 'was "Where did you get those eyes?" and he kept lining us up and instead of pulling faces we had to pull eyes. Uh, John and George didn't oblige. Listen, do you think this boy Avedon will do things for us? Because we'll hire him.'

'Right now we're using Freeman. He's sort of in-betweens-ville,' said John.

We talked about Liverpool. Paul said, 'There is a certain awareness about some people in Liverpool. Like Ringo; he's never been to school except two days. Three times they told his mum he was going to die.'

'Anyway,' said John, looking at Ringo, 'to be so aware with so little education is rather unnerving to someone who's been to school since he was fucking two onwards.'

Ringo looked up and said, 'My grandad used to ask whether my hair was too long for butting because he'd do it if I gave him any cheek.'

'Butting is a Liverpool term for hitting with your head,' said Paul. 'I remember a little hooligan boy saying to my brother, "If you don't watch out I'll butt you", which he did.'

'Butting,' said John, 'is the first move used by the Liverpool lout. I only tried it once but my opponent moved and I nearly cracked my head open.'

I said that sometimes a poor childhood was fortunate, that it could be a real handicap to have a famous father.

'Uh, I don't agree,' said John. 'I could have stood a famous father rather more than the ignoble Alf, actually.'

Paul said, 'I think it would have been a drag if my father was famous.'

'I would have enjoyed the money,' said John. 'Never mind the fame. I think it is a working-class fallacy that you have to fight your way up. I think there must be people who have enjoyed a happy and fruitful life without having to fight for it. People who are made great are only made great by people of the class they leave. Let's say there are five people from the working class and one makes it. He's only great in the eyes of the other four.'

Paul said, 'Frank Sinatra didn't have wealthy parents but he's recognized by rich people.'

On the subject of children they agreed that they would probably make the same mistakes with theirs as their parents did with them. 'I know when my kid is about sixteen,' said John, 'and I say, "Come in at such and such a time" and he does, I'll be saying, "At my age when I was told to come in I didn't." I'll say, "When they told me not to have sex I did; when they told me not to smoke I smoked." If he turns out to be one of them who does everything he's told, I'll be dead choked.'

'I mean, what's wrong with us?' says Paul. 'Our parents used all the old clichés and look how we turned out.'

John asked Ringo, 'Why don't you ever say anything except "I'm the drummer?" '

'I don't like talking,' says Ringo. 'It's how I'm built. Some people gab all day and some people play it smogo. I don't mind talking or smiling, it's just I don't do it very much. I haven't got a smiling face or a talking mouth.'

Paul (whispering): 'Shakespeare's songs – you like Shakespeare's songs – go on' (to me) 'ask him what kind of music he likes.'

I asked him what kind of music he liked.

'I like real blues.' (They laugh.)

'And what kind of poetry?'

'Mozart's poetry.'

'One more ciggy,' says John, 'and I'm gonna hit the sack; "hit the sack" being an American thing we got off Gary Coople as he struggled along with a clock in *Hi, Goons*. But I really never liked "sack", it's, uh, something you put potatoes in over here.'

'The whole thought of hitting the sack,' says Paul, 'it's so – so dirty, and it can mean a lot of things.'

'You can sack Rome,' says John, 'or you can sack cloth – or you can sacrilege, or saxophone, if you like, or saccharine.'

'Or sacrifice,' says Ringo.

* * * *

London

A few days later I visited John at his flat. His wife Cynthia sat with us round the fire, hardly talking, but occasionally getting up to look at their young son or to make tea. Toys that had been sent to the child lay scattered about. In a corner was a suitcase, holding John's stage outfits. Piles of records were on the gramophone and the Miracles and the Shirelles played during our conversation. John was wearing a T-shirt and the heavy horn-rimmed glasses he never uses on stage. He sat sprawled over a chair, looking relaxed, but he was still feeling depressed about their cabaret performance.

'The sound is so important and we just didn't have it at Grosvenor House,' he says. 'I remember when we made our first recording. We didn't sound natural. Paul sang "Till there was you", and he sounded like a woman. I sang "Money", and I sounded like a madman. By the time we made our demos of "Hello, Little Girl" and "Love of the Loved" we were okay, I think.'

I ask him whether he thinks the Beatles' success depends more on their sound or on the way they look. 'We could have managed, looking like we look,' he replies, 'and making worse records, or we could have managed, looking like the average pop singer and making our noise. But the combination makes a better impact. We have always looked different from the rest of the mob. We're clean-cut now but originally we were anti-clean-cut. I mean if we looked like Presley we'd look stupid. Before he came nobody here looked like him. But when we started there were already people like art students who looked like us.'

We talk about Presley whom John says he admires. 'Of course,' he says, 'he's doing the same thing in films that he did on stage but he's made a million and that's what he started out to do. I like him but I don't want to imitate him. Some of our songs are American but when we sang them American they just didn't come off. We learnt you just can't be American. When we first sang "From Me to You" it sounded American and we didn't want it.'

He starts to talk about the film the Beatles would be making. 'After this film,' he says, 'they'll find out we're not actors and that will be that. If we had a year to do it it might be good. But we're going to race through it and I'll probably lose all confidence by the time it's over unless something happens quick.

'I mean, none of us are going to learn our lines. I'm not, for a start, I just don't have the concentration. They're going to have to catch us and there's always one of us who will not, y'know, help.'

I suggest that maybe they could improvise their parts instead of learning lines. 'We're not really capable of ad-libbing,' says John, 'unless it's among ourselves, and that's too personal. I mean, I can count the people on my fingers who can understand what we're about all the time. No, the film will start out as one thing and I hope by the end that they will have gathered that we're going to do what we do.'

He takes a drink of Scotch and sprawls even more. 'Anyway,' he says, 'I hate the first one. Like I hated doing the first record. If we could only make this our first and fifth film.' He thinks for a moment. 'The trouble is,' he say, 'it's only us who can write for us.' He explains that his first line in the script is one he is supposed to say when Paul enters with an old man. 'I'm supposed to say, "Uh, who's your friend, Paul?" I wouldn't say that. I'd just say, "Who's the old crip?" '

Cynthia left the room for a moment. 'Uh, can I just go and get this thing I wrote and see how it affects you,' he says. He returns with a couple of pieces of hotel note-paper. On them, scrawled on both sides, was a story called 'No Flies on Frank'.

'There were no flies on Frank that morning,' it began. 'After all, why not? He was a responsible citizen with a wife and a child, wasn't he? It was a typical Frank morning and with an agility that defied description he leapt into the bathroom on to the scales. To his great harold he discovered he was twelve inches more tall-heavy!'

When I have finished reading he says that he has written thirteen or fourteen similar stories while on tour. 'When I have about fifteen more I'd like to get them published. Right now, I just like showing them to people. It knocks me out to see what different people laugh at. I mean, *I* laugh at it all and everybody laughs at something different. What it is, is really our humour on paper. I mean, mine, more than Paul's and George's. It's easy for me to write them. If people like them I can write them till I'm blue in the face.'

He wants to call the book *John Lennon in his Own Write*, a title suggested by Paul. I say that since he also plans to do sketches for the book it should be called *John Lennon in his Own Write and Draw*.

'Right-hand draw,' says John.

I tell him that parts of his writing are very much like *Ulysses*. He says he has never read Joyce and the only influence on his writing that he knows of is Lewis Carroll. 'I don't go in for much of those culture things, like Paul,' he says. 'Just drop a name and Paul will go; I'd rather stay at home when I'm not working but Paul goes out to Harry Secombe and *Lovely War*. I suppose I *should* like those things, but I just don't.'

I ask him what he eventually wants to do – whether he wants to continue in show business.

'Well, first of all,' he says, 'we're not going to fizzle out in half a day. But afterwards I'm going to change into a tap-dancing musical. I'll just develop what I'm doing at the moment, although whatever I say now I'll change my mind next week. I mean, we all know that bit about it won't be the same when you're twenty-five. I couldn't care less. This isn't show business. It's something else. This is different from anything that anybody imagines. You don't go on from this. You do this and then you finish.'

He starts talking with Cynthia about a series the *News of the World* is running on the Beatles. John is worried because he thinks there may be something about his father whom he hasn't seen since his mother died when he was fifteen. He was brought up by an aunt and hadn't heard from his father until the paper received a letter from someone who claimed to know him.

'I don't want to think about it,' says John. 'I don't feel as if I owe him anything. He never helped me. I got here by myself, and this is the longest I've ever done anything, except being at school, and that was false.'

George and Ringo share a flat in Mayfair. Although the building is kept spotless, the flat is filled with overflowing ashtrays and record jackets strewn over the floor. In one corner the hi-fi set blasts music continuously. This is punctuated by the ringing of the telephone. Their number is unlisted but when they pick up the phone they hear giggles or a sigh and the sound of the receiver being placed back down.

The Beatles have a few days free and Ringo has gone to Liverpool.

It is now midday and George has just woken up. He wanders into the sitting-room where he is fitted for a suit by the Beatles' tailor, Dougie Kingman. He then gets dressed and prepares to go out for lunch. Once in the street he keeps looking around for fans and seems both annoyed and pleased when one of them finally asks him for his autograph in Park Lane.

At lunch he tells about a television programme the Beatles have appeared on. The host, a Liverpool comedian called Ken Dodd, had said he was thinking of becoming a pop singer and wanted a 'down-to-earth name'. George had suggested 'sod'.

After lunch he produces a copy of a contract the Beatles made in Germany. He is taking it to their music publisher to find out how much they are owed in royalties. He has been carrying it in his pocket for two weeks. Before that it lay in a suitcase in Liverpool and London for three years.

A few days later John is in a taxi, passing a store that has a red night-shirt in the window. He tells the cab to stop, goes inside, and asks how much the night-shirt costs. 'Six pounds,' he is told. 'That's a lot,' he says, 'but I think Cyn would like it.' While it is being wrapped the clerk asks him to look at some jackets that have just arrived. He winds up buying three and a coat. The bill comes to £107, but he doesn't have his cheque-book with him. The store presents a blank cheque but he can't remember what branch his account is at.

* * * *

The next day the Beatles are an hour early for a recording at the BBC. Rather than return to their flats, George says he needs a shirt. They send Sommerville into Simpson's to announce their arrival and are then ushered into a room next to the executive offices, where, as a store executive informs them, 'The royal family does its shopping'. George gets his shirt and between them they spend several hundred pounds on clothes they cannot possibly get the chance to wear.

Dr Richard Asher is a physician who runs a psychiatric clinic at London's Middlesex Hospital. The study of his house in Welbeck Street is filled with paintings and books. Copies of scientific journals lie scattered about. Tonight, his daughter Jane is sitting in the study talking to a friend of her brother's, a young Cambridge student called John Dunbar.

Paul walks in. Jane says that since stories about them have appeared in the papers she has been receiving many telephone calls from girls who ask for Paul and then hang up. She says that her father must keep his number public because of his practice and that he is getting annoyed with the calls.

Her brother Peter comes in with his friend Gordon. They have just finished playing jazz at the Pickwick Club, and they start talking about a record they are about to make of a song written by Paul and John. Paul goes out, and I tell Peter about the Beatles' shopping expedition. He seems particularly interested in the fact that George spent so much money on clothes. Dunbar remarks that his only problem about clothes is that his parents don't like him to wear jeans all the time.

When Paul returns, Dunbar, who is reading psychology at Cambridge, starts talking about dreams and their interpretation. Paul tells about a recurring dream he has, with a discus thrower in it. Jane and Dunbar try to analyse it, but Paul seems content merely to relate it. Peter and Gordon leave to play chemmy in a Soho club, and Dunbar and Jane continue to talk about the interpretation of dreams. As they talk Paul suddenly stands up and announces, 'Well, I've had a very tiring day making lots of people happy. I'm going to bed.'

THE FIRST TYCOON OF TEEN

Phil Spector by Tom Wolfe

Phil Spector is sitting in a little cream room in his office suite at 440 East 62nd Street with his back to a window that is practically on top of the East Side Drive. Twenty-four years old, he has a complex of corporations known as Phil Spector Productions. One of them is Mother Bertha Productions, named after his mother, Bertha. She works for his office in Los Angeles, but only because she wants to. The main organization is Philles Records. Spector has produced twenty-one 'single' Philles records since October 1962 and sold more than 13,000,000 copies. All rock & roll. His current hit, 'Walking In The Rain' by the Ronettes, has gone as high as number 20 on the 'Cashbox' chart and has sold more than 250,000 copies. His latest record 'You've Lost That Lovin' Feelin', by the Righteous Brothers, rose from the seventies to number 37 with a 'bullet' beside it, meaning 'going up fast'. He has produced seven albums. The first teenage tycoon! He is leaning back in the chair. He has on a suede jerkin, Italian pants, a pair of pointy British boots with Cuban heels. His hair hangs down to his shoulders in back. The beard is shaved off, however.

Danny Davis, his promotion man, is talking on the phone in the inner office. A fellow sits across from Spector with his legs crossed and a huge chocolate brown Borsalino hat over his bent knee, as if he were just trying it on. He says, 'Phil, why do you do—'

'I'm moving the whole thing to California,' says Phil Spector. 'I can't stand flying any more.'

'Why do you do these things?'

Spector – without his beard, Spector has a small chin, a small head; his face looks at first like all those little kids with bad hair and reedy voices from the Bronx, where he was born. But – an ordinary Phil Spector? Phil Spector has the only pure American voice. He was brought up not in the Bronx, but in California. His voice meanders, quietly, shaking, through his doldrum fury out to somewhere beyond cynical, beyond cool, beyond teenage world-weary. It is thin, broken and soft. He is only twenty-four years old, the first millionaire businessman to rise up out of the teenage netherworld, king of the rock & roll record producers.

Spector jumps out of the chair. 'Wait a minute,' he says, 'just a minute. They're making deals in here.'

Spector walks into the inner office gingerly, like a cowboy, because of the way the English boots lift him up off the floor. He is slight, five foot seven, 130 pounds. His hair shakes faintly behind. It is a big room, like a living-room, all beige except for eight gold-plated rock & roll records on the wall – some of Phil Spector's 'goldies', 1,000,000 sales each. 'He's A Rebel' by the Crystals. 'Zip-a-dee-doo-dah' by Bob B. Soxx and the Blue Jeans. 'Be My Baby' by the Ronettes. 'Da Do Ron Ron', 'Then He Kissed Me', 'Uptown', 'He's Sure The Boy I Love', all by the Crystals. 'Wait Till My Baby Gets Home' by Darlene Love. And beige walls, beige telephones all over the place, a beige upright piano, beige paintings, beige tables, with Danny Davis crowding over a beige desk, talking on the telephone.

'Sure, Sal,' says Danny, 'I'll ask Phil. Maybe we can work something out on that.'

Spector starts motioning thumbs down.

'Just a minute, Sal.' Danny puts his hand over the mouthpiece and says, 'We need this guy, Phil. He's the biggest distributor out there. He wants the 1,000 guarantee.'

Phil's hands go up as if he were lifting a slaughtered lamb up on top of an icebox. 'I don't care. I'm not interested in the money, I've got millions, I don't care who needs this animal. I'm interested in selling records, OK? Why should I give him a guarantee? He orders the records, I guarantee I'll buy 1,000 back from him if he can't sell them; he sells them, then after the record dies he buys up five hundred cut-rate from somebody, sends them back and cries for his money. Why should we have to be eating his singles later?'

Danny takes his hand away and says into the mouthpiece, 'Look, Sal, there's one thing I forgot. Phil says this record he can't give the guarantee. But you don't have anything to worry about . . . I know what I said, but Phil says . . . Look, Sal, don't worry, "Walking in the Rain", this is a tremendous record – tremendous, a very big record . . . What? . . . I'm not reading off a paper, Sal . . . Wait a minute, Sal—'

'Who needs these animals?' Spector tells Danny.

'Look, Sal,' Danny says, 'this man never made a bad record in his life. You tell me one. Nothing but hits.'

'Tell him I'm not in,' says Spector.

'Sal—'

'Who needs these animals!' says Spector, so loud this time that Danny cups his hand around the receiver and puts his mouth down close.

'Nothing, Sal,' says Danny, 'that was somebody came in.'

'Joan,' says Phil, and a girl, Joan Berg, comes in out of another room. 'Will you turn the lights off?' he says.

She turns the lights off, and now in the middle of the day the offices of Philles Records and Mother Bertha Productions are all dark except for the light from Danny Davis's lamp. Danny crowds into the pool of light, hunched over the phone, talking to Sal.

Phil puts his fingers between his eyes and wraps his eyebrows around them.

'Phil, it's dark in here,' says the fellow with the large hat. 'Why do you do these things?'

'I'm paying a doctor six hundred dollars a week to find out,' says Phil, without looking up.

He sits there in the dark, his fingers buried between his eyes. Just over his head one can make out a painting. The painting is kind of came-with-the-frame surrealist. It shows a single musical note, a half note, suspended over what looks like the desert outside Las Vegas. Danny has to sit there huddled in his own pool of light talking to this 'animal' on the telephone.

'This is a primitive country,' says Spector. 'I was at Shepheard's, the discotheque, and these guys start saying these things. It's unbelievable. These people are animals.'

'What kind of things, Phil?'

'I don't know. They look at, you know, my hair. My wife and I are dancing, and – I mean it's unbelievable – I feel somebody yanking on my hair in the back. I turn around, and here's this guy, a grown man, and he is saying these unbelievable things to me. So I tell him, like this, "I'm going to tell you this one time, that's all: don't ever try that again." And the guy it's unbelievable – he shoved me with the heel of his hand and I go sprawling back into a table –'

Spector pauses.

'I mean, I've studied karate for years. I could literally kill a guy like that. You know? Size means nothing. A couple of these' – he cocks his elbow in the gloom and brings up the flat of his forearm – 'but what am I going to do, start a fight every time I go out? Why should I even have to listen to anything from these animals? I find this country very condemning. I don't have this kind of trouble in Europe. The people of America are just not born with culture.'

Not born with culture! If only David Susskind and William B. Williams could hear that. Susskind invited Phil Spector to the *Open End* television program one evening to talk about the record business. Suddenly Susskind and William B., station WNEW's old-nostalgia disc jockey, were condemning Spector as one kind of sharpie poisoning American Culture, rotting the minds of youth, and so forth. That was how it all hit Spector. It was as if he were some kind of old short-armed fatty in the Brill Building, the music centre on Broadway, with a spreadcollar shirt and a bald olive skull with strands of black hair pulled up over it from above one ear. There was something very ironic about that. Spector is the one record producer who wouldn't go near Broadway. His set-up is practically out in the East River, up by the Rockefeller Institute.

Susskind and Williams kept throwing Spector's songs at him – 'He's a Rebel', 'Da Do Ron Ron', 'Be My Baby', 'Fine Fine Boy', 'Breakin' Up' – as if he were astutely conning millions of the cretins out there with this stuff. Spector didn't know exactly what to tell them. He likes the music he produces. He writes it himself. He is something new: the first teenage millionaire, the first boy to become a millionaire within America's teenage netherworld. It was never a simple question of his taking a look at the rock & roll universe from the outside and exploiting it. He stayed within it himself. He liked the music.

Spector, while still in his teens, seemed to comprehend the prole vitality of rock & roll that has made it the kind of daring holy beast of intellectuals in the United States, England and France. Intellectuals, generally, no longer take jazz seriously. Monk, Mingus, Ferguson – it has all been left to little executive trainees with their first apartment and a mahogany African mask from the free-port shop in Haiti and a hi-fi. But rock & roll! Poor old arteriosclerotic lawyers with poky layers of fat over their ribs are out there right now twisting clumsily to rock & roll. Their wives wear stretch pants to the seafood shop. A style of life!

There have been teenagers who have made a million dollars before, but invariably they are entertainers; they are steered by older people, such as the good Colonel Tom Parker who steers Elvis Presley. But Phil Spector is the bona fide genius of teen. Every baroque period has a flowering genius who rises up as the most glorious expression of its style of life – in latterday Rome, the Emperor Commodus; in Renaissance Italy, Benvenuto Cellini; in late Augustan England, the Earl of Chesterfield; in the sad, volatile Victorian age, Dante Gabriel Rossetti; in late-fancy neo-Greek Federal America, Thomas Jefferson; and in teen America, Phil Spector.

In point of fact, he had turned twenty-one when he made his first million. But it was as a teenager, working within the teenage milieu, starting at the age of seventeen, that Phil Spector developed into a great American businessman, the greatest of the independent rock & roll record producers. Spector's mother, Bertha, took him from the Bronx to California when he was nine. California! Teen heaven! By the time he was sixteen he was playing jazz guitar with some group. Then he got interested in rock & roll, which he does not call rock & roll but 'pop blues'. That is because – well, that's a complicated subject. Anyway, Phil Spector likes this music. He genuinely likes it. He is not a short-armed fatty hustling nutball fads.

'I get a little angry when people say it's bad music,' Spector tells the man with the brown hat. 'This music has a spontaneity that doesn't exist in any other kind of music, and it's what is here now. It's unfair to classify it as rock & roll and condemn it. It has limited chord changes, and people are always saying the words are banal and why doesn't anybody write lyrics like Cole Porter any more, but we don't have any presidents like Lincoln any more, either. You know? Actually, it's more like the blues. It's pop blues. I feel it's very American. It's very today. It's what people respond to today. It's not just the kids. I hear cab-drivers, everybody, listening to it.'

And Susskind sits there on his show reading one of Spector's songs out loud – no music, just reading the words, from the Top 60 or whatever it is – 'Fine Fine Boy', to show how banal rock & roll is. The song just keeps repeating, 'He's a fine fine boy'. So Spector starts drumming on the big coffee-table there with the flat of his hands in time to Susskind's voice and says, 'What you're missing is the beat.' Blam blam.

Everybody is getting a little sore, with Susskind reading these simple lyrics and Spector blamming away on the coffee-table. Finally Spector starts asking Williams how many times he plays Verdi on his show? – Monteverdi? – D. Scarlatti? – A. Scarletti? 'That's good music, why don't you play that? You keep saying you play only good music. I don't hear you playing that.' Williams doesn't know what to say. Spector tells Susskind he didn't come on the show to listen to somebody tell him he was corrupting the youth of America – he could be home making money. Susskind: 'Well, ah, all right, Phil.' Everybody is testy.

Making money. Yes! At the age of seventeen Spector wrote a

rock & roll song called 'To Know Him Is To Love Him'. He took the title off his father's tombstone. That was what his mother had had engraved on his father's tombstone out in Beth David Cemetery in Elmont, Long Island. He doesn't say much about his father, just that he was 'average lower-middle class'. Spector wrote the song, sang it, and played the guitar in the recording with a group called the Teddy Bears. He made $20,000 on that record, but somebody ran off with $17,000 of it and . . . well, no use going into that. Then he was going to UCLA, but he couldn't afford it and became a court reporter – one of the people who sit at the shorthand machine taking down testimony. He decided to come to New York and get a job as interpreter at the UN. His mother had taught him French. But he got to New York, and the night before the interview he fell in with some musicians and never got there. Instead he wrote another hit that year, 'Spanish Harlem'. And then – only nineteen – he became head of A&R, Artists and Repertoire, for Atlantic Records. By 1961 he was a freelance producer, producing records for the companies, working with Connie Francis, Elvis Presley, Ray Peterson, the Paris Sisters.

All this time, Spector would write a song and run all phases of making records, get the artists, direct the recording sessions – everything. Spector would work with these kids who make these records because he was a kid himself, in one sense. God knows what the music business biggies thought of Phil Spector – he already wore his hair like Salvador Dali did at that age, or like an old mezzotint of Mozart or something. And he was somehow one of them – the natives, the kids who sang and responded to this . . . music. Phil Spector could get in one of those studios with the heron microphones, a representative of the adult world what makes money from records, and it became all one thing: the kids comprehended him.

Spector had an ideal: Archie Bleyer. Bleyer was a bandleader who founded a record company. Cadence Records. Spector formed a partnership with two other people in 1961, then bought them out and went on his own as Philles Records in October of 1962. His first big hit was 'He's A Rebel' by the Crystals. Spector had a system. The big record companies put out records like buckshot – ten, maybe fifteen rock & roll records a month – and if one of them catches on, they can make money. Spector's system is to put them out one at a time and pour everything into each one. Spector does the whole thing. He writes the words and the music, scouts and signs up the talent. He takes them out to a recording studio in Los Angeles and runs the recording session himself. He puts them through hours and days of recording to get the two or three minutes he wants. Two or three minutes out of the whole struggle. He handles the control dials like an electronic maestro, tuning various instruments or sounds up, down, out, every which way, using things like two pianos, a harpsichord, and three guitars on one record; then re-recording the whole thing with esoteric dubbing and overdubbing effects – reinforcing instruments or voices – coming out with what is known through the industry as 'the Spector Sound'. The only thing he doesn't keep control of is the actual manufacture, the pressing of the records and the distribution.

The only people around to give him any trouble all this time are the distributors, cigar-chewing fatties, and . . . well, to be honest, there is a lot that gives Phil Spector trouble, and it's not so much any kind of or any group of people as much as his status. A teenage tycoon! He is betwixt and between. He identifies with the teenage netherworld, he defends it, but he is already too mature for it. As a millionaire, a business genius, living in a penthouse twenty-two stories up over the East River, with his wife, Annette, who is twenty, a student at Hunter College, and with a four-room suite downstairs on the ground floor as his office, and a limousine, and a chauffeur, and a bodyguard, and a staff – Danny and Joan Berg and everybody – and a doorman who directs people to Mr Spector's office . . . well, that makes Phil Spector one of them, the universe of arteriosclerotic, hypocritical, cigar-chewing, hopeless, larded adults, infracted vultures one meets in the music business. And so here in the dark is a 24-year-old man with a Shelley visage, a suede shirt, a kind of page-boy bob and winkle-picker boots – the symbol of the teen world – sitting in the dark in this great beige office – the symbol of the tycoon world – in the middle of the day, in the dark, tapping his frontal lobes with his fingers in the gloom.

One of the beige phones rings and Danny answers. Then he presses the 'hold' button and tells Phil Spector, 'It's the Rolling Stones. They just got in.'

Spector comes alive with that. He gets up on his ginger toes and goes to the telephone. He is lively, and he spins on the balls of his feet a little as he stands by the phone.

'Hello, Andrew,' he says. He is talking with Andrew Oldham, the manager of the Rolling Stones. And then he puts on a cockney accent, 'Are you all in?' he says.

The Rolling Stones – all right. The Rolling Stones, English group, and Andrew Oldham, are like him. They grew up in the teenage netherworld and made it, and they all want to have it all too, the kids' style of life and the adults' – money – and not cop-out on one side or the other, larded and arteriosclerotic. Phil Spector's British trip! That was where suddenly he had it all.

Phil Spector is here! The British had the ability to look at all sorts of rebel baddies and alienated thin young fellows and say coo and absorb them like a great soggy, lukewarm, mother's poultice. The Beatles, Beatlemania, rock & roll – suddenly it is all absorbed into the centre of things as if it could have been there all along if it only asked. Phil Spector arrives at London Airport and, Santa Barranza, there are photographers all over the place, for him, Phil Spector, and the next morning he is all over the centrefold of the London *Daily Mirror*, the biggest newspaper in the Western World, 5,000,000 circulation: 'The 23-year-old American rock & roll magnate.' He is in the magazines as the 'US Recording Tycoon'. Invitations go out to come to the receptions to meet 'America's outstanding hit-maker, Phil Spector'. And then he lands back at Idlewild and waiting are, yes, the same bunch of cheese-breath cabbies, and he takes a cab on back to 440 East 62nd Street and goes into his beige world – the phones are ringing and it is all the same, the same . . .

'Cigar-smoking sharpies,' says Phil Spector. He is in a livelier mood after the talk with Andrew Oldham. 'They're a bunch of cigar-smoking sharpies in record distribution. They've all been in the business for years, and they resent you if you're young. That's one reason so many kids go broke in this business. They're always starting new record companies – or they used to, the business is very soft right now. They start a company and pour all their money into a record, and it can be successful and they're still broke, because these characters don't even pay you until you've had three or four hit records in a row. They order the records and sell them and don't pay you. They don't pay you because they know they don't have to. You start yelling for the money and they tell you "What-ya mean, I have all these records coming back from the retailers, and what about my right to return records and blah-blah!" What are you going to do? Sue twenty guys in twenty different courts in the United States?

'They look at everything as a product. They don't care about the work and sweat you put into a record. They respect me now because I keep turning out hits, and after that they become sort of honest . . . in their own decayed way.'

Where does a man find friends, comrades, anything, in a world like that? They resent his youth. They resent his success. But it is no better with the kids. He is so much more mature and more . . . eminent . . . they all want to form 'the father thing' with him. Or else they want to fawn over him, cozen him, cajole, fall down before him, whistle, shout, stomp, bang him on the head – anything to get his attention and get 'the break', just one chance. Or one more chance. Spector can't go near the Brill Building, the centre of the music business, because the place is crawling with kids with winkle-picker shoes cracking in the folds who made one hit record five years ago and still can't realize that they are now, forever, in oblivion. They crawl all over the place, the way the small-time balding fatty promoters and managers used to in the days when A. J. Liebling wrote about the place as the Jollity Building.

Phil Spector steps on to an elevator in the Brill Building. The elevator is packed, and suddenly he feels this arm hooking through his in the most hideously cozy way and a mouth is closing in on his ear and saying 'Phil, baby, wait'll you hear this one: "Ooh-oom-bah-ay",' and Phil Spector is imprisoned there with the elevator inching up, ' "vah ump nooby poon fan ooh-ooh ayub bay-ay" – you dig that, Phil? You dig that, don't you Phil? Phil, babes!' He walks down the hall and kids sneak up behind him and slip songs, music, lyrics into his coat pocket. He finds the stuff in there, all this ratty paper, when he gets home. Or he is leaving the Brill Building and he feels a great whack on the back of his head and wheels around, and there are four kids, in the singing stance, their heads angled in together, saying 'Just one bar, Phil: "Say wonna love boo-uh-ay-yay-bubby" ' – while the guy on the end sings bass with his chin mashed into a pulpy squash down over his collarbone – '. . . "beh-unggh, beh-ungggh".'

Status! What is his status? He produces rock & roll and therefore he is not a serious person and he won't join the Young Presidents or whatever kind of organization jaycee geniuses would join for their own good.

'Phil,' says the man with the hat, 'why don't you hire a press agent, a PR man?'

Phil is tapping his frontal lobes in the gloom. Danny Davis is hunched up in the little pool of light on his desk. Danny is doing his level best for Phil.

'Jack? Danny Davis . . . Yeah . . . No, I'm with Phil Spector now . . . Right! It's the best move I ever made. You know Phil . . . I'm in the best shape of my career . . . Jack, I just want to tell you we've got—'

'A press agent?' Phil says to the man in the hat. 'In the first place, I couldn't stand to hear what he'd say about me.'

'Got two tremendous records going, Jack, "Walking In The Rain", the Ronettes, and—'

'In the second place,' Phil says, 'there's no way my image can be bought.'

'And "You've Lost That Lovin' Feeling" by the Righteous Brothers,' says Danny. '. . . Right, Jack . . . I appreciate that, Jack . . .'

'The only thing I could do – you know what I'd like to do? I'd like to do a recording session in the office of *Life* or *Esquire* or

Time, and then they could see it. That's the only chance I've got. Because I'm dealing in rock & roll, it's like I'm not a bona fide human being.'

'. . . Absolutely! . . . If there's anything we can do for you on this end, Jack, let us know. OK? Great, Jack . . .'

'And I even have trouble with people who should never say anything. I go over to Gristede's to get a quart of milk or something, and the woman at the cash register has to start in. So I tell her, "There's a war in Vietnam, they've fired Khrushchev, the Republican party is falling to pieces, the Ku Klux Klan is running around loose, and you're worrying about my hair!" '

America's first teenage tycoon – a business genius, a musical genius – and it is as if he were still on the corner of Hoffman Street in the Bronx when the big kids come by in hideous fraternity, the way these people act. What is he now? Who is he in this weird country? Danny talks in the phone in the little pool of light; Joan is typing up whatever it is; Phil is tapping his frontal lobes.

DIRTY BLUE SUEDE SHOES

Carl Perkins by Michael Lydon

'If it weren't for the rocks in its bed, the stream would have no song,' said Carl Perkins with a comic dolefulness. He had just put down his well-thumbed copy of *The Power of Positive Thinking* and was staring out at the brown miles of West Texas prairie that slipped by the mobile home bus.

Carl, now 36, his extensive bald spot covered by a toupee, and his front teeth replaced with a plate, was on tour with the Johnny Cash Spectacular. He's been with Cash for two years, opening the show with some uptempo pickin' and singin' to warm things up, and since the accidental death last summer of Johnny's long time guitarist, Luther Perkins, has also been backing Johnny.

He doesn't exactly have the 'how the mighty are fallen' blues – his own days at the top were too brief, and steady work with a big country music tour isn't the bottom – but Carl, author of 'Blue Suede Shoes', has had his vicissitudes and they've made him philosophical.

'I'll tell you true,' he said that afternoon as the bus rolled from Lubbock to El Paso, 'I've been at the top of the bill and now I'm at the bottom and there's no comparin' 'em. The top beats the bottom everytime.

'At the top you know the people came for you. At the bottom, you're something between the crowd and what they came for, and you gotta work real hard to make it seem worth it to yourself being out there.'

'Oh, Carl, don't be blue,' said honey-blonde and honey-voiced June Carter Cash. 'Why, you know the people enjoy hearing you. You're an indispensable part of this show – isn't he, Johnny?'

'Sure is,' said Johnny Cash, lounging back in his seat and edging his voice with mock sarcasm, 'I don't know what we'd do without you, Rock King.'

'Laugh,' said Carl, 'but that's what they called me, and that's what some still call me, the King of Rock and Roll.'

They all laughed. Carl Perkins is a natural born straight man, his inferiority complex his comic device. He reads *Positive Thinking* seriously, but it's like Mr Peepers reading Charles Atlas. Yet he is never pathetic. 'We all love Carl,' said June. 'He has been through some hard times, but they never soured him. Think what it means for a man who was number one to be working behind someone, but Carl can do it because he's a big man.'

One of the crop of country singers who broke open the pop-market in the mid-Fifties and created rock and roll – Haley, Presley, Roy Orbison, Gene Vincent, Jerry Lee Lewis, and to some extent Cash himself – Carl was always an entertainer against his better judgment.

'I've always been the shyest person I know,' he said. 'When I was in school in Jackson, Tennessee, I'd have another kid sharpen my pencil, 'cause I was too scared to get out of my seat. I had an old guitar my pappy bought me – I painted that thing so many times that it had paint an inch thick and you could throw it against a wall and not make a dent – and one day my teacher asked me didn't I have a guitar and wouldn't I play it at assembly. I was too scared to say no, but before that show I was almost sick I was so scared and when I did it I could barely sing a note.

' 'Course the applause was nice, that made it better, but since then, though I made this my profession, I've always liked best just singing and playing in my home or in the dressing room best. That's where it's fun. Playing before people isn't bad exactly, but it's work.'

Like dozens of other hopefuls, Carl and his two brothers made it to Memphis to audition for Sam Phillips of Sun Records. 'Sam is filthy rich and slowed down now, but then Sun was exciting. We heard about his little recording studio and tried to get in. We were playing this music that wasn't country and it wasn't pop and it wasn't rhythm and blues, but somewhere in between. Some called it rockabilly, but we called it country rock.'

'Blue Suede Shoes' was the second song he recorded, his first hit, and his greatest song. It's still his closing number, and though a hunting accident which shattered his left foot has cut his hot-footed dancing down to little hops, it still brings it to rollicking life. '*You can burn my house,*' he sings, standing in a Fifties drugstore hood pose,

Steal my car,
Drink my liquor from an old fruit jar,
But uh-uh honey, lay off a them shoes,
Don't you,
Step on my blue suede shoes
You can do anything,
But lay off a them blue suede shoes

It's one of rock and roll's fundamental songs, one that showed the way. With a good dancing beat, clean and snappy guitar, and funny-serious lyrics, it has the 'teen feel' of defiant and narcissistic self-assertion. Songs like 'Blue Suede Shoes' literally created the concept of 'teenager': every rock in a leather jacket and T-shirt, who had dice hanging from the mirror of his chopped, blocked, and dropped '51 Ford, who spent hours trying to get that Sal Mineo curl in his DA, and who used a lot of Saturday afternoons catching Marlon Brando in 'The Wild One' – every one grooved on 'Blue Suede Shoes'. The millions of kids who listened joyously to the radio stations that played it straight for hours were suddenly linked up and could say, 'This song is *us*, what we wanna say is: lay off our blue suede shoes.'

Carl's version sold one and a half million copies; it was, he remembers proudly, one of the few songs ever to top the pop, country, and R&B charts simultaneously. For a few months in early 1956, Carl had everything: twenty-four years old with a smash hit, he was good looking, a good dancer, writer, singer, and guitarist, and he was riding the beginning of an enormous musical and cultural wave.

But the wave that year belonged to the Pelvis, and it drowned poor ole Carl. His managers, trying to milk every penny from 'BSS', waited eight months before releasing his next record. By then Elvis, whose 'Heartbreak Hotel' came out after 'BSS', had racked up half a dozen million-sellers (plus doing well with a cover of 'BSS'). On one hand he was raunchier than Carl, and grabbed the market that way; on the other hand he was a more malleable commercial property. By the end of 1956, with 'Love Me Tender', Elvis was on the way to becoming the widely appealing ballad singer with the carefully sculpted, non-offensive image. But they could never take the country out of Carl; he was just too 'Tennessee' to sell big.

Smaller hits followed – great songs like 'Matchbox' and masterpieces like 'You've Got the Right String, Baby, But the Wrong Yo-Yo' – and for about five years he did well on the country circuit. Even that success was too much for him.

'When you're a country boy just a month from the plow, and suddenly you're a star with money in your pocket, cars, women, big cities, crowds, the change is just too fast. You're the same person inside, but you're a star outside, so you don't know how to act. You're embarrassed about the way you talk, the way you eat, the way you look. You can't take the strain without a crutch. For me it was booze – I've seen the bottom of a lot of bottles. I was a mess, a wreck for years. Never knew where the money went, didn't get paid all of it, even from Sun.'

And in the early Sixties Carl, with other fading and faded stars like Gene Vincent and Bill Haley, was touring the provincial dance halls of Europe, making fair money but knowing he was there because he couldn't make it at home. 'People are ruined by that touring, like Chuck Berry. Maybe it was those years in prison, but when I first knew him he was an easy guy who'd swap guitar ideas with me in the dressing room. I saw him last on an English tour. He had gone all cold, wouldn't hardly talk.'

The Beatles were among the foreign kids who dug Carl, and they paid full tribute by recording 'Matchbox', 'Honey, Don't', and 'Everybody's Trying to Be My Baby'. Carl met them when they were getting big and they gave a party for him. 'They know all about me and idolized my songs. I was in the studio when they did "Matchbox" and played guitar with George on one cut of it, but it's never been released. Their versions are okay, but the royalty checks were nicer.'

Those checks, about $50,000 worth, carried him out of his slump until he signed with Cash, joining his old drummer, W. S. 'Fluke' Holland, whom he had had to let go years before. The Cash Spectacular (which also includes the Carter Family – Mother Maybell and her daughters, Anita, Helen, and June – and the Statler Brothers) tours ten to 15 days a month; Carl, Fluke, and bassist Marshall Grant triple up in motel rooms to save money, but otherwise it's comfortable traveling. They're all country boys to the marrow, and they have a good time.

They talk about the old days, Elvis ('He had a project to see how many girls he could make. He did okay,' said Johnny), and sing Jimmy Rodgers' song, cracking up on each yodel; they exchange Nashville gossip, swap car info, and tell jokes. ('Hear about the girl who said "Give me nine inches and hurt me"?' said Carl. 'So the guy screwed her three times and punched her in the mouth.')

But Carl still hates the road. 'People'll tell you how great it is, but I won't. I do it 'cause I have to. All I'm hoping for in the world is to get to where I can close the case on that Epiphone and not open it until *I* want to open it.'

Three days out on the road and he's wildly homesick, moaning about his wife, 'poor ole Valda' and how he can't stand being without her.

'When I call Valda, I make sure I'm at a window where I can see the moon. When I talk to her, I say, "Valda, can you see that moon?" and she says, "Yes, I can, Carl, it's beautiful, isn't it," and I say, "Sure is, Valda," and then our love goes from each of us, to the moon, and then to the other.'

Carl paused while the others laughed. 'I don't think true ladies and gentlemen would laugh at the tender outpourings of a man's heart,' he said, his lantern jawed face twisted with woe, and they laughed even harder.

He misses his two sons almost as bitterly. When he's away they often stay at Carl's father's farm, and Carl is glad they're learning country ways. 'I think the happiest time in my life was when I was a little boy in the country in the summer. Then I thought time was standing still and the world was mine.'

He's getting things set up for Valda and the kids. They've just moved into a new house, and with Carl's drinking days behind him, they're piling up a nest egg. Columbia is considering putting out an LP of Carl's biggest Sun hits, to be produced by Bob Johnston. Cash's latest single, 'Daddy Sing Bass', an easy swinging country-religious song, is a Perkins tune, and Carl has high hopes that a tune he's just written, 'Lovin' You Constantly', a really beautiful ballad, could become a pop-country standard.

'It's all in how you look at things,' Carl finished, picking up *Positive Thinking* again. 'I figure I went from low to high to low to just about right in the middle. That's an advance, isn't it, and maybe now I'm inching forward again.'

'Poor ole Carl,' said June, batting her long lashes and grinning warmly.

MISSIONARIES OF APOCALYPTIC SEX

The Doors by Joan Didion

It was six, seven o'clock of an early spring evening in 1968 and I was sitting on the cold vinyl floor of a sound studio on Sunset Boulevard, watching a band called The Doors record a rhythm track. On the whole my attention was only minimally engaged by the preoccupations of rock-and-roll bands (I had already heard about acid as a transitional stage and also about the Maharishi and even about Universal Love, and after a while it all sounded like marmalade skies to me), but The Doors were different, The Doors interested me. The Doors seemed unconvinced that love was brotherhood and the Kama Sutra. The Doors' music insisted that love was sex and sex was death and therein lay salvation. The Doors were the Norman Mailers of the Top Forty, missionaries of apocalyptic sex. *Break on through*, their lyrics urged, and *Light my fire*, and:

Come on baby, gonna take a little ride
Goin' down by the ocean side
Gonna get real close
Get real tight
Baby gonna drown tonight –
Goin' down, down, down.

On this evening in 1968 they were gathered together in uneasy symbiosis to make their third album, and the studio was too cold and the lights were too bright and there were masses of wires and banks of the ominous blinking electronic circuitry with which musicians live so easily. There were three of the four Doors. There was a bass player borrowed from a band called Clear Light. There were the producer and the engineer and the road manager and a couple of girls and a Siberian husky named Nikki with one gray eye and one gold. There were paper bags half filled with hard-boiled eggs and chicken livers and cheeseburgers and empty bottles of apple juice and California rosé. There was everything and everybody The Doors needed to cut the rest of this third album except one thing, the fourth Door, the lead singer, Jim Morrison, a 24-year-old graduate of UCLA who wore black vinyl pants and no underwear and tended to suggest some range of the possible just beyond a suicide pact. It was Morrison who had described The Doors as 'erotic politicians'. It was Morrison who had defined the group's interests as 'anything about revolt, disorder, chaos, about activity that appears to have no meaning'. It was Morrison who got arrested in Miami in December of 1967 for giving an 'indecent' performance. It was Morrison who wrote most of The Doors' lyrics, the peculiar character of which was to reflect either an ambiguous paranoia or a quite unambiguous insistence upon the love-death as the ultimate high. And it was Morrison who was missing. It was Ray Manzarek and Robby Krieger and John Densmore who made The Doors sound the way they sounded, and maybe it was Manzarek and Krieger and Densmore who made seventeen out of twenty interviewees on *American Bandstand* prefer The Doors over all other bands, but it was Morrison who got up there in his black vinyl pants with no underwear and projected the idea, and it was Morrison they were waiting for now.

'Hey, listen,' the engineer said. 'I was listening to an FM station on the way over here, they played three Doors songs, first they played "Back Door Man" and then "Love Me Two Times" and "Light My Fire".'

'I heard it,' Densmore muttered. 'I heard it.'

'So what's wrong with somebody playing three of your songs?'

'This cat dedicates it to his family.'

'Yeah? To his family?'

'To his family. Really crass.'

Ray Manzarek was hunched over a Gibson keyboard. 'You think *Morrison*'s going to come back?' he asked to no one in particular.

No one answered.

'So we can do some *vocals*?' Manzarek said.

The producer was working with the tape of the rhythm track they had just recorded. 'I hope so,' he said without looking up.

'Yeah,' Manzarek said. 'So do I.'

My leg had gone to sleep, but I did not stand up; unspecific tensions seemed to be rendering everyone in the room catatonic. The producer played back the rhythm track. The engineer said that he wanted to do his deep-breathing exercise. Manzarek ate a hard-boiled egg. 'Tennyson made a mantra out of his own name,' he said to the engineer. 'I don't know if he said "Tennyson Tennyson Tennyson" or "Alfred Alfred Alfred" or "Alfred Lord Tennyson", but anyway, he did it. Maybe he just said "Lord Lord Lord".'

'Groovy,' the Clear Light bass player said. He was an amiable enthusiast, not at all a Door in spirit.

'I wonder what Blake said,' Manzarek mused. 'Too bad *Morrison*'s not here. *Morrison* would know.'

It was a long while later. Morrison arrived. He had on his black vinyl pants and he sat down on a leather couch in front of the four big blank speakers and he closed his eyes. The curious aspect of Morrison's arrival was this: no one acknowledged it. Robby Krieger continued working out a guitar passage. John Densmore tuned his drums. Manzarek sat at the control console and twirled a corkscrew and let a girl rub his shoulders. The girl did not look at Morrison, although he was in her direct line of sight. An hour or so passed, and still no one had spoken to Morrison. Then Morrison spoke to Manzarek. He spoke almost in a whisper, as if he were wresting the words from behind some disabling aphasia.

'It's an hour to West Covina,' he said. 'I was thinking maybe we should spend the night out there after we play.'

Manzarek put down the corkscrew. 'Why?' he said.

'Instead of coming back.'

Manzarek shrugged. 'We were planning to come back.'

'Well, I was thinking, we could rehearse out there.'

Manzarek said nothing.

'We could get in a rehearsal, there's a Holiday Inn next door.'

'We could do that,' Manzarek said. 'Or we could rehearse Sunday, in town.'

'I guess so.' Morrison paused. 'Will the place be ready to rehearse Sunday?'

Manzarek looked at him for a while. 'No,' he said then.

I counted the control knobs on the electronic console. There were seventy-six. I was unsure in whose favour the dialogue had been resolved, or if it had been at all. Robby Krieger picked at his guitar, and said that he needed a fuzz box. The producer suggested that he borrow one from the Buffalo Springfield, who were recording in the next studio. Krieger shrugged. Morrison sat down again on the leather couch and leaned back. He lit a match. He studied the flame awhile and then slowly, deliberately, lowered it to the fly of his black vinyl pants. Manzarek watched him. The girl who was rubbing Manzarek's shoulders did not look at anyone. There was a sense that no one was going to leave the room, ever. It would be some weeks before The Doors finished recording this album. I did not see it through.

THE YEAR OF THE SHARK

Led Zeppelin by Stephen Davis

Zeppelin, flieg!	*Zeppelin fly!*
Hilf uns im Krieg	*Help us in war*
Fliege nach England	*Fly to England*
England wird abgebrannt	*England will be burnt up*
Zeppelin, flieg!	*Zeppelin fly!*

German children's rhyme, 1915

Peter Grant was going for America's throat. With no album out yet, Led Zeppelin was taking a calculated risk in going to America. But Peter Grant was basing his strategy on years of experience and his lupine, instinctive savvy for the unslaked cravings of American youth for English rock. Relying on Jimmy's name, Peter and his agent, Frank Barsalona of Premier Talent, booked Led Zeppelin into the key regional venues for breaking in a new act – Bill Grahams' Fillmores West and East, the Whiskey in Los Angeles, the Kinetic Circus in Chicago, the Boston Tea Party, and others. Then Atlantic sent out 500 white-label promo copies of *Led Zeppelin* to FM stereo rock stations and record stores, which generated a 50,000-copy advance order (excellent business for a first LP by a new band) and genuine listener interest in the newest band to emerge from the late, lamented Yardbirds. Once in the States, Peter Grant, doing his own promotion, would call ahead to the FM station in the next town the band would play in, reminding the programme director that Led Zeppelin was coming and asking what cuts from the new album his listeners were responding to. The Yardbirds had been getting $2,500 a night, but Led Zeppelin was happy to take gigs at $1,500, and as low as $200. The idea was simple: go out and play.

The product of Grant's strategy was phenomenal success. Led Zeppelin spent the next year and a half on the road (including six separate tours of America), earning their fortune and trying to shake a deserved reputation for bawdy mayhem and excess. The real cause of this reputation, road manager *extraordinaire* Richard Cole, first met the four members of Led Zeppelin in October at Peter's office on Oxford Street. He had just left the New Vaudeville Band in Canada and was about to pick up Terry Reid in the States, who was opening shows for Eric Clapton's new 'supergroup', Blind Faith. Richard, buccaneering veteran of myriad rock voyages, immediately took to the new band, especially the eager, inexperienced young drummer Bonzo. The shrewd Cold also foresaw big things ahead for Jimmy: 'I knew he was going to be a big leader in rock. You could tell. When the Yardbirds finished – somehow, although he'd only been in the group for a year – he ended up owning the name. Don't ask me how, but he owned the name, and it was a gold mine and he *knew* it. He also knew what he wanted to do with a group and he just needed the people to complement him. I'm sure he was born with a fucking gold nugget up his arse – and he's probably still got that fucking original gold nugget, with two coats of paint on it. He's the meanest in the world, that's why they call him Led Wallet.'

On 23 December 1968, Richard Cole met Jimmy, Robert, Bonzo and Peter Grant's flight from London at the Los Angeles airport. John Paul Jones, who with his wife had spent Christmas with singer Madeline Bell in New York, arrived separately. Los Angeles was a funhouse for English rock bands. Robert Plant and Bonzo, who had hardly even been out of England, were incredulous. Robert kept remarking about how he'd never seen a policeman with a gun before. Even before they played a note in Hollywood, Led Zeppelin became the darlings of the main Hollywood groupie clique, Girls Together Outrageously, or the GTOs. Unlike most English stars, Led Zeppelin actually liked to go to sleazy rock clubs and just *hang out*. Jimmy was an old hand at this, but Robert and Bonzo – country bumpkins from the Midlands – were amazed to find themselves pursued by beautiful young GTOs with kohl-rimmed eyes and big heaving bosoms hanging out of their brazen, near-frontless frocks. Influenced by Richard Cole's relentless philosophy of sex and booze, Led Zeppelin found themselves keeping company with the starlets of the groupie scene and such novelties as Dahlia the Dog Act, who would bring her Great Dane to the band's hotel for special shows.

Right after Christmas the band flew to Denver to make its American debut, accompanied by its two-man crew, Richard Cole and roadie Kenny Pickett, whom the band called Pissquick. It was the first time Cole had heard Led Zeppelin. 'Fucking monsters,' he thought. But they weren't even listed on the bill. Two days later they were in Boston to play the Tea Party, which Grant considered a key show in the key American taste-making college town. Here the group had its first inkling of Zeppelin hysteria when, after they had already expanded their hour-long show by half an hour, they were called back for seven encores by the cheering crowd. With their brand-new LA hippy regalia drenched in sweat, they had to play unrehearsed jams on Elvis Presley, old Yardbirds warhorses and Chuck Berry classics. At one point, during a reprise of 'How Many More Times', Jimmy nudged John Paul to look down in front, where the entire first row of boys were banging their heads against the rim of the stage.

Led Zeppelin next touched down in New York and met the press. Atlantic's publicist took them on the obligatory visit to *Billboard* magazine, where one of the staff kidded the group about their hair, unusually long even for that era. Jimmy was also interviewed by *Hit Parader*; he described Led Zeppelin as an improvisatory blues group, defended himself from charges that he was stealing ideas from Hendrix and Clapton, and held forth on his bowing technique and his new acquisition, a pedal steel guitar, which he had used on the forthcoming album. Asked what advice he would give to aspiring guitarists, he was succinct: use lighter strings.

The Yardbirds' old stronghold had been the West Coast, and Peter Grant had booked a heavy concentration of gigs there, usually opening for Vanilla Fudge. (On other dates they opened for the rabble-rousing Detroit band, the MC5). On the last day of the year, the group played in Portland, Oregon, and then found itself unable to fly to Los Angeles because an arctic blizzard had closed the airport. But all were adamant that they make the date at the Whiskey, the main rock showcase in Los Angeles. The show *had* to go on. So Richard Cole rented a station wagon and started to drive the group to Seattle through the worst snowstorm in local memory in order to catch a plane at Seattle's still-open airport.

The Whiskey engagement was a wild success, and Hollywood embraced Led Zeppelin as it had the Yardbirds four years earlier. On 9 January, Jimmy's twenty-fifth birthday, the band began three days at the Fillmore West in San Francisco, supporting Country Joe and the Fish. Taj Mahal opened the show. In spite of the headbangers in Boston and the enthusiasm in LA, it was this Fillmore West weekend that showed the musicians they were going to be very big. Here they ran out of Elvis medleys and were forced to play unrehearsed Garnet Mimms tunes and improvise current hits like Spirit's 'Fresh Garbage'. Through all this, Jimmy suffered with flu and a fever, reminiscent of his glandular fever in the Crusaders days.

As Led Zeppelin headed for the hinterlands, Atlantic geared up its hype machine. Thousands of posters were distributed showing a bushy-headed Jimmy reaching out, palm extended (copied from the Doors' first poster), while the three hairy 'sidemen' glowered behind him. *Led Zeppelin* was released in America in the last week of January, while the band played the Image Club in Miami. But, on progressive rock stations like WBCN in Boston and KSAN in San Francisco, the album had already been an underground hit for several weeks, with disc jockeys mostly leaning on 'Communication Breakdown', 'Babe . . .' and 'Dazed and Confused'. (In New York, singer Jake Holmes heard Jimmy's version of his song and wondered what to do. Jimmy had lifted intact the title, bass line and *gestalt* from Holmes's song, but the words were completely different. Years later, Holmes recollected: 'I said, what the hell, let him have it.')

After three weeks of honing their show at provincial clubs and colleges, Led Zeppelin finished its first American tour opening for Iron Butterfly at the Fillmore East in New York on 31 January. Before the show, Peter Grant told Jimmy that Led Zeppelin's job was to blow the clumsy Butterfly off its own stage. So Jimmy went on in his red velvet suit and played for two hours before the by-now expected half-dozen encores, with Bonzo leaping in the air above his drums. By the time they had brought the crowd to its last explosive climax and finished 'Train Kept A-Rollin', Iron Butterfly refused to go on, realizing that Led Zeppelin – fellow musicians, hip brethren and label-mates – had left them nothing.

The band returned to England in February, flushed with success.

But England was a disappointment. Led Zeppelin had tasted its power in America, which now beckoned to them with money, girls and fame. So on 20 April they flew back to Los Angeles for another tour, again shepherded by Richard Cole. Back on the first tour, at the Carousel Ballroom in San Francisco, Cole had made an unusual request of Peter Grant. 'I said, "Look, let me stay with this band and not do all the others. Let me stay with one fucking band instead of jumpin' about, let me have a bit of the glory." Because I *knew* they were gonna make the money. I *knew* they were gonna be monsters. And they were.'

The tour opened with four nights at the Fillmore West. Twenty-nine shows in thirty-one days, co-headlining with Vanilla Fudge, which meant that whichever band was strongest in that market went on last. By then Led Zeppelin's act was growing out of proportion. Their original hour-long show had expanded to an hour and a half on stage. When they added their utility Ben E. King and Garnet Mimms numbers, they played for two hours. The encores demanded in America expanded the show to two and a half hours, and the new riffs and songs Led Zeppelin were writing on the road added an hour to that. Even Vanilla Fudge, who the band were friends with, was leery about going on after Zeppelin had wrung a crowd for three and a half hours of non-stop crunch.

In Los Angeles, Cole installed the group in bungalows at the Chateau Marmont Hotel, where Led Zeppelin's orgies wouldn't disturb the other guests. Everyone in the band but Jimmy was married, which only heightened the forbidden pleasures that Hollywood nightlife offered the band. At one point Bonzo dressed up as a waiter, laid Jimmy on a room service cart, and wheeled him into a suite full of tumescent girls, whom Jimmy fancied on the youngish side. 'I don't think you will ever find an English musician who would ever put down those girls who were called groupies,' Cole says. ' 'Cos those girls were not *sluts* or *slags* or whatever. They fucking saved my arse as far as patience goes, 'cos you're talking about twenty-year-old guys away from home. The girls took care of them and were like a second home. You could trust them. They wouldn't steal from you. Most of them are dead now.'

By early May, *Led Zeppelin* had entered the American Top 10, and the band was raging. The long shows usually began with 'Communication Breakdown', and segued into 'I Can't Quit You Baby' with Robert's yawping howls and Jimmy's delicate blues fugues. Often the shows would bog down in the bombastic sludge of 'Killing Floor'/'Lemon Song' and 'Babe I'm Gonna Leave You' before ending with the usual oldies medley. At one show at Winterland, this started with Garnet Mimms' 'As Long As I Have You' and ran through an improbable melange of the lullaby 'Hush Little Baby', 'Bags Groove', 'Shake' à la Otis Redding, and 'Fresh Garbage'.

Two days later, Led Zeppelin's sojourn in Seattle proved to be the end of their reputation as normal humans. Seattle was where the Shark Episode took place.

The show itself was another success. Playing at an open-air

festival, Robert and Bonzo were thrilled to be on the same bill with Chuck Berry (whom the jaded Jimmy knew from Yardbirds tours as a moody recluse). Their awe was increased when they beheld the brown-eyed handsome man emerge from his dusty Cadillac, which he'd driven up from St Louis, unpack his guitar and play a set with a strange pick-up band, and then deposit his cash fee in his briefcase and drive off. Led Zeppelin took the stage after the Doors had finished their set, made anti-climactic by Jim Morrison's disconnected rambling, and then revived the faded audience with their punchy, explosive rhythms. It was no contest, and Led Zeppelin gave no quarter.

Back at the hotel, the band started drinking. Richard Cole says that what happened later was his fault. 'The sharks thing happened at the Edgewater Inn in Seattle. How it came about is that in 1968 I was with Terry Reid, supporting the Moody Blues in Seattle, and their road manager told me the band should stay at the Edgewater Inn, because there's a tackle shop in the lobby and you can fish right out the window of the hotel. I said, "Go on, fuck off ya cunt." He said, "Come on Richard, I'm not kidding, it's true." So the next time I was in Seattle was with Led Zeppelin and Vanilla Fudge, and we started to catch sharks out the window. By this time the tours were more and more risqué, and you could do what you liked with the girls who showed up at the hotel. For me, that second fucking Led Zeppelin tour was the fucking best time of my life. *That* was the one. We were hot and on our way up, but no one was watching too closely. So you could fucking *play*. And these birds were coming up to my suite wanting to fuck, and me and Bonzo were quite serious about catching these fish.' What happened next isn't really clear. One girl, a pretty young groupie with red hair, was disrobed and tied to the bed. According to legend, Led Zeppelin then proceeded to stuff pieces of shark into her vagina and rectum.

Richard Cole says it didn't happen that way. 'It wasn't Bonzo, it was *me*. Robert and Bonzo didn't know *anything*, they were kids. It wasn't shark parts anyway: it was the nose that got put in. Yeah, the shark was *alive*! It wasn't dead! We caught a big lot of sharks, at least two dozen, stuck coat hangers through the gills and left 'em in the closet . . . But the *true* shark story was that it wasn't even a shark. It was a red snapper and the chick happened to be a fucking redheaded broad with a ginger pussy. And that is the truth. Bonzo was in the room, but I did it. Mark Stein [of Vanilla Fudge] filmed the whole thing. And she *loved* it. It was like, "You'd like a bit of fucking, eh? Let's see how *your* red snapper likes *this* red snapper!" That was it. It was the *nose* of the fish, and that girl must have come twenty times. I'm not saying the chick wasn't drunk, I'm not saying that *any* of us weren't drunk. But it was nothing malicious or harmful, no way! No one was *ever* hurt. She might have been *hit* by a shark a few times for disobeying orders, but she didn't get hurt.'

In this incredible year-long spurt of debauchery, the musicians and management of Led Zeppelin, according to Richard Cole, often kiddingly reminded each other that silent film star Fatty Arbuckle's career had been ruined when he was alleged to have mistakenly killed a girl he was rogering with a champagne bottle. This was often talked about, because Led Zeppelin quickly discovered that *lots* of girls wanted to be fucked with champagne bottles. Cole blames it all on alcoholism. 'I'll tell you how much we used to drink. I think we bankrupted Steve Paul's Scene in New York because we *never* paid our bar bills. All the so-called Led Zeppelin depravity took place the first two years in an alcoholic fog. After that we got older and grew out of it. It became a realistic business.'

Meanwhile, the tour madness only increased. In British Columbia, they discovered that their two dates were 500 miles and one day apart. The distance had to be driven overnight. From there they flew to Hawaii and a couple of days of rest before plunging back into battle with shows in Detroit. After flying all night, the group staggered into their Detroit motel at seven in the morning and stumbled onto a gruesome murder scene. The corpse was being taken out as the band walked in, and steam was rising from a pool of blackened blood on the carpet. A man had been shot to death just a few moments before. Robert grabbed his bags and his room key and headed for some sleep. 'I only knew I'd spew if I looked at it for another second,' he said.

In Detroit, Led Zeppelin's entourage was joined by its first writer/photographer team, covering the band for *Life* magazine. Back in Los Angeles, the band had been upset by its decidedly mixed reviews in the local press. A Hollywood press agent was hired to correct that situation, and *Life* was convinced to assign a team to the tour. Writer Ellen Sander and her photographer had originally proposed covering the Who, also touring America that summer (they were one of the few English bands to play at Woodstock), but that had fallen through and Sander and *Life* had settled on Zeppelin instead. It was Ellen Sander's first job for *Life* and a plum for Zeppelin, since new bands weren't often afforded such mainstream press coverage. It was decided that Ellen Sander would join the band in Detroit. There Richard Cole organized an informal betting pool based on which of them would sleep with her first.

As Sander travelled with the band, she recorded her impressions for her article. Robert was 'woolly, handsome in an obscenely rugged way'. Jimmy was 'ethereal, effeminate, pale and frail', Bonzo 'played ferocious drums, often shirtless and sweating like some gorilla on a rampage'. John Paul Jones held the whole thing together and stayed in the shadows. 'No matter how miserably the group failed to keep their behaviour up to a basic human level,' Sander noted, 'they played well almost every night of the tour. If they were only one of the many British rock groups touring at the time, they were also one of the finest. The stamina they found each night at curtain-time was amazing, in the face of every conceivable foul-up with equipment, timing, transportation and organization at every date. They had that fire and musicianship going for them and a big burst of incentive; this time around, on their second tour, from the very beginning, they were almost stars.'

Sander couldn't help noticing the frantic air of sexual tension and competition between the members of the group. Jimmy didn't like to approach girls himself, preferring to have Richard Cole solicit for him. But Sanders was not a groupie and Richard was too dangerous, so instead Jimmy had his publicity agent tell Sander to call him. And Sander did end up spending the most time with Page, since Robert was too wild and preoccupied with sex, Bonzo was too drunk, and Jones was never around. One night Cole burst into her room to tell her that the group was leaving for a gig, and noticed that both beds were unmade. 'Pagey's been with you then,' he yelled, and rushed out to tell the rest. But it wasn't true.

When Robert Plant awoke from his daytime nap in Detroit, he stank so badly he was dispatched to buy some shampoo and deodorant for himself. As he stepped out of the motel onto the street, a motorist stopped at a light cursed his long hair and spat in his face. Robert was upset. 'I'm white,' he said later. 'I can imagine how a spade feels here.'

That night the show was at the Grande Ballroom, an old warehouse that was one of the original rock palaces. The house was packed and restless; armed police were arresting customers for lighting joints. The house loudspeakers failed during the first set, which sounded terrible. Backstage, the dingy dressing-room was crowded with groupies angling for a shot at the band. According to Sander: 'A pair of grotesquely painted, greasy-cheeked, overweight sexbombs in their late twenties pushed their way through the young things to Robert Plant. One placed her hand on his thigh and brassily declared: "You're spending the night with *me*." Robert grimaced and exploded. "Hey wot, you bloody tart, old Robert's a married man!" The others tittered as he squirmed away, pausing to shoot them a leering wink.' Huddling together for protection, the band discussed the situation. The two older groupies were dubbed 'the ugly sisters' but it was decided they did possess a certain slatternly allure. A plot was hatched to get them back to the motel, gang-bang them and then stuff them full of cream-filled doughnuts. Pleasant memories of the Shark Episode still danced in their fevered brains. In fact, once Led Zeppelin acquired a taste for abusing groupies, it just got worse. With smug self-justification, Jimmy explained it to Sander: 'Girls come around and pose like starlets, teasing and acting haughty. If you humiliate them a bit they tend to come on all right after that. Everyone knows what they come for . . . I haven't got time to deal with it.'

Just then John Paul Jones walked in the door, looked in the room full of girls and dope-dealers, and walked out again, sulking miserably outside while fans pestered him. Jimmy Page, 'with that febrile, forlorn look that brought out perversity in fifteen-year-olds' (according to Sander), sat inside and chatted with whoever spoke to him, neither offering not accepting any sexual invitations.

The following morning the group met outside the hotel, waiting for Richard to show up with the station wagon. Robert was annoyed. Not only had the cream doughnut event fallen through when they couldn't find a store after the gig, but Robert had been with one of the ugly sisters and she wouldn't come all night. 'Can you believe that?' he asked. 'I was embarrassed.'

The next gig was in Athens, Ohio. Between his own hectic sexual escapades (he often wound up with the girls he solicited for others), Richard Cole got the band to the airport, handled the reservation and tickets, got them drunk on the flight so they wouldn't complain, rented a car at the next airport and got them to their next motel and gig. No time for supper, just visits to the motel bar before and after the show. Then he got them up in the morning, and the musicians collapsed into a sleepy stupor, heads lolling with the turns, as Cole drove them through springtime Ohio farmland back to the airport and the next gig in Minneapolis. When Robert got on the plane he galloped down the aisle like a demented ape, shouting 'Toilets! TOILETS FOR OLD ROBERT!' The other passengers gaped as the big hippy with the blond mane clawed at the door of the lavatory.

The plane was delayed, and the band was late getting onstage at the staid Guthrie Memorial Theatre, where the audience chuckled in genteel chagrin at Robert's climaxing orgasm sequence during the new song, 'Whole Lotta Love'. Afterwards the band was obliged to attend a party for the country club set at the promoter's suburban manse, where the exhausted Englishmen got quietly drunk and were gaped at by the locals for several excruciating hours. The next morning Richard Cole convened a meeting. There were four days before the next show in Chicago; everyone wanted out of Minneapolis. Jimmy decided the band should go to New York to work on the new album, rehearse, and do interviews.

Work had started on *Led Zeppelin II* the previous January, with riffs left over from the original act and new riffs developed during the constant playing, rehearsal and improvisation of the tour. *Led Zeppelin II* was the product of an English band's insane life on the road, written in snatches in motel rooms, dressing-rooms and studios all over North America. Since English musicians were allowed only six months per year in America, they were under constant pressure to make every day pay. But actually working in the studio became a problem when word spread among the groupies that Jimmy Page and his hunky band were in town. There was one thirty-ish groupie queen who was particularly annoying to Jimmy. She'd shown up at the studio where Jimmy was trying to mix 'Bring It On Home', claiming to be the ex-wife of a famous producer, dressing the part – dyed blond hair, black leather mini-skirt, tall boots, a cowboy hat. The most intelligent of the groupies had the foresight to check the studio schedules so they could arrive early to get the best seats: it was this group the blonde tried to intimidate, loudly announcing that Jimmy was so *marvellous* in bed last night. Finally a distracted Page could take no more. He went out in the hall and found the most pathetic of all the aspirant groupies. Cuddling her protectively, he led this wretch back into the studio and demanded the older woman give up her seat for her. Staring straight ahead, her pancaked face crumbling, the blonde got up and left. That night the group saw her cruising Steve Paul's Scene like a barracuda, sniffing fresh blood.

The next stop, Chicago, was old Yardbirds turf. The massive Kinetic Circus was packed; also on the bill were Vanilla Fudge, and in the dressing-room the gory details of the Shark Episode were rehearsed again with great mirth, Led Zeppelin tore it down that night, and the hall echoed to repeated ovations. 'Dazed and Confused' was now stretching into twenty minutes, with Jimmy's bow exhibition drawing much awe for its ritualistic connotations of diabolism. Snooping at the back door, Peter Grant caught the hall's manager surreptitiously selling tickets to an already sold-out show and confiscated the cash. Something else felt wrong. Neither Grant nor Cole believed the tally of heads and cash. In the office, Richard Cole took apart the wastebin and came up with ticket stubs of the wrong colour. Again, Grant demanded and received whatever illicit cash was due the band. Grant's tenacious instinct for the scent of cash eventually meant that his clients Led Zeppelin would earn (and keep) more money than any rock musicians before them.

Next show: the Boston Tea Party, where before the kids had been banging their heads on the stage. This time, with all the Atlantic people up from New York to see the show, the Zeppelin soared and were called back for the usual multiple encores by the oversold, throbbing rock freaks. After five encores, the group is backstage, swigging Watney's Red Barrel ale, about to drop but still high on adrenalin. Outside, the crowd is *bonkers*. Robert urges, 'Let's give 'em another.' Jimmy Page shakes his head, laughing. 'We don't *know* any others,' he gasps. But as Robert walked out again, the crowd began to roar and the others followed him into an unrehearsed, sloppy medley of Beatles and Stones songs. Backstage after the show, the band was limp. Robert was enraged because a fan had stolen his favourite shirt. Jonesy lovingly wiped his bass down with a towel before carefully depositing it in its plush-lined case. They were besieged by groupies as usual. Earlier, a bridegroom had gone to the group's motel where his bride had tried to find Led Zeppelin, and had beaten her up on the street outside while the band ate in the restaurant, ignorant of the whole incident. This time, too tired to cope, they asked a DJ from the Boston FM station to find them some nice girls.

The second tour of the States ended with two shows at the Fillmore East on 30 and 31 May. On the last night, Ellen Sander from *Life* showed up backstage to thank the band for letting her travel with them, and to say goodbye. She walked into Led Zeppelin's dressing room, she remembers, unprepared for what happened next. 'Two members of the group attacked me, shrieking and grabbing at my clothes, totally over the edge . . . Bonzo came at me first, and then there were a couple more . . .

after that I didn't see much. All of a sudden there were all these hands on me, and all these big guys. My clothes were half torn off; they were in a frenzy. I was absolutely terrified that I was going to be raped and really angry . . . And then I saw Peter Grant – who was bigger than all of them – and I thought, "Him too? Oh no, I'm gonna be *killed*!" But what he did was pull Bonham off me. Peter Grant just picked me up and pulled him off me, so all they did was tear my clothes. They didn't hurt me, except for my feelings.'

Led Zeppelin never did get their pictures in *Life*; Ellen Sander refused to write the story. And when she later published her bitter account of Led Zeppelin's second American tour, she concluded: 'If you walk inside the cages of the zoo you get to see the animals close up, stroke the captive pelts, and mingle with the energy behind the mystique. You also get to smell the shit firsthand.'

THE TRUE ADVENTURES OF THE ROLLING STONES

Altamont by Stanley Booth

Some people were dancing. Angels dancing with their dirty bouffant women. A pall of wariness and fear seemed to be upon the people who were not too stoned to be aware, but the music was pounding on and though the drums were not properly miked and the guitar seemed to separate and disappear in places and you couldn't really hear Wyman's bass, it was hanging together.

'Ooh, yah,' Mick said as the song ended. He stopped dancing, looked into the distance, and his voice, which had been subdued, now began to sound pacific, as he glimpsed for the first time the enormity of what he had created. One surge forward and people would be crushed. Half a million people together, with neither rules nor regulations as to how they must conduct themselves, can through sheer physical weight create terrible destruction. 'Oooh, babies – ' low motherly tone ' – there are so many of you – just be cool down front now, don't push around – just keep still.' He laughed as if he were talking to a child, looking down at the pretty stoned faces before him. 'Keep together – oh yah.'

Keith tested the first three notes of 'Carol', unleashed the riff, and Mick leaned back to sing

Oh, Carol! Don't ever steal your heart away
I'm gonna learn to dance if it takes me all night and day

The sound was better, drums and bass clearer, guitars stronger. At the end Mick said, 'Whoo! Whoo! Aw, yes!' He hoisted a bottle of Jack Daniels' that was sitting in front of the drums. 'I'd like to drink, ah, drink one to you all.'

Keith set out on 'Sympathy for the Devil'. As Mick sang, 'I was around when Jesus Christ had his moment of doubt and pain,' there was a low explosive *thump!* in the crowd to the right of the stage, and oily blue-white smoke swirled up as if someone had thrown a toad into a witches' cauldron. People were pushing, falling, a great hole opening as they moved instantly away from the centre of the trouble. I had no idea people in a crowd could move so fast. Mick stopped singing but the music chugged on, four bars, eight, then Mick shouted: 'Hey! Heeey! Hey! Keith – Keith – *Keith!*' By now only Keith was playing, but he was playing as loud and hard as ever, the way the band is supposed to do until the audience tears down the chicken wire and comes onstage with chairs and broken bottles. 'Will you cool it and I'll try and stop it,' Mick said, so Keith stopped.

'Hey – hey, peo-ple,' Mick said. 'Sisters – brothers and sisters – *brothers* and *sisters* – come *on* now.' He was offering the social contract to a twister of flailing dark shapes. 'That means everybody just cool *out* – will ya cool out, everybody – '

'Somebody's bike blew up, man,' Keith said.

'I know,' Mick said. 'I'm hip. Everybody be cool now, come on – all right? Can we still make it down in the front? Can we still collect ourselves, everybody? Can everybody just – I don't know what happened, I couldn't see, but I hope ya all right – are ya all right?' The trouble spot seemed still. Charlie was making eager drum flutters, Keith playing stray notes.

'Okay,' Mick said. 'Let's just give ourselves – we'll give ourselves another half a minute before we get our breath back, everyone just cool down and easy – is there anyone there who's hurt – huh? – everyone all right – okay – all right.' The music was starting again. 'Good, we can groove – summink very funny happens when we start that numbah – ah, ha!'

Keith and Charlie had the rhythm pattern going, tight and expert, and Mick asked again to be allowed to introduce himself, a man of wealth and taste, but not about to lay anybody's soul to waste. Keith's solo cut like a scream into the brain, as Mick chanted, 'Everybody got to cool out – everybody has got to cool right out – yeah! Aw right!'

Sounding like one instrument, a wild whirling bagpipe, the Stones chugged to a halt. But the crowd didn't stop, we could see Hell's Angels spinning like madmen, swinging at people. By stage right a tall white boy with a black cloud of electric hair was dancing, shaking, infuriating the Angels by having too good a time. He was beside an Angel when I first saw him, and I wondered how he could be so loose, nearly touching one of those monsters. He went on dancing and the Angel pushed him and another Angel started laying into the crowd with a pool cue and then a number of Angels were grabbing people, hitting and kicking, the crowd falling back from the fury with fantastic speed, the dancer running away from the stage, the crowd parting before him like the Red Sea, the Angels catching him from behind, the heavy end of a pool cue in one long arc crashing into the side of his head, felling him like a sapling so that he lay straight and didn't move and I thought, My God, they've killed him. But they weren't through. When we went down they were all over him, pounding with fists and cues, and when he was just lying there they stood for a while kicking him like kicking the dead carcass of an animal, the meat shaking on the bones.

The song was over and Mick was saying, 'Who – who – I mean like people, who's fighting and what for? Hey, peo-ple – I mean, who's fighting and what for? Why are we fighting? Why are we fighting?' His voice was strong, emphasizing each word. 'We don't want to fight. Come on – do we want, who wants to fight? Hey – I – you know, I mean like – every other scene has been cool. Like we've gotta stop right now. We've gotta stop them right now. You know, we can't, there's no point.'

Sam took the microphone. 'Could I suggest a compromise, please.' He was a bit more awake now and the soul of peace and reason. 'Can I ask please to speak to the – ' He stopped then because the logical conclusion was, ' – to the Hell's Angels and ask them please to stop performing mayhem on people.'

'Either those cats cool it,' Keith said, 'or we don't play. I mean, there's not that many of 'em.'

It was a fine brave thing to say, but I had made up my mind about fighting the Hell's Angels while one of them had me in the air, and probably the rest of the people present had concluded some time ago that the first man who touched an Angel would surely die. Even as Keith spoke an Angel was ripping into someone in front of stage left. 'That guy there,' Keith said, 'if he doesn't stop it – '

There was a pause while another Angel did slowly stop him. Still another Angel yelled to ask Keith what he wanted. 'I just want him to stop pushin' people around,' Keith said.

An Angel came to the mike and bellowed into it. 'Hey, if you don't cool it you ain't gonna hear no more music! Now, you wanta all go home, or what?' It was like blaming the pigs in a slaughterhouse for bleeding on the floor.

Horowitz was leading some of the women in our group back to the trailer. Michael Lydon asked me, 'Can I use your notes later? My old lady's had a bad acid trip and she cut her foot and I need to get her out of here.' Later Michael wrote of the Angels, 'Their absolute solidarity mocks our fearful hope of community, their open appetite for violence our unfocused love of peace.' At the time I thought, Notes? He thinks I'm taking notes?

Stu, in his blue windbreaker, was at the mike, saying in a cool but unhappy voice, 'We need doctors down here *now*, please. Can we have a doctor down here now to the front?'

You felt that in the next seconds or minutes you could die, and there was nothing you could do to prevent it, to improve the odds for survival. A bad dream, but we were all in it.

I looked around, checking my position, which if not the worst was not good, and saw David Maysles on top of a truck behind the stage. Ethan Russell and Al Maysles were up there with their cameras, and more people, including a couple of Hell's Angels sitting in front dangling their legs over the side like little boys fishing at a creek in the nineteenth century.

'Hey! David!' I said.

'You want to get up here?'

'Sure.' I stuck my notebook behind my belt and swung aboard, being careful not to jostle the Angels. At least now I would be behind them, instead of having it the other way round, which had given me worse chills than the wind did up here. It was cold away from the warm amps but this was, I hoped, a safer place and better to see from.

Hunkered behind the Angels, I noticed that only one wore colors, the other one in his cowboy hat and motorcycle boots was just a sympathizer. Sam was saying, 'The doctor is going through in a green jumper and he's just here – ' pointing in front 'wavin' his hand in the air, look.' The mass, like a dumb aquatic beast, had closed up again except for a little space around the body. (The boy didn't die, to my – and probably his – surprise.) 'Can you let the doctor go through please and let him get to the person who's hurt?' Someone in front spoke to Sam, who added wearily, 'We have also – lost in the front here – a little girl who's five years old.'

Charlie was playing soft rolls, Keith was playing a slow blues riff. 'Let's play cool-out music,' Keith said to Mick.

They played a repeating twelve-bear pattern that stopped in half a minute. 'Keep going,' Mick said, and it started again, a meditative walking-bass line, the Stones trying to orient themselves by playing an Elmore James/Jimmy Reed song they had played in damp London caverns. 'The sun is shining on both sides of the street,' Mick sang. 'I got a smile on my face for every little girl I meet.' The slow blues did seem to help things, a little. A huge Angel with long blond hair, brown suede vest, no shirt, blue jeans, was standing behind gentle Charlie, patting his foot, one giant hand resting on Charlie's white pullover. The song ended without event and Mick said, 'We all dressed up, we got no place to go,' which was all too true.

'Stray Cat,' Keith said, but there was another flurry of fighting stage right, partly hidden from us by the PA scaffold, a tower of speakers.

'Hey – Heyheyhey look,' Mick said. Then to Keith or to no one he said, 'Those *scenes* down there.'

I leaned forward and spoke to the cowboy hat. 'What's

happening, man,' I asked. 'Why are they fighting?'

Over his shoulder, out of the corner of his mouth, he said, 'Some smart asshole, man, some wise guy wants to start trouble – and these guys are tired, man, they been here all night, some wise guy starts something they don't like it – arhh, I can't tell you what happened.' Taking a jug of acid-apple juice from his Angel friend, he drank till his eyes looked, as Wynonie Harris used to say, like two cherries in a glass of buttermilk. Me, I lay low.

'Stray Cat' started, Mick sounding perfunctory, forgetting the words here and there, Keith playing madly.

A girl down front was shaking with the music and crying as if her dream of life had ended. In the backstage aisle between the trunks, the Angels and their women were doing their stiff jerking dance. Most of the women were hard-looking tattooed types with shellacked hairdoes, but one of them, no more than fourteen, with a dirty, pretty-baby face, wearing a black leather jacket, was moving the seat of her greasy jeans wildly, and I thought of the little guerrilla in Fort Collins and was glad she wasn't in this crowd.

The Angel standing with his hand on Charlie's shoulder was being asked to step down off the stage by one of the New York heavies, a red-faced, red-haired, beefy man dressed in the light golf-jacket uniform. You could follow what they were saying by their gestures. The cop told the Angel to step down, the Angel shook his head, the cop told him again and pushed him a little. The cop had a cigarette in his mouth and the Angel took it out, just plucked it from between the cop's lips like taking a rose from the mouth of the fair Carmen, causing the cop to regard the Angel with a sorrowful countenance. It was only when two more men in golf jackets turned around and faced the Angel with expressions equally dolorous that he went down the steps. He came back a minute later but stayed at the rear of the stage, dancing, twitching like a frog attached to electrodes.

As 'Stray Cat' ended, Mick said, 'Ooh baby,' looking up as if for deliverance and finding a shapeless human mass reaching into the darkness as far as he could see. 'Baby – all along a hillside – hey, everybody, ah – we gone do, we gone do, ah – what are we gonna do?'

'Love in Vain,' Keith said. The slow elegant Robert Johnson line began, building slowly. 'I followed her to the station with my suitcase in my hand – oh, it's hard to tell, when all your love's in vain.' The Stones had not forgotten how to play, but nobody seemed to be enjoying the music, at least nobody who could be seen in the lights that made the stage the glowing center of a world of night. Too many people were still too close together and the Angels were still surly. At stage right an Angel with a skinful of acid was writhing and wringing his hands in a pantomime of twisting Mick's neck. At stage left Timothy Leary huddled with his wife and daughter, looking as if he'd taken better trips. The stage skirts were so crowded that Mick had only a limited area to work. He looked cramped, smaller than ever and cowed, frightened, but he kept on singing.

Things were quiet during 'Love in Vain' except for some heavy jostling down front, the prevailing mood of impending death, and the fear and anguish you could see in the faces. 'Aw yeah,' Mick said as the song ended. 'Hey, I think – I think, I think, that there was one good idea came out of that number, which was, that I really think the only way you're gonna keep yourself cool is to *sit down*. If you can make it I think you'll find it's better. So when you're sitting comfortably – now, boys and girls – ' withdrawing the social contract – 'Are you sitting comfortably? When, when we get to really like the end and we all want to go absolutely crazy and like jump on each other then we'll stand up again, d'you know what I mean – but we can't seem to keep it together, standing up – okay?'

In the background Keith was tooling up the opening chords of 'Under My Thumb'. A few people in front of the stage were sitting, going along with Mick, who for the first time in his life had asked an audience to sit down. The anarchist was telling people what to do. Then, just before he began to sing, he said, 'But it ain't a rule.'

'Under My Thumb' started – 'Hey! Hey! Under my thumb is a girl who once had me down – ' and Mick had sung only the first line of the song when there was a sudden movement in the crowd at stage left. I looked away from Mick and saw, with that now-familiar instant space around him, bordered with falling bodies, a Beale Street nigger in a black hat, black shirt, iridescent blue-green suit, arms and legs stuck out at crazy angles, a nickle-plated revolver in his hand. The gun waved in the lights for a second, two, then he was hit, so hard, by so many Angels, that I didn't see the first one – short, Mexican-looking, the one who led me onstage? – as he jumped. I saw him as he came down, burying a long knife in the black man's back. Angels covered the black man like flies on a stinking carcass. The attack carried the victim behind the stack of the speakers, and I never saw him again.

The black man, Meredith Hunter, nicknamed Murdock, was eighteen years old. He had come to Altamont with his girlfriend, Patty Bredehoft, a blond Berkeley High School student, and another couple. They had arrived in Hunter's car at about two o'clock in the afternoon, parked on the highway and walked over to hear the bands. Near the end of the day Patty Bredehoft and the other couple were back at the car when Hunter who had been hanging around the stage area, came to get her to go hear the Rolling Stones. Later she told the Alameda County Grand Jury, 'When we finally worked our way up to the front of the crowd and the Rolling Stones started playing, there was a lot of pushing and there were Angels on the stage. And Murdock kept trying to go farther up toward the front. I couldn't keep up with him because I wasn't strong so I sort of waited back, didn't try to get as far as he did. He was as close as he could get, where there were some boxes with people standing on the boxes. I'd say there was about five people in between me and him, estimating, because the crowd was moving around, but I could see the upper part of his body.

'I was getting pushed around, and as I glanced up there, I saw either he had hit Murdock or pushed him or something, but this Hell's Angel who was standing, pushed him or knocked him back. It didn't knock him down, but knocked him back over the stage, and as he started to come back forward towards the Hell's

Angel, another Hell's Angel who was on the stage grabbed him around the neck. They were scuffling around. I'm not sure which Hell's Angel it was, but I just remembered he was scuffling around and there was a couple of people blocking my view of him because he was down on the ground. I couldn't really see him. As the people backed away, Murdock came around by my side and pulled a gun out. Then they came toward – well, a group of Hell's Angels – I'm not sure they were all Hell's Angels, but I know most of them were – they came toward him and they reached for his arm and then they were all kicking and fighting and stuff, Murdock and the Hell's Angels, and the fight more or less moved around towards where the scaffold was on the edge of the stage.

'I followed them around and then I was standing there watching them fight, or watching whatever – I couldn't really tell what was going on underneath the scaffold, and the Hell's Angel – I thought he was, was a Hell's Angel, but I wasn't quite sure because he had the jeans jacket on, but I couldn't see the back to see if it had colors on. He was holding the gun in his hand, laying in the palm of his hand, to show it to me, and he said something like, "This is what we took from him. He was going to kill innocent people, so he deserved to be dead".'

A young man named Paul Cox, who had been standing beside Meredith Hunter before the violence started, talked to the grand jury and to *Rolling Stone*. 'An Angel kept looking over at me and I tried to keep ignoring him and I didn't want to look at him at all, because I was very scared of them and seeing what they were doing all day and because he kept trying to cause a fight or something and kept staring at us. He kept on looking over, and the next thing I know he's hassling this Negro boy on the side of me. And I was trying not to look at him, and then he reached over and shook this boy by the side of the head, thinking it was fun, laughing, and I noticed something was going to happen so I kind of backed off.

'The boy yanked away, and when he yanked away, next thing I know he was flying in the air, right on the ground, just like all the other people it happened to. He scrambled to his feet, and he's backing up and he's trying to run from the Angels, and all these Angels are – a couple jumped off the stage and a couple was running alongside the stage, and his girlfriend was screaming to him not to shoot, because he pulled out his gun. And when he pulled it out, he held it in the air and his girlfriend is like climbing on him and pushing him back and he's trying to get away and these Angels are coming at him and he turns around and starts running. And then some Angel snuck up from right out of the crowd and leaped up and brought this knife down in his back. And then I saw him stab him again, and while he's stabbing him, he's running. This Negro boy is running into the crowd, and you could see him stiffen up when he's being stabbed.

'He came running toward me. I grabbed onto the scaffold, and he came running kind of toward me and fell down on his knees, and the Hell's Angel grabbed onto both of his shoulders and started kicking him in the face about five times or so and then he fell down on his face. He let go and he fell down on his face. And then one of them kicked him on the side and he rolled over, and he muttered some words. He said, "I wasn't going to shoot you." That was the last words he muttered.

'If some other people would have jumped in I would have jumped in. But nobody jumped in and after he said, "I wasn't going to shoot you," one of the Hell's Angels said, "Why did you have a gun?" He didn't give him time to say anything. He grabbed one of those garbage cans, the cardboard ones with the metal rimming, and he smashed him over the head with it, and then he kicked the garbage can out of the way and started kicking his head in. Five of them started kicking his head in. Kicked him all over the place. And then the guy that started the whole thing stood on his head for a minute or so and then walked off. And then the one I was talking about, he wouldn't let us touch him for about two or three minutes. Like, "Don't touch him, he's going to die anyway, let him die, he's going to die."

'Chicks were just screaming. It was all confusion. I jumped down anyway to grab him and some other dude jumped down and grabbed him, and then the Hell's Angel just stood over him for a little bit and then walked away. We turned him over and ripped off his shirt. We rubbed his back up and down to get the blood off so we could see, and there was a big hole in his spine and a big hole on the side and there was a big hole in his temple. A big open slice. You could see all the way in. You could see inside. You could see at least an inch down. And then there was a big hole right where there's no ribs on his back – and then the side of his head was just sliced open – you couldn't see so far in – it was bleeding quite heavily – but his back wasn't bleeding too heavy after that – there – all of us were drenched in blood.

'I picked up his legs and someone else . . . this guy said he was a doctor or something . . . I don't know who he was . . . he picked up his arms and he said, "Got to get him some help because he's going to die. We've got fifteen or twenty minutes, if we can get him some help . . ." And so we tried to carry him on the stage. Tell Mick Jagger to stop playing so we could get him on the stage and get some attention for him. No one told Jagger that, but someone was trying to tell him to stop and he kept leaning over and looking out at the crowd like he was paying attention and trying to figure out what was happening. He kept leaning over with his ear trying to hear what somebody was telling him, but he couldn't hear. So they kept on playing and the Hell's Angels wouldn't let us through . . . get on the stage. They kept blocking us, saying go around, go through some other way. They knew he was going to die in a matter of minutes. They wanted him to die probably so he couldn't talk. And so we carried . . . we turned around and went the other way. It took about fifteen minutes to get him behind the stage. We went around that whole thing and got behind where there was a Red Cross truck, something like that. And someone brought out a metal stretcher and laid him on that. Well, first we laid him on the ground. And then we felt his pulse and it was just barely doing it . . . real slow and real weak. His whole mouth and stuff is bashed up into his nose and stuff and he couldn't breathe out of his nose. He was trying to breathe out of his mouth. There really wasn't anything you could do. We carried him over to some station wagon and then whoever owned the car hopped in and some other people hopped in and I stayed there. I went over and they had this thing of coffee and I had it . . . poured it all over to wipe off all the blood.'

The doctor who helped to carry Hunter backstage was Robert Hiatt, a medical resident at the Public Health Hospital in San Francisco. 'He was limp in my hands and unconscious,' Hiatt said. 'He was still breathing then, though quite shallowly, and he had a very weak pulse. It was obvious he wasn't going to make it, but if anything could be done, he would have to get to a hospital quickly. He had very serious sounds.'

Dr Richard Baldwin, a general practitioner from Point Reyes who saw Hunter backstage said, 'He got a bad injury in that they got him in the back and it went in between the ribs and the side of the spine, and there's nothing but big arteries in there, the aorta, the main artery in the body, and a couple kidney arteries. And if you hit one of those you're dead. You're dead in less than a minute and there's nothing anyone can do. In other words, if you're standing in front of the hospital or even if he was stabbed in an operating room, there's nothing they could have done to save him. That's one of those injuries that's just irreparable.'

When the trouble with the boy in the green suit started, the Stones had stopped playing. 'Okay, man,' Keith said, 'look, we're splitting, if those cats, if you can't – we're splitting, if those people don't stop beating everybody up in sight – I want 'em *out of the way.*'

An Angel in front of the stage was trying to tell Keith something, but Keith wouldn't listen. 'I don't like *you* to tell me – ' he went on, but another Angel, onstage, stopped him. 'Look, man,' the Angel said, 'a guy's got a gun out there, and he's shootin' at the stage – '

'Got a gun,' someone else yelled.

Mike Lang, one of the organizers of Woodstock, who had been helping with this concert, took the microphone. 'People – hey people – c'mon let's be cool – people, please – there's no reason to hassle anybody, please don't be mad at anybody – please relax and sit down . . .'

Sam, who'd been standing by with his hands jammed in his

pockets, took over. 'If you move back and sit down,' he said, 'we can continue and we will continue. We need a doctor under the left-hand scaffold as soon as possible please.' He was listening to shouts from the front of the crowd. He listened to a girl for a few seconds and went on: 'There's a Red Cross building at the top of the stage and there's been lots of lost children, children, under the scaffold – if you've lost a child go and collect him or her there please – it's a Red Cross van . . .'

After another pause during which no one onstage did anything but look anxiously around, Mick said, 'It seems to be stuck down to me – will you listen to me for a minute – please listen to me just for one second a'right? First of all, everyone is gonna get to the side of the stage who's on it now except for the Stones who are playing. Please, everyone – everyone, please, can you get to the side of the stage who's not playing. Right? That's a start. Now, the thing is, I can't see what's going on, who is doing wot, it's just a scuffle. All I can ask you, San Francisco, is like the whole thing – this could be the most beautiful evening we've had this winter. We really – y'know, why, why – don't let's fuck it up, man, come on – let's get it together – everyone – come *on* now – I can't see you up on the hillsides, you're probably very cool. Down here we're not so cool, we've got a lot of hassles goin' on. I just – every cat . . .'

There were shouts from the darkness. Mick peered out blindly past the stage lights and answered, 'Yeah, I know, we can't even see you but I know you're there – you're cool. We're just trying to keep it together. I can't do any more than ask you – beg you, just to keep it together. You can do it, it's within your power – everyone – Hell's Angels, everybody. Let's just keep ourselves together.

'You know,' Mick said with a sudden burst of passion, 'if we *are* all one, let's fucking well *show* we're all one. Now there's one thing we need – Sam, we need an ambulance – we need a doctor by that scaffold there, if there's a doctor can he get to there. Okay, we're gonna, we gonna do – I don't know what the fuck we gonna do. Everyone just sit down. Keep cool. Let's just *relax*, let's get into a groove. Come on, we can get it together. Come on.'

'Under my Thumb' was starting to churn again. The band sounded amazingly sharp. The crowd was more still. Without knowing exactly what, we all felt that something bad had happened. I assumed, and I was not given to flights of horrible imaginings, that the Angels had killed several people. Gram told me later that he saw Meredith Hunter lifted up, with a great spreading ketchup-colored stain on the back of his suit. Ronnie was running to the First Aid tent, outdistancing the Hell's Angel who had been leading him. Hunter was there when Ronnie came up, calling for a doctor. A cop said, 'You don't have to scream for a doctor for this guy, he's dead.'

Over the last notes of 'Under My Thumb,' Mick sang, 'It's all right – I pray that it's all right – I pray that it's all right – it's all right – '

'Let's do "Brown Sugar",' Mick Taylor said.

' *"Brown Sugar"*?' Keith said.

" "Brown Sugar"?' Bill said.

'What?' Charlie said.

'He wants to do "Brown Sugar", ' Mick said.

'Wait, let me change guitars,' Keith said.

'Thank you,' Mick said to the crowd. Charlie was playing rolls. 'Thank you. Are we well, yeah, we're gettin' it together – we gonna do one for you which we just ah –' pausing, remembering that making the record was breaking the law ' – we just ah – you've never heard it before because we just written it – we've written it for you – ' as Keith was tuning – 'I dunno how good this is gonna be, baby – ah, this is the first time we've played it – the very first time we've played it.' Keith finished tuning and played the song's first chords. Mick shouted, *'We gonna do one f'you now which we did for you, which we haven't ever played ever before, we gonna play it for you for the very first time, it's called "Brown Sugar".'*

Stacked like cordwood at the sides of the stage were bouquets of red and yellow long-stemmed roses. As the Stones played, Angels threw the bouquets into the crowd as if pitching babies out of airplane windows.

Scarred old slaver knows he's doin' all right
Hear him whip the women, just around midnight

Oh – brown sugar – how come you taste so good
Oh – brown sugar – just like a black girl should

It was a song of sadism, savagery, race hate/love, a song of redemption, a song that accepted the fear of night, blackness, chaos, the unknown – the fear that the mad-eyed Norsemen, transplanted from Odin-drunk mead halls to California desert, were still seeking mad-eyed to escape.

'Ahhh, one mo' time – whoo, baby, Yeah 'ang you – awww –' Taking a harp from Stu, Mick played a few menacing riffs of 'Midnight Rambler.' Keith had changed guitars and was tuning again. Mick played soft harp notes that trailed off as, head bent over the mike, he began singing lullaby phrases, trying to soothe and gentle the great beast. 'Aw now, baby baby – hush now, don't you cry.' His voice was tender, a tone of voice that Mick Jagger had never before used in public and maybe never in his life. 'Hush now, don't you cry –' A few more notes on the harp, and then, as if he were coming out of a reverie, gaining strength with each word, Mick said, 'We gonna do you one which we hope you'll *dig* – which is called "The Midnight Rambler". Wshoo!' (expostulation of a field hand stripping the sweat off his forehead with a dusty forefinger)

Sighing down the wind so sadly –
Listen and you'll hear him moan

The song had scared me when I first heard it, because it was true, as nobody at Altamont could deny, the dark is filled with terror, murder and evil ride the night air. 'I'll stick my knife right down your throat, honey, and it hurts!'

Things seemed to be settling down, as if the killer-lover lament had worked some psychic release on the crowd.

'Aw yah! Aw yah! Stand up if you can stand up,' Mick said. 'Stand up if you can keep it cool.' He raised the Jack Daniel's bottle. 'One more drink to you all.' He drank and spoke again in his lullaby tone, 'Awww, babies.' Then, as if he were coming to again, he said, 'It's so – sssweet! It's really sssweet! Would you like to live with – each other? I mean, you're really close to each other.' He stared into the crowd and seemed to drift away again. 'Wow,' he said.

'You ready?' Keith asked.

'Yeah, I'm ready,' Mick said.

'One two three faw,' Keith snarled, and they started 'Live with Me.'

Around the stage people were dancing, but in front of the stage, staring at Mick, one curly-haired boy in a watch cap was saying, Mick, Mick, no – I could read his lips. Behind the boy a fat black-haired girl, naked to the waist, was dancing, squeezing her enormous breasts, mouth open, eyes focused on a point somewhere north of her forehead. As the song ended, the girl, her skin rose-florid, blinking off and on like a pinball machine in orgasmic acid flashes, tried to take the stage like Grant took Richmond. Completely naked now, she was trying to climb over the crowd to get a foot onstage, where five Angels were at once between her and the Stones, kicking and punching her back, her smothering weight falling on the people behind her.

'Hold it,' Mick said.

'Stop that one,' Keith said.

'Hey – heyheyheyheyheyhey*hey!* One cat can control that chick, y'know wot oi mean. Hey fellows, hey fellows. One of you can control her, man,' Mick said, speaking the last sentence to the Angel nearest him onstage.

'Yeah, we're gonna do it,' the Angel said, in a world of his own, as were all the Angels looking down into the crowd, trying to reach the girl with fists or boots, wanting to get down there and smash her face, stomp her throat, kick her tits off and send them sailing over the heads of this dumb sheeplike crowd, and kick her in the pussy till she bleeds to death.

I NEED MORE

A True Confessional by Iggy Pop

Why I Do What I Do

I'm sure the constant exposure to amplifiers and electric guitars, and hearing my own voice amplified, has altered my body chemistry, in which, after all, the life lives.

I often try to examine the reasons why I am doing what I do – working with electric guitars and drums and singing – or what I'm trying to do with it. But I feel so umbilically connected to the thing itself, the process is far more important than the result. It is the proximity of the electric hum in the background and just the tremendous feeling of buoyancy and power, you know. When you start being in the presence of this power, you also become its witness. When guitars are played properly, hitting the same sound at the same time, a joyful thing happens; that's good backing. You are dangerously abandoned. It is the most honest experience I have ever encountered. Gotta have it. Once I started playing on stage, maybe even after the first gig, it was like a wolf after getting his first blood or something. As soon as I had a taste of that I just abandoned all interest in music and went right straight for the throat. I was really determined to use the noises on myself, as if I were a scientist experimenting on himself, like Dr Jekyll or the Hulk. Sometimes I feel like the Hulk, actually. I really didn't have any use for rationality or harmony – that was right out, you know. Stated harmonies, I didn't want. I wanted more overtones. Really good music isn't just to be heard, you know? It's almost like an hallucination. So I've always liked chance overtones. What I do is either abstract to you or it's POW!

Goose Lake

One typical sort of gig was the Goose Lake Festival. It was the Dead Festival days, about 100,000 people. It's me and the Stooges, the Burrito Brothers, the Faces, and some others, maybe Canned Heat. So we're on just after dark, right? It's the second day, and I've been there since the festival started. And I've just been rolling from tent to tent getting more and more out of it, right, with this friend of mine.

I'm in this tent, and I'm snorting something. I wasn't very selective in those days, and all of a sudden I have amnesia: total amnesia. To be honest, this is very painful for me to talk about. I've had some heavy moments in life, and this is one. I can almost feel it. I'm sitting there, and all of a sudden I have no idea not only who I am or where I am but beyond that I don't know what anything is. Everything within my view screen is racing, and my entire world is confined to the inside of this tent, which had a door so you've got daylight out there. I'm crosslegged on the floor. It's exactly like when the vertical goes on your TV, spinning around at the rate of ¾ of a second. The picture keeps flipping over. So we had a problem. I'm told that at the time I was just out, eyes gazing and mouth gaping. I was terrified. Then I remember thinking that I had something important to do, but I couldn't quite remember what it was. Aha! the music. And suddenly I knew what things were, that these were people – by this time about eight people had crowded in my view screen, and the vertical was still going – the vertical hadn't stopped. And then I realized that I had to realize who I was and then I remembered who I was, and, at the same time, the view screen returned to normal – the vertical hold took effect. That's scary, isn't it? I like TV, and it's a drag when your TV don't work right. It should be so simple to bring into focus. So I got up and said,

'Good day,' and got in the Corvette and took off for backstage. And that was that.

Allman Roadies

One time the Stooges played in Nasheville, Tennessee, at a joint called Mother's. And the support band to play with us were the roadies of the Allman Brothers, who were then very big, right? These guys had muscles on their muscles, and they were everything you think of as shit-kicking, badassed, top drawer roadies – for that sort of group – right? I mean these guys were tough and mean and long-haired, lantern-jawed, cowboyed out, and everything.

So they were doing their sound check when we come in, and James Williamson is dressed up in this outfit that has a diamond-shaped piece cut out in the middle exposing his skin, like Spider Man or something. It's weird looking. It shows his belly button and his breasts, and he looks a bit like a parrot or something, like a faggot, I guess – not to me of course. I was wearing a sarong, just a simple sarong over Cabaretta knee boots and a little shawl. And they looked at us and said, 'Wow! Isn't that some fuckin nice, finger licking good, wet pussy! Oh, look at that! Oooh-wee, hidee-hey, you girls got some pussy in there? I bet you do little honey,' la de da, and everything.

We were scared and locked ourselves in the bathroom, right? Locked the door, and they were pounding on the door of the bathroom. 'Come on outta there puss. We're gonna be real good, good lovin for you.' They were getting nastier and nastier.

But then it was time to go on, and we went out and played our gig. When we came off and hit the dressing trailer, there they were to apologize to us. Yeah, they apologized, 'We all didn't know that you all could play like that.'

There seems to be this discrepancy between badass music and really being a badass. Ha, because I AIN'T, you know, a badass.

After that gig James cleared the entire dressing room of every radio: he liked to steal things at gigs. That was his kick.

Fuckin' on Location

One thing that's really strange is fucking before or after, actually IN the place where you're playing, like in the halls or something. I am VERY rarely involved in that sort of thing, but . . .

One time I was in a place called the 'Joint in the Woods', New Jersey, with the Stooges – James Williamson on guitar, Ron was over on bass, Rock Action (formally Scott Asheton) on the beat, and me. We were in the Joint in the Woods, and there's this chick hanging around backstage. Like, I'm just trying to concentrate on the gig, right? This chick has this strong perfume on – it's really awful – she's got these really sleazed out brown nylons and is wearing a mini skirt with a garter belt. She was a plump girl, dressed in black with a very fussy blouse and just begging to be fucked. And I know I shouldn't fuck before a gig. I can't help it. So I just take her in the bathroom and lay her down on the floor, you know, and just fuck her. And then I hear from outside, 'Come on, Jim.' The whole band's laughing and everything: 'Come on, you're late.'

It was time to go on, so I just got up and I was still hard and had all this trouble – you know the situation – I'm trying to put my cock back in my pants. I wore very tight pants, right? And I'm trying to shove it in, and meantime Ron's dressed up in his SS outfit. I had goaded Ron into doing a German language introduction to our set. I told him people would love it, in full SS gear, right? So he comes out in his authentic, full dress, mint condition, superb detail, black SS colonel's outfit, with jodhpur riding boots and full accessories, and a good fit, too.

He's introducing the band in German and I'm trying to stick my pecker back in my pants, and this girl is going, 'Oh, no!' She's just laying there on the bottom of this john and gazing up – in the men's room.

I get on the stage and – it was some night – a couple of people really freaked at the German introduction. The JDL (Jewish Defense League) shut us down after that, as a matter of fact. I didn't do it, Ron did it. Anyway it didn't faze me. There was a little kid in front saying, 'How could you do this?' pointing at the

SS gear. It must have been an Italian kid. But it didn't faze me. I was very relaxed. It's all part of the show. But I wasn't very good that night.

There's this other chick in Wisconsin who really likes it in the dirt, too. Can't remember her name.

Butcher Cuts

One time in DC this chick – this biker chick, about 250 pounds – was with three of the Stooges – I wasn't involved. But they told me to come over and look. And I cracked up. They took this girl and using their belts tied her arms and legs to the four corners of the Sealy posturepedic. Then with these big magic markers they divided her entire nude body into amazingly accurate illustrated butcher cuts – like shank, prime rib, spare rib – just like the charts on the wall at the butcher shop, only with arrows pointing this way to beaver with little slogans and everything. She had been unconscious, and when she woke up she was so DESPERATE to have a good time – party at any cost – that as long as we would ignore the fact that she was covered with this graffiti she could accept it. The fact that she happened to be tied down and couldn't move didn't bother her and her groove. She had arrived with an ounce of angel dust and was smoking plenty. She was pretty cool. But if we were disrespectful to her verbally in her position she'd start to panic; the pathos of her forced gaiety would creep in. The guys didn't want her upset because they figured she MUST have some humongous biker old man around somewhere. I went back to my room.

Frisco

In 1970 I played a fun gig with Alice Cooper. I was first bill, Alice Cooper was second bill, and third bill was some unknown, the Flaming Groovies – a faddy rock group that wasn't funny.

I had a good gig, and afterwards this guy came over and introduced himself to me and gives me this enormous speech about rock. He introduced himself to me as Stan Owsley, the acid king. Oh, great. So what, you know. He was giving me this weird rap about all these people he knew and how they knew I was in league with the devil – you know, really weird shit. He told me about how he does sound for the Grateful Dead.

During the gig, there had been all these people in the front row dressed in strange Arabian garments – quite fascinating – with bananas on their heads. It was our first time in Frisco (or California, for that matter), and after the gig I went over to the house of these people from the front row, and they turned out to be from Hybiscus – a bunch of drag queens. I had no idea what it was going to be like. I'd never been to a gay home.

I remember how penetrating and strange the house felt and how three of them were peering at me – very strange. I had never been exposed to either homosexuality or opiate behaviour. There was this chick, Tina, who was a real sick chick. She was about 14 and was the one who turned the straight tricks for money to buy heroin – absolutely tiny, all the way from San Bernardino, very beautiful, Latin-type girl, with a beautiful Roman bridge and pronounced eyebrows, large brown eyes, and a wanton mouth. I hung out with them for the night and was just getting disgusted with the stench of it all. So I took Tina and went home. She was raving on and on about I don't know what. I had a big hard-on to fuck her, and it was the first time anybody ever said, 'Hurt me – hurt me!' I had never encountered that before, you see. I was learning something.

So loveless,
so pretty,
so what?

THE LEGENDARY TROGGS TAPES

Transcribed by Mat Snow

Long before there was Spinal Tap, there was something else that stood for all that is inept in rock'n'roll. A fading pop group assembled in a studio, in 1970, to record a single. They failed disastrously. Ever since then, tapes of that session have kept musicians' undertrousers moist with mirth. It is our pleasure – nay, our duty – to present the legendary Troggs Tapes.

The year is 1970. It is the year the samba skills of Pele, Jairzinho and Rivelino sweep Brazil to World Cup victory in Mexico City. In the same year, perhaps a little less light on his feet, Mr Heath drones his way to Number 10 at the expense of Mr Wilson. Also that year, the Americans carry the Vietnam War into Cambodia, and with the break-up of The Beatles and the deaths of Jimi and Janis, the curtain falls on rock's golden age. And just by way of a footnote, 1970 is a year that falls a long way after the sell-by date of a certain band from Andover, Hampshire. Yet, for The Troggs, their finest hour is only just round the corner . . .

As The Troggs gathered for a recording session in the studio of Dick James Music in London, a once-glittering future lay some distance behind them. Carefully steered by their manager and producer Larry Page (who'd sought to invest them with that same combination of brutishness and camp he had successfully brought out in The Kinks), Hampshire's finest had scored on both sides of the Atlantic with their second single, a cover of Chip Taylor's Wild Thing (currently enjoying a revival extolling the ferocious chocolatiness of Lion bars). The Troggs had followed this immortal slice of rifferama with more hit 45s: I Can't Control Myself (the lines 'Your slacks are low and your hips are showing' earned it a ban from the BBC), With A Girl Like You, Give It To Me, Night Of The Long Grass and Love Is All Around.

But in summer 1967, following an offer of £100,000 to sign to MGM in America, The Troggs split from Larry Page amid much litigation and bitterness, and their hit career ebbed away within a year.

1970, then, found The Troggs plying their trade on the British cabaret circuit – a living, but hardly the glory game of yore. That year, however, they were persuaded back into the studio by their record company, Dick James Music, to try to recover that hit-making magic. Once again, opportunity knocked for singer/ songwriter Reg Presley (as Reginald Ball had been cheekily renamed in 1966), drummer Ronnie Bond (alias one Ronald Bullis), guitarist Chris Britton and newly acquired bassist Tony Murray. Thus the foursome gathered in DJM's London studio – an inconvenient crucible for music-making, seeing as how the actual recording room was separated by a corridor from the control room, with communication only possible by closed-circuit TV and the Tannoy system, unless one preferred the old-fashioned method of going to the door and having a good shout.

In the recording room, then, we find The Troggs' three instrumentalists labouring to 'lay down' a backing track, while in the back seat of the control booth, producer Dennis Berger and the inimitable Reg Presley offer advice and encouragement. The song, as fate would have it, is called Tranquility – but it will never see the light of day. Instead, the engineer keeps the tape rolling during the band's discussions, and it's this – the overnight sensation that they call The Troggs Tapes – that secures the legendary status the band had looked so in danger of losing.

The Transcript

Ronnie Bond: 'That is a fuckin' Number 1! If that baaa-stard don't go, then Oi'll fuckin' retoire. Oi fuckin' do!'
Dennis Berger, (producer): 'I agree – I think it is a good song.'
Ronnie: 'But it fuckin' well won't be unless we spend a little bit of fuckin' thought and imagination to fuckin' make it a fuckin' Number 1. You've got to put a little bit of fuckin' fairy dust over the baaa-stard!'
Dennis: 'Well, we'll put some fairy dust over it – I'll piss over the tape.'
Ronnie: 'Oi don't know what it needs, Den . . .'
Dennis: 'Aaah! I know that it needs strings – that I do know.'
Reg Presley: 'You've got to have a fuckin' bloke who says, Oi've got a fuckin' sound in here that's fuckin' great.'
Tony Murray: 'We need a producer who says, You're not doing that; you're fuckin' doing this.'
Dennis: 'Did you do exactly what Larry Page said?'
Chorus: 'Yep!'
Tony: 'That's how they had hit records.'
Reg: 'Because there was just one fuckin' mind on it – not fuckin' seven or eight.'
Ronnie: 'We didn't even fuckin' get a say in it – it was fuckin', wham, it was in the can regardless. You reckon that was bad? Fuck me! One take, that's it, finish. You never 'ad a fuckin' say – it was out. As weak and fuckin' insipid we used to think.'
Reg: 'We thought With A Girl Like You was fuckin' terrible and let's go and do it again. And that was the only fuckin' time he let us fuckin' have our way. And could we get anything fuckin' better?'
Ronnie: 'No.'
Reg: 'Fuckin' . . . the first thing he fuckin' did was it.'
Ronnie: 'All fuckin' day. We went in there at nine o'clock and we didn't come out till, fuck, about three o'clock the next fuckin' morning, and they had Mick Jagger, you name it, they were fuckin' in there to try and make it better.'

Reg: 'What about a fuckin' 12-string on it?'
Dennis: 'Play the beginning again, Barry.'
(*The identity of 'Barry' is now lost in the mists of time. Vigorously strummed guitar chords are affirmed as just the ticket by a slightly demented shriek of 'Yeah! . . . No!!' from Reg.*)
Reg: 'You 'ad it there at the beginning, Ron. It was soundin' good. Ron? Ronnie? Just listen fer a sec . . .'
Ronnie: 'You can say that all fuckin' night, but Oi just cannot feel it any other way than what Oi've been fuckin' doing it.'
Reg: 'You have played it tonight.'
Ronnie: 'Don't expect fuckin' miracles just like that, Reg. It's fuckin' there – better than there. Oi can't fuckin' hear it any other way but that.'
Reg: 'But you have done it. You did it.'
Tony: 'Play duh-duh duh-duh duh chuh.'
Reg: 'No, no more beats.'
Tony: 'Play duh-duh duh-duh duh chuh on whatever drum you were playing it on originally.'
Reg: 'You did it. You went duh-duh duh-duh duh chuh.'
Ronnie: 'You can say that all fuckin' night, but you won't listen.'
Tony: 'We can keep on trying . . .'
Ronnie: 'Yeah – well just shut your fuckin' mouth for five minutes and give me a fuckin' chance to do it. Don't keep fuckin', right into that fuckin' microphone. Duh duh derh duh duh derh. Fuck me, Reg. Just fuck off, in there, and just keep going fuckin' do i', doan' just . . .'
Reg: 'Well, just fuckin' think then.'
Ronnie: '. . . don't just keep saying they're not loud enough. Oi know they're fuckin' right, Oi can hear it ain't right you cunt. Weeeell, fuck me.'
Reg: 'You can hear it's fuckin' not right too.'
Ronnie: 'Oi fuckin' can, and Oi'm the cunt that's playing it so Oi don't want to hear . . . fuck . . . fuck . . . in me fuckin' head that's what Oi gotta fuckin' do, then Oi'll do it. Yer big pranny.'
(*Tum-tum-tum-ti-tum, goes the bass guitar. Tum-tum-tum-ti-tum, tum-tum-tum-ti-tum . . .*)

Reg: (*quietly*) 'Fuckin' drummer. Oi shit 'im. Duh duh derh duh duh derh, duh duh derh duh duh derh.'
(*Enter the guitar*)
Reg: 'One, two, a one two three four... Yer doing it fuckin' wrong!'
Ronnie: 'Oi know Oi am.'
Reg: 'Dubba dubba dubba chah, dubba dubba dubba chah, dubba dubba dubba chah, dubba dubba... You did i' in the beginning. Bloody hell, Oi can't play to thar.'
Ronnie: 'Nor can Oi.'
Reg: 'Eh?'
Ronnie: 'Nor can fuckin' Oi.'
Reg: 'Well, you're fuckin' doin' i'!'
Ronnie: 'Well Oi can't fuckin' play to it either.'
Reg: 'Hahahaha. Why don't you just do what you fuckin' started ou' doing – dubba dubba dubba chah. On your top one, dubba dubba dubba chah. Dubba dubba dubba chah.'
(*On tom tom, Ronnie attempts to follow his singer's sage advice. It sounds hopeless.*)
Reg: 'Nooooo!'
Ronnie: (*very heatedly*) 'Why don't you fuckin' ... You're talking out of the back of your fuckin' aaaarse because all you want then is the same fuckin' thing that Oi was playing fuckin' originally in that baaa-stard.'
Reg: 'But on different fuckin' drums!'
Ronnie: (*agitatedly*) 'Then all you want, then, is fuckin' tha' one, and the fuckin' bass drum playing the same thing.'
Reg: 'You're the fuckin' drummer!'
Ronnie: 'Yes, you fuckin' do, 'cos that's all you're fuckin' doing. You ain't playing any fuckin' thing else – orl roi', Oi'll play tha'. Oi'm goin' nah-nah-nah-nah-nah-bomp, nah-nah-nah-nah-nah-bomp, nah-nah-nah-nah-nah-bomp...' (he thumps in dull accompaniment, sarcastically).
Reg: 'You don't fuckin' listen, that's your trouble Oi'm only asking you to do half of it on one drum, half of it on the other and the bang wherever you want to bang... Ronnie, can you 'ear me? Wha' abeou' tryin' i' not just on that top skin floor and

then your floor tom-tom, but split your hands so's that one beat is doin' it on the top drum, one's doin' it on the floor tom tom, then your bass.'
(*A tinny tattoo beats out gamely.*)
Reg: (*philosophically*) 'Fuckin' drummer. Oi shit 'im . . .'

KEITH MOON: THE ROLLING STONE INTERVIEW

The Who by Jerry Hopkins

It is probably fitting that Keith Moon plays the most aggressive instrument, drums, in the most explosive of groups, the Who, for Moon clearly seems more outrageous and more violent than any of his contemporaries. Behind him for a period of ten years, for more than a third of his life, he has left a trail of empty Courvoisier bottles, splintered drum kits, wrecked automobiles and gutted hotel rooms, punctuating every conceivable incident with a bark of total pleasure and amusement.

There are uncounted Keith Moon stories floating around. Keith tells several here. Unfortunately, much is lost in translating Moon to print. His energetic sprints around the room, his dozen or so precise vocal impressions and dialects, the rubbery, gap-toothed face, the singing and dancing, the infectious volleys of laughter – all must be experienced. So must his $150,000 modern house, set on the site of an ancient monastery nearly an hour from London in the green, suburban stockbroker belt. The walls of the bar are painted in a Marvel Comics hero-villain motif, and the ceiling is draped like a sultan's tent. The sitting room is a huge, richly cushioned 'conversation pit', with a colour television and a stainless-steel fireplace that's never been used. There is almost no furniture. But there is a stuffed albatross, a polar-bear rug, several rifles, an old jukebox and a sound system that will send multidecibel music far beyond the boundaries of his seven-acre estate.

From the outside, the house looks to be a collection of square pyramids painted a glaring white. On one side is a tree so large it had to be lowered in by two helicopters. On the other side workmen are presently excavating a swimming pool that will be lined with marble and will offer the underwater swimmer the latest recorded melodies.

When I arrived, the live-in housekeeper – Moon's mother-in-law – was in Spain on holiday. His long-haired mechanic and driver, Dougal, was working on the engine of the 1936 Chrysler, which was parked between the XKE Jaguar and the Dino Ferrari. The missus, Kim, and the child, Mandy, 6, were out. And the lord of the manor was banging away with a shotgun, firing randomly into the tall, leafy reaches of a horse-chestnut tree.

How did you come to the group to begin with?

First they were called the Detours, then the Who, then the High Numbers, then the Who again. I joined in the second phase, when they were changing from the Detours to the Who. I was in another group on the same pub circuit called the Beachcombers.

Did that mean surfing music?

It did when I joined, yeah. Ah-ha-ha-ha.

So the Beachcombers was a surfing band, sort of?

Sort of. It relied on vocals more than instruments. As I'm a disgusting singer . . . I mean, the boys don't let me sing. I don't blame them. I sometimes forget meself and join in, and they have to come down on me: 'Moon . . . out!' I mean, I even get sent offstage during 'Behind Blue Eyes' just in case I forget meself. It's the only number of the Who's that really requires precise harmony. The rest of it's all 'YEEEEAAAHHHH – magic bus!' We shout. It doesn't matter. So they send me off during 'Blue Eyes', because either I'm buggering about and I put the boys off or I try to sing and really put them off.

Anyway, I'd decided my talent as a drummer was wasted in a tight-knit harmony group like the Beachcombers, and the only band that I heard of that sounded as loud as I did was the Detours. So when I heard their drummer had left, I had plans to insinuate meself into the group. They were playing at a pub near me, the Oldfield. I went there, and they had a session drummer sitting in with them. I got up onstage and said, 'Well, I can do better than him.' They said go ahead and got behind this other guy's drums, and I did one song, 'Road Runner'. I'd had several drinks to get me courage up, and when I got onstage, I went *arrrrrrrrggggggghhhhhhhhh* on the drums, broke the base-drum pedal and two skins and got off. I figured that was it. I was scared to death.

Afterward, I was sitting at the bar, and Pete came over. He said, 'You . . . come 'ere'. I said, mild as you please: 'Yesyes?' And Roger, who was the spokesman then, said, 'What're you doing next Monday?' I said, 'Nothing.' I was working during the day, selling plaster. He said, 'You'll have to give up work. There's this gig on Monday. If you want to come, we'll pick you up in the van.' I said, 'Right.' They said they'd come by at seven. And that was it. Nobody ever said, 'You're in.' They just said, 'What are you doing Monday?'

The first American tour. Do you remember it with fondness?

For me it was a tour of discovery. It was three months with 'Erman's 'Ermits. Backing up the 'Ermits was ideal. It was a position that suited us. We weren't on the line. If the place sold only a portion of what it could have sold, the disaster was never blamed on us, it was blamed on 'Erman's 'Ermits. We didn't have the responsibility. We had time to discover. We found the good towns.

Which ones are they?

For the Who they're New York, Chicago, Detroit, Los Angeles, San Francisco and Cleveland. They have the best audiences for us.

Was it on this tour you had your infamous birthday party?

Yes. That's how I lost me front tooth. In Flint, Michigan. We had a show that night. We were all around the 'Oliday Inn pool, 'Erman's 'Ermits and meself. I was twenty-one and they started giving me presents. Somebody gave me a portable bar, and somebody else the portable booze. I'd started drinking about ten o'clock in the morning, and I can't remember the show. Then the record company 'ad booked a big room in the 'otel, one of the conference rooms, for a party. As the hours went on, it got louder and louder, and everybody started getting well out of their minds, well stoned. The pool was the obvious target. Everybody started jumping in the pool with their clothes on.

The Premier Drum Company 'ad given me a 'uge birthday cake, with like five drums stacked up on top of each other. As the party degenerated into a slanging, I picked up the cake, all five tiers, and hurled it at the throng. People started picking up the pieces and 'urling it about. Everybody was covered in marzipan and icing sugar and fruitcake. The manager 'eard the fracas and came in. There it was, his great carpet, stained irrevocably with marzipan and fruitcake trodden in, and everybody dancing about with their trousers off. By the time the sheriff came in, I was standing there in me underpants. I ran out, jumped into the first car I came to, which was a brand-new Lincoln Continental. It was parked on a slight hill, and when I took the hand brake off, it started to roll. It smashed straight through this pool surround [fence], and the whole Lincoln Continental went into the 'Oliday Inn swimming pool, with me in it. Ah-ha-ha-ha!

So there I was, sitting in the eight-foot-six in the driver's seat of a Lincoln Continental, underwater. And the water was pouring in – coming in through the bloody pedal 'oles in the floorboard, you know, squirting in through the windows. In a startling moment of logical, I said, 'Well, I can't open the doors until the pressure is the same . . .' It's amazing 'ow I remembered those things from my physics class! I knew I'd have to wait until the pressure was the same.

So I'm sitting there, thinking about me situation, as the water creeps up me nose. Today I can think of less outrageous ways of going than drowning in a Lincoln Continental in a 'Oliday Inn swimming pool, but at that time I had no thoughts of death whatsoever. There was none of that all-me-life-passing-before-me-eyes-in-a-flash. I was busy planning. I knew if I panicked, I'd 'ave 'ad it. So when there's just enough air in the top of the car to take a gulp, I fill up me lungs, throw open the door and go rising to the top of the pool. I figured there'd be quite a crowd gathered by now. After all, I'd been down there underwater for some time. I figured they'd be so grateful I was alive, they'd overlook the Lincoln Continental. But no. There's only one person standing there, and 'e's the pool cleaner, and 'e's got to have the pool clean in the morning, and he's furious.

So I went back to the party, streaming water, still in me underpants. The first person I see is the sheriff, and 'e's got 'is 'and on 'is gun. Sod this! And I ran, I started to leg it out the door, and I slipped on a piece of marzipan and fell flat on me face and knocked out me tooth. Ah-ha-ha-ha!

I spent the remainder of the night under the custody of the sheriff at a dentist's. The dentist couldn't give me any anesthetic because I was pissed out me mind. So 'e 'ad to rip out what was left of the tooth and put a false one in, and the next day I spent a couple of hours in the nick. The boys had chartered me a plane because they had to leave on an earlier flight. The sheriff took me out in the law car, and he puts me on the plane and says [*American accent*], 'Son, don't ever dock in Flint, Michigan again.' I said, 'Dear boy, I wouldn't dream of it.' And I was lisping around the new tooth. Ah-ha-ha-ha!

By now I'd learned 'ow destructive we'd all been. During the merriment someone 'ad upset all the fire extinguishers and turned them on all the cars in the car park. Six of them 'ad to 'ave new paint jobs; the paint all peeled off. We'd also destroyed a piano. Completely destroyed it. Reduced to kindling. And don't forget the carpet. And the Lincoln Continental in the bottom of the pool. So I got a bill for £24,000. Ah-ha-ha-ha! I wasn't earning 'alf that on the tour, and I'd spent everything by the time I'd got to Flint, Michigan. I was in debt up past me eyebrows before this 'appened. Luckily, 'Erman's 'Ermits and the boys split it up, about thirty of us gave a thousand dollars each. It was like a religious ceremony as we all came up and dropped a thousand dollars into a big 'at and sent it off to the 'Oliday Inn with a small compliments card with BALLS written across it and the words SEE YOU SOON. Ah-ha-ha-ha!

You can't have destroyed as many rooms as legend has it.

You want to bet?

Have there been other times when . . .

Lots. Yes. I get bored, you see. There was a time in Saskatoon, in Canada. It was another 'Oliday Inn, and I was bored. Now, when I get bored, I rebel. I said, *'Fuck it! Fuck the lot of ya!'* And I took out me 'atchet and chopped the 'otel room to bits. The television, the chairs, the dresser, the cupboard doors, the bed – the lot of it. Ah-ha-ha-ha! It happens all the time.

I've always heard it was Pete who started the destruction onstage, but you make it sound as if it might've been your idea. Was it?

The way the story goes, Pete put the neck of his guitar through a low ceiling when he jumped too 'igh, but that's not it. It 'appened when somebody got pissed off with the gig, with the way things were going. When Pete smashed his guitar it was because 'e was pissed off. When I smashed me drums, it was because I was pissed off. We were frustrated. You're working as hard as you can to get that fucking song across, to get that audience by the balls, to make it an event. When you've done all that, when you've worked your balls off and you've given the audience everything you can give, and they don't give anything back, that's when the fucking instruments go, because, 'You fucking bastards! We've worked our fucking balls off! And you've given us nothing back!'

That's one way the instruments got smashed. Another way was if a member of the group was too fuckin' stoned to give it their best. Then he was letting down the other three. In a lot of cases it was me, through drinking too much. You know, just getting out of it at the wrong time. Then Pete or Roger or John says, 'You cunt! You fucking let us down! You fucking bastard, if you want to get pissed, why don't you wait until after the show!'

You all seem to be fairly available to the press.

We're doing fuck-all else. Ah-ha-ha-ha! Some people say I'll do anything for the press, it's true . . . that I make meself too available. I just like to 'ave fun. There was this time Keith Altham and Chris Williams, who look after our PR, phoned me up and said I 'ad to be at their office at three o'clock for an interview. Well, you know, the pubs shut at three, so I was rather delayed, because they don't turn out until ha'past. So it was quarter to four before I eventually started. I was back up in my office at Track [Records] and finally I remembered; I'd forgotten all about it. So, uhhh, 'Oh, Christ, they're gonna be angry.' Right opposite the office is a chemist's, so I sent Dougal, me driver, over there to pick up some rolls of bandages and plaster, and I did all me leg up, strapped me arms up and purchased a stick, a walking stick. Then I went over to the office: 'Sorry I'm late, but the 'ospital delayed me.'

I'd called earlier and told them I'd been run over by a bus on Oxford Street. They didn't think that unlikely. I think they've adopted the attitude that anything's likely with Moon, y'see. So I walk into the office . . . 'obble in, actually . . . and they say, ' 'Ow did it 'appen?' I said, 'I was just crossing Oxford Street and a Number Eight from Shepherd's Bush 'it me right up the arse and sent me spinning across Oxford Circus.' So Keith and Chris say they'll cancel the interview. I say no, but maybe they'd be so kind as to carry me down the four flights of steps to the street. They thought I'd come up by meself, on me walking stick, y'see.

So they carried me down the stairs, and we're walking along. I'm 'obbling along the street again, and this bloody lorry comes along as I'm crossing the street, and it screams to a 'alt in front of me. I say, ''Ang on, mate, I can't go fast on these legs,' and Keith has a go at the lorry driver: 'You 'eartless bastard, can't you see this man's injured! 'Ave you no 'eart, 'ave you no soul, you bastard! Trying to run over a cripple!'

We went on to the interview, and in the middle, after about four brandies, I just ripped off all the plaster and jumped up on the seat and started dancing. Ah-ha-ha-ha!

Have you ever been injured in any of your stunts? Aside from the missing front tooth?

I broke me collarbone once. That was in me own 'otel, the one I own, one Christmas. I collapsed in front of the fire at four o'clock one morning, and some friends of mine decided to put me to bed, and they were in as bad a state as I was, but they were still on their feet. Just about. One of them got 'old of me 'ead, the other got 'old of me feet, and they attempted to drag me up the stairs. They got me up two flights and then promptly dropped me down both of them, breaking me collarbone, y'see. But I didn't know this until I woke up in the morning and tried to put me fucking shirt on. I went through the fuckin' roof.

Now . . . I was supposed to do a television show, the *Top of the Pops New Year's Eve Special*, and two days before I 'ave me arm all strapped up so I can't drum. I went to me doctor, dear Dr Robert, and he gave me a shot on the day of the gig so I wouldn't feel anything. I put a shirt over the cast, fastened the drumsticks to my wrist with a sticking plaster, sat down behind the drum kit, and got Mr Vivian Stanshall to tie a rope around me wrist. We then threw the rope over the lighting pipe overhead, the one that holds the floods and all, and I kept an eye on the television monitor. Every time I was on camera, I'd give the signal to Viv, and he'd give a pull on the rope, which caused me right arm to shoot up and then come crashing down on the cymbal. Ah-ha-ha-ha!

These farcical situations . . . I'm always tied up in them. They're always like Laurel and Hardy sketches. And they always 'appen to me! Ah-ha-ha-ha! I think unconsciously I want them to 'appen, and they do.

Is that the image you have of yourself?

I suppose to most people I'm probably seen as an amiable idiot . . . a genial twit. I think I must be a victim of circumstance, really. Most of it's me own doing. I'm a victim of me own practical jokes. I suppose that reflects a rather selfish attitude: I like to be the recipient of me own doings. Nine times out of ten I am. I set traps and fall into them. Oh-ha-ha-ha-HA-HA-HA-HA! Of course the biggest danger is becoming a parody.

Your wife, Kim, must be extraordinarily sympathetic and patient.

She is. She sort of takes it in 'er stride.

How did you meet her?

Heh-heh-eh-eh. Ah-ha-ha-ha! I met her in Bournemouth when I was playing a show. She was sixteen and she hung out at the club where we worked, the Disc. Sometime later when I went down to see her, I was on a train, and Rod Stewart was on the train. This was about ten years ago. We got chatting, and we went to the bar car. It was Rod 'The Mod' Stewart in those glorious days, and he'd just been working with Long John Baldry. He was playing a lot of small discotheques and pubs, doing the sort of work we were doing. I said to Rod, 'Where are you going?' He said, 'Bournemouth.' 'So'm I,' I said. 'I'm going down there to see my chick.' He said, 'So'm I.' So I showed Rod a picture of Kim, and he said, 'Yeah . . . that's 'er.' Ah-ha-ha-ha!

What happened?

I don't remember. We were in the bar car, and we both got paralytic. I only remember the trip back. Oh-hee-ha-ha-ha!

How'd your mother-in-law come to live with you?

She's me 'ousekeeper. And she's a great cook. You see, I was cradle snatching. I snatched her daughter at sixteen, right out of convent school, and she 'adn't learned 'ow to cook yet, so I said, 'Get your mother up 'ere.' She's been living with us for about a year now. She's not the accepted idea of a mother-in-law. At my 'ouse there's no real accepted idea of anything.

Do you have favourite drummers?

Not many. D. J. Fontana [Elvis' original drummer] is one. Let's see . . . the drummers I respect are Eric Delany and Bob Henrit [from Argent] and . . . I got a 'uge list, really, and all for different reasons. Technically, Joe Morello is perfect. I don't really have a favourite drummer. I have favourite drum pieces, and that's it. I would never put on an LP of a drummer and say everything he did I love, because that's not true.

How'd you start on drums?

Jesus Christ, I think I got a free drum kit in a packet of corn flakes. Ah-ha-ha-ha! But no . . . drum solos are fucking boring. Any kind of solo is. It detracts from the group identity.

How much of a group effort are the songs? How much do you change those demos when you record?

Not a hell of a lot. Because Pete knows. When Pete writes something, it sounds like the Who. The drum phrases are my phrases, even though it's Pete playing drums. He's playing the way I play. He's playing my flourishes. The same thing for the bass part, and the guitar of course is 'is own. Only the vocals change some.

Two years later, how do you look back on 'Tommy'?

With disbelief. Ah-ha-ha-ha! I can't believe we spent six months doing it. It took six months to make. That's studio time, and that's talking about it, discussing it, arranging it, producing it and writing it. Getting it all together. Recording it, and then saying we could so it better and recording it again.

Other than with disbelief, how do you remember it?

Well, it is disbelief. I just can't believe that we did that album. It was an amazing album to do. It was, at the time, very un-Who-like. A lot of the songs were sort of soft. We never played like that. And we didn't have an idea then as to how it was all going to turn out. Here we were, spending all this time on a project that none of us really knew all that much about.

Then came the 'Tommy' tours . . .

Because we'd been in the studio so long, we immediately went on an American tour. We incorporated a lot of *Tommy*. In fact, the act was mostly *Tommy*. After that, on the opera 'ouse tour, we played just two numbers to warm up – we'd do 'Summertime Blues' and 'I Can't Explain' or something – and then we'd do the opera. We did about six or seven opera 'ouses. I enjoyed them. Nice sound. But it was a bit strange. It was rather like playing to an oil painting.

The Who's always been a working band, a touring band. Do you still enjoy the road?

[*Using soft voice, as if delivering a eulogy*] I love it. It's my life. If I was to be deprived of touring . . . I love being responsible for the enjoyment of a packed 'ouse. Knowing the four of us can go onstage and give enjoyment to that many thousand people, that's fucking something, man, that does me right in. If I'm good and the group is good, you can get 14,000 . . . 140,000! . . . get them on their fucking feet. Yeah. That's where it's at. That's what it's all about for me.

Can you tell me what you're worth?

I don't know. Now now. Some time ago me accountant told me I 'ad a lot of money. I said, ' 'Ow much?' He said, 'Well, you're very well fixed.' I said, ' 'Ow much? I mean, am I a millionaire?' 'Well, technically, yes.' So I said. 'What should I do about it?' and he said, 'Well, obviously if you've got that much money, and you've got these tax bills, it's logical to spend money so that you can claim it against the tax that's owed.' 'I see . . . so I should spend money?' 'Well, yes, you should.' So six weeks later I'd spent it all. Ah-ha-ha-ha! I'd bought four 'ouses, a 'otel, eight cars, a swimming pool, tennis courts, expensive wristwatches that fall apart, a riverside bungalow just five minutes away, furnished in French renay-sance-period furniture. I'd spent it all. It was gone. Ah-ha-ha-ha!

I get accused of being a capitalist bastard, because, you know: 'How many cars you got?' 'Eight.' 'Big 'ouse?' 'Yes.' Well, I love all that; I enjoy it. I have lots of friends over, and we sit up, drinking and partying. I need the room to entertain. I enjoy seeing other people enjoy themselves. That's where I get my kicks. I'm kinky that way. I have the amount of cars I do because I smash them up a lot. Six are always in the garage; it's a fact. They're always saying I'm a capitalist pig. I suppose I am. But, ah . . . it ah . . . it's good for me drumming, I think. Oh-ho-ho-ha-ha!

You really do have troubles with cars?

I came off the road in the AC Cobra at one hundred and ten. We flew over a canal and sort of collapsed in a mangled heap in a field about ten foot from a reservoir. The Cobra people were very unhappy when I took the wreckage into their garage. They only made about ninety-eight of them and they're touchy about how they're driven. Ha-ha-ha! I've tried to bump-start the 1936 Chrysler several times, always with disastrous results. Once I tried to bump-start it with my X-type Jag, which is built so low to the ground, it slid under the Chrysler. Another time I tried to bump-start with the Rolls . . . forgetting there was nobody sitting in the Chrysler. I pushed it right into the fish pond on the front lawn.

When did the group swing away from drugs towards booze?

Ah-ha . . . a change-of-pace question. Ah-ha-ha-ha! I think we just sort of grew out of drugs. The drugs aren't necessary now. They were then, as a crutch. We went through just about everything. Not Roger so much. He smoked, but that was it. The rest of us went through the same stages everybody goes through – the bloody drug corridor. You know. We were no exception. Eventually we stopped fucking about with the chemicals and started on the grape. Drinking suited the group a lot better. When we started drinking, that's when it all started getting together.

We're all pretty good drinkers. After the show there's always the celebration drink, or the noncelebration drink. Then there's always the clubs. John and I, generally, go clubbing. We just like the social side of drinking. Everybody I know is a drinker. I've met some of my best friends in pubs.

You've been in two films without the others . . .

Yeah, one was *200 Motels* with Frank Zappa. The other was *Countdown* with Harry Nilsson, both with Ringo.

I was at the Speakeasy with Pete, and Frank 'appened to be at the next table. He overheard some of our conversation and leaned over and said [*American accent*], 'How'd you guys like to be in a film?' We said [*English accent*], 'Okay, Frank.' And he said [*back to American accent*], 'Okay, be at the Kensington Palace Hotel at seven o'clock tomorrow morning.' I was the one who turned up. Pete was writing and sent his apologies, and I was given the part Mick Jagger was to play – that of a nun. Mick didn't want to do it.

Then there was a bit in one of the local papers that said Ringo was making *Countdown* with Peter Frampton and Harry Nilsson and a lot of others, so I called Ringo up and said, 'Is there a part in it for me?' He said yes, and I turned up. I do some drumming.

Was that your first meeting with Nilsson?

Yes. We were supposed to be on the set at six, but it was nine before everyone was there. Then somebody brought out a bottle of brandy. Me, I think. Ah-ha-ha-ha! And Peter Frampton said, no, no, too early, and some of the others said no. But 'Arry was standing there with an 'alf-pint mug. I knew at that moment it was destiny put us together. Ah-ha-ha-ha!

So we were drinking brandy at nine and, thanks to Mal Evans, white wine all the rest of the day. Then about six o'clock somebody came round and slipped little envelopes into our hands. It was a pay packet! I 'adn't 'ad a pay packet in ten years. And 'Arry'd never 'ad one. We were pretty well out of it, and we looked at each other and then tore up 170 pounds in one-pound notes, threw it up in the air and danced about, cackling like schoolboys. Ah-ha-ha-ha! Dancing and leaping about, clutching bottles of Blue Nun Liebfraumilch in our hands, singing, 'We're millionaires, aren't we?'

MAMA'S DREAMAWAY LOUNGE

Bob Dylan by Sam Shepard

This was one of the most amazing days on the tour and seemed to come out of pure chance. Through Arlo Guthrie, Ken had contacted an eighty-year-old gypsy lady, known in the vicinity as plain Mama. She ran a small bar / diner-former brothel somewhere out in the extreme boondocks of Massachusetts, a place called Becket. We pulled in on a warm, sunny afternoon after having stopped periodically along the back-country roads to leave little white notes pinned to trees for the buses to follow. 'Lay Lady Lay' is softly drifting out of a shack behind a bulging apple tree. Guthrie's funky half-ton Ford is parked in front of the Lounge, a place that immediately gives the impression of eccentricity and oddball taste. There's nothing imposing about it, just a kind of eclectic atmosphere to the trimmings. Inside, every inch of wall space is taken up with ancient photography, mostly images of Mama in various stages of her adventurous life. In some she's posing with a group of chorus girls, guitar strapped to her shoulders, dressed in full gypsy regalia. One of her cheek-to-cheek with a sea captain. Mixed in with the photos are all kinds of religious artifacts, rosaries, crucifixes, Virgin Marys, Last Suppers, Crowns of Thorns, etc. All of them either based in plastic or swimming in faded synthetic three-dimensional lamination like you find a lot in the Deep South. Still, it's not altogether that depressing. In fact the rich smells of Mama's home cooking coming from a tiny kitchen behind the bar make everything seem real promising and warm. We're introduced to Mama right off, and she makes no shortcuts in lambasting you with her generous personality. She's a very wide woman, not very tall but definitely broad and beefy, white hair pulled up and waved and wearing one of those Hawaiian muumuus that stop halfway between her knees and her leathery bare feet. She wears a tiny silver chain around one ankle with a small silver heart resting on a blue vein. She stares up at you from below with an expression halfway between tears and a kind of sentimental good wishing. Later, it turns out that she breaks into sudden fits of tears and sobbing for no apparent reason other than her memory of past love suddenly welling up into the present. Then she immediately cures herself and goes on to show you some tiny object she's collected in her travels, only to break down again in the same emotion-choked delirium. The results are similar to following a slightly demented but benevolent relative around a sanatorium, all the time pretending that everything's okay and masking your true reactions to these manic shifts in her state. There's two recordings of her singing which she brings to our attention, right there on the home juke box. I slide a quarter in and punch the buttons. The first selection is an unending little ditty in a foreign tongue which sounds like a mixture of Spanish and Italian, called 'Mama and God'. The juke is wired up to an old tin speaker mounted outside on the front porch so that Great Nature can take part in Mama's gifts. There's something fantastic about all this in the way that this woman's life has evolved to this place in the middle of the sticks. Her satisfaction with things as they are and the way she's drawn it all into this tiny world inside the Lounge. A collection of her past which she keeps snugly around her without making her numb to the present.

As soon as Baez shows up, things really start pumping. Mama immediately relates to Joan's Catholic features and bursts into a series of giggles, sobbing and bear-hugging Joan, then standing arm's length with a firm grip on her shoulders and staring up into her eyes, tears streaming down both cheeks. She squeezes

Joan's hand, lifts up her muumuu, and starts sprinting up a narrow flight of carpeted stairs. 'Come, I have something to show you. Something I want you to have. Come.' Baez is towed into Mama's bedroom, placed on the billowy blue bed just below a large colour portrait of Christ while Mama rummages through an old dresser and hauls out a white sequined wedding gown. She wheels the gown around and holds it out to Joan. There is a silent moment of almost religious proportions as Mama slowly tiptoes toward Baez with the dress.

Joan is squirming halfway between embarrassment and glee at the old woman's generosity. 'I couldn't take that, Mama. That's yours.'

'I want you to have it. It was mine when I was a girl and now I want you to have it.'

Joan ducks into a closet and starts changing as Mama forages anew into other drawers for more relics. She pulls out glittering blue necklaces with earrings to match, jeweled brooches, even a green guitar. Joan emerges from the closet in glistening white. The dress fits her like a snake. Mama starts crying at this vision and showers Joan with the jewelry. The cameramen are freaking out from lack of film. Gaffers are running up and down the stairs trying to reload the magazines at atomic speeds. The lights are being changed. Mama starts rambling on about God and Christ and 'luck' and healing and medicine and church and love, and Joan is trying to remain upright through it all. Finally she asks Mama if she'd like to hear a song. Mama nods and Joan goes into a lilting country tune that has Mama mesmerized to the floorboards. She rocks in slow motion on her barefoot heels, eyes rolling back into herself, both hands clasped across her dumpling of a stomach, an expression of pure audio-ecstasy melting down her broad face. Joan's tremolos are ringing off every corner of the old woman's crowded bedroom. For a second everything stands still and just listens.

Downstairs, Dylan and the second bus have arrived. He's already in the midst of an impromptu scene at the bar with Ronee Blakely. Something about him being her groupie. Her a famous singer, and him dogging her shadow clear across the country just to get a glimpse of her in the flesh. Howard's upside down in one corner, dripping sweat, with the camera held between his knees. His crew seems to be in the same frenzied state of unreadiness. The sound man is throwing his equipment across the floor in a desperate effort to reload the tape machine while the lighting guys are strapping spotlights to the hatrack with huge strips of gaffer's tape. Dylan is cruising through his second brandy and seems to be having a good time. He shifts from one leg to the other and bops language over Ronee's head. She does her best to establish a repartee, but there's something stilted about the situation. Then suddenly Baez unfolds in her white visionary elegance and the whole air gets zipped. Here is where the pure chance of things has taken the upper hand and turned out better than anything we could have possibly planned in advance. Joan plants herself at one end of the bar with Dylan at the opposite end. She bears down on him through her black eyes. Dylan twitches slightly, orders another brandy, and grins at the situation sideways. The cameras are rolling for sure. Joan plunges straight into it. 'Why did you always lie?'

'I never lied. That was that other guy.'

'You're lying now.'

The cameras are crackling. Everyone's tiptoeing heavily, doing pantomime slaps on his knees at the outrageousness of this moment. Joan presses on.

'You were always calling me up and lying to me.'

'Aw, come off it. You think everything's bullshit. Now I'll admit, there's some things that are definite bullshit but not everything.'

'Stop lying, Bobby. You want them to turn the cameras off, don't you?'

'What ever happened to that boyfriend of yours?'

'Don't change the subject.'

'I'm making conversation.'

Baez beams at him, white teeth flashing over the top of Mama's blue necklace.

'What would've happened if we got married, Bob?'

'I married the woman I love.'

'And I married the man I thought I loved.'

This is turning into either the worst melodrama on earth or the best head-to-head confessional ever put on film. Dylan is dancing around, soaked in brandy, doing his best to dodge the Baez kidney punches. She just stands there, planted, hoisting one-liners at him like cherry bombs. Producers are wincing in the background. Musicians are tittering. Cameras are doing double time.

'Didn't you used to play the guitar?'

'No, that was that other guy.'

'What other guy, Bob?'

'That little short guy. I forget his name.'

'Oh, you mean that little Jewish brat from Minnesota? His name was Zimmerman.'

'Yeah.'

'Why'd you change your name, Bob?'

'Just for a change.'

'Do you still play the guitar?'

'Yeah. Every once in a while. We've got a road show.'

'Oh, yeah, I heard about that. What's it called? Rumbling something?'

'Something like that.'

'Where are you playing?'

'Little places. Just around.'

Arlo finally announces that dinner is ready. Dylan's not hungry. He wants to go on with the shooting. It's hard to resist the smells of Mama's fish gumbo, so we all pack it in for a while to dive into huge plates of the stuff. Bob is really hot for the film now. He takes his plate into another room and sets up a scene of him eating with Scarlet Rivera, Ginsberg, and Rob Stoner, and Arlo sits down at an old beat upright piano. Dylan starts talking to Scarlet at the table, asking her what goes on in this town. Scarlet picks right up on it and starts winding her way through a 'hometown girl' routine. Arlo does a soft piano, silent movie back-up to the dialogue. The camera crews are going bananas trying to keep up with all this shift of scenery, light changes and at the same time balancing plates of gumbo off their elbows, sneaking forkfuls at the same time they're adjusting camera angles. Mama is handing out black-and-white postcards of herself in her younger days. The scene at the table picks up momentum and begins to turn into full-tilt Max Sennett routine with Jack Elliot appearing in the window singing sea chanties, then Ginsberg reading from *Moby Dick*, then Dylan crawling across the table, out the window and disappearing. Then Stoner appearing with the green guitar doing his Gene Vincent impersonation, then Barry's dog, Miller, appears, crawls through the window, across the table, through plates of fish bones, and leaps to the ground.

Outside, Joan and Dylan are having an intimate scene under a green apple tree, then moving down to a pond and throwing rocks, leaving cameramen broken in their wake. The whole thing has busted loose into this chain reaction of insanity and good times. The film is really happening to the point of almost causing all this collage of inspired events. This stuff wouldn't be going on without a camera around. Not like this anyway.

All of a sudden it's nighttime and someone remembers we have to be somewhere. Another concert somewhere. Mama's Lounge is glowing in the dark, as though the special energies from the day have been transmitted to it, seeping into its walls and boards somehow, causing it to throb with life in the middle of the Massachusetts woods. The bus drivers come out of hibernation behind the wheels. The gear's packed up and we're rolling off again, leaving Mama doing dishes in her muumuu.

A DAY ON THE RIVER

The Sex Pistols' Boat Trip by Peter York

We're back at the pier early. The police want us off. They want everyone off the boat. I don't mind either way; I've had a nice day and it's the man's boat after all. But I stay on because I want to see fair play – see what happens. Branson's arguing with the top cop, he's in his Merry Prankster element, throwing the ginger locks around and grinning hugely. But there *are* people getting off here and there. Branson is mainly on about the fact that they've booked the boat *for the day* and the police are saying, well, the owner wants you off. There are Black Marias all round the Embankment and on the bridge and a tidy little crowd waiting – all to celebrate Virgin Records promotional Sex Pistols Jubilee up-river boat trip.

After some more in this vein and some megaphone work the police come on. They're going straight for whatever look like the trouble types. I stay on until the little whirling scrums around you mean you just have to move. This is no particular bother because they're not going at everyone – it's hardly the S.P.G., various people around are having their own little fights. I slip off with Jon Savage from *Sounds*, Stephen Lavers the Bionic Boy, and Zecca, who's the pianist for one of the more dreadful 'punk' bands in the world, Cherry Vanilla and her lot, ex-Warholites.

People say afterwards that the police have had it in for Malcolm ever since the business of the Lonesome Cowboys –

he'd been had up for selling those cowboy T-shirts with the guys with the duelling dicks. But they don't seem to be doing anything very systematic. Back at Waterloo Pier we go up the stone steps and watch from the top. It's chaos, the police are coming back dragging a few by the ears with them, including Vivienne Westwood who's gone dead-dog, still shouting. They're hauling her up the steps. I'm not really worried for her because it doesn't look as if she's getting hurt, and she dearly loves an argy-bargy (like with Judy Nylon who actually applauded at Ferry's Albert Hall concert. Anti-Ferry had been a *cause*.) So this little tableau of wildcat Vivienne Westwood and the coppers is coming up the steps towards us, when Zecca, who is basically a short-haired hippie and a gent, starts saying how they're being brutal with her and so on and we're saying 'Oh, come on, Zecca'. We can't stop him, he's off to her rescue. 'For Christ's sake, that's a woman you've got there.' So they take him in too (obstruction). Then, of course, we *have* to stay around because we're going to have to bail him out or do the necessary – he could be deported otherwise.

On the Embankment I feel very blank – all around there are kid's shouting 'They've got Malcolm' and 'They're doing Malcolm over in a corner' and so on, having a little gossip about it and having the time of their lives. What I feel mainly is that I'd heard this before – at Archway with the black kids outside the police station, and at the Carnival, and compared with that this is all play power gone sour. Savage drives up to the station where there is absolutely nothing to be done, we're far too early, they've barely got them in. They've got to do their stuff first.

On the steps outside is Roadent, this suitably rat-featured creature, the 1977 Face, who's a famous part of the Clash organization. He has a name for various bits of self-laceration – and unlikely parentage they say. And we do what one does – have another little outraged gossip about it all and go for a drink. By now we're four, which is Savage, Lavers and someone I've never seen around before and certainly heard a lot about – that Tony Parsons from N.M.E. We've never exactly met, and we hardly exchange two words this time either. He's OK but I reckon he glowers too much.

The pub is real madness, a bigger jolt than anything we've seen today which included, one has to admit, one or two little fights on the boat – but absolutely nothing compared to what you see at gigs – all the Fascist police shock horror and so on. The pub is the most absolute 1984/1948 Jubilee time warp possible, because in there they're all doing their high summer, 1977 colour supplement, street-party number. They've got an old girl in a boater at the mike, singing all the old songs to the old crowd in the old cracked voice. Where they get them from in trendy, up-market Covent Garden I can't think, all swaying about like a kind of cheerful cosy Jack Warner Cockney crowd scene who'd kill on sight. I know Savage, who is well into these paranoid montages – London's Outrage, tower blocks and fifties ads – will pick up on the 1984 number. I can *see* his copy for next week's *Sounds*.

We're not welcome; Parsons is looking like what the Average *Mirror* Reader would see as proto-typical punk, i.e. he has the God Save The Queen T-shirt on and a black leather jacket, and the others look fairly *defined*. (I look fairly *general* – white Lee drainies, white socks, brogues, white Arrow button-down.) We were served, there's no excuse not to, but since we're not joining in it's pretty much like draft dodging, and a certain amount of nudging's going on.

At our table the talk seems to centre on social control and repression. I can't go along with this. We break off in a desultory way. I take Savage to the Zanzibar and we have a drink while we wait to see what's to be done about Zecca. Zecca had been very talkative on the boat, very interesting about his background; hippie to punk. He was telling us about the Anvil in New York where the really grotesque stuff went on. He'd been saying at that point he started asking himself what he was doing – 'Is this decadence? . . . this *is* decadence . . .' *Idiot*, we can't leave him there.

In the Zanzibar, as ever, the LA sun shines at cocktail hour in the other time warp, the graphic design Café Society 10CC world. Nick, who runs it, had already told me how they had to have a *policy* about punks after a couple had sliced themselves in the lavatories and upset the patrons – that's really it, so far as he's concerned. I find this incontrovertible. So it's a Brandy Alexander and a Pina Colada.

* * * *

In his account in next week's *Sounds*, Savage says we go into 'the sickening cutesy-poo decadence of the Zanzibar'. That's the last time I'm taking him there.

RETURN TO SENDER

The Elvis Suicide by Albert Goldman

Almost from the moment my book *Elvis* appeared, I began receiving a mass of fresh information. But much of it – like reports of an illegitimate child in Louisiana or of Elvis's ties to organized crime – proved impossible to confirm. Then, in August 1989, I read an article in a British tabloid that said Elvis had taken his own life.

The source for the story was David Stanley, the youngest of Elvis's three stepbrothers, all of whom went to work for him between 1971 and '72 when they were teenagers. David and his brother Rick (along with Al Strada, a former security guard) were Elvis's closest aides during his declining years. They called themselves the lifers. Not only were they Elvis's pistol-packing bodyguards, they were literally his lifeguards, maintaining an around-the-clock vigil in his bedroom and witnessing daily the most intimate details of their boss's slide into oblivion. Nobody got closer to Elvis than these three.

When I began work on my book in 1979, two years after Elvis died at the age of 42, David was one of the first people I interviewed. He came across as tough and honest. If he was claiming now that Elvis had killed himself, I wanted to hear the whole story from David's own lips. What had been printed in the British press struck me as inconclusive.

My first question would be: why didn't you tell me about Elvis's suicide 11 years ago?

While tracking David down, I went to the warehouse where my files lie stacked in dusty, old boxes. Rereading my 1979 interview with David, I discovered to my surprise that he *had* told me: 'When Elvis took that last pill, he knew he was going to die. So, if you want to call it suicide, OK, call it that.'

At the same time I recalled a sharply worded letter I had received from John P. Morgan, MD, Programme Director of Pharmacology at the City University of New York Medical School and my principal authority on drugs. He had taken issue with my interpretation of Elvis's death, insisting that the evidence pointed clearly to suicide, and stressing the importance of the two anti-depressants, Elavil and Avcntyl, that were discovered in the star's body. According to Morgan, these drugs testified to Elvis's gloomy state of mind; nobody takes them for pleasure.

(The toxicology report disclosed that Elvis's body also contained the following drugs, all of which he had to have consumed within the preceding 24 hours: codeine – at a concentration of ten times higher than the toxic level; Metaqualone – Quaalude, above toxic level; diazepam – Valium; diazepam metabolic; ethinamate – Valmid; Ethchiorvynol – Placidyl; amobarbital – Amytal; penfobarbital – Nembutal; pentobarbital – Carbrital; meperidine – Demerol; phenyltoloxamine – Sinutab, a decongestant, and morphine.)

Professor Morgan's interpretation is supported by two other equally important facts. First, Elvis had to have known what he was doing when he took the drugs that caused his death. Few laymen were more familiar with the danger of mixing barbiturates and tranquilizers with ten times the toxic dose of codeine. It was no secret that for years Elvis's favourite book, apart from the Bible, was the *Physicians' Desk Reference*. This handbook is illustrated with colour photos of tablets, capsules and spansules, and offers precise descriptions of how drugs act and interact in the body. Elvis had committed many of these explanations to memory. Nevertheless, in the latter part of his life he frequently overdosed.

The case for suicide is strengthened further by the timing of

Elvis's death. Elvis OD'd only hours before he was scheduled to depart on a ten-city tour that would have followed closely the publication of *Elvis: What Happened?* Based on interviews with three former bodyguards – Red West, Sonny West and Dave Hebler – this book ripped the lid of Elvis's private life, portraying him as a drug addict, a sex freak and a ghoulish weirdo who liked to visit the Memphis morgue in the dead of night to brood over the corpses. How would his fans react to these revelations? Would they look at him onstage and wonder: 'Is he on the stuff? Is that why he's so fat and out of breath?' There is firsthand evidence that Elvis, always hypersensitive, was appalled by the demolition of his image.

Despite all these clues, I never doubted that Elvis's death was unintentional. Because Elvis had a history of accidental overdoses, I saw no compelling reason to think that his last OD differed in any way from the others – except for the fact that there was nobody around to rescue him.

I realize now that I was guilty of a flagrant error in logic. How could I be sure that all those earlier ODs were accidental? Suppose some of them had been unsuccessful suicide attempts?

Then I got a call from David Stanley. He and his brother Rick, he explained, had been circulating a proposal for a book that would contain information they had withheld from a previous volume, *Elvis, We Love You Tender*, a valentine that made no mention of suicide. For various reasons they had abandoned their project, and David said he was now willing to provide me with all his new information. We then embarked on a series of interviews that paint the clearest picture yet presented of Elvis's final days.

The basic theme of my biography was the total incongruity between Elvis the man and Elvis the myth. That incongruity is far more striking now. In the old days, when the public knew virtually nothing about Elvis's private life, it was possible to accept the myth. Today, when we know so much, the refusal to acknowledge the facts has assumed the character of a mass delusion surpassed only by the stubborn conviction that he is still alive. The evidence supplied by David Stanley may not explode these delusions – but it should. Holed up in his palace, The King in the last months of his life was trapped inside a nightmare from which the only escape was death.

The engine that drove Elvis to destruction was his prodigious appetite for prescription drugs. But until Elvis's personal physician, Dr George Nichopoulos, went on trial in 1981 for overprescribing drugs, we had no official evidence of how much Elvis had actually consumed. Though Dr Nichopoulos was acquitted, the trial provided some startling testimony: during his last two-and-a-half years, Elvis obtained from Dr Nichopoulos more than 19,000 doses of narcotics, stimulants, sedatives and anti-depressants. Yet even this staggering number fails to indicate the full measure of Elvis's addiction. He had many other suppliers, including doctors, dentists and pharmacists located in every corner of the country, but especially in his favourite haunts – Memphis, Las Vegas and Hawaii. Whenever one source dried up, Elvis would board his private plane, fly off to another city and lay in a fresh supply. The rate at which he ingested these powerful pharmaceuticals can be deduced from the appalling drug protocol that was used to assure Elvis of a good night's sleep.

Elvis's day was night. By 4 a.m. he had been lucid for perhaps eight hours. Now it was time for him to tune out. When he had slipped into his blue nylon pyjamas and installed himself in his immense bed with its built-in plastic backrest and retractable armrests of speckled metal, he would turn to the aide on duty and say: 'Gimme my first attack.'

The attendant would break open a small yellow envelope containing 11 different pills and three shots of Demerol. Elvis would hold out a cupped hand, and the attendant would fill it with brightly coloured tablets and capsules. He would swallow the pills one by one with a glass of water. Next, he would stand up and remove his pyjama top, exposing his back, into which – on either side of the spine beneath the shoulder blades – were thrust the little needles of the plastic disposable syringes. Occasionally Elvis would instruct the aide on duty to leave the pills and the syringes so he could use them at his leisure.

The pills were mostly downers, among them a lot of

barbiturates: Amytal, Carbrital, Membutal or Seconal. All these drugs are habit-forming and all lose their effectiveness quickly as the user develops a tolerance, obliging him to step up his dose. This progression is risky because the increase in tolerance is not matched by an increase in the level needed for a fatal dose. The yellow envelope also contained Placidyl and Quaalude, chemically different from the barbiturates but similar in their effect and just as dangerous. Of Elvis's other drugs, Valmid is usually prescribed for insomnia, Demerol is a substitute for morphine and equally addictive. Mixing any of these drugs requires great caution. By taking them all at once, Elvis was risking his life every day. He was also becoming a pharmaceutical freak. Dr Norman Weissman, the pathologist who complied the toxicology report after Elvis's death, testified that he had never seen so many drugs in one body.

After Elvis had received his first attack, he was ready to eat supper – at about 4.30 a.m. From the kitchen, manned 24 hours a day, would arrive three huge cheeseburgers and six or seven banana splits. Now the question was: could Elvis consume all this food before the drugs hit him, or would he nod off with a mouth full of hamburger that could easily choke him to death? Many times his aides rescued him by reaching down his throat to extract the food that was blocking his windpipe.

Once The King had fallen asleep, the aide would settle back in the dimly-lit bedroom and watch television. In about four hours Elvis would begin to stir. Though he was so drugged he couldn't speak, his feeble efforts to get out of bed would indicate that he wanted to go to the bathroom. With great difficulty, the aide would then hoist Elvis's 250 lb body on to his back, transport him in a fireman's carry, deposit him on the toilet, then carry him back to bed again. Supine once more, Elvis would tug at his attendant's shirt. This was the signal for his second attack. Another yellow envelope (inscribed 'second attack') would appear, but this time the job of administering all these drugs was difficult. The aide had to insert the pills one by one into Elvis's mouth and gingerly manipulate the water glass, taking great care not to choke him.

Elvis would quickly fall asleep again. At 10 a.m. he received his third attack. This final load would sink him until mid-afternoon, when he woke up groggy and disoriented. At this point he needed a different type of drug. Elvis would grab from his drug-strewn bedside table a handful of Dexedrines to jump-start his heart, then insert cotton swabs soaked in liquid cocaine into his nostrils.

When asked what could possibly justify such a monstrous, life-threatening routine, David Stanley answers by quoting Elvis himself: 'I'd rather be unconscious than miserable.'

Miserable is the best word to describe Elvis's condition during those brief hours when he wasn't zonked out. After the triumph of his early years, he suffered throughout the rest of his life from a series of frustrations, misfortunes and failures that steadily darkened his outlook and eventually plunged him into despair. His greatest ambition was to become a serious film actor, like Bing Crosby or Frank Sinatra. But under the tyrannical, self-serving management of Colonel Tom Parker – a wily, greedy pitchman who charged Elvis monstrous fees and then gambled millions away – Elvis's dreams were drowned in a swamp of moronic exploitation movies. His fame as a rock star waned in the Sixties, when he went for five years without a newly recorded hit. Even his longing to travel overseas and experience new scenes and audiences was thwarted by Colonel Parker's ban on foreign engagements, no matter how lucrative.

Instead, as Elvis grew older and more disillusioned, he was condemned to a treadmill of concert and nightclub dates, as many as 150 a year, which he regarded as sheer torture. He found these mechanically programmed shows terribly boring, and they were also a severe test of his stamina. Burdened by excess weight and debilitated by drugs, he could never have sustained such a taxing schedule without the help of Dr Nichopoulos, who accompanied him on tour. According to David, Elvis was cranked up with powerful uppers before each performance and then let down to resume his somnolent existence in a hotel room or in his flying bedroom aboard the Lisa Marie.

Dr Nichopoulos's help was bought at a steep price. Like Colonel Parker, he kept carving himself a bigger and bigger piece of the Presley pie, thus contributing to the financial difficulties that bedeviled Elvis's last days. Eventually, he persuaded Elvis to underwrite and lend his name to a chain of racquetball courts. When the enterprise got into financial troubles, Elvis had to dig deeper into his pockets, even putting up Graceland as collateral for a £1.3 million bank loan. But the debt kept growing. If Elvis had lived another year, he may have had to file for bankruptcy.

Even more demoralizing for Elvis was the breakdown of his cherished lifestyle. The King used women the same way he used drugs – to numb the agony of being – and he took them as he took pills, in large numbers. For 20 years, beautiful young girls had thrown themselves into his arms in Los Angeles, Las Vegas and Memphis, desperate to please and grateful for his slightest favours. But in his last years Elvis found himself in a humiliating condition. The legendary lover was impotent.

The effects of his decline were evident in his affair with 20-year-old Ginger Alden, the voluptuous young woman he was planning to marry. Elvis flung himself into this affair, purchasing an 11-carat ring and proposing marriage on bended knee. Ginger accepted the ring – and a Cadillac Seville – but she refused to accompany him everywhere he went. Often, when Elvis sank into a drugged stupor, she would return to her own home rather than spend the night in his bed. She had no intention of leaving her family and living with Elvis until she became Mrs Presley.

This enraged Elvis, who interpreted any disagreement as an act of betrayal. Yet he could not relinquish his romantic dream of marrying the perfect girl and finally exorcising the ghost of Priscilla. There were nights when Elvis would praise Ginger to his aides, petting her fondly and holding out her hand to display the gleaming diamond. There were other nights when, waking to see her gone, he would denounce her violently and accuse her family of being leeches. To console himself, Elvis would sometimes spend an evening with a companion from the past, or with a Memphis belle one of his aides had recruited. Minde Miller, a Los Angeles model, was one of his old flames. Her dark good looks and full figure appealed to Elvis's taste for the exotic. His dilapidated condition appealed to her motherly instincts, but she soon realized that as a reclamation project Elvis was a lost cause. Another dark-haired beauty, Alicia Gerwin, turned up during the summer of 1977. She accompanied Elvis on his final flight to Las Vegas, where he picked up a huge stash of drugs. Disturbed by Elvis's alarming state, she soon stopped visiting Graceland.

Always a cradle snatcher – Priscilla was only 14 when they met – Elvis indulged in a final fling with Rise Smith, a Memphis schoolgirl who was 15 when she met Elvis. But Rise was soon gone, having only briefly relieved The King's gathering gloom.

Elvis was also plagued by family worries. His father, Vernon Presley, had left his wife, Dee, for a young nurse named Sandy Miller, and Elvis was convinced that the stress of divorce would prove fatal to a man who had suffered two heart attacks. Days before he died, Elvis said to David, 'Tell Dee I'll give her £10,000 if she'll come here and talk about getting back with Daddy.'

His daughter Lisa Marie, who frequently visited Graceland, was also a problem. Elvis was too self-absorbed to give Lisa Marie the attention she needed – she was nine when he died – but he salved his conscience by showering her with expensive toys. Towards the end, however, dogged by guilt, he would burst into tears and sob: 'I wish I could be a better father!'

And there was another family matter that troubled Elvis's conscience. Two weeks before his death, like a man closing accounts before going out of business, Elvis summoned Billy Stanley to Graceland and tearfully begged his eldest stepbrother to forgive him for having seduced his wife several years earlier.

As he neared the end, Elvis spoke about death constantly. When he saw a tape of his last television special, which showed him looking bloated, he said: 'I may not look good now, but I'll look good in my coffin.'

When Ginger's grandmother died, Elvis was at the funeral. Contemplating the body, he said: 'It won't be long till I'm there.'

When Elvis visited Priscilla for the last time, they had a consoling moment of intimacy. In the car coming home, he told David: 'Everything's all right. Lisa will be fine.'

'Why are you talking like that?' David asked. 'You'll see her again.'

Elvis replied, 'We'll see.'

Watching the films of President Kennedy's assassination, Elvis talked admiringly of the kahunas, the Hawaiian sorcerers and healers who claimed they could predict the precise time of their deaths. He also began to pray passionately. It was not unusual for David to walk into Elvis's bedroom and find him down on his knees, crying in a loud voice, 'God, have mercy on me! Forgive me! God, help me! I can't go on!'

In David's opinion: 'His overall attitude was die, die, die. He talked himself to death.'

Most ominous of all were the last words Elvis spoke to David. Two days before Elvis's death, David announced that he was going off to Nashville for a quiet visit with his estranged wife. As he was leaving, he recalls, 'Elvis put his arms around me and hugged me as hard as he ever had, weeping, crying. I said, "Well, Elvis, take care. Are you sure you don't need anything?" And he said, "No, I'll be all right, David. I just wanna tell you, I will never see you again. The next time I see you will be in a better place, a higher plane. I love you very much." '

David also disclosed for the first time that Elvis had a history of suicidal behaviour. In 1967, shortly before his marriage to Priscilla, he came perilously close to killing himself. He had grave doubts abut the marriage and had tried to delay it. This angered Colonel Parker, who coerced Elvis into making a final commitment, warning him that if he jilted Priscilla, he would be publicly exposed by her stepfather for living with an under-age girl. Feeling the pressure, Elvis got into a violent fight one night with Priscilla and afterwards gulped a large handful of barbiturates. Some time later he was found unconscious in his bedroom. David remembers Vernon, his stepfather, answering the phone in their home and screaming, 'My son tried to kill himself!' Herding his family into the car, Vernon roared off to Graceland, where he ran up the stairs bawling, 'Son, please don't die! Don't die!' David says he saw Elvis laid out on his bed, comatose and ghostly pale, as paramedics laboured to revive him – a scene he saw repeated with tragic results ten years later.

* * * *

Clearly, in his last grim weeks, Elvis was possessed by the thought of death. What transformed the thought into the deed, David is firmly convinced, was the conjunction of two intolerable prospects: public reaction to the bodyguards' book and the public exposure of a new tour. David says Elvis was outraged and horrified when he read a purloined manuscript of *Elvis: What Happened?* One minute he would moan, 'My life is over!' The next he would snarl, 'I'll *kill* Red and Sonny!'

As for the upcoming tour, Elvis had been saying ever since his last ordeal on the concert circuit that he would never go on the road again. Nobody paid much attention to the threat – after all, Elvis's concert appearances were virtually his only remaining source of income. In any case, greedy old Colonel Parker wasn't about to let his meal ticket turn into a rain check. The Colonel was awaiting Elvis's arrival in Portland, Maine, when he received word that The King was dead.

On his last night, Elvis left Graceland at around 11 and went to a dentist's office. (As David notes with an ironic smile, 'Elvis had more toothaches than any human being alive.') Was it the dentist who gave Elvis the codeine – not a regular drug in his daily protocol – that was later found at a lethal level in his body? No-one knows for sure.

As the sun rose on the morning of August 16, 1977, Elvis retired to his bedroom with Ginger. A short time later he ordered Rick to go to a local pharmacy and pick up some Dilaudid pills – two-and-a-half times stronger than pure heroin – that had been prescribed by Dr Nichopoulos the night before. When Rick returned, he was told to take Elvis his first attack.

Rick reports that he found Elvis alone in the bedroom. He was holding a manuscript of the bodyguards' book, and he was in a state of extreme agitation. 'How are the fans gonna take this stuff?' he demanded. 'How is Lisa Marie gonna feel about her daddy?' At the climax of his anxious interrogation, Elvis insisted that Rick pray with him. 'God, forgive me for my sins,' he pleaded. 'Let the people have compassion and understanding of the things that I have done. Amen.'

By now, Elvis was in no mood for his first attack. So Rick

handed him the yellow envelope, assuming that he would swallow the pills when he was ready. As Rick left, Elvis gave him an unusual order: 'Tell David [who came on duty at noon] not to disturb me until four o'clock *under any circumstances.*'

When Rick returned to the bedroom at 8 a.m., bringing the second attack, he found Ginger there and Elvis still awake. So he handed Elvis the yellow envelope and went away. Downstairs, Rick proceeded to get high, and by 9 a.m. he was too wasted to deliver the third attack to his boss. So the last drug delivery was made by Graceland's housekeeper, Elvis's Aunt Delta Mae, who simply handed over the packet and left.

That's how matters stood at 9 a.m. Elvis had been given three envelopes, each containing 11 pills and three plastic syringes, and no-one had seen him swallow or inject a single dose. He also had in his possession a lethal quantity of codeine.

At around 9.30 Ginger awoke in time to see Elvis pick up a book on the Shroud of Turin – revered by the credulous as the garment Jesus Christ wore in the tomb – and head toward the bathroom, where he kept a reading chair. 'Precious, I'm gonna go read a while,' he explained. 'OK,' she sighed, 'but don't fall asleep.' He smiled and replied, 'I won't.'

At around 2.30 that afternoon, according to Ginger, she awoke and went to look for Elvis. She found him doubled over on the bathroom floor. Unable to rouse him and alarmed by his blood-engorged face, she called for help. Aides and family members responded immediately and worked desperately to revive Elvis. David was one of the first to arrive. Scanning the room for evidence of drug use, he spotted the three yellow attack envelopes on the floor. All of them were empty, he remembers, and one had been wadded up. He also saw three or four empty or half-empty syringes (others were found by the bed) and six spilled pills.

David and Rick quickly figured out what had happened. Instead of taking his three attacks in the customary span of six to eight hours, Elvis had consumed this huge load of drugs all at once – and on top of that he had swallowed the large quantity of codeine. Nobody could have withstood such a concentrated assault – and Elvis knew it. It was obvious to David that Elvis had taken his own life.

Right there in the bathroom a cover-up began. David reports: 'All the traces that might point to the real horror of Elvis or confirm that this was no accident were removed. Nobody thought it was strange. It was just the thing we had always done. Elvis had lived a lie and now he had died a lie.'

The lie was insidiously perpetuated. When a team of paramedics failed to revive Elvis, he was rushed to Baptist Memorial Hospital in an ambulance that also held the frantic Dr Nichopoulos. What happened in Trauma Room No 1 is a subject of some dispute. David says he caught a glimpse of Elvis laid out naked on a steel table with an incision running from his neck to his abdomen. Dr Eric Muirhead, who presided at the autopsy, says there was no such incision. David, however, claims he saw doctors working inside Elvis's body – he assumed they were massaging his heart. At any rate, according to Dr Muirhead, someone pumped out the contents of Elvis's stomach. The substances that could have provided convincing evidence of suicidal intent were then presumably destroyed.

That same afternoon Dr Nichopoulos obtained a note from Vernon requesting a private autopsy whose findings would be sealed for 50 years. Ask for a copy of the autopsy report and all you get are three pages on which all the revealing passages have been blacked out. Exactly what the doctors discovered is a mystery, yet despite the suspicious nature of Elvis's death – and despite the fact that Dr Nichopoulos and members of Elvis's family were aware of his drug abuse – the Shelby County coroner, Dr Jerry T. Trancisco, appeared on television the night Elvis died and announced to the world that the singer had succumbed to 'cardiac arrhythmia'.

The truth began to come out two years later, when the sensational revelations of the Nichopoulos trial and ABC's airing of the toxicologist's report strongly suggested that Elvis died of a massive drug overdose. The faithful, blindly believing The King could do no wrong, blandly ignored the evidence of Elvis's sordid private life and canonized the man as a martyr.

Fourteen years after his death, Elvis is bigger than ever. Elvis clones appear by the dozen on stage, screen and television, and the man himself (if you believe the tabloids) has been seen in a Michigan supermarket and even on Mars. What's more, Elvis is worth more dead than alive. In 1989 his estate earned more than $15 million from the sales of records, souvenirs and the 500,000 adoring fans who took guided tours of Graceland.

Not even Elvis could kill Elvis.

SCUM ALSO RISES

Sid Vicious by Nick Kent

Jan 1978, Sticksville, USA, through whose dark heart a bus travels bearing the fabulous Sex Pistols on a tour that will conclude with the group's self-detonation. A deluxe vehicle, its inhabitants comprise the four Pistols, one Malcolm McLaren, some roadies, a Warner Brothers exec and two photographers. Anyway, Sid Vicious is staring out the window – the obligatory beer can in one paw, a sandwich in the other, a blowjob on his mind and dreams of a syringe in his arm – when he turns and those scrawny eyes alight on a wondrous vision. *Motorcycle boots* to be precise, but not just any old motorcycle boots – *these*, like, *unbelievably* heavy-duty storm-trooping creations of leather and steel. They were, however, being worn by one of the photographers; some *blinkin' Yank* called *Bob* that McLaren was matey with or something. Sid didn't dislike this bloke, mind, didn't much like him probably. He meant fuck all to Sid really, he was just, like, there. But the boots were espied and Sid was smitten. He got well intimate then. Nothing extravagant of course, just yer basic, 'Alright then mate? Uh, bet you got some fucking good snaps eh?' Then, with nary a pause, Vicious asked the fellow to flog him his boots *'cos, like, he really fancied 'em.*

Unfortunately, there was a problem here which Sid would have instantly recognised as 'insurmountable' were he, Sid Vicious, capable of comprehending the concept, never mind understanding the word. Bob wasn't some biker fop: it was just that, so spacious were the boots that a whole camera, simply dismantled, would fit snugly inside the lining. They had become a necessary appendage to his vocation. Sid took this in. It's debatable whether he fully grasped the reasons, but he understood a guy saying 'no'. Bob stemmed the tide of pleading he sensed fast approaching by allowing Sid to wear his boots onstage that night at whatever redneck club the group were scheduled to trash.

Once Sid got his feet in Bob's boots he felt himself undergoing a considerable transformation. On the stage that night Sid felt his whole stance increased. The fact that he was performing the wrong bass parts for most of the set was inconsequential. Lydon was acting like a stuck-up wanker, a bloody ponced-up pop star who wasn't, like, even *involved* in the spirit of the thing. In those boots, those precious boots, Sid felt himself invincible. Still, they weren't his.

Bob again allowed Vicious to wear them the next night that the Pistols performed, and *again,* the fact was made resolutely manifest: Sid and these boots were made for each other. He struggled to find the right solution. Bob wasn't budging – this was clear. The boots were back on Bob's feet so stealing them was not feasible. The answer struck home: in order to get those boots, Sid would have to kill him.

It was approaching three a.m. and virtually every passenger on this downbound bus was sprawled in positions appropriate to some condition of sleep. Providential indeed, then, that one of the party should awake just in time to look upon a chilling spectacle. Bob was sound asleep in a vaguely upright position, his backbone curved against the slight dip in the posture sprung seating. Directly behind his prone form stood Sid Vicious, his right hand brandishing a Bowie knife.

Amassing what strength he could muster, our interloper managed to tackle Vicious from behind, jerking both arms up behind his (Vicious') head and removing the weapon almost at once. Vicious didn't scream or attempt to unfasten his gangling limbs from the hammerlock. Amazingly, the action itself roused not a soul, not even Bob. The interloper, a longstanding colleague of McLaren, had encountered Sid on various occasions, though never remotely in such circumstances. He was stunned. Vicious was also stunned: the interloper's shocked stare bore down on him. The first person to break the silence was Sid. Shamefaced, he pleaded with an earnestness that undermined any possibility of it being a humorous remark.

'I would have woken him up before I slit his throat,' he kept repeating.

That is my favourite Sid Vicious story, not simply because it packs that good hearty *thwack* of sensationalism, but more because it is a perfect example of the psychological bomb-site upon which John Simon Ritchie invented his own Action Man in the persona of Sid Vicious.

Ritchie was born in May 1958, a suitably turbulent year, that witnessed the lascivious rise and fall of Jerry Lee Lewis, infamy's most indomitable living practitioner, the slaying of young Nebraskan Charlie Starkweather, and the celluloid vision of Elvis Presley, a young god, explaining his physical predilections to some cornfed belle thus: '*That ain't tactics, baby, that's the beast in me*'. In a way, the stage was set.

He grew up in and around the outskirts of London – principally the East End – the only child of a single parent and, in those crucial seven years of life, well, one can surmise. Imagine claustrophobic estate blocks, spurious influences, and the presence of something inexplicably disturbing, impersonal and sickly-scented; the sight of some stranger laying comatose against a bean-bag. Children around junkies are given few options in life. Our little prince was given two: he could stare at the wall, or he could throw himself against it. He chose the latter, time and time again.

Most rock stars of the rebellious mould use their parents' values as the sourcepoint of their desire for reinvention. John Simon Ritchie used the world as a whole, but, lacking vision and the potential to apply himself, his alter-ego was fashioned more by a colleague, John Lydon. He, Lydon and others were a gang – sneering and puerile, with Lydon the brains and the rest the brawn and banter. Because virtually all this mob were called John, making it hard to know whose round it was, nicknames were compulsory. Lydon rechristened our lad Sid – a name he loathed, but duly lived with.

Sid initially adored Lydon, with his higher intellect and a clear cutting-edge to his loathing. When the latter was asked to join the Sex Pistols, Sid and the others became a leering gestapo for Lydon's Top Cat persona. Fuelled on leapers (favoured by 90% of bank robbers) they were the big noise now, *they knew the truth* and anyone threatening that autonomy was needful of a lesson in intimidation.

In June of 1976, Sid was dispatched to give such a lesson to a journalist at a Pistols gig taking place in the 100 Club. Assisted by a psychopath accomplice, who held a knife some two inches, no more, from this music writer's face, Sid landed five good scalp-lacerating direct hits with his rusty bike chain. Only once did he hit his mark, causing much bloodletting, but little damage. The blow, however, warranted an ebullient Lydon to grant Sid a new surname: 'Vicious'.

Infamy was now calling the shots: Sid was quoted at length in punk exposés: he abhorred 'sex', 'uniforms', 'hypocritical bastards', 'hippies', 'poseurs', prescribing 'a good kicking for all and sundry'. An exact century earlier, another young hellion had struck fear into the hearts of the law abiding. Billy the Kid, like Sid (Ritchie or Beverley) boasted two conflicting surnames: Bonney or Harrigan. Also, like Sid, he first killed at age 14. Bill's victim was a drink-sodden 'hombre', one Belisano Villagrán, a gun fighter of local renown in New Mexico. Sid's victim was a cat: swinging its tail repeatedly, he beat the feline's brains to mush against a brick wall. Both also died aged 20 or 21. Billy the Kid, however, had cold-blooded guile and the application to back up his reputation as the fastest gun in the West: 21 victims were notched on his holster ('not counting Mexicans'). Sid Vicious, however, only managed to foul up everything he got involved in. No stamina, no gumption. As one quarter of the Sex Pistols – at their best the musical equivalent of a car wreck – he displayed all the dexterity of a one-legged man at an arse kicking contest. As a hellion, he was feeble. Where the desperado or snake-eyed boy let his weapon do the talking, Vicious would solemnly intone, 'Well, I think that I'm not, like, *really, really* vicious, y'know . . .' He'd pause, lost in half-baked exegesis, 'but I'm pretty wild!'

Sid Vicious was a dirty fighter. He couldn't throw a punch and lacked the bearing, the stance, of a good scrapper. A good scrapper works from his heels, uses his wits, develops a technique for felling the opponent. Vicious just bottled in, all gangly limbs and mock sneer. He was dangerous because pain – physical pain – wasn't a concern he seemed remotely aware of. Instead he would wantonly gouge his torso with broken glass, razor blades, knife cuts. He would do this when he was 'bored'. Boredom was intolerable as the great George Sanders pointed out in his suicide note.

Love, for Sid, was another wretched contrivance, be it 'universal harmony' or the more intimate variant. By the autumn of '76, as an oft-quoted celebrity in the vanguard of punk's disaffected youth, he boasted that he was the most sexless creature in the world. Then, some four months on, he encountered Nancy Spungen and duly revised his opinion.

Vicious first tried heroin not in the company of Spungen but in the company of Heartbreakers' Johnny Thunders and Jerry Nolan. The former would wave a syringe in the face of some uninitiated, impressionable shill. 'Are you a boy or a man?' he would tease, turning the issue into a matter of machismo. Vicious, of course, tried it – twice, in fact, whilst in their company. He threw up a lot and found the experience less than awe-inspiring. However, when Spungen, a maladjusted harridan who'd flown to London in the vain hope of recommencing her fleeting affair with drummer Nolan, found herself in Vicious' company, she sensed the malleable nature of Vicious' hedonistic potential and steered him into the murky precincts of filtered cottons; and that same acrid stench he must have recalled offending his senses as a child. For a short while there was a sexual rapport that Vicious had never believed could exist. The archetypal mixed-up restless little boy and his maladjusted, self-fixated little girl looking for that golden-armed handshake from a white-knuckled world. Some would call it 'love' – but I prefer to concur with Lou Reed in 'Street Hassle': '*It's called bad luck*'.

Infamy is a flint-hearted vocation to live with, requiring lightning reflexes and an abundance of quick-wittedness. Vicious and Spungen had neither. Two months of enchantment curdled overnight into a year of entrapment. Romeo and Juliet they weren't: their relationship was closer to the hopelessly juvenile version of Jack Lemmon and Lee Remick in *Days of Wine and Roses*. On October 12th, 1978, ten months after the Pistols detonation, during which time Vicious had alienated everyone he'd ever known but his soul-mate, the affair came to a predictably gore-spattered conclusion. At 10.50 a.m., a barely coherent English accent phoned the Chelsea Hotel switchboard asking someone to check room 100 because 'someone is seriously injured'. The Manhattan police arrived to find Vicious stunned, seated on the bed while in the bathroom the dead body of Nancy Spungen lay under the sink, a trail of blood running from the bed to her final resting place. When probed, Vicious stated that the fatality had occurred because he was 'a dog, a dirty dog'. A moment later, suddenly acquainted with the enormity of his circumstances, he said, 'You can't arrest me. I'm a rock'n'roll star'.

Ten days later Sid was free on bail. Old acquaintances had sprung to his aid. His mother had flown over; Malcolm McLaren (who, weeks earlier, had refused to take a phone call from his former client) was in town, determined to free 'his boy' even if it meant employing the services of F. Lee Bailey, America's most prestigious defence lawyer. Conspiracy theories were being tossed around: Spungen had been the victim of a drug syndicate hit; a mugger had attacked her while Vicious slept. Optimism reigned, or so it seemed, but Vicious was far from jubilant. His metabolism had been through hell while he was ensconced at Ryker's Island jail. Also, his conscience was riddled with a gnawing remorse.

That evening, he locked the door to the bathroom and, finding only a Bic razor and a broken lightbulb, he slashed away at every vein in his arms and legs. His mother respected her son's wish to die and sat by him as the blood seeped from his body. By the time McLaren and Joe Stevens, Vicious' unofficial minder, arrived they were confronted with a scene of extraordinary hideousness. Vicious was so far gone he could no longer control his bladder and urine spurted onto the blood-soaked sheets. Mrs Beverly immediately rounded on a dazed McLaren, informing him that this was a suicide pact and not to interfere. Sid meanwhile, still conscious, begged his manager to go out and score some downers so as to stop the pain. McLaren walked to the door not knowing what to do. Stevens meanwhile knelt next to Vicious and, a small cassette recorder in his hand, pressed 'record'. The first words are his. 'So, Sid, on that night, what really happened?'

The tape lasted half an hour, lapses occurred, the voice receded yet the clarity of recollection was consistent.

They'd been waiting to score having received a wad of dollar bills – over 1,000 in cash – for an upcoming gig. However, no narcotics could be found. Their dealer, Robert, gave them Tuinol, a heavy barbiturate which, mixed with alcohol, caused Vicious' withdrawal symptoms to worsen. At one point he left the room and began knocking on all the doors of the Chelsea Hotel, screaming for drugs.

This alerted a suitably imposing black custodian, who, having verbally warned Vicious – only to be called 'a fuckin' nigger' – began striking the puny twerp; in the process breaking his nose. Vicious crawled back to the room to be confronted by Spungen, equally enraged. She slapped his face, striking the broken nose and causing the brutish pain to intensify. Vicious, standing by the table on which a seven-inch knife was placed, reciprocated. One clean lunge at the stomach of his beloved: it was hopeless, stupid and typical of their relationship. Minutes later they were embracing, reconciled. Unfortunately, Spungen removed the blade and omitted to cover the wound with a bandage of any sort. She lay down on the bed, while Vicious, similarly negligent in matters of basic hygiene, dashed off to keep an appointment at the Methadone clinic. When he returned, his beloved Nancy was deceased. She was not yet 21. Police duly noted that her corpse was already beginning to decompose a mere seven hours after death.

As Vicious finished the halting recitation, McLaren returned, not with a handful of downers but with an ambulance. Two weeks in Bellevue Hospital had Vicious patched up. His morale also changed: guilt and remorse were no longer concerns worthy of a wild and crazy desperado like Sid Vicious. Like all hopelessly self-absorbed rock stars, he detoured away from moral considerations and believed what he and his fans wanted. He wasn't guilty and the realization that he was once more a big noise – possibly capable of literally getting away with murder – excited him. He had a new girlfriend, Michelle Robinson, another groupie, and that cocky psychopathic attitude – *'I'm a rock'n'roll star. You can't arrest me'* – was suddenly back to the forefront.

It ended on the second week of December '78. Vicious, back to his initial kamikaze oafishness, had lewdly propositioned the girlfriend of Todd Smith, brother of Patti. Smith had verbally reprimanded him only to have Vicious smash a broken bottle into his face, almost blinding him. Smith pressed charges and Vicious was back in Ryker's Island alongside the 'niggers' who beat him bloody, the 'spicks' who spat at him, the hardcore badarse elite who took no truck from some fucked-up limey pop star whose choices and options they never had. In Ryker's Island, punks weren't spikey-haired rebels with guitars and wild, crazy attitudes. They were the broken spirits, the losers who could only survive via homosexual liaisons that would offer them protection.

Vicious was released almost two months later, on February 2nd. He boasted to Jerry Nolan that he'd gotten on well with his cohabitants; that these desperados could see that he, Vicious, was cut from the same leathery fabric as themselves. In reality, he had been treated like scum. Arriving at a celebratory bash, clean and in good spirits, he injected some heroin his mother had bought for him, fearing that he'd try scoring himself, thus jeopardising his bail *again*. He immediately blacked out, his complexion tinged with the blue signs of overdose – but, after a short exercise, he came to and continued, in good spirits, to muse about the future.

Yes, he could still fantasize. But then reality would impinge and he'd realize that no matter which defence lawyer was involved, no matter how much he could kid himself he was innocent, it was over. No, Ryker's Island was not going to see him languishing with the other lifers, perverts and losers. While Robinson slept, he found another packet of the deadly powder. This time there was no-one conscious to awaken him from falling into the abyss. He heated the spoon, filtered the cotton and – his life revolving around him – returned to dust. The scum that also rises sank into an unmarked grave.

Decomposing was their greatest achievement. A mere seven hours after expiring, Nancy Spungen was already *smelling* of death. It takes up to 48 hours before the putrifying odour commences in the corpses of the old. At the age of 20, both had wasted themselves beyond belief. Let them rot.

WHEN WE WERE GLASS

The Futurists by Adair Nye & David Quantick

A while ago Eric B guested as a video judge on *Night Network*; there was none of the leg-crossing or persona-switching or constant references to *Blade Runner* one associates with British pop stars. Eric B sat stolidly and affably through the proceedings, speaking when spoken to, conveying the air of an urban king surrounded by craven representatives from Chrysler showrooms; nothing moved the guest judge until one particularly murky video. By British standards this clip wasn't all that novel – in fact, it was a fairly palsied example of the haunting-images-of-decay-super-imposed-over-sleeping-girls genre – but Eric B clearly thought it decadent. 'No way could you show this in the States,' he said, staring.

The reason, of course, stems from the fact that Americans have never embraced GARY NUMAN, and all things that sprang from his lugubrious works. Americans have no gift for pretention. Americans don't aim for art cred. They have too much pep to send songs about lassitude and despair straight into the top ten and have little or no desire to face the camera dressed entirely in flawless white, extending one perfect dead fish to the viewer à la DAVID SYLVIAN. Musically, the only real aesthetic of excess in America is sentimentality – where the Brits love the sound of breaking glass the Yanks are sobbing over little green apples.

The sleeve of 'The Pleasure Principle' shows Gary Numan

sitting fascinated/repelled at a mirrored table; a grown man in mascara and a business suit rendered helpless by a small plastic pyramid with a red light inside. All the usual British pop obsessions are here: sex (the title), loss of identity (the reflective table), restriction (say, there's no door in here!). But it's Gary's *gaze* that makes the whole thing so miraculously corny, so resplendent with true British pretension. Gary's looking at the pyramid like he's half in love with it. He's making a Statement About Technology – like: *it's alluring, sure, but it might take me over!*

From 1979–83 British musicians produced the most pretentious lyrics, imagery, and minor chords the pop world has ever known, surpassing even the Pre-Raphaelite aspirations and bogus rock operas of the Sixties and Seventies. Step forward ULTRAVOX, JAPAN, HUMAN LEAGUE, BEF, POSITIVE NOISE, (early) CURE, (early) SIMPLE MINDS, GARY NUMAN, DEPECHE MODE, OMD, FAD GADGET and innumerable others who were called at the time 'futurist' or 'atmospheric' (as opposed to the more arcane 'industrial' or the too-chummy 'synthi-pop'). Confusingly some 'industrial' bands like JOY DIVISION, WIRE, and THROBBING GRISTLE – really *were* Art, and not merely Art Damaged, which tended to make competition for the critical honours quiet but deadly.

Sometimes the difference between suggesting a genuine heart of darkness and manufacturing a flapdoodle approximation of same balanced on the narrowest of margins. Compare, say, '*here are the young men/the weight on their shoulders*' (Joy Division, almost alchemically gripping) with '*but things were different then/for the Quiet Men*' (Ultravox – were the Quiet Men elegant enigmas or just bookish guys scared of girls?). It soon became clear that some bands could transform a motorway underpass into an instrument of nausea and terror, while others, Gazza-like, inspired laffs all around ('Underpants!' cried JOHN FOXX, like a character out of *Carry On Up The Terminal Beach*).

Pretentious bands cared about looking controlled and opaque, and so were never photographed near baby showers or Club Mediterranée rhumba lines. Pretentious bands cared about landscape and order, and so issued sleeve designs that seemed to say: *Help! I'm trapped inside some evocative spatial arrangements*

– *details inside!* Pretentious bands use concepts like 'alienation' and 'epic sweep' like water in a squirt tie: first you were seduced by the look of it all, then – bap! – right in the retina with another song about fragments of things, or how we're all connected by machines. But the pompous boys' most endearing trait was that they conducted themselves like heroes in an art film *at all times*, vain enough to believe that they were under constant surveillance and misguided enough to believe that geniuses never lose their dignity.

Like all great cultural movements, the Pretentious Era was about sharing the pain. As with punks, the big issue for the pompous bands was the breakdown of modernism. As the Seventies ended, the art-school boys grasped that Britain was kidding itself about a lot of things. Brooding types discovered that image was more real than substance; that media was a matter of who's looking at who, and with what equipment; that nostalgia was pathetic; and that news footage on TV could appear grotesquely sensual. Everyone was suffering from the same industrial jaundice, but, surprisingly, the art-damaged set turned out to be much more prescient than the punks, if not quite as sexy.

The punks were old-fashioned romantic Lefties – they loved Britain enough to give it an exciting old age. The pretentious bands foresaw something different – Britain as an ordered, creepily pristine pathology lab. The punks took a look around Britain and thought it best to behave like terrorists; John Foxx took a look around Britain and thought it best to behave like a *liquid*.

The point is, if you were young, white, male, heartstick and British in the late Seventies, you'd be pretentious too. Pretentiousness – being possessed by naff, disturbing visions, and then getting them on *Top Of The Pops* – is the traditional British way of Being Heard. Britain is a class-bound, print-oriented, Druid-worshipping country; therefore, one good method of proving yourself more shriek-worthy than your peers is to be extra-literate, extra-superior, extra-visionary. Whereas the Americans buy or fight their way out of nerd status, in 1979 the Brits were trekking out to Shepperton to visit J. G. Ballard, where they could talk about the eroticism of helicopters.

By late 1983 the electricity had gone out of the movement, and so the good ship Pretension left the crackling pylons of Sheffield for the fleshpots of London, to the Blitz club to try on new attitudes with a new bunch of disaffected boys. Audiences switched from being interested in lyrics about threatening rooms and cenotaphs to wanting to see pictures of them instead. Inevitably, there came a point when supremely gassy 'poetry' collided with equally over-the-top visuals, and that point was the video for 'Vienna'. Not only did you get pictures of tubercular Euro-decadents, but also wavering chords and lyrics like '*the cold empty silence*'. But video made the 'atmospheric' bands less and less necessary – now the pictures were on tap, ready-made, and not a mental by-product of squonking synth lines.

Pretentious bands believed that everything is a lie except for Art. Soul boys, on the other hand, believe that everything is a lie except for love. Disco tekkies believe that everything is a lie except for their own bodies. But the trouble with abandoning Art – however silly and tacky it may be – for flesh and flowers is that Tories make mincemeat out of love. In the charts, love-glorious-love ends up conforming pro-lad, pro-showbiz, pro-'enterprise' values. Singing about love gives you tabloid pop. Singing about discordant ideas gives you, um, discordant ideas.

Tragically, British musicians have stopped trying to mystify people. The pretension of today is of the kissy-kissy strain – that it's better to persuade people that you're a great lover rather than a great brooder; that you're a brill dancer rather than a collector of BURROUGHS first editions; that the past is safer that the future; that it is better to be American and rich than British and interesting. From car crash to car wash – only one of these infatuations ever distinguished us from the least pretentious nation on earth.

THE GREAT GREENLAND MYSTERY

Michael Jackson by Danny Baker

> *'Comrade Jackson,' he said, 'This is well met. The one man of all others I would have wished to encounter. We will pop off somewhere, Comrade Jackson, should your engagements permit, and restore our tissues with a cup of tea. I had hoped to touch the Jackson family for some refreshment . . .'*

The introduction of Michael Jackson into P G Wodehouse's Leave It to Psmith (1923).

Greenland. If you think nothing happens in your town you should throw an eyeball around Greenland.

From five miles above it looks like the kind of terrain that made Captain Oates cry Uncle. Impossible mountain ranges scar snow-bound grey granite and as far as I can see there's no houses, no roads, no people, not even the obligatory polar bear cutting holes in the floes. Just grey, grey and more grey. (Those readers living in Kidbrook will have a more vivid picture of what I mean.)

I fell asleep for an hour and when I awoke the view was as if we'd remained motionless. As I begin formulating a theory about how punk rock may have actually started in Greenland wastes an even more staggering statistic occurs. It may well be that down below me, within that endless papier mache freeze, lies the only nation on this earth that hasn't presented Michael Jackson with a platinum disc for thirty zillion sales of his album

'Off The Wall'. Sure, if they have a chart there it's number one without a doubt, but it's equally certain that there can't be enough people on the island to make it actually go platinum, thus, making Greenland quite unique. And the little headphones round my ears go:

'Ah wawna raark with you/(All right)/ Dance you into day/ (Sunlight)/Ah wawna raark with you/(All night)/Daance the night awayhay . . .'

Britain's unique for 'Off The Wall' too. No other land pulled *five* tracks from the album as 45s. Four yes, but we snuck 'Girlfriend' out in extra time and y'know what? All five were big hits. I bet Greenland had a struggle following up 'Don't Stop Till You Get Enough' – I mean, we had a hard enough time breaking *NME* there so that gives you some idea how tough these cookies are to part with their hard earned cruzeiros. (*NME* is now the number two highest selling publication amongst Greenlanders, a few issues behind *A Thousand Things To Do With Slush Weekly.*) It's unlikely The Jacksons have ever toured down there even though The Stranglers were received enthusiastically I'm told.

Click, click. The muffled onomatopoeia tells me the flight cap'n is about to say a few words.

'Ah, ladies and gentlemen if you look out your windows right now you will see, uh' – there's a pause while he checks his watch – 'uh, the prairies of Canada. Pretty soon you'll be able to see a lake or two and we'll be coming down through Utah over . . .'

Canada? Canada? Stewardess!

'Yes sir?'

'Are you going to tell me that's not Greenland down there?'

'I'm afraid that's Canada, sir. Why? Did you need to get off at Greenland or something?'

'Enough of the wisecracks already.' I squinted at her name tag. 'So tell me, er, Rayleen. Given that that is Canada hurtling beneath us would you think it probable that they sell many copies of "Off The Wall" to their countrymen?'

'Sexist!'

'OK, OK, country*people*.'

'Oh yes, sir. I should think it very likely. It wouldn't surprise if it were triple platinum by now, at least. Of course, sir, in Greenland it barely turned a miserable Gold.'

'Yes I know, don't rub it in. Now be off with you and fetch me a fresh Motion Discomforture bag – I've already filled these two.'

As she scuttled off toward the bulkhead I sat further back in my excruciatingly narrow solid-stone chair and sighed. Canada. Not Greenland at all. Ah well, there goes the opening to my Jacksons feature . . .

But this *is* Los Angeles. The most geographically beautiful place I've ever seen and the centre of hatred and scorn for just about every thinking rock fan the world over. Carted over here to record an interview, it can near tear the heart out of an old punk rocker. I'm carrying attitudes around inside me like worms.

At every opportunity I position on the aggressive. Somebody say politics? Well back home we do it this way! Rock music? We *own* rock music bub! Sport? You folks wouldn't dare go to a real, proper *football* match. You say red, I'll say black. You wind up twisted and, well, guilt-ridden.

What am I doing with these people? Snarling with the gnawing fear alright. It's daft but understandable. After being accustomed to the pressure cooker of UK, to be dropped slap pow from the wooden horse into the smiling sumptuous greenery of polite society, well it can put you on edge to say the least.

'Feel, feel, Resist, resist,' you go, 'this isn't how it is!' But then you phone a friend back and they screech 'You lucky, jammy, soft belly bastard. It is absolutely pissing down and you'll be back in it sooner than you think.'

Gotcha. Kicking against this is like setting off a smoke bomb in Woolworths just because it's rag week. Hell, some people are getting on with things here – what's your problem, brother? Roll with it. A long exhalation and two loosening twists on the valves – let's shed this slug, smug rock journalist obsession with 'real life'. Nothing's *your* fault, idiot. So get out there and soak it up with your eyes open – it's a beautiful day in the lush gorgeous resort. Just don't be grateful, that's all. And the little headphones round my ears go: . . .

'Let's daance/Let's shout/

Shakeyabarrdy downto
thegroun'/Let's daance!/Let's shout!/
Shakeyabarrdy downto thegroun'!'

So I'm here to do The Jacksons. (That's the trouble with having photos accompany a feature – they give the game away too soon.)

The Jacksons, and we know we're all being incredibly polite to four of them here, are the world's premier soul dance band. From chic (small c) disco across to electronic funk that might, hopefully, make a dozen or so British outfits take the cloth before they totally commit themselves to a life of pretence. When The Jacksons turn to funk they use no guitars. They have made the use of percussion into an unmatchable style – the intro to 'Shake Your Body', or 'Don't Stop Till You Get Enough' or the handclaps on the 45 version 'Rock With You'. It's what goes on in those pauses that makes it funk, not because there are a thousand drums keeping the rhythm alive.

Listen to 'You Got Me Working' on 'Off The Wall' for proof positive.

But far and above all else, there is The Voice of Michael Jackson. The greatest voice in pop music. Leaving the actual lyric treatment aside, it's those chirps and squeals between the lines that score. Play the track 'Off The Wall'.

'You can shut out all you want to – Ah DAH/Cos there ain't no sin in folks getting loud Tah/If you take the chance and do it HHIIIIT/Then there ain't no one who's gonna put you down AH . . .'

There's barely a line on the track that isn't punctuated with some urgent, throwaway bit of breath. And if you think they're unimportant then you've never seen the girls on the dancefloor mouth them to each other with expressions that the boys around could never hope to cause in a millennium. No matter how soapy the actual words may be, Michael Jackson blows sax through them.

And though countless grands get splashed on increasingly whacky videos, those plain old-fashioned bits of *film* of MJ on *Top Of The Pops* capture the show. Like the unchained, word-perfect – including all the little tail enders! – miming of 'Don't Stop' he performed against one of the cheesiest backdrops ever seen on TV. Or the stoic rendering of 'She's Out Of My Life' that climaxed with *real tears*. What? Stuff your futurist white studios after that, kiddies, the effect of watching the star cry one Thursday night must've stenciled 'Michael' on more emotions than there are in a cellarful of Steve Stranges.

And the killer is, as I'll try and illuminate later, that he probably *really was* crying!

Still, amongst all the ham let's not lose sight here of the fact that The Jacksons make some of the best records on this planet. (Really. Look at the writing credits and on eight out of ten there will be one bro' or ano' lurking 'tween the brackets. And now production!)

Enough of my barking. Suffice to note that the family have fans from King's Cross to Kuala Lumpur to me and you. Now, what shall we talk about, as the little headphones round my ears go:

I'm melting (I'm melting) like hot candle wax/Sensation (ah sensation) lovely where we're at OOH/keep on the force/Don't stop till you get enough/Woooh!'

There's about an hour or so before the car arrives and I'm whisked to meet the group. (Actually, 'car' is far too weak a word for something that rolls down the boulevards like Windsor Castle on castors.) I buy a notebook and tear it in half. One section I label 'Light' and the other I call 'dark'. I figure that as soon as my subjects become too uncomfortable with questions that require long answers – and with US bands I've found that lasts about 34 seconds – I can dip into the 'light' and pep them up:

'Who's your favourite actor, Mike? Whaddya have for brunch, Tito? What's six and eight, Marlon?'

You know, the type of stuff pop groups usually figure you've flown eight thousand miles to ask them. (I'm not lying!)

I go for a walk along Sunset Boulevard, my head turning from a fifty-foot ad for Johnny Mathis, to a 75-foot ad for *The Elephant Man* to the even bigger blurb for Robin Williams as Popeye. REO Speedwagon, Dr Hook, Neil Diamond, *Raging Bull*, Jack Daniels Whiskey and Elvis Costello all inflated airship size and sitting moored under 85 degrees.

I need some sunglasses and manage to get a pair that don't

actually cover half my face in Schwabb's drugstore, a curious airhangar place which sells everything from expensive perfumes through medication and also serves breakfast. Tucking into temptation – a 'black & white' ice-cream soda – I find myself sitting next to a man with a German accent who shows me a photograph in which, he claims, a large steel rod on the right is from outer space. 'It vas not dere ven ze photograph vas took so vy does it show up now? Huh? Vot is it, can you explain?' Well, I could have said it looks like an old curtain rod falling down but, y'know, some people can see the Messiah in an ounce of Golden Virginia shag and it's far too hot to debate with some Schwab schwizzle head. For the next twenty minutes he heckles me with ESP mumbo jumbo and I leave him with a heavy heart and ear-ache.

Two minutes later, I swear this is true, I come upon a red London bus in a roadside forecourt. That this should be in California is odd enough, but on inspecting the front of it I discover that the vehicle was destined to drive past my front door before it became exiled.

Considering the previous conversation, I get to feeling most odd and ponder three possibilities: 1) The old German sensed my incredulity and zapped this bus here to warp my head in. 2) CBS have settled for super-economy with my home travel. 3) We are all descended from London Transport ticket inspectors.

Anyway, if anyone's waiting on a 192 calling at Surrey Docks, Deptford and all stops to Catford Garage, you might consider starting to walk. I think the driver got a tad confused at the Elephant & Castle . . .

Dzzzsshoooom. Windsor Castle glides up. I climb in and make my way down the corridor into the back seat. I'm touched *NME* have been given an exclusive 'one on one' interview with the boys after which the boys will face the world at a press conference.

Now having faced Village People, Dynasty, Shalamar, Rose Royce, Chic and a whole bunch of other such acts, I know that Ma Jackson's brood ain't about to risk nothing.

'We are dedicated to crushing fascism and oppression anywhere in the world. We feel strongly on the lack of identity in US music and also about the sickening star system which exploits so many and denies millions access to recording facilities. We are worth millions but will not rest until we see justice in our land. We believe it can be achieved through a strong music message even if it makes us unpopular and even if it costs us every last cent.'

Are you kidding? The day a US superstar – any superstar – says that and means it I'll show my arse again in the Vatican. No, we all know what the outline is even before we start talking. But the press conference, ah, I feel the press conference could be fun . . .

My driver reaches for his megaphone and yells back to me that we have arrived in Century City. That's where CBS live – in Century City. (City in this place means much the same as village. They're named after the big film studios. This being 20th Century Fox's layout. There's also Universal City too which houses the funpalace studios where I spent yesterday afternoon. But that's another feature.)

Up on the seventh floor I sit cradling my two notebooks and a glass of Heineken. As 'the boys' arrive one by one I'm struck by a terrible thought. Jesus wept, I can't place the names to the faces.

Let's see. There's Michael and Tito and Marlon and . . . and . . . oh sure, Randy the little one and uh . . . er . . . Dopey, Happy and Doc. No this is serious, help. I'm shaking hands with each member as they arrive, grinning away, and I'm trying to think of the album credits. So far there are three here but which three? Everyone knows Michael but mein host has only used my name in intros, believing all the others to be instantaneously recognised. Then, God be praised, somebody in the next room is talking into a phone and I overhear that we're only waiting on Michael and *Jackie*. Good ol' Jackie Jackson, who can forget he of the double surname!

OK, so I figure that the young one sitting in the shorts is Randy – yes, we all laughed at his name, don't fret – and by merely asking Tito about the weather I assumed that the one who didn't answer me was Morty. Sorry, that's Marlon. OK, we're nearly off. In bounds Jackie in a track-suit – Jackie in a trackie? Are you nuts? – saying hi to all and taking a seat over by the window where he will remain throughout our hour saying very little.

The Jackson brothers don't live together. That much is made plain by their enthusiastic gossipping while we await the arrival of Michael. Ten minutes slip by in which Tito manages to slip in the fact that he's recently taken ownership of a new white Rolls Royce. Not his first either. A white Rolls – what a hoary old cliche, but then, this is Hollywood.

Suddenly I hear a raising of vocal octaves and an increase in the nervous giggling from the outer office. Michael's here. In he comes waving meekly to the kin and smiling benignly at my forehead as we shake hands,

He shakes hands like I imagine the Queen Mother might.

All united, the family begin requesting all manner of manna from the press office people. I see they may be a few seconds yet so I take a stroll outside the room. Here, Jim from Epic catches my arm.

'Hey, Danny, you OK?'

Sure, great.

'Now you know there are a couple of subjects that are strictly *out*, don't you?'

No, I don't. I'm dying to know.

'OK, so one is the Osmonds.'

The what?

'The Osmonds. The boys are fed up with questions putting them with The Osmonds.'

I'm staggered. Two-thirds of my interview just peeled away.

'The other thing is astrology, you know – signs and stuff.'

Well there goes the other third. Goodbye.

'No, you see they are followers of Jehovah and they don't hold with anything like astrology – dates, birthdays, Christmas, nothing like that. They keep it all very private and have been known to walk out of interviews because they objected to the questions.'

Good grief.

'And has anyone told you about Michael?'

I'm beginning to go numb. No, Jim, nobody's 'told me' about Michael.

'Well.' He sighs as if before a major declaration. 'Be easy with him. He's very, very shy but has got a lot better.'

Better? I'm bewildered.

'He can seem odd to people who don't know him. Like you may find that once you've asked him a question he'll need one of his brothers – usually his sister Janet – to whisper it in his ear. He might seem to drift off but he's still with it – it's just the way he is. He likes to have one of the family explain questions to him before answering. I think it's down to confidence.'

I float back into the meeting with my thoughts all of a heap. It seems that one peep outa line and I'm gonna be conducting this piece with five empty chairs and a rubber plant. It's not as though it's going to be tough – there they all are smiling and joking, genuinely wanting to meet their fans – as they put it – through the press. But all of a sudden they don't seem like the five funky kids who fought their way up from Gary, Indiana, the gritty sharp Jacksons of the wizard pop and sex appeal. God forgive me, but they've taken on the sheen of . . . of . . . so help me, The Osmonds.

I sit and fix a grin like a man who's just been slipped a note that his dinner guest is a schizophrenic axe murderer. One of the press office attendants closes the door – but remains in the room – and announces that the interview may begin. Half expecting a gong or a starting pistol, I take off.

You don't think much to interviews do you?

Marlon: 'No, the brothers don't like them. Ain't that right, fellows?'

General hubbub of agreement. (A phrase which sounds like a civil war veteran.)

Why do you do them?

Marlon: 'We like to talk to our fans. Let them know how we feel. We feel we have to do that.'
Tito: 'Y'see we know we *have* to do 'em but we don't get into, uh, interviews that much because they will misquote you.'
Jackie: 'Definitely.'
Tito: 'But like he says – you have to speak to the fans . . . every so often.'

Why do you think 'they' misquote you?

Tito: 'Strictly because they wanna sell their papers and bad news sells better than good you see.'

The brothers are gathered around a table, except Jackie who sits behind on a chair and Michael who is reclining over by the wall on a square couch affair. He speaks, in his light almost feminine voice.

'What paper you from.'

I tell him.

'The *NME*? Enemy? Oh wow! Haha.'

Somebody chips in with the obligatory 'enema' and there's much suppressed giggling. Happy days.

Do you scream at each other much?

Marlon: 'Very seldom. We don't scream.'
Tito: 'You can take more stuff from your brother. Like if you told me something, well we might get into a fist-fight. But it must help when you've grown up together, y'know, slept together, peed the same bed.'
Marlon: 'Ah, he did the peeing, I didn't.'

They all erupt into small verbal exchanges. At the back, Michael cuts in.

'Yellow Mattress, that's a good album title.'

It's already becoming pretty clear that they'd all rather be some place else. Before we began, they'd all been extremely keen to find out when they'd be free to get off that day. They're all crazed baseball followers and get to most games they can. It occurs to me that they mightn't feel safe out in the open like that.
Tito: 'It's cool. In this town it's cool.'

So how do stars of your bracket react to something like the Lennon murder?

Pow! The room goes still, punctuated only by a few 'Oh God that's awfuls'.

Michael: 'We . . . we don't even like to think of it. We don't wanna talk of it.'

OK so let's get some stories rolling. What was it like growing up in public as The Jackson 5?

Marlon: 'The good part of it was we got off school. We had just three hours school a day which is great compared to six hours, right? It was great getting to all those different cities – hey we even met the Royal Family! Then again it was work. We do the Apollo Theatre and stuff, making all those runs to Chicago and Philadelphia. Seven shows a night.'

Seven shows a *night?* Seven shows a night for two weeks each date. That's right. Just waiting to be noticed by the world.

Tito: 'Those were fun days.'

Michael: 'We talkin' bout Motown?'

Tito: 'Naw, I'm talking about the Peppermint Lounge, Guys and Gals . . .'

Michael: 'Oh yeah . . .'

Tito: 'I'm surprised *you* remember it.'

Tito: 'See, Michael and Marlon were known as the dancers and, OK, when your good people'd throw money on the floor – these are not dimes, these are *bills* we're talking about – so they'd do spins and then splits and grab a ten and stick it in their pockets.'

Marlon: 'Me and Mike we used to sell our photos. Can you believe that? Who would want our photo then? This is when we were working the night clubs till four, five in the morning and be up for school at eight. Yes sir.'

What did your schoolmates think of your life?

Tito: 'They'd tease us – actually laff at us. Saying really cruel things like you guys'll never get anywhere, what are you practising for? We were barely being paid – our first performance was eight dollars. Mr Lucky's club.'

Jackie: 'But that's a lot of candy in those days.'

What sort of material did you start with?

Marlon: 'Temptations, James Brown . . .'
Michael: 'I think the song that really tears the house down was "Skinny Legs And All" by Joe Tex.'

With all the theatrics?

Michael: 'Oh yeah. You know I used to go in the audience and lift all the girls' legs up! God I'm so embarrassed about that. I would never dream of . . .'

He trails off in a chuckle, raising his hands to his cheeks.
Marlon: 'Favourite part of the act – lifting up all them skirts.'

Five minutes of bandying about tales of yore seems to perk them up. It's Tito and Marlon who do most of the answering from here, and although there's no signs yet of Michael getting whispered assurance, he does seem to wander mentally sometimes. Transcribing the tape was a pretty dull affair I might tell you. Unlabelled, I figure it could be any one of a hundred bands yakking. It's the way US Big Bands see the whole much-maligned beauty, dynamics and power of music as just so many shades of grey.

They really do believe that repeating those non-committal line-walking platitudes in their songs amounts to some sort of 'message'. Maybe it eases consciences to think that they're all doing their bit. Fortunately The Jacksons' records have strength enough to carry the wish-wash. Nobody turns to The Jacksons for political backbone, that's granted. But while we're talking of it . . .
Marlon: 'If you listen to the lyrics on 'Can You Feel It?' we're not pretending everything is alright. We're saying everyone's got to get together.'
Michael: 'There is hope.'
Tito: 'Our main effort is to bring everyone together.'

But how??

Marlon: 'It's easy. It's the easiest thing in the world if they wanna do it.'

Tito: 'But a lot don't want to.'

I give Sham 69 fans six seconds to complete the line.

All this simplistic 'if only' nursery rhyming is like the Monty Python track from 'Previous Album' where the *Blue Peter* team tell all the jolly viewers how to unite the Russians and the Chinese as well as cure all known diseases from the earth in cheerful two-syllable sentences. Y'know – '*Got that all you little people? Jolly good, well toddle off and disband the KKK then like good citizens will you.*'

However, Tito and Marlon do have a point when they say:

'Disco music was one of the greatest things that happened in the world. Never before did we see blacks and whites under the same roof dancing to the same songs. It stopped people giving attention to the colour of a performer's skin. It did that. They all had a good time – and it wasn't just on the night either. I believe they took that attitude outside and home with them.'

Tito: 'A black music? It's . . . Well it's not . . . I dunno, there's . . . er, yes.'

Marlon: 'I call black music the blues. The old blues songs.'

Michael: 'Or jazz or how rock and roll started. But like that Blondie song 'Rapture' – that was originally done by a black artist but it didn't cross over. She did it and it became a big hit.'

Don't you resent that somehow?

Michael: 'Resent it? No, I don't resent it. I'm proud for her but I wish they were more equal.' He struggles for the right phrase. 'Just . . . more equal . . .'

OK, so do you think these are good times we're living through?

Tito: 'Naw. No times is good times. I don't think it's as bad as yesterday, but not good times.'

What keeps you going?

Marlon: 'Trying to sell more records. Sell more than the last one.'

And if they don't?

Tito: 'We never think about that.'

But just say it happened.

Tito: 'Well . . . I wouldn't think it was because people didn't like it. I'd think it was mistakes in marketing and those things.'

How much of an ego do you have?

Tito: 'Well, we don't walk on air. I know if I step out that window I'm going to the bottom.'

Well then, who are your rivals?

Marlon: 'Everybody. Everyone.'
Tito: 'Whoever is in that number one spot, that's who we gotta beat. We gotta move 'em out.'
Jackie: 'Rod Stewart, Mick Jagger.'

The Jacksons refer to what they do as 'showbusiness'. I wondered if they pay the same attention as film people to awards. They grab at it.
Michael: 'We like Grammys.'
Tito: 'Oh boy, we want a Grammy badly. Whew, I tell you.'

Why?

Tito: 'Why? We've put a lot of years into this business, a lotta years. And we want one. We want it.'
Jackie: 'We like awards.'

When you make an album, do you ever ask yourself about risks in your style – what you can get away with?

Marlon: 'We never put junk on our albums. Everything is from the heart.'

Tito: 'See, you can't just write. A good dee can come in the shower!'

Dee?

Tito: 'I say good dee – I mean melody.'
Everyone laffs at parrot 'dee' street jive style.
Jackie: 'I've got a tape recorder by my bed and many times I've woken from dreams and written down a song.'

What did they sound like in the morning?

'Well,' he says sitting back in his seat, 'they weren't hits.'
Michael Jackson is allegedly a big fan of classical music. He fails to elaborate on why but Tito puts in a nice angle.
Tito: 'I don't like that. Well actually, I heard some classical music once – I can't remember it now – but it really impressed me and I didn't expect it. But I don't think I can waltz with my wife to it though . . .'

The opening to the new album is quite grandiose though, right?

Tito: 'Well, Michael wrote that bit – hey, Michael. Y'wanna tell him how you wrote that?'
(Here's a doozy.)
Michael: 'Ah well, that opening . . . I thought . . . would be a good opening for an album.'
Full stop.
You may have found it hard to distinguish between my earlier mentioned 'light' and 'dark' posers. So have I. However, these must have come from the light.
Anybody got favourite actors?
They all agree on Richard Pryor. Michael goes further. 'De Niro for me. And Brando and Pacino.'
I find this list-ette surprising from somebody who, I hear, is very DOWN on swearing. The boys go on to list James Earl Jones

and Diana Ross. 'You know,' they say. 'The Greats.'

Alright, Michael, so just what's all this about you and Diana Ross?

He looks to the floor and flounders a bit.

'We're just good friends.'

All my life I've been waiting for an interview that contained that exchange. Now, I feel, I am a proper journalist.

What, or rather who, makes The Jacksons laff is in little debate. Especially with Michael who *really* springs to life for the first time here.

'Oh wow, Benny Hill!'

Really?

'Uh! Are you kidding – every day! I love Benny Hill. I like him better than Monty Python!'

What is it you like?

'He just *do* things. You think, how can *he* think that way to come out with that joke! You never know. He just cracks me up – a genius.'

The Benny Hill thrill causes me to realise that Michael has put down the telephone receiver that he has had to his ear for a good stretch of the interview. He never spoke into it, just had it to his head. Several times, when I particularly wanted his answer to something he would apologise for it. What he was listening for/to remains unclear.

Just before the press officer called a close to our audience I couldn't resist one purely selfish – for us smug Brits – question.

I wonder what ya'll made of the Sex Pistols?

Marlon: 'The Sex . . . ?'
Tito: 'I don't remember them.'
Randy: 'Sex Pistols?'

Jackie: 'Sure. I think we were in London when that shooting happened.'
Michael: 'They never broke open big here.'
Maybe not broke open but they certainly broke up.
Michael: 'They broke up?'
Jackie: 'You remember that shooting, Marlon?'
I explain the confusion vis-a-vis the sordid deed.
Michael: 'Ha! I love that name – Sid Vicious.'
It was at this point that an ugly flavour crept into their comfortable cheery manner. You see, we needed some photographs and . . .
Michael: 'You want some pictures, like, now? Will we get to see these first? How come you're not using CBS's pictures?'
The excellent folk at Epic press try and explain the *NME* to a risingly alarmed MJ.
Michael: 'Oh come on, look the only thing is we don't like the way covers come out because they're not what we like them to be. How come . . . I mean we don't have make-up on! I'm sorry really, but we wanna look good for the girls. I don't wanna be photographed like this.'
He looks healthier, better and thinner than you've ever seen. But I guess when you're *used* to make-up and the whole bit you need them for more than just covering zits. It's not *safe* without them.
Anyway, off go the boys to get ready for the impending press conference and Epic promise to arrange another photo sesh tomorrow or maybe Thursday. Looks like we're staying, Joey . . .

I love press conferences. Nobody says anything for the first ten minutes and then, when someone does, questions fly about in little spurts. In the gaps, hungry hacks eye up and down their comrades' columns to see if someone is going to ask a question a split second before they open their own cake-holes, thus shutting down their own effort in its first syllable.
Then there's the all-out strain to see who can project the best image of the seen-it-all pressman. Never admit it's your first PC. Also sort out where the majors are present. No one wants to

admit they're from the *Basildon Non-Ferrous Metals Weekly* when you're sandwiched between the *Times* and the *Telegraph*.

It's wonderful to spot potential questioners. You can see their lips moving as they run over and over the question, ironing it out for a full quarter-hour before popping it. And worse! If some bastard creep gets in *your* query first, they usually get approving nods from all around and you feel like screeching '*But I was going to ask that!*'

Anyway, today is no exception and the world's press – literally – are setting about selecting the right and proper seat. Hundreds of shapes of microphone come out from dozens of shoulder bags. You never see anyone slap down a £17.50 Wondertroid compact cassette with built-in mike – even though that'd pick it all up. No, here it gets to look like Jodrell Bank. Booms, snubs and long rangers hang taut from arrangements of scaffolding that would challenge McAlpines for quick construction.

Then there's the well-used but still fresh-looking note-pad that on every page has the standard four lines of shorthand at the top. You have to rattle a pencil around your teeth – never chew it! – until you get an 'idea'. Then you add another half line of shorthand culminating in finally slamming your notebook shut with a disturbing air of confidence. Then you just sit back, arms folded, surveying the lesser hacks who've yet to complete the preliminaries.

A good time to help yourself to the completely tasteless – but gratis – niblets in the ashtray-like bowls. This is done by taking a generous handful and, by opening the thumb from your fist, throwing two or three at a time into your constantly chewing gums. Never look directly at your food and drink – it's beneath contempt.

Once the artists enter you're treated to a stampede of photographers – forming tight bundles like mating-crazed frogs. The sound of motor-driven cameras whines worse than the cliffs at Folkestone during gull nesting time. All the smudges yell 'This way please Cecil' even though Cecil never does. They usually nick a glance from somebody else's successful bid.

Before photographers do all this, they pick straws to see who will be the one who goes around behind the artists and takes a shot or two of All The Other Photographers Taking Photos of Cecil. The runner-up gets to be the essential smudge who stands firm snapping away after the others have retreated. He carries this on until a bouncer leads him away.

During the questioning, the photographers have two options. They can either peer downward at the lenses of the machine around their neck making finicky alterations. Or they can occupy their time writing indecipherable squiggles on little black plastic pill-boxes containing 'shot' film.

If you meet someone you know at a press conference, you always ask each other what you're doing here. Then you both decide 'It's a giggle', the subject is only fit to be sent up, and ask who was that berk who asked such and such a question halfway through. Then you destroy the berk's paper.

The Jacksons re-emerging smiling but all sporting huge jam-tart sized sun-glasses. Michael's are very mirrored. Ninety five per cent of the questions are aimed at him and this time Randy really does whisper in his ear the whole time.

The questions are real tat. 'Ven fill hue be wisiting Sweden, Michael?' 'Are you a close family, Michael?' (to which the family Michael showed a keen drollery in snapping back 'No sir'), 'Can you give us information about your new record?'

It was pretty bleak until this one poor wretched Japanese looking bloke committed the cardinal sin of any press conference – he tried to crack a joke. Oh, but he did. Y'see there's a track on their new LP called 'Heartbreak Hotel' and this bloke – who had little command of English anyway – thought he had cooked up a real zinger.

'Ah Michael,' he stuttered, seizing his chance. 'Ah if you had not been a hit with your LP, ah, would you have gone to, ah, Heartbreak Hotel?'

In the ensuing silence, the wind blew, crickets chirped and you could plainly hear the guy swallow hard as the apologetic grin froze on his chops. It turns out that nobody understood him. Tito asks him to repeat the 'question'.

'Ah Michael, i-if your LP had n-not been success . . . w-would you have, ah, have gone t-to Heartbreak Hotel?'

By now most of us hacks have caught on to what's being said and the less valiant turn away and clear their throats. The guy is still grinning although he has stopped blinking by now and is wobbling perceptibly.

A Jacksons aide steps in. 'Er Yoshi, what do you mean?'

'Ah Michael. If your album h-h-had not been su-su-su-success wouldyouhavegonetoHeartbreakHotel?'

Michael shakes his head and Jackie tries. 'OK, I got Heartbreak Hotel but that was on our LP – what's it to do with Michael?'

Poor old Yoshi is drenched in flop-sweat. He's darting his eyes around looking for an ally. His neck has gone to semolina and his palms perspire like the Boulder Dam.

'I-I-I'm playing with words you see.'

Nobody sees and Yoshi's grasp of the lingo falls an inch short of the word 'joke'.

'P-P-Playing with words . . . words.'

The eyes of the world are burrowing deep inside that tweed jacket of his. He's trembling like a sapling in monsoon and smoke is starting to belch from his ears. Then – a voice at the back ends the torture.

'I think the guy's trying to make a funny.'

'Yis! Yis! That's it!' babbles the released spirit. 'I'm making funny! Funny!'

As he begins to appeal for clemency, the final cruel blow sounds. Amidst the unnecessary sighing the aide says:

'Hey Yoshi. This is a press conference, man. Save the funnies, huh?'

The dumb questions resumed but I couldn't take my eyes from the broken Japanese. Ruined, he never heard another word all afternoon. Today, I suspect he sits in a bathchair in some far off sanatorium, grey haired and twitching, mumbling to anyone who will listen: 'The words. Playing with the words you see . . . is funny . . .'

Meanwhile over on the dark side, I'll never forget how the

writer from South Africa informed Michael Jackson that his LP was number one back home.

'Yeah I saw that,' beamed MJ. 'Number one. It made me really happy, I smiled, number one, ha ha.'

Jackson laughed but showed no signs of appreciating the significance of being lauded in Johannesburg any more than if the guy had been Danish or Greenlandic. Even when they went on to explain their peacock motif, some deep patter about 'incorporating all colours', not once did the boys show any sign of letting go of their firm belief in shallow gestures.

Some fellah goes out of his way to say what a large clout his radio show pulls, then reveals himself to be a purveyor of 'spiritual songs, gospel or positive message music'. He asks whether the band have any plans to make a gospel album. I'd clean forgotten about the Jehovah nix and I swing to catch Michael's answer. The answer is long, bland and professional. About 'music coming from within' and 'personal messages'. Nothing is given away.

The guy tries again – quite innocently – and Michael nearly lets it slip.

'We have positive messages in all our songs. We don't use terminology like *Jesus* or whatever, although he's good – we all love Jesus, God, nature – but, like the song "Can You Feel It" is saying it all for us. The peacock and what it represents. What more can I say? We just made an animated film for that song. But I don't feel we have to use the word Jesus . . . ah, it's all in the lyric.'

Michael Jackson has a room full of scripts. He likes the part he's been offered in *A Chorus Line* and the story of dancer Bill 'Bojangles' Robinson. He's keeping up with *his* dancing too. Most of his idols are dancers – Russian dancers especially. He's happy enough.

But a cloak of secrecy and protection – over-protection – seems to surround the heart-throb. Whatever lies at its core won't be penetrated in a decade. From all the advice and semi-apologies that accompanies my meeting with him, I might deduce a kid on the edge. He *is* vague, he is in possession of a butterfly thought pattern, and externally he is painfully fragile. Quite unlike his brothers. He's certainly not a Star, *a la* wonky Streisand. His aloofness stems more from a childlike shyness and apparent lack of confidence in his own conversational voice.

As for all the whispering, phone listening, and attention wandering, well, I'm beat. He struck me at times as having just a touch of the character that Peter Sellers played in *Being There*.

This was never more evident than when we parted. He shook my hand very lightly.

'See you, Michael,' I said. 'Mind howya go, eh?'

He stood for a second, unblinking and with that ever-present almost hippyfied smile.

'Thank you,' he began with absent-minded sincerity. 'Thank you, I will. I will mind how I go.'

And he slowly walked toward the lift.

Although Joe and me were there the next day, and the next day and the next, as were Marlon, Tito, Jackie and Randy at times, Michael never showed up for that photo session. One day he was 'ill' and on the Friday he'd 'hurt his back and couldn't be available for at least a week'. So it was blown out. Sorry, 'girls'. That's showbusiness.

And what about The Jacksons as a group? Well, I won't bore you with another, albeit sincere, plug for their excellent product. They may be from Gary, Indiana, but they're honorary Californians now. I know that because of exchanges like the one when I asked what their greatest dream was:

'My great dream,' Marlon bubbled, 'would be to sit in the seats and watch us perform.'

Tito jumped in. 'Right. You know I actually did dream that once?'

Michael looked over.

'Oh really? Was it sold out?'

LONG TIME GONE

A True Confessional by David Crosby & Carl Gottlieb

The nature of base smoking is that once you get started, you do it a lot. After your first taste, the next day you do it a lot. It's a peculiar drug that way. You become obsessive with it immediately. It doesn't take a week and it gets worse. You get obsessive and want to do it until you fall out. A lot of times it happens to people the very first time – base gets you loaded if it's made properly. It's a quick rush and then it's gone. So you want to do some more right away and then you want to do some more and then you want to do some more and some more and some more.

There is a human mechanism that says, 'I want it, I want it, I want it, I got it!' It's the one that gets built up in humans when we want cigarettes or sugar or any of the other addictives. You can build an addictive cycle on a lot of different stuff. I'm just now being able to beat the one on sugar. I beat the one on cigarettes many years ago. Beating the one on heroin was difficult because it involved physical illness. You get very sick when you kick heroin and your endorphins are nonexistent so you feel terminally fucking awful, but the psychological dependency on base is the most obsessive of all. I used to smoke some base that wasn't good, feel sick, and want some more. That's totally fucking crazy. The point that is best learned from the whole experience is the craziness, the completely illogical short-circuiting of the normal human mental process that takes place in obsessive addiction. You no longer have control of your mind or your spirit or your choices. You just don't. When you become severely addicted you do stuff that doesn't show any sense at all. There are definitions for addictive behavior: one of them is doing the same thing repeatedly and expecting different results. Another is doing something that you know is self-damaging and doing it anyway. Another is deliberately destroying your social circumstance, knowing that you're blowing your job, you're wiping out your savings, you're smoking yourself out of house and home, you're selling the car, and you're doing it anyway – just so you can do more dope. That's what being an addict is really about.

I had chippied with heroin for a long time, but that's when I started doing it more seriously. I started scoring from different people: coke from coke dealers and smack from others because heroin dealers generally deal only in heroin. I can even remember one heroin dealer that I liked, a nice man who eventually committed suicide because he didn't like what he was doing. Heroin dealers are usually not nice people – to put it mildly. Heroin became serious for me when I discovered Persian or Pakistani dope: it's called Persian Brown. I was turned on to a way of smoking called Chasing the Dragon. I've always been terrified of needles. Toward the end of my addiction, I overcame my fear and became an intravenous drug user, as well as snorting China White (which I had done all along). I have probably shot up a couple of dozen times in my life. I had somebody else do it because I couldn't do it to myself. One time I overdosed in Novato; I turned blue and was dying and woke up to find my friend's old lady with her hand down my pants with a handful of ice cubes. I heard angel's wings. That's what you hear when you're going out: a rushing noise, like wind in the trees, as you lose consciousness.

Heroin has always been the big villain, the bottom-line worst drug of all time. It's not. In my opinion, cocaine is more dangerous than heroin because you can kick heroin faster. You get sick, but you can beat it. Freebase cocaine is more addictive on a more dangerous level. The numbers say I'm wrong; figures on recidivism and the ability of people who are addicted to kick are worse for heroin than for cocaine. But if you factor into the equation people who are smoking base, not snorting cocaine, the base smokers' rates of recovery are even worse than those of people on heroin.

The brain has a lot of voices, a lot of levels, and apparently they all get to have a vote on your behaviour. What I have found is that my verbal crystallization level, the one that's speaking here, is the articulate one. In most people, it's the one closest to the steering wheel and has the biggest vote – or one of the two or three biggest votes. You have a lot of other levels in your head: emotional, spiritual, imaginative, intuitive, clear back to baby ones, just saying, 'I am.' What happens with hard drugs is that they take over, level after level. They're like a little guerrilla unit that moves through a big apartment building, taking over floor after floor, until you can't stop your elevator on those floors. You open the doors on those levels and it's not good. More and more levels of your head will vote for: 'I'll do whatever I have to do to put some more drugs in my face,' without looking at the situation or what the drugs are doing to you or how your health is deteriorating or how you're not doing what you want to do.

On the conscious level I'd say, 'I can't do this anymore. I'm going to put myself in the hospital.' Then I'd pick up the pipe and take another toke. Now I'm not sure who in my head said, 'Let's go to the hospital,' and I'm not sure who said, 'Let's take the next toke,' but they clearly weren't talking to each other, not those two. I would take my life's steering wheel and turn it to the right and my life would veer sharply to the left. That's a helpless feeling. Jan and I tried to change because we didn't like how it was. We had frequent moments of utter despair. I thank God that neither of us is suicidal because I most assuredly would have committed suicide. The depression that hits you when you've been doing cocaine for twenty years and during the last year, let's say, you haven't stopped once, just the minimal amount to get enough sleep to enable you to pick up the pipe again. The only limiting factor is that after six or seven days you'll nod out with the pipe and a lit torch in your hands and burn yourself with the torch. I have scars from those burns all over my body.

While David was awake, which was for inhumanly long periods of time, he would be smoking freebase. He would smoke in airplanes; not just on private charter flights, but on commercial airliners, sitting in first-class. He could ignite a propane torch behind his parka and, under the pretense of sleeping or pulling the coat over his head, take hits from a glass pipe between meal and beverage service at thirty thousand feet. David could smoke at the wheel of a car he was driving; using both hands to manage torch and pipe, he would steer with his knees. 'I'm the best no-hands knee-steering driver in the world,' he would reassure startled passengers, this author included, as he took a hit from the pipe while doing seventy on the highway. As disturbing as this might have been to others, it was a way of life to David and Jan, even though they had both experienced grand mal seizures while basing. On March 28, 1982, Crosby was driving a rented car to Orange County to play at a No Nukes rally outside the San Onofre nuclear power plant in Southern California. He had been smoking freebase, although he probably had both hands on the wheel when the seizure took him. Police reports describe what happened next:

STATEMENT BY WITNESS: *Witness related he was southbound on 405 approx. 20 car lengths behind V-1 [Crosby's car]. V-1 was in one of the righthand lanes when it suddenly went to the left, as if to change lanes. V-1 kept going left and struck the center divider. DR-1 [Crosby] made no attempt to brake or swerve. Witness thought DR-1 had a heart attack or fell asleep.*

OFFICER BAECKEL (COSTA MESA POLICE DEPARTMENT): *I arrived and saw Crosby sitting in the driver's seat of the red Granada, which had collided into the center divider fence. I asked Crosby if he was all right [he had blood on his face]. Crosby told me he was late for a 'gig' and had to go. I told him he had been involved in a collision. Crosby said he hadn't. He then started the car and was preparing to leave. I reached in and turned off the car. Paramedic assisted me in taking Crosby out of the car. Crosby did not know what today was or where he was or what had happened. I looked inside the car and in plain sight, on the driver's floorboard, I saw a propane bottle and 'bong'. I left these in place. Highway Patrol arrived and took over the collision scene and investigation.*

CHP OFFICER GLIDDEN: *When I looked in the vehicle, I noticed a glass bottle with two pipes extending from it and a glass tube sitting on the driver's floorboard. Both had a brownish residue within them . . . When I went to the right passenger door to look for registration, I saw a leather zipper bag on the right floorboard. The center portion of the bag was open, exposing a chrome .45 cal. automatic (#310543). When I lifted the bag, I noticed in a side compartment several small glass bottles containing a white powder residue . . . Bag contained numerous drug paraphernalia items (razors, glass tubes, matches, instruments, etc.). A gray plastic film canister was found to contain a white powder, which was later determined to be baking soda. The contents of the bag and the items found on the floor are commonly used for 'freebasing' cocaine . . . based on the nature of the T/C (drifting off the road into c/d fence), witness statements on the subj's incoherent manner and the drug items found, I determined the subj was possibly under the influence of drugs. He was placed under arrest for 20152(A) V.C.*

> From the emergency medical facility, David was transported to the Orange County Jail in Santa Ana, where he was formally charged with driving under the influence of drugs or alcohol and carrying a concealed weapon. He was released on twenty-five hundred dollars' bail, but he missed the gig. Graham and Stephen went on without him.

I had a seizure from toxic saturation in the fast lane doing sixty-five miles an hour on the San Diego Freeway. One minute I was driving along, going south to play a concert. The next thing I knew I was parked facing into the center divider fence, talking to a California Highway Patrol officer and a paramedic and there was about a hundred yards of fence torn up behind me and the front of my car was a mess. The worst part was not being busted or having a gun or being charged with possession of drug paraphernalia, but realizing it wasn't just me that was in danger. What if I had jumped the fence and crossed into the opposing lanes of traffic? The luckiest thing that would have happened would have been dying alone. What if I hit a family and wiped out three kids? Could I have lived with that? Seizures from toxic saturation were not only a danger to myself and Jan. If I had one in a car, I became the kind of menace that I dreaded, someone out of control who could cross the center line and hit my daughter or my friends, someone who could kill innocent people. I had a night in jail to think about that, then I got bailed out, but not without notice by the press: the story made the wire services.

WASHINGTON POST: *Rock singer David Crosby, who was arrested and charged last weekend with driving while intoxicated and concealing a weapon, will face narcotics charges as well, according to authorities in Santa Ana, Calif. Crosby's rented car hit a freeway divider while he was en route to a demonstration at the San Onofre nuclear power plant. He was to perform with rock singers Graham Nash and Stephen Stills, his partners in the 60's group Crosby, Stills, and Nash. Lt. Wyatt Hart of the Santa Ana Sheriff's Office said that in addition to a gun, Quaaludes, cocaine, and drug paraphernalia were found in the singer's car. Asked why he was carrying a load .45-caliber pistol, Crosby said simply, 'John Lennon.'*

SIMON LEBON: THE FACE INTERVIEW

Duran Duran by Fiona Russell Powell

It's the day before Christmas Eve and I'm on my way to The Savoy hotel, 15 minutes late already for my interview with Simon le Bon, the man who once said: 'If I was rich and I wasn't doing this, I'd pay to do it! Just to get up on stage and have all those people looking at you! And some even listening to you!'

For a lot of girls, six hours spent with the singer of Duran Duran would be the perfect stocking filler, but although Simon is a fairly charming person, Martini adverts just aren't my cup of tea. My late arrival went unnoticed because Simon was screaming over a newly-discovered spot during the early stages of his make-up session: 'Oh God, a spot! It travels all around my body; three weeks ago it was heading south down my back towards my bum. It's the bane of my life!'

We are introduced. Si doesn't let my hand drop for about five minutes and the first thing he asks me is whether I'm wearing tights or stockings. He then tells two jokes, one vaguely racist and one vaguely anti-semitic, neither of which I get, so there is an embarrassed silence after the punchlines. Undaunted, he turns round and says 'Bison Melon' followed by 'Eno Slim Nob' . . . Pardon? 'I'm just making anagrams of my name,' he explains. 'Eno Slim Nob,' I reply, 'that's not what I've heard.' He looks astonished for a second and then grins as I continue. 'Now you've got an idea of what my line of questioning is going to be!' And so have you.

Down the corridor now to the photo session which takes forever and nearly all of my allotted interview time. I learn all sorts of things about Simon and other people while I sit in and watch. For instance, did you know that Simon's favourite parts of his body are his eyebrows and his feet? And he likes to make his hair fluff out because otherwise he looks like 'a pinhead' but he doesn't like to wear too much hairspray because it 'makes you look a bit dilly (puffy)'.

Only ten minutes left and I haven't asked him the colour of his underpants! But Simon smoothly chips in and says: 'We'll go to the soundcheck in a cab together, come back to the hotel after and if you've still got any questions left, finish the interview in my room.' That's fine by me. I'm sure I'll have run out of questions on the way back. Si and I make our way to the lobby and for some peculiar reason he dawdles all the way behind me until we're sitting down waiting for our cab . . .

FRP: Your mother left England didn't she? When did she move?

SL: She went to Florida about two years ago.

And your father's still living in London?

Yes.

So your parents have split up?

Well, um – the taxi's here now.

At this point we are summoned to the front door of The Savoy where a black cab is waiting to take us to Wembley Arena. Simon's security guard follows behind in another cab. We slip past the 30 or so waiting fans who have kept up a long vigil outside the hotel, clutching flowers, chocolates and other gifts for the band. Travelling slowly through the heavy Christmas traffic, we continue the conversation . . .

You were about to elaborate on the break-up of your parents' marriage.

Ah well, I miss my mother a lot, but I miss the whole family because I don't see them much. Jonathon – he's my youngest brother – he's always going off sailing in the Caribbean . . . I come from a very middle-class family.

Why did your mother move so far away from her three children?

Just to get a bit of head space and to get a better job I suppose.

From the interviews I've read, you're obviously very attached to your mother. Do you hold with the cliché that children who are nurtured from birth for showbiz stardom by their parents miss out on a normal childhood?

Oh no – my mother *did* get me a lot of acting work when I was a kid but I object to the suggestion that I was moulded. That's a bit of an insult really. I wasn't a 'child star', I wasn't forced to go to stage school or anything like that. I just did the work because I had a pretty face, I suppose. Before she got married, my mother was involved in acting but when she had three kids it was a bit difficult for her to carry on with it.

So she pursued her ambitions through you?

I'll admit that if it wasn't for her I certainly wouldn't have carried on doing drama and if she hadn't pushed me I wouldn't have gone to university to study drama.

Do *you* believe in the sanctity of marriage?

I believe that if you make big promises like that, you should keep them.

And you're marrying your girlfriend Clare soon, aren't you?
(Here I made a gentleman's agreement with Simon not to reveal his denial.)

Do you expect a nuclear war within your lifetime?

I expect a bomb will go off but I don't expect a world-wide holocaust.

Have you taken any precautions like installing a bunker at the bottom of the garden?

No, certainly not. If there was a war and if England was involved in any way, I wouldn't like to come out of my shelter six months later to find a totally flat, black land. I just wouldn't want to survive.

Do you support the CND?

(*Carefully*) I believe that disarmament will never happen. I think there's a lot of other facets of CND which I wouldn't like to associate myself with. They're not just involved in getting rid of nuclear weapons – they bring party politics into the issue which they shouldn't do.

Would you do a charity gig for the Greenham Common women?

Err . . . we're not going to do any charity gigs for a long time! I think the Greenham Common have got a lot of guts and I've got a great deal of admiration for them but I've heard that they won't let any men join the lines. I'm not sure if that's true, but if it is, I think they're a bit silly.

The last charity gig you did for Mencap didn't come off too well, did it?

No, it was just a major fuck-up on a lot of fronts basically. What really happened was that we over-estimated the amount of people that would come to the show. It was at Villa Park, Birmingham, and we thought we'd be getting people from all over England but about 90% of the people there came from within a 40 mile radius of Birmingham, so we actually had about 7,000 people less than we'd hoped for and those 7,000 were the ones that were going to make the profit for Mencap . . . We ended up giving Mencap a lot of money out of our own pockets; all in all, with the band and our two managers, it cost £70,000 between the seven of us.

In your current tour programme, there is a listing of events connected with the group. For June this year, it says you stayed in the South of France getting ideas for the new LP, playing tennis, attending the Cannes Film Festival and 'reflecting on the nature of life'. What conclusion did you reach?

There are some funny things in that programme. That sounds very intellectual and philosophical, which isn't us at all. What an odd thing to write. No, really, we were just mixing business with pleasure.

And rubbing your fans' noses in it. So, what is the meaning of life, Simon?

(*laughs*) Um, well, for me, very busy – for some others, not so busy!

So basically, Kaspar de Graaf, who wrote the tour programme, was just being pretentious?

I think it's one of his little jokes really; Kaspar's got a big sense of humour.

Therefore he's making fun of thirteen-year-olds and you're condoning it.

It doesn't worry me.

What happened behind the bike sheds?

What!! How do you know about that?

You mentioned it in a *Flexipop* interview just before 'Planet Earth' was a hit.

That was a long time ago and only me and two other people know about it, and one of them only a little bit. I'm not going to give those kind of secrets away!

You were obviously still at school so you must have been very young.

I wasn't *very* young. I mean, I was old enough!

Is it true that Nick Rhodes (real name Nick Bates) was nick-named Master Bates at school so he decided to name himself after his favourite synthesiser?

Ha ha: It's a piano actually, not a synth. A Fender Rhodes piano! I think he liked the name Rhodes because of the Greek island connection and also because of the music business connection as in Bernie (*laughs at what must be an 'in' joke*). If I was going to change my name I think I'd call myself something like Jet Cane or Peter Smith or something.

Have you ever been gobbed on?

Gobbed on? Don't you mean spat at? Well, actually yes, quite a few times, mostly on stage.

Really? I can't quite imagine all those sweet young girls in the front row –

We did the Hazel O'Connor tour and there weren't so many little girls in that audience, let me tell you. I usually see it coming and I tend to get out of the way in time. In fact, I've never had a direct hit.

Do you like Test Department?

Pardon?

I said: do you like Test Department?

What's a test department?

Oh dear, how long have you been away? *(Simon looks worried)* **They're part of the latest craze that's sweeping the country . . .** *(At this point, dear reader, you may fast-forward the interview button, because of course we all know who Test Dept. are.)*

Oh yeah, I think I've heard a bit about it. I have heard some music like that but quite a long time ago; you used to get bands who used washboards and brooms with bits of string tied to boxes, things like that . . .

You mean like The Chevalier Brothers. No, it's not like that, let me explain it to you again. *(I try to capture the essence of Test Dept., SPK and Einsturzende Neubauten in a nutshell which is rather hard and Simon still looks blank).*

Er, yeah. What I think about Test Department is this: Great, if the music that comes from it sounds good or they can get good tunes from it – fine, but it sounds a bit gimmicky to me.

Have you ever been told that you look like a young Elvis Presley?

Yes, I've also been compared to the bloody bloated Las Vegas Presley – that was a down-right insult . . . do you think I do?

Actually, yes.

(*Looking glum*) I think it must be because we pull the same expressions when we're singing. I must admit I've never been a big Elvis fan, although I think what he did for music was brilliant, but I don't like his voice that much. I think the best things he ever did were 'Jailhouse Rock' and 'King Creole'.

Are you planning any similar film ventures?

Well, I'd like to do films but not like that.

What's your sexual fantasy?

I'm a bit shy about it to be honest . . . I don't think I'm a pervert at all, not compared to some of the stories I've heard.

Is it a recurring fantasy?

No, they change all the time.

I noticed in a list of likes and dislikes, you once wrote for likes: women, rubber, water and leather.

Women – yes, but I've definitely gone off rubber. I don't like the smell very much. When I used to go caving and pot-holing, which I'm sure must have awful connotations, I used to have to wear a neoprene suit. The fantasy at the moment is definitely a hot one because of all the cold weather. Have you ever seen the film *Walkabout?* There are some amazingly erotic scenes in that with trees. There's some beautiful trees that only grow in Australia and they look just like women's parts; the way the branches split is incredibly erotic. I mean, don't get me wrong, I'm not into trees, I really like women, I just find the imagery erotic . . . I'd like to make love in a poppy field and eat strawberries at the same time and then ride away on two dapple-grey horses.

It sounds just like one of your videos!

(*Laughing*) Yeah, okay, 'Hungry Like A Wolf' just happened to be one of my fantasies!! What's *your* fantasy then – you did promise you'd tell me.

Oh, I've got so many! Mostly bondage, buggery and water sports with greasy bikers. (*Of course, I was only joking*).

(*Eyes gleaming, mouth grinning*) I'm fairly dominant! As the band has developed over the last three-and-a-half years, I've become a lost more confident in many ways, including sexually!

John Taylor was once quoted claiming you wrote the video story-lines just so you 'could get to work with more chicks'. Is that true?

I think that was a kind of a joke. But take 'Girls On Film' for example. When we first talked about making a soft-core porn video, I must admit that one of the, er, attractions of doing it, would be to actually see it being filmed and to actually be there.

Why does every member of the band, with the exception of Andy Taylor, go out with a model? Isn't that a bit of a cliché: popstar-goes-out-with-brainless-beauty?

Doesn't Battersea Power Station remind you of an upside-down table with those legs? I really like it, it's the oddest-looking building there is.

Talking about legs –

Have you noticed that they've wrapped up Big Ben? It looked just like a big Christmas present, it's great. Apparently they're cleaning the clock-face because its eroding.

Would you like to do a duet with somebody?

Vocally? I'm not at that stage yet. I'd love to work with Dolly Parton though; I think she's so funny. I'm not really into that song, the one she did with the old git with the grey hair, but she's so funny in the video. She looks great and she has the most incredible bosom. What else can you call it? That's a bosom if ever I saw one. I think all that working with other people, like The Assembly and Paul McCartney with Michael Jackson, is a bit naff . . . I think they're doing it because they're running out of ideas and they want other people to help them basically. You can't deny it's working in a very sweet way with McCartney and Jackson, but I grind my teeth whenever I hear 'The Girl Is Mine'.

Which member of the band are you closest to?

It changes a lot. In the studio, I'm closest to Nick, we do a lot of work together . . . Socially, I'm probably closer to Andy or John.

How would you describe them individually, given one word each?

Nick – desperately intelligent; John – desperately sociable; Andy's like that as well but he's got a very dry sense of humour, he's very cynical sometimes. He can be really mean to you one moment and then the next he'll come up and say he didn't mean it. Andy's a really nice guy. Roger – John once said 'he's the earth that cannot be shaken,' but I see him as the branch that cannot sink.

How does it feel to know that you are the masturbation fixation of thousands and thousands of pubescent girls all around the world?

No-one's ever put it that way before! It sounds quite exciting; it doesn't appeal to me but it does flatter me. There's pros and cons to that; the public property thing can get too much. When everybody thinks that they know you personally, they can get really fresh and forward with you. I mean, I know I do this for a living and I go out and give a lot of myself on stage and on record, but I don't give *that* much. It's very disconcerting when somebody comes up to you and grabs your arse or something. I may be public property but there are some parts of me which aren't, and that's one of them.

But you do concentrate on your sexuality in the most blatant way possible. Take your first album cover for example; it could be concluded from the group photo on the front that you're well-endowed. I thought it was probably unintentional until I turned over to the back cover, where there's a zoom-in shot of just your crotch next to a car-engine – the symbolism is rather obvious, isn't it?

(*Laughs*) I noticed that as well. I couldn't believe they'd used that photo. Of course I'm not going to deny that I *am* well-endowed. It has been pointed out to me before – about the photo I mean. Uh, you know, it's very hard to do an interview about the size of your dick! Look, I've gone all pink.

(*Unrelenting*) **Yet I noticed on the large video screen at your gig on Sunday that your flies were half undone. It wasn't accidental because someone I know who is on the tour with you said the zip was at half-mast every night.**

Oh, er, *blah*, aah, what actually happened is that I did a jump and the buttons popped off. I didn't get around to having the trousers mended until the other day; they have now been altered slightly with a heavy-duty zip.

What do you think about when you masturbate? Don't pretend you don't!

I wasn't going to! If I can't think of anything I just look through my fan-mail till I find something good. I've had some great suggestions from secretaries who want to get me between the filing cabinets.

Do you ever feel limited in any creative way with Duran Duran?

Limited only by my own limitations. No, there's plenty of room for development while it's still huge, it's very difficult to discipline yourself to try not to run before you can crawl, if anything, I only feel limited by my own creativity.

Where did you get the nickname Muscles?

That was really stupid. I was doing a show in London ages ago, before I joined the band, and some choreographer started calling me Muscles. The band all call me Charlie, because it's my middle name. Imagine being called Jimmy the Hoover! What a bad-news name for a band. It reminds me of someone I know called Jimmy the Con. He's a bouncer at the Cedar Club, Birmingham; he's a real laugh. Once, he lifted me up above his head and just twirled me round. He's a real funny guy . . .

We have now arrived at Wembley Arena and the taxi-driver takes us round to an obscure back entrance where there are a handful of female fans hanging around the security fence. It's about 5.30 and the gig doesn't start until 9. As we wait for the gates to be opened, one of the girls recognises Simon who isn't exactly crouching in the corner. 'Ohmigod! I don't believe it, look, it's Simon!' All of a sudden, all these faces are pressed against the window and fists are beating on the roof and thin screams pierce the freezing air. I've never been in this situation before; it's so unreal, like monkeys in a zoo, but Simon completely ignores the commotion outside and carries on talking while signing his autograph for the taxi driver's two daughters.

Simon carries my coat, bag and tape-recorder into the backstage area, then hands me over to his bodyguard. The sound-check takes about 45 minutes; Duran Duran are doing Cockney Rebel's 'Come Up And See Me' which they do so well, it ends up sounding just like a Duran Duran song. The soundcheck over, we climb into the back of an extremely luxurious coach which is going back to The Savoy. About a hundred girls run after us as the coach sets off. I can hear them screaming and part the curtain to watch. Simon shrugs his shoulders. 'The exercise will do them good.' He offers me a chocolate from one of the many boxes lying on the floor.

Were *you* ever a fan.

Not in that way, no. I didn't start going to concerts until about '76 or '77. The first concert I ever went to was Genesis' 'Lamb

Lies Down On Broadway' tour at Earls Court. I think Peter Gabriel's brilliant . . . I also like The Cramps and Big Country.

How much money have you made this year?

I don't know. We don't find out until about five years later. I'm really bad at business and accounts, that's why we have Andy Taylor in the band.

How important is money to you?

I think it will be one day but it isn't at the moment because we're having a great time just being in the band and it pays for itself.

What satisfies you more than anything else?

Being on stage. It's a really big challenge – it's really dangerous in a way. Every night before I go on, I have a kind of trauma about whether I can do it tonight.

Would you rather have achieved fame through acting than through the (according to some) less credible medium of being a pop star?

At one point, my parents and a lot of other people thought I was mad joining a group and psychologically I rebelled against that kind of prejudice. A lot of people think that being in a group is a lower form of art than acting. I disagree with that attitude completely. There's a lot to be said about going on stage and performing what is basically your own script, something that you've come up with totally by yourself. When you're acting, you're working with someone else's script and someone else's character and you're being directed by other people as well. There's a lot of pride attached to being able to work the whole thing out yourself . . . But I'm really looking forward to seeing Sting in *Dune*. My favourite actor is Donald Sutherland – I love his face, it's not a fashionable or handsome face but it's so charismatic. I'd like to play a part that I could really get my teeth into, not necessarily something deep and meaningful, but something with good words in it. I'm very fond of Shakespeare because of the words.

I expect you like Mervyn Peake then?

Yes, how did you know? That's very perceptive, I feel like I've been stripped naked. I love the Gormenghast trilogy – they're my favourite books.

Do you respect your audience?

Yes, I do very much and for a lot of different reasons as well. Because they've got the common sense to like decent music like ours and for sticking by us in the face of great adversity.

How would you define your audience?

It's very widespread. It's not just made up of 13-year-olds.

What does 'Seven And The Ragged Tiger' mean?

It's like a commando team. Seven is a really special number for us because it's the number of the actual unit of our success, the five members of the band and the two guys that manage us who are a very integral part of everything. The ragged tiger symbolises luck and success.

Do you stay on good terms with your old girlfriends?

Some I do, some I don't. Some you end up with big bashes, some you can write letters to.

Have you ever hit a girl?

Yes but I haven't *hit* a girl, I've smacked one. I would never hit a girl on her face. If I was going to hit one, I'd hit her on the bottom.

Before I met you, I was convinced that I was being sent to interview a megalomaniac!

I wouldn't call myself that although I like my one-and-a-half hours of power that I have every night. I enjoy that. If I told them to get up and smash up the place and not go to school tomorrow, some of them would do it unquestionably... You know, I'm really enjoying this interview.

Good. Why?

Because you're so cute and sexy and you've got nice legs. That's why I walked all the way behind you at the Savoy!

The coach has come to a hydraulic halt outside the main entrance of The Savoy. Simon and I descend into a crowd of girls; I get away as fast as possible, and five minutes later Simon escapes loaded with gifts, kisses and phone numbers.

Would you consider seeing a psycho-analyst?

No. I'd rather find out about myself through myself. To start with, I'm very happy with myself. I don't think there's anything wrong with me. It also seems very vain to pay someone else to talk about you. On the subject of ego, I think it's really very important to keep a good balance between what I'm doing for a living, which is like walking a tightrope between charisma and bullshit, and to know what I really am, which is basically the same as everybody else, but just lucky enough to have a decent job . . . Have you heard that joke? How many psychologists does it take to change a light-bulb? *One*. It takes a very long time and the light-bulb has to want to change.

That's the best one you've told all day.

I like telling jokes and stories. You know, I used to lie a lot when I was young, well up into my teens actually. I used to tell people that my parents were Russian refugees or that I was a gypsy, I used to really over-romanticize and over-glamourize everything because I thought I was a really boring slightly overweight youngster, which is what I was. I was so embarrassed when they did my life story in *No. 1*. It had all my mother's quotes and my mother would never let you think I was boring. Those pictures of me sitting in that bloody tweed jacket – I cringed then and I cringe now when I see it. I had a really hard time at school when I was in the local newspaper.

Have you taken speed to keep your weight down?

I used to but I don't touch drugs now. Heroin is getting so fucking trendy in this country again, it's frightening. And it makes me sick that people are still being led to believe that it's fashionable or glamorous . . . You can't even enjoy it the first time, you have to do it two or three times before you stop puking up – what's the attraction of that?

How long do you see the success of Duran Duran lasting?

I'm a big optimist. I do believe in the future of the band. A band has to make a very big effort these days to be able to change enough to be fashionable but also be able to please yourself which is more important. You can't approach anything if you're not totally satisfied with what you're doing.

Finally, Simon, can you think of any question which I've neglected to ask, which you feel could be important?

Well, you haven't asked me any questions about our music . . .

THE STRANGE & MYSTERIOUS DEATH OF MRS JERRY LEE LEWIS

The Killer by Richard Ben Cramer

'YOU SCARED OF ME?' LEWIS ONCE ASKED HIS WIFE'S SISTER.
'YOU SHOULD BE. WHY DO YOU THINK THEY CALL ME THE KILLER?'

How was I out to lunch? Let me count the ways. I was new to magazines, never having written for a national publication, much less for *Rolling Stone*. I was a newspaperman, just returned from the Middle East – a bit unsteady, still, in America. The provenance of rock & roll I had traced as far back as the record store. Past that lay a great sea of unknowing.

All of a sudden, I was in Hernando, Mississippi, where no restaurant order was complete until the waitress asked, 'You wan' gravy?' Where the leading candidate for sheriff was known as Big Dog Riley. Where Jerry Lee Lewis was a legend and a power, not to mention the spendigest man in the country, which spending had bought for almost a decade the quiet cooperation of local authorities who would perform all kinds of 'community service', like towing the Killer's car out of a ditch without checking his blood for alcohol, or bargaining his drug charge down to a simple fine, or shipping off the bruised body of his dead fifth bride for a private autopsy, with no coroner's jury and little public inquiry into the cause of her death.

And I was proposing to penetrate this long-closed world, to find out how that girl died?

Truly, I was out to lunch.

But God looks after his children who were tardy on brain day. He introduced me to a splendid couple of folks who owned the local weekly newspaper, and then to the local prosecutor, who wanted to help me honorably, even though the resulting story could not reflect well on his grand-jury presentation. And then there were the ambulance drivers, the local cops, local merchants and matrons, meetings at midnight, anonymous notes left at my motel. Bit by bit, they made a picture of life where Jerry Lee lived.

Then, too, I was led to Hernando's Hide-A-Way, the Killer's favourite nightclub, fifteen miles north of Memphis, Tennessee, and to the lubricious owner of that nightclub, Kenny Rodgers; in Memphis, too, there was Elvis's old doctor chum, Dr Nick; there was Jerry Lee's manager, J. W. Whitten, and Whitten's little dogs, Nickie and Kai; there was J. W.'s former wife; and there were former band members, club bartenders, former girlfriends, bouncers, strippers, whores . . .

Quickly, it became apparent that this unexpected, inexplicable death was not out of the ordinary in the world of Jerry Lee. And not long after, it would become equally clear that the official version of events diverged early and often from the facts. Something went violently wrong at the Killer's mansion on the night of Shawn Lewis's death. And as soon as that death was disclosed, everything went wrong with the investigation. A grand jury was quickly led to conclude that no crime had occurred. But I was sure Shawn's death was no suicide, no mistaken handful of pills. No one would ever prove what happened: Only two people were in the house that night. One was dead and buried before the appropriate tests could be made. The other was Jerry Lee Lewis.

First, I had to learn something about where Jerry Lee's music came from – and about the stark choices presented to a boy at the Assembly of God church in Ferriday, Louisiana. In a hundred times of trouble, he had vowed he would dedicate his soul and music to the Lord's work, forevermore, but he never could make that stick. And then the millions of miles and the thousands of nightclub dates – the rage they required, the drinks and drugs – took their toll. He ate away at himself. By the terms of his church, Jerry Lee made his living with the devil's dance on his piano. 'Great Balls of Fire' was his anthem not by happenstance.

And he ate through the lives of his women. His third wife, his cousin Myra Gale Brown, won divorce with horrific tales of how Jerry Lee beat her up in view of their little daughter. His fourth wife, Jaren Gunn, also won divorce, but she ended up dead, mysteriously drowned in a Memphis swimming pool, just before her settlement came through. Shawn Michelle Stephens was the fifth. A sharp and spunky twenty-five-year-old from Garden City, Michigan, she thought Jerry Lee was her ticket to the good life. They married on June 7th, 1983, and seventy-seven days later, she was dead.

It seemed to me unlikely that the magazine of rock & roll would greet this harsh story with enthusiasm. I thought, in fact, that if I meant to question Jerry Lee's clean escape from this case, I'd have to possess a ton of stonehard facts and present them as a wall, every stone immovable. It took weeks in Mississippi, Memphis and Detroit – more weeks in New York. It seemed to me a miracle that I never heard a discouraging word from my editor, Susan Murcko. I thought perhaps I hadn't made exactly clear what it was I thought I'd found. I wrote with trepidation. I saw every word raising a wall that might fall back on me. It was months after the assignment when, at last, I presented to Murcko a thick sheaf of pages.

Too thick!

Murcko started thinning the wall. She worked with the infinite patience of a medieval mason. Thousands of words were chiseled to dust. And nothing was lost. Murcko, God bless her, was all dogged delicacy.

Then Jann Wenner looked it over. Too thick!

To hell with delicacy! More thousands of words, whole interviews, whole characters, were dust, mere dust. Murcko brushed the wall smooth again.

Then fact checkers . . .
The copy editors . . .
Then lawyers!

I was unprepared for this woe. I was a newspaperman. The way I was brought up, you wrote the thing, you sent it in, it ran that night. Next day, it was over. This was months. This was murder.

February 1984, finally, the story was in type. Ten pages in the magazine. I looked it over as if it were some strange geode, compressed as it was by time and tread. I was shocked to discover that it said what I meant.

The county's inquiry into Shawn's death never was reopened. The feds took up the scent for a while, but they never made a case on the death of Jerry Lee's wife. They put all their eggs into the Internal Revenue basket and actually charged Lewis under the tax laws. But as far as I know, nothing much came of it. Some bargaining went on – more judgments against Jerry Lee, more liens. What the hell, he already had enough judgments against him to pave the road to Tupelo.

Jerry Lee got married again – to a cute young thing. The tabloids attended and wrote about her ring.

The Killer's only reaction to my story came through his manager, J. W. Whitten. He said Jerry Lee was 'just surprised . . . that ROLLING STONE would do that kind of thing on us.'

Well, so was I.

* * * *

The Killer was in his bedroom, behind the door of iron bars, as Sonny Daniels, the first ambulance man, moved down the long hall to the guest bedroom to check the report: 'Unconscious party at the Jerry Lee Lewis residence.'

Lottie Jackson, the housekeeper, showed Sonny into a spotless room: Gauzy drapes filtered the noonday light; there was nothing on the tables, no clothes strewn about, no dust; just a body on the bed, turned away slightly toward the wall, with the covers drawn up to the neck. Sonny probed with his big, blunt fingers at a slender wrist: it was cold. 'It's Miz Lewis,' Lottie said.

'I came in . . . I couldn't wake her up . . .' Sonny already had the covers back, his thick hand on the woman's neck where the carotid pulse should be: The neck retained its body warmth, but no pulse. Now he bent his pink moon-face with its sandy fuzz of first beard over her pale lips: no breath. He checked the eyes. 'Her eyes were all dilated. That's an automatic sign that her brain has done died completely.'

Matthew Snyder, the second ambulance man, had barely finished Emergency Medical Technician school. He was twenty, blond, beefy, even younger than Sonny, and just starting with the Hernando, Mississippi, ambulance team. Even rookies knew there wasn't anything uncommon about a run to Jerry Lee's to wake up some passed-out person. But Matthew saw there was something uncommonly wrong now, as he caught the look of worry and excitement from Sonny over at the bed. 'Go ahead and check her over,' said Sonny, and Matthew restarted the process with the woman's delicate wrist. He saw, up on her forearm, the row of angry little bruises, like someone had grabbed her hard. He saw the little stain of dried blood on the web of her hand. He shook his head at Sonny: no pulse.

Lottie knew it was wrong, too. She was a stolid, hard-working black woman who'd taken care of Jerry Lee since before he moved down here from Memphis – more than ten years, that made it. She was crying as she moved down the hall and knocked at the door with the iron bars.

The Killer was there within seconds. If he'd been sleeping on the big canopied bed, he must have been sleeping in his bathrobe. For now, he came into the hall, with the white terry-cloth lapels pulled tight across his skinny chest, and he looked surprised to find Lottie in tears. Then he looked a silent question into Sonny Daniels' eyes.

'Mr Lewis, your wife . . .' Sonny averted his gaze. He said: 'I just checked her over in there . . .'

Still, he didn't meet the question in Jerry Lee's hard eyes. He saw the two bright red scratches on the back of Jerry Lee's hand, like a cat had gouged him from the wrist to the knuckles. When Sonny looked up at last, his own eyes grew, his whole face seemed to grow larger, rounder, younger.

'Mr Lewis,' he said. 'I'm sorry. Miz Lewis is dead.'

The autopsy that cleared Jerry Lee Lewis called Shawn Michelle Lewis, 25, 'a well-developed, well-nourished, white female, measuring sixty-four inches in length, weighing 107 pounds. The hair is brown, the eyes are green . . .' It hardly did her justice. She was a honey blond with a tan, small and full of bounce, with a grin that made everybody smile and had turned male heads since junior high.

'Everybody liked her. She was like the stepchild of the club. Everybody looked out for her,' says Mike DeFour, the manager of DB's, a fancy nightclub in the Hyatt Regency Hotel in Dearborn, Michigan, where Shawn Michelle Stephens worked as a cocktail waitress. DeFour treated his waitresses, 'the DB's girls,' like family – he loved them all, took care of them, saw to it that they made good money – even the new girls, like Shawn, who had started part time about four years ago. 'Some of the girls I gave nicknames to. Shawn was "Little Buzz," because she was always buzzing around, you know, half buzzed . . .

'No, not like that. Drugs weren't a big problem. You know, a hit on a joint or two, no problem. It was around. Or a shot from a bottle of schnapps – okay, I'd look the other way.'

Shawn loved working there. The money was great – sometimes $150 a night. But it wasn't just that: It was upscale, crowded with people who dressed and threw money around. It was something more for a girl from Garden City, a suburb of little boxes built for the auto workers of the Fifties. There, *more* was the stuff of dreams.

But somehow, in Garden City, Shawn never seemed to get much more. Her mother's divorce had only made it harder. Shawn had been in and out of jobs, mostly waitressing, since she graduated in 1975. She dreamed of marrying Scott, her boyfriend, but his parents were strict, and they never thought much of Shawn. So DB's was fine for the moment – great, in fact. She loved the people. It almost wasn't like work. The musicians took them to parties after hours – great parties. One DB's girl,

Pam Brewer, took up with J. W. Whitten, the wiry bantam of a road manager for the Jerry Lee Lewis band. Pam flew off to Memphis, and when she came back the next year, she was soon to be Mrs J. W. Whitten, travelling with the band, flying in Learjets and shopping from a limo! That's when it happened to Shawn.

Jerry Lee, performing for a week at the Dearborn Hyatt, picked Shawn out from among the girls. Pam Brewer set it up: She told Shawn that Jerry Lee wanted to take her to a party in his suite. It wasn't like Shawn had been looking for it. In fact, the first time she'd seen Jerry Lee, she'd told her mother: 'Mom, he's a lone man, and he's about your age. You ought to come and try to meet him . . .' Instead, it was Shawn who went. 'I always thought Shawn'd be good for Jerry,' says Pam. 'She was so cute, petite, and he likes little women. And she was so much fun to be with. I introduced them. I thought she was flexible enough to understand his moods.'

Jerry Lee wasn't showing his moods the night of that first party. A great party, Shawn told her friends. Actually, it was just a few drinks in his suite. A couple of other women were already up there. Jerry Lee played piano and sang, while Pam's little Chinese Shih Tzu dog sat up with him on the stool. Shawn knew she was looking good, in her jeans, cowboy boots and a huggy little white rabbit jacket. And Jerry Lee treated her so nice! He'd turn away from the keyboard as he'd slow down his rhythm for a snatch of a love song. She felt him sing straight to her. It was February 1981. Shawn was twenty-three.

'Dead. You sure?' said the Killer, as he crossed the hall to the guest room. He grabbed Shawn's wrist, as if to feel her pulse, then dropped it and just stood staring at her.

'Anything you can do?' Jerry Lee said, mostly to Sonny. 'In the hospital?'

'No, sir, we woulda took her already,' said Sonny. He was real polite.

Jack McCauley, a deputy sheriff, came into the room at that moment. By happenstance, he said, he'd been patrolling on

Malone Road as the ambulance made the turn for Jerry Lee's house. Of course, his ordinary patrol area was miles away, but nothing about Jack McCauley seemed to fit the ordinary. McCauley, 48, certainly was the sharpest deputy in DeSoto County: a college man, a Yankee transplanted to Mississippi, a man who said he'd made a small fortune on developments like the industrial park in the northeast corner of the county. John Burgess McCauley lived in a hideaway house that made Jerry Lee's look modest – it must have been worth $200,000, according to realtors who'd seen it. Nobody quite knew what Jack was doing, fooling around in patrol cars with a deputy's job that paid $12,000 a year. And the way he'd take your head off for the smallest little thing, start shouting and get red all the way up to his crew-cut, no one asked Jack.

Sonny was going to explain to Jerry Lee the need for an inquest, but Jack McCauley took over from there. He had that air of command about him. McCauley announced he was going to clear the room. He wasn't real polite like Sonny – more familiar. 'Come to think of it,' says Sonny, 'I don't recall Jack introducing himself. Maybe he knew Jerry Lee.'

Maybe, but it's hard to tell now. McCauley won't talk about the case. And Jerry Lee never said much of anything about it, except that day, when he had a long talk with McCauley. They were alone in Jerry Lee's little den for more than an hour before the state investigators or anybody else arrived at the house. McCauley never filed any report on that long conversation. He did write a report that told how he came in the wake of the ambulance, just after 12:30 p.m., August 24th, 1983, and how he got delayed in the driveway by two employees of Goldsmith's department store, who'd come to the house to hang drapes, and then how Matthew Snyder told him 'that a female subject was dead in one of the bedrooms.' His report continues:

> Upon entering a small bedroom on the east side of the residence, Mr Lewis was bending over the bed where a white female was lying partially covered by a bedspread. She was clad in a negligee . . . When I first arrived, Mr Lewis' speech

was heavily slurred, but he was alert and coherent. I telephoned the sheriff's office and requested a justice of the peace if the coroner could not be located, and an investigator. The latter was requested because there were no visible causes of death and because Mr Lewis' bathrobe contained apparent bloodstains and he had a cut on his wrist.

At 13:51 hours I advised Mr Lewis that his manager J. W. Whitten had arrived but would not be allowed to enter the residence until the investigation was completed. Mr Lewis commented we need to 'find out who killed – how she died,' so funeral arrangements can be made.

So McCauley was the first to report that Jerry Lee's robe was spotted with blood. Surely, McCauley must have seen, as well, the blood on Shawn Lewis, on her hand, on her hair, on clothes and a bra in another room, on a lamp, in a spot on the carpet. He must have seen the film of dirt on her, and the bruises on her arms and hip, maybe her broken fingernails with something that looked like dried blood underneath. None of this was in his report. But it didn't matter much. For McCauley's report never made it into the investigative file, never left the sheriff's department until after the grand jury had decided no crime had occurred.

Shawn hadn't been a great fan of the Killer's, not until that first night in his suite. She was tiny in her mother's womb when his 'Whole Lotta Shakin' Goin' On' threatened to knock Elvis himself off the throne of rock & roll. At forty-five, Jerry Lee was still riveting – a star, and he seemed to like her. He'd make funny faces and twist his head around, trying to understand her funny Yankee way of talking. Then he'd understand and try to mimic, and everybody'd laugh – Jerry, too. Of course, girls were never a problem for the Killer. They were always around. Often, Jerry left the details of his trysting to others; now, in February 1981, it was Pam who issued another invitation, this time with a free ticket to Memphis: 'Jerry was gettin' ready to go to Europe, and I figured it was a good time to bring Shawn down. Because I figured he'd take her with him. Which he did . . .'

Clever girl! Pam Brewer is twenty-six now, and although she's split up with J. W. Whitten, she still lives in Memphis. She talks in a molasses drawl (well, a girl's got to fit in!) about Shawn's springtime trip to Europe.

'He bought a beautiful gold watch for her. I don't know how many thousands he spent on it. It was his first gift to her . . . They'd send her out, and she's get herself a bunch of beautiful suits, and she'd come back and just look at herself in the mirror, because she couldn't believe that was her in all those beautiful things . . .

'How could you not get taken by it? I was in heaven all the time I was, uh, involved.'

It was heaven – most of the time. Then there were the times Jerry was speeding so bad after a show: He couldn't come down, and he'd bully Shawn to stay up with him. God, they never slept. And then it was kind of disgusting when Jerry would stick that big needle with the Talwin narcotic right into his stomach. He said his stomach was killing him, and no wonder, the way he lived.

It was better, sort of, back in Nesbit, Mississippi, in the big brick house – at least you could relax. There was the pool shaped like a piano, and the lake out back with the Jet Ski, a sort of kicky little snowmobile for the water. Shawn loved the sun, and she'd lie out there all afternoon, before Jerry woke up. Then at night, they'd go to Hernando's Hide-A-Way, Jerry's home club, fifteen miles north, up in Memphis. They'd roll in about midnight, and Jerry Lee would sort of dance to his table, announcing. 'The Killer is here.' They'd always drink, or have a pipe or two back in a little office by the bandstand. Sometimes, Hernando's owner, Kenny Rodgers, would get up to the mike, straighten his pearly tie under the vest of his gray business suit and announce: 'Ladies an' gentlemen! The greates' ennataina inna worl' . . . the Killa . . . Jerra Lee!' And then Jerry'd screw around for hours, while the house band wilted behind him, and Jerry would work to his own private rhythms, singing a snatch of this or that, cutting off songs in midverse, making the whole club dance to his tune.

That could get ugly, too, like the time some patrons left the floor in disgust when Jerry Lee cut off another song. 'You stupid ignorant sonsabitches,' Jerry Lee screamed from the piano bench. 'You got a $20,000 show here, and y'all walkin' off from the Killer!'

Shawn said she knew how to handle him. For one thing, you just had to pay attention. Shawn said she knew, too, how to handle other women. A friend and former DB's girl, Beverly Lithgow, says: 'Shawn told about one of the first times they went out to dinner down there near Memphis, and this girl came over to the table and asked for Jerry Lee's autograph. So he gave it to her. She came back again and started talking with him. So the third time she came back, Shawn finally just grabbed her by the hair and pulled her down, and said, "He's with *me* tonight. Leave him alone." Shawn said Jerry Lee loved it because she was so forceful.'

She had spunk – 'She wasn't a pansy,' says Bev – enough to leave him when her younger sister, Shelley, came down to visit, and Jerry started showing his moods. Shelley, 20, drove down with their brother, Thomas, and his friend, Dave Lipke. Jerry Lee got jealous; he thought Shelley was bringing a young man for Shawn. Then he got mad, according to Shelley, and started knocking Shawn around. Shelley says the real problem was Jerry Lee's insistence that she and Shawn have sex with him.

'I knew what he wanted, and I wouldn't do it,' Shelley says. 'He made us leave, but he didn't actually tell us to go. He made Shawn tell us. So she said, "Well, if you're leaving, so am I."

'It was really crazy. Jerry Lee was wild. He ended up accusing us of stealing his Jet Ski. But the Jet Ski is big, like a snowmobile. I mean, I only had a Camaro. And he saw us drive away. He parted the curtains. We saw him looking through the bars on his window. I kept saying, "Duck! Duck!" We all thought he was going to shoot us.'

The Killer wore a white tuxedo and a red, ruffled shirt to his wedding on the patio of the big Nesbit house. Shawn shone in ivory-colored silk, and she spoke her vows bravely to Justice of the Peace Bill Bailey, who presided. In the rush, they hadn't been able to find a preacher to do the honours. (Well, J. W. Whitten found one, but he was black and Jerry might not have liked that, so J. W. got the judge.) In the rush, no one thought about the blood test for the license and the three days' wait required by Mississippi law, until Lottie Jackson brought it up on the morning of the wedding. For a while, it looked like Jerry Lee would have to pack the whole party off to Tennessee, where things could be done with less wait and bother. But J. W. fixed the license, too. 'I made a phone call,' he says, with evident pride. 'Just somebody I knew down there.' J. W. winks. 'In the business, it's called "juice".'

Shelley arrived in Mississippi in the first days of June, driving a brand-new red Corvette that Shawn had asked her to deliver for her.

Shelley's mother said the family would drive down, too, but Shawn insisted that they spring for one-way air fare. No problem, Shawn said: Jerry Lee could send them home in the Learjet.

When at last they got it together, it didn't seem to want to start. Shawn's mother walked down the hall to find out what was keeping Jerry. He was almost ready: He was sitting in the master bedroom with his friend, Dr George Nichopoulos. Dr Nick had his medical license suspended in 1980 for over-prescribing addictive drugs. He was Elvis' personal physician on part of the King's long slide into drug oblivion. Dr Nick testified at hearings that he also wrote narcotic prescriptions for Jerry Lee Lewis. Dr Nick was still a frequent guest at the Nesbit house. On the wedding day, Shawn's mother says, she found Jerry regarding three pairs of pills, laid out neatly on a bed table: two of each, three different colors. Jerry Lee said he'd be up in a moment.

J. W. Whitten had invited the *National Enquirer*, which supplied this account of the big day, June 7th, 1983:

> Despite Jerry's experience at saying, 'I do,' he was a bundle of nerves during the ceremony... And three times the

nervous groom flubbed the line 'according to God's holy ordinance.' Eventually, Jerry held up his hand to the judge and said, 'Just a minute, sir. I'm going to get that right,' and went on to complete his vows perfectly.

Then he slipped a ring on the finger of the honey-blonde bride . . . The magnificent $6000 ring glittered with a two-carat diamond surrounded by smaller diamonds, all set in silver.

'Oh, Lord, was I nervous,' laughed the legendary hell-raiser, known to friends and fans as 'the Killer'. . .

'It was love at first sight,' Jerry recalled. 'I've never believed in that sort of thing, but there it was: The Killer fell in love.'

There it was . . . and Shawn, was it there for her, too?

Well, she clipped the *Enquirer*'s story and sent it to friends and family. On each copy, she crossed out '$6000' and wrote in the margin, '$7000'.

Her father stood in the hallway shouting: 'What's the deal here? You marry my daughter, then you can't even come out and see us?' Thomas Stephens was steamed; the morning after the wedding, he'd arrived with the rest of the family at the house at eleven. They'd sat outside the locked doors at the pool for more than an hour, before Shawn could emerge from the bedroom to let them in the house. Now, after another hour, Jerry Lee still hadn't made an appearance.

Jerry Lee showed a half-hour later, with a mumbled apology. He was buzzed. They couldn't understand him. He wasn't in a very good mood. 'I went into the kitchen,' says Shelley,' and he yelled at me, "What do you want?" I said, "I just came in for a couple of beers." He started pounding his fist on the counter, screaming: "You scared of me? You should be. Why do you think they call me the Killer? How'd I get that name, huh?" Then he slapped my face. I was trying not to cry. I couldn't tell my father. Shawn took us to a hotel there, near the airport, and dropped us off.'

The family didn't have tickets home, and they didn't have the money to buy them. Gone was the easy promise of the Learjet.

Shawn's mother, Janice Kleinhans, says there weren't any rental cars available at the airport that day. At last, she had to call Jerry Lee. 'I said, "I don't know where this mix-up come from, but if you can get us home, you'll have this money back right away." '

Jerry Lee said: 'I don't want no money back from you.' He and Shawn came by a couple of hours later. Shawn was crying as she met her mother in the airport and laid $1000 cash in her hand. Jerry Lee kept the motor running.

In phone calls back to Michigan, Shawn seldom spoke of troubles. Still, at one point, she told a friend that her life with the Killer was just like jail – she couldn't stand his jealousy, she felt like she was watched all the time. Once, she called home all excited about her new Lhasa apso – a $500 dog! In her next call, she sadly reported that she had to give up the pet because Jerry Lee got jealous. Later in the seventy-seven-day marriage, most of the calls were about a homecoming, a Jerry Lee concert Sunday, August 28th, in Nashville, Michigan. The family planned to convene – even Shawn's grandfather, who'd been too infirm to make it to the wedding, was planning to go. 'Don't forget that Sunday,' Shawn reminded them a dozen times.

She couldn't wait to see her sister Shelley and called in the middle of August to invite her down for a visit. Shelley, who had left her apartment and had to wait a month before moving into her new one, delightedly agreed to a long vacation. 'Perfect,' said Shawn. 'I'll send you a ticket.'

Her first night there, they went to Hernando's Hide-A-Way. Jerry was in a good mood, joking and dancing with Shawn, trying to charm Shelley. When they left at four in the morning, Jerry Lee was still flying. He played some piano back at the house, then put on the cassette of his new unreleased album. 'No one has ever heard any of these before,' the Killer told Shelley and Shawn. When the song 'One and Only You' started playing on the tape, Jerry Lee smiled and murmured, 'This is dedicated to you.'

He said it to both the sisters, but Shelley felt he was pressuring her. She didn't want him coming on. She didn't go for group sex. She said she'd better get to bed. Shawn said: 'Oh, stay up a little longer.' Shelley didn't want to be put on the spot. She said good night and went to bed.

When she got up at two the next afternoon, Jerry Lee was still up, drinking in his den. His sister, Linda Gail, and her children were over at the house for a visit. Shawn and Shelley sat in the sun at the pool, until Jerry Lee came out, looking mean and slurring his words. 'He said something like, "I think you girls better get your shit together," and then he hit me on the thigh and slapped me across the face. Shawn sat up to say something, and he hauled off and backhanded her across the face. He hit her hard, too. Then he just looked at us really crazy and walked off into the house again.

'I just looked at Shawn, and she asked me, "Did he hit you hard? Did it hurt?" I said, "You're damn right it hurt!" I said, "I'm leaving. I don't care who he is. Nobody can . . ." And then I stared to cry. "He can't hit me like that . . ." I said I was going to the police

'Shawn said it wouldn't be a good idea to go to the police down there, because they were with Jerry, and they'd be trying to find a way to get me for trying to cause trouble for him. So I just said I was going. I was really upset. And she said, "Just wait a little, Shel, 'cause I'm leaving too. I'm not staying if you don't. I know what he'll do to me if I go back in that house." I said, "Get your stuff, 'cause I'm leaving, with you or without you." '

They passed through the den on their way in, and Shelley said, trying not to cry, 'I think I'm going to go now.'

Jerry Lee said, 'Go. Get your ass outta here. Get walkin'.' He mumbled something about her being trouble.

'Then Shawn said, "Shelley's been as quiet as a mouse since she's been here." Jerry didn't hear her. She was over by the record shelf. He started yelling: "Speak up! Whaddya say about me?" He grabbed some albums out from under her hands, and he smashed them on the floor. Then he knocked her across the room. Linda Gail grabbed up her two kids and left.

'Shawn was, like, whimpering: "You're so mean. What's wrong with you?" She was sunk down into the big brown chair. He picked up a set of keys and whipped 'em at her, hit her in the forehead. She bent down to get the keys, and she told him: "I'm leavin' with Shel. I'm not stayin' here with you." So he tells her, "I'll show ya leavin'." He grabs her by the front of her robe, and he hauls her off down the hall. He says, "You're my wife. I'll kill you before you leave me." '

Shelley left the house on foot. She hitched a ride to the nearest store and called her father.

Back in Detroit, Shelley called her mother to recount the fight, but she omitted any mention of group sex, 'Well, there may be things you didn't know about,' her mother said. 'Maybe she was making him mad somehow. There's two sides to everything. One night, when you're over here, we'll call her together and all talk about it.' But before they made that call, Shawn wakened her mother with a phone call at 3:30 a.m., August 23rd.

'She said, "I'm leaving him," ' her mother recalls, ' "if and when I can get away from him . . ." '

'I said, "Shawn, it's three o'clock in the morning. Call me tomorrow."

'She said, "I don't know if I can. Whatever you do, make sure nobody calls for me here."

' "Honey, call me tomorrow, okay?"

' "I don't know if I can, but I'll be in touch, Mom."

' "Okay, talk to you later . . ." '

The next day, Shawn was dead.

TROUBLE MAN

Marvin Gaye by David Ritz

Now, 16 years later, I understand how I manipulated my first meeting with Marvin Gaye. It was 1978, and he had just released 'Here, My Dear', a full-blown soul suite delivered to a California judge as payment in a bitterly contested divorce from his first wife, Anna. In the most musical judgement in the history of domestic conflict, Anna was to receive the profits from the record while Marvin, lacking cash but never irony, simply said, 'Here, my dear.' The songs themselves – filled with rancour, self-pity, piety, wisdom and astonishing candour – told the story of the painful break-up. I became obsessed.

I listened to nothing else for weeks. His voice touched my heart and excited my head with such intensity that when the *Los Angeles Times* attacked the album, I knocked out a spirited response, comparing 'Here, My Dear' to the better works of Duke Ellington and Stevie Wonder. I realize now that, though the letter was public, I was really writing to Marvin himself, hoping my defence of his masterpiece would elicit a personal thanks – which is exactly what happened.

Like Miles Davis, Martin's troubled soul was covered with a mysterious, intriguing cool. Unlike Miles, he was open and friendly and seemingly colour blind. His secrets were subtle. When I met him that winter afternoon in his Sunset Strip studio, I had just completed a two-year project co-writing the autobiography of Ray Charles, an inspiring collaborator, but an authoritative and often distant figure. Marvin came on like a brother. He was warm, witty and quick to laugh. He spoke like he sang, in whisper-quiet melodies and soft falsettos. His conversation had a lyricism all its own. His affectations – a slight British accent when he was feeling aristocratic – were counter-balanced by disarming sincerity. Like his music, the singer was seductive. He thrived on intimacy. He used your first name. 'David,' he'd ask, 'do you read philosophy? What about philosophical dialogues? What about *musical* dialogues?' Then he'd sing a half-finished song in which the Devil played chess with God for the soul of man. 'I'm thinking of becoming a monk,' he'd declare, only half-jokingly, 'to free myself of the flesh.' From there he'd ponder the intricacies of a *Playboy* centrefold before stopping everything and breaking into meditation or prayer, all conducted under a heavy cloud of marijuana.

Marvin loved grass. He lived high. It's probably romantic musing on my part, but I like to think that pot made him mellow while cocaine – and certainly crack – made him mad.

I've long since stopped, but in those days I never passed up a joint offered by Marvin. I'm not saying it either improved or damaged our efforts, but the truth is that we worked under the influence. The lazy haze of herb suited his style, rounding out the edges of what I would eventually see as the manic corners of his jagged personality.

We became friends. I was privileged to watch him work and play up-close. It soon became clear that, like his music, his personal life was filled with dramatic contradictions, a combination of charm and chaos. As his second marriage unravelled with even greater melodrama than his first. I kept thinking of a line from the 'What's Goin' On' song 'Right On'. '*Right on*,' he wrote, '*for those who got drowned in the sea of happiness*.' Because he was a hero of mine, and because his art was so dazzlingly beautiful – so self-contained, so accomplished, so utterly slick – it took me a while to realize my hero was drowning.

On the other hand, it took very little time to see how Gaye's musical fantasies followed fact. By instinct, he wrote out of immediate experience. At the same time, the high theatre of his private life, like Woody Allen's, would become more compelling than any of his artistic confections. If autobiography was his strength, the more undiluted the better. When he suggested that I co-author his autobiography, I soon saw that my only chance of writing that book was to become a character in the ongoing narrative. Unlike my experience with Ray Charles, who would calmly sit in a room and entertain questions, I would have to entangle myself in Marvin Gaye's adventure in order to give his life literary form.

It was painful to see his cool façade crumble. For a man whose charm seemed to border on the divine, he harboured enormous insecurities and fears. Because his charisma was so sweetly engaging, I was fooled into thinking that he had evolved into a state of high consciousness. No doubt he had the potential. But, in truth, his soul was ripped apart by opposing forces. And although he loved being looked on as a man in control of his fate, his candour was stronger than his pride. 'The battle is between good and evil,' he said to me in one of many allusions to his own demise. 'And there's no doubt,' he added, 'evil will win.'

On the run, I researched the book which would be titled *Divided Soul* and published in 1985, a year after his death. In those first years, my method of gathering information reflected the mayhem of Marvin's life. I was scribbling notes scrambling to keep up with him, getting to know his mother and father, his siblings, his sweethearts, riding on his tour bus as he drifted from city to city, cancelling gigs, dropping in at discos, discussing his childhood in spurts, reading the Bible or the Koran, reaffirming his belief in Jesus while insisting that the Devil was winning, that the End – for him, for the civilized world – was near.

At the end of the Seventies, his career was in a shambles, his finances a mess. To punish his second wife, Janis, and to escape the tax man, who had already repossessed his studio and home for non-payment, he escaped to Hawaii with his young son Frankie. There he lived in a bread van, ate fruits off the trees, tripped on magic mushrooms and came close to overdosing on cocaine. A promoter brought him to England where his tour came to a crashing halt when Gaye failed to appear for a command performance before Princess Margaret. His 20-year marriage to Motown ended that same season; the company released 'In Our Lifetime' – a wonderfully eccentric album of philosophical musings – without Marvin's final approval.

I caught up with him in Ostende, Belgium, where he was living off the largesse of yet another European promoter. Walking along the North Sea, strolling through the Grand Place in old Brussels, Marvin described being down and out in London. 'I used the cocaine pipe,' he said, 'to explore the limits of sanity.' Now he was interested in healing. 'Sexual healing,' I suggested, was what he needed when I looked at the violent pornography with which he surrounded himself. He embraced the concept, and within a few minutes we wrote the song together. Now, a dozen years later, I wonder whether he ever understood the meaning.

The success of the song simultaneously led to his resurgence and doom. He returned to America to repeat patterns which had haunted him from the start. His theological sophistication never overcame his Christian fundamentalism, personified by his cross-dressing storefront preacher father. For Marvin Gaye, it was either/or – either sex or salvation, either Jesus or Satan, either heaven or hell. He turned the last months of his life into hell.

As a witness and part-time participant in the drama, I was alternately excited and depressed, amazed and surprised. My friendship with Marvin suffered when he failed to credit me as a co-writer on 'Sexual Healing', a decision that was eventually overturned in my favour. It was agony fighting with my hero, even worse watching my hero slowly lose his mind, knowing there was nothing that I, his biographer, could do except accurately record the poignant facts.

Leave it to Marvin Gaye – crafty, brilliant, unrelentingly

autobiographical – to forge an ending worthy of Sophocles, and even go one better. Desperate to escape his head and leave his body, Trouble Man provoked his father into committing the single act he could never quite execute himself.

Several years before, I had realized that Gaye's heroics were restricted to art, not life. As a college teacher, I used to begin my course by paraphrasing D. H. Lawrence. 'Don't trust the teller,' I'd tell my students, 'trust the tale.' It was a lesson I would have to learn for myself. Marvin Gaye was a teacher. Like his father, he was a frustrated preacher whose humanitarian ambitions remained unfulfilled. As an artist – a rebel against conformity, a social critic, a proud black man who insisted on forging art from the landscape of the ghetto – he was powerful. As a romantic, a man whose music sprang from private heartache and joy, he was irresistible. And as a singer, he was simply magnificent. No-one has ever sculpted harmonies with such subtlety. His split personality was reflected in his many voices – a mellow mid-range, a growling bottom, a silky falsetto. Along with 'I Heard It Through The Grapevine', his multitracked masterpieces – 'What's Goin' On', 'Let's Get It On', 'I Want You' and 'Here, My Dear' – endure as timeless expressions of deep longing and ageless beauty.

I think of Marvin every day, the great enthusiast who, in the blink of an eye, moved so quickly from the light of love to dark despair. Like the man, his music remains fascinating and involved. In the decade after his death, his reputation has grown even greater. The obsession with his sound will not fade. I miss him, not as a hero, but as a human being, fabulous, flawed, wildly creative.

FRONTLINES

Annie Lennox by Julie Burchill

One of the nicest things about 1985 was the rise of Madonna and her cartoon capers, and the decline of the Eurythmics and their neurotic doodlings. I don't know if you remember, but both 1983 and 1984 (the year and the soundtrack) were *lousy* with the Eurythmics. Absolutely everyone loved them. If Leavis had come back to life, his first essay would have been ANNIE LENNOX: GOD OR DEMITASSE? When I saw a shooting star, my wish was invariably a simple one – 'Please, let the Eurythmics die painlessly in a plane crash.' All bad things come to an end, though, and now the Eurythmics boat looks well and truly scuppered. Replaced by Dire Straits as the great consensus sound of last year, everything they touched turned to treading water.

The Eurythmics were the '60s version of the '80s performed by strictly '70s people. He might as well have had HIPPIE tattooed across his forehead, while *she* was a smorgasbord of swinging hang-ups – interest in religions full of Eastern bullshit and marriage to a cult fruitcake (very short, very sweet, very '70s), tax exile in France, erratic and incontinent feminism (one minute insisting that sisters were doing it to themselves, the next collapsing in a heap of well-publicised tears – Margaret O'Brien to director; 'Do you want me to cry out of the left eye, or the right eye, or both at once?' – and telling the world how much she relied on Her Man). Of all the hippies with haircuts – Police, Thompson Twins – to step into the breach after punk, they were the worst.

The power pop cover in 1979; the gender bending and synthesisers in 1983, the famous friends in the 'Who's That Girl?' video; '1984'; the 'authentic' rocking out in 1985; the hitch-your-wagon-to-a-tar (Annie and Dave are Mr and Mrs Beige; any black artist they get their sweaty mitts on is immediately blanched, bleached, blanded into a funky fondue as sure as if they'd been indulging in that face-rot you can buy over the counter in Dalston chemists) usage of Aretha Franklin and Stevie Wonder – such a blatant shopping list of opportunism being in evidence, why do people feel so fondly towards them and give them credit for an integrity they so obviously possess less than zero of?

One reason is The Voice, always spoken of with crypto-religious reverence. People remark on its 'purity' and 'clarity' – but really, who wants purity or clarity from a monster as big bold and brassy and beautiful as pop music? Clarity and purity are what you look for when you're shopping for olive oil. Someone who cried when Sandy Denny died – *that's* the sort of person who likes Annie Lennox's voice.

There are two main schools of chanteuserie; pure and dirty. Dirty is Veronica Bennett, Deborah Harry, Madonna. Pure is Judy Collins, Joni Mitchell, Joan Baez, Annie Lennox. These pure voices are much loved by wimps for the simple reason that they are so unthreatening – they are the voice of the female eunuch. The efforts that some people make to see Miss Lennox as a standard bearer of '80s feminism are perhaps the saddest of the lot, considering her dependence and her much-flaunted instability. She bends over backwards not to offend the boys – 'I love men, I'm mad about them,' she said in a 1983 *Face* interview, adding 'I'm not gay.' What next? – 'I want to travel, meet people and save myself for Mr Right'?

Lennox is the anti-Madonna; tasteful where Miss M is tacky, nervous where she is assured, in need of care and protection where Madonna is tough. It's the difference between Mary

Pickford and Theda Bara, between wimp and vamp. And where Madonna embodies a lot of what is good about pop – honest to goodness blood, sweat and lipgloss – Lennox stands for a lot that is rotten – particularly the crawling conceit inherent in the public display of psychic wounds – 'MINE are special!' – to an extent not seen since the days of whine and neuroses singer-songwriter early '70s.

Madonna presents herself unelaborately, slashed boldly in a few primary-coloured strokes as a cartoon character – gambler, material girl – with simple needs – a holiday, an angel, to dress you up. Her ego is all surface flash. With Annie Lennox, the self-regarding selling-point goes all the way through, like a stick of rock. A genuinely interesting person doesn't mind being seen as a cartoon character; a frigging bore, on the other hand, will have 19 nervous breakdowns in order to prove to the world how uniquely intricate and complex they are.

As Peter York pointed out in a conversation about American Presidents in *The Hudson*, it is much less Me Generation to present yourself in a very self-assured way – Reagan/Madonna – then it is to present yourself as a *human being* with a whole megillah of *doubts* and *crises* – Carter/Lennox. A typically self-centred only child, Miss Lennox left classical music because there was no room for personal expression (tell that to Yitzhak Perlman), explaining a song, she said 'Once I had a boyfriend, and he died. I tried to think about the little things that summed him up and it ended up being about me.' It is fair to expect that if Miss Lennox was asked to copy a map of Kurdistan on to a piece of paper, it would end up being about her. She is just that sort of person. Where Jean Brodie meets Yoko Ono, you have Annie Lennox – roving ambassador of that past, that foreign country, the Annie Hall Years. You listen, Me Gen.

(They are 'Dave' and 'Annie', not David and Anne – note the instant intimacy, the Nescafe sincerity – very creepy-crawly touchy-feelie, *very Annie Hall*.)

Curiously, it is being such aesthetic horrors that makes them essential to a great many people, the sort of person who *really doesn't believe* that Diane Keaton should be hung from a meat hook and poked with electric cattle prods for her heinous crimes against civilisation and celluloid. Like Sting, Dire Straits and Phil Collins they are there to help the grey-haired blue-jeaned boys sleep safely at night, singing Horlicks. They are the Consensus Sound, here to blank out the scary/sexy sound of spitting boys and screaming girls. The only thing that punk and teenthrob had in common was that they both threatened to repossess El Pop as the property of the young, to make a pop playground safe for under-25s. The Consensus Sound changed all that, making, as another of their crummy number had it, music for penthouse *and* pavement, playground *and* poolside. What matters is that everyone can understand it; what doesn't seem to matter, and should be the only criterion in pop, is that this music as well as being classless and mindless is sexless and soulless. Just look at the Consensus Soundsters; not one of them – with the possible exception of Sting, if you like men who look like Malcolm McDowell after a car crash – is yummy. They all look like social workers.

Of course, there's nothing wrong with our pop stars looking like social workers – if you think the big beat started with Clifford T. Ward rather than Elvis Presley. Personally, I believe that pop is about EEK! and POW! and WHAM! and all those other vulgar pop art noises. But then, I wouldn't vote SDP either – so who am I to make judgements about today's Consensus sound?

HOME THOUGHTS FROM ABROAD

Morrissey by Frank Owen

It's a long way from Whalley Range, is Cleveland. A long way indeed from the Collyhurst cut-throats, city hobgoblins and the Stretford beer monsters so central to Morrissey's waking nightmares. What of Central Library, Whitworth Street gent's toilets, the Arndale Centre, Piccadilly all night bus station? What of the fluttering hearts and flashing Stanley Knives? We'll come to that later. But first, ladies and gentlemen, I present Cleveland.

The Smiths are encamped in the middle of a civic pride that burns about them like a beacon aspiring to light up the rest of America. No longer is this city content to be known as 'the armpit of the USA', to be the butt of a thousand Johnny Carson jokes, to be lampooned for its dullness by 'Saturday Night Live' with their 'Cleveland Vice' skit. No longer the Stoke-On-Trent of the Midwest, the 'mistake on the lake' (Cleveland is on the shores of Lake Erie) now proclaims itself as the 'best location in the nation'. Paper hats, mugs, tee-shirts that read 'If you don't believe in your city, no-one else will' are piled high in the shops.

The mayor refers to his domain as the 'ALL AMERICAN CITY'. The propaganda surges out of the City Hall printing presses with all the fervour of a micropatriotism hot on the campaign trail. No longer will naughty old Randy Newman sing 'Burn On' – a paean to Cleveland's Cuyahoga River which, a decade ago, was so full of chemicals that a spark from a broken

Zippa lighter would have sent the whole thing up. The city is resurging – and how.

Part of Cleveland's renewed civic pride is its rock'n'roll past. 'The rock'n'roll capital of the world' runs the legend. The local radio station, WMMS, has won the Rolling Stone readers' poll for the best radio station seven years on the trot. Clevelanders frequently boast of the superstars that launched their Stateside careers in Cleveland: David Bowie, Fleetwood Mac and the Boss himself. With fervour, if not funk, on their side, the Cleveland self-improvement campaign has paid off.

Soon to be set in the city crown is what they regard as their most glittering gem to date: The Rock And Roll Hall Of Fame. This august edifice will house both museum and auditorium, and will provide lectures and academic programmes on rock's rich tapestry. Cleveland, Ohio (population 558,000), collected 650,000 signatures on petitions demanding this honour and, at the same time, lodged 110,000 phone calls to America's national daily, USA Today. In pursuit of its objective, Cleveland presented the following persuasive arguments: deejay Alan Freed first coined the phrase 'rock'n'roll' in Cleveland in 1951 and, a year later, Cleveland hosted the nation's first rock'n'roll concert, The Moondog Coronation Ball. Perhaps when the place is built they'll invite Professor Steven Morrissey to give a lecture on how he made rock'n'roll celibacy sexy and, in the process, made a fortune.

The other dominating manifestation of this civic pride is the accommodation of the yuppie that can be seen everywhere in the city. The Flats is the equivalent of London's Dockland: warehouse apartments, expensive antique shops, nautical stores, sculpture galleries and posh restaurants arising out of the city's industrial poor image past. This gentrification has produced places like the Burgess Grand Cafe, a favoured location for the pasta and Perrier set. Amid the fin de siecle decor – somewhere between Victoriana and Art Nouveau, but precisely where I'm not sure – Cleveland's yupward mobiles power breakfast. But even the tall canvas panels of willowy nymphs, the corner mural after Gustav Klimt or the smell of nouvelle-Ohio cuisine can't re-write history. Now and again the corners of the new city peel off, the blue collar past showing through to the present.

To the rear of The Smiths' Music Hall venue, the National Rib Cook-Off is in full grill. 'More like National Slaughter Day,' mutters Meat-Is-Murder drummer, Mike Joyce. Some kind of national showcase for those in the barbeque trade, big men with big appetites eat big meat and the aroma of roasting ribs and other meaty hunks drifts over to irritate the noses of The Smiths fans waiting to be ushered into the Queen's presence.

Smith fandom, USA style, is nothing like its British counterpart. Dressed in punky fancy dress, with orthodontic braces appearing to be the main fashion accessory, this lot had none of the grubby self-righteousness of their British equivalents. The ones I talked to I liked. I especially liked their obsessive dedication – 'The Smiths' scrawled in felt tip on their arms, the way they had professed to have given up meat as soon as they heard 'Meat Is Murder'. It reminded me of the Osmonds fans I used to know who had renounced the C of E in order to become Mormons.

A brief taped intro (Prokofiev's 'Romeo And Juliet' culture vultures) and The Smiths hit the stage with 'There Is A Light That Never Goes Out' – all thrills and spills and chills down the spine.

With his off-the-bum jeans and off-the-shoulder shirts, Morrissey is as gorgeously camp as ever, assaulting the male myths of rock idolatry with his usual little-bit-of-delicate-sleaze-and-a-lot-of-tease routine – the missing link between Norman Wisdom and Joe Dallesandro. Morrissey doesn't need to have sex in private because he does it all on stage. Don't be fooled by the coy boy, Miss Goody Two Shoes pronouncements: Morrissey owes more to Little Richard than he would care to admit.

In the past, The Smiths have erred on the side of private gloom. Not tonight. With their best ever album behind them, The Smiths have now achieved something approaching the perfect pitch with a collective voice that is funny, fluent and profound. Morrissey's switches of register – one moment coming on all wry and ironic, with a keen eye for the comic detail, the next, deadly serious, delicately recording certain feelings and stripping them down to the bare bones – are now beguiling rather than gauche. What strikes you most about The Smiths, these days, is Morrissey's longing for passionate speech – the desire to say something that matters, to say something that above all else, will *move* the listener.

In an ironic age, this is a difficult task and, in the past, it has left The Smiths wide open to charges of a wayward, wimpy mooniness. But Morrissey the lovelorn dickhead is no more. Welcome, Morrissey, the possessor of a generously comic higher intuition. As somebody who hated the majority of 'Meat Is Murder' that is something that I thought I would never admit to.

The band climax the set with 'The Queen Is Dead' against a giant image of the most beautiful man in the world, Alain Delon. A swift dash back to the hotel and Morrissey spends most of the night politely answering calls from swooning fans.

Defunkt sex

'Sex is hard work just like everything else. I'd rather laugh in bed than do it.' Andy Warhol

The Sexual Hangover, No Sex, Defunkt Sex, Post-Sexual Sex, call it what you will, but sex just isn't sexy anymore. In America, No Sex has reached epidemic proportions and it's not just the fear of AIDS and herpes. For 30 years we've had sex saturation in the guise of a sexual revolution and candid sex has now become candied sex – sex as the boundless sweetshop of sexual identity and consumption. It was inevitable that, after the Grand Bouffe, abstinence would set in. Some people like to try a new thing just for the heck of it and No Sex is the new thing.

As Sylvia Lotringer has written: 'Revolutions are never good news for queens. When everything is permitted, nothing is extraordinary. Sex has ceased to be extraordinary.' And if there is one thing that Little Mo wants to be, then it's extraordinary. Along with the likes of Germaine Greer and Andy Warhol,

Morrissey has been a key propagandist for the Celibate Tendency. Giving up sex has become a declaration of independence. Sex is such a hassle, such a bore, such a waste – think of all the time and energy spent in the search and consummation. But can anyone really overcome sex? While you can live without sex (after all, monks do it), can you live without desire? But we'll come to that later.

Meanwhile I'm sitting in my hotel room at Stoufers Inn On The Square, waiting to be summoned to the 11th floor to interview the Great One. On the telly Doctor Ruth, America's renowned down-home sex therapist, is counselling Bert from Ohio about the lumps on his penis. Doctor Ruth offers firm but frank advice: 'Go to the Doctor, Bert.'

The phone rings. It's Morrissey awaiting my presence. So I collect my tape recorder, my notebook, my best knowing smile and a new packet of Kleenex and set off to meet him.

Morrissey's propensity to speak about No Sex has become such an explicit, expected and expedient feature of The Smiths' interview experience that it takes a certain amount of courage on behalf of the interviewer not to touch the subject. Me, I'm a born coward so I ask him has liberation from sex replaced sexual liberation as a radical demand? First off I get the coyboy routine.

'That's difficult for me to answer, because, personally, I have nothing to do with sex, nothing whatsoever. I'm not a tremendous authority on sexuality in general, so I can't really say.'

Oh come on, Morrissey. You harp on about sex all the time. Is it just a pose or is it born out of a reaction against the way rock'n'roll masculinity is traditionally presented?

'Mmm, well, yes. There's all those very tangled bits of seaweed but, in essence, I don't think, without wanting to sound self-congratulatory, that anyone with views such as mine has been successful in the rock'n'roll sense. And that makes me, if you like, vaguely unique but really I'm not plotting anything I'm just dramatically, supernaturally, non-sexual.

'In The Smiths song, "Stretch Out And Wait", there is a line

"God, how sex implores you". To make choices, to change and to be different, to do something and make a stand, and I always found that very, very encroaching on any feelings that I felt that I just wanted to be me, which was somewhere between this world and the next world, somewhere between this sex and the next sex, but nothing really political, but nothing really threatening to anybody on earth and nothing really dramatic. Just being me as an individual and not wishing to make any elaborate, strangulating statements.'

Do you like strong women?

'Yes I do . . . Germaine Greer for instance. I would like to eventually turn into Germaine Greer.'

At the moment, she's been harping on about how, in this post-pill age, women are treated like do-nuts and that sex is a waste of time.

'It is! It's a waste of batteries. If we all had to face each other as individuals, as human beings, we'd all be petrified. People thrive on barriers and descriptions and loopholes.'

Isn't this asexual chic merely a refusal of maturity – a fey, adolescent form of sexuality that speaks of sweaty socks and masturbation in locked bedrooms?

Morrissey is indignant. 'Not at all because you make it sound slightly retarded and it certainly isn't. I think that's a wrong image, I think that's a deliberate slur. I certainly never had smelly socks . . . but don't ask me about masturbation.' He laughs.

Free at last. Free at last. Free from sex. But can we ever really be free? Morrissey's genital continence might be strategy to rise above the debased form or rock'n'roll sexuality we know today with its obsessive phallic focus. Asexuality might restore sexuality to its fullness as a non-goal-orientated experience. Asexuality might be a form of sex strike, a consumer boycott, something radical and special. But, more likely, it's just another swing of the pendulum – after sex comes No Sex. It wouldn't surprise me to find, in a couple of years time, Morrissey eulogising the joys of fist-fucking and water sports.

Black pop conspiracy

'POP has never been this divided,' wrote Simon Reynolds in his much-lauded, recent piece on the indie scene, referring to the chasm that now exists between indie-pop and black pop. The detestation that your average indie fan feels for black music can be gauged by the countless letters they write to the music press whenever a black act is featured on the front page.

It's a bit like the late Sixties all over again with a burgeoning Head culture insisting that theirs is the 'real' radical music, an intelligent and subversive music that provides an alternative to the crude showbiz values of black pop.

Morrissey has further widened this divide with the recent single, 'Panic' – where 'Metal Guru' meets the most explicit denunciation yet of black pop. 'Hang the deejay' urges Morrissey. So is the music of The Smiths and their ilk racist, as Green claims?

'Reggae, for example, is to me the most racist music in the entire world. It's an absolute total glorification of black supremacy... There is a line when defence of one's race becomes an attack on another race and, because of black history and oppression, we realise quite clearly that there has to be a very strong defence. But I think it becomes very extreme sometimes.

'But, ultimately, I don't have very cast iron opinions on black music other than black modern music which I *detest*. I detest Stevie Wonder. I think Diana Ross is awful. I hate all those records in the Top 40 – Janet Jackson, Whitney Houston. I think they're vile in the extreme. In essence this music doesn't say anything whatsoever.'

But it does, it does. What it says can't necessarily be verbalised easily. It doesn't seek to change the world like rock music by speaking grand truths about politics, sex and the human condition. It works at a much more subtle level – at the level of the body and the shared abandon of the dancefloor. It won't change the world, but it's been said it may well change the way you walk through the world.

'I don't think there's any time any more to be subtle about anything, you have to get straight to the point. Obviously to get on 'Top Of The Pops' these days, one has to be, by law, black. I think something political has occurred among Michael Hurl and his friends and there has been a hefty pushing of all these black artists and all this discofied nonsense into the Top 40. I think, as a result, that very aware younger groups that speak for now are being gagged.'

You seem to be saying that you believe that there is some sort of black pop conspiracy being organised to keep white indie groups down.

'Yes. I really do.'

Morrissey goes on: 'The charts have been constructed quite clearly as an absolute form of escapism rather than anything anyone can gain any knowledge by. I find that very disheartening because it wasn't always that way. Isn't it curious that practically none of these records reflect life as we live it? Isn't it curious that 93½ per cent of these records reflect life as it isn't lived? That foxes me!

'If you compare the exposure that records by the likes of Janet Jackson and the stream of other anonymous Jacksons get to the level of daily airplay that The Smiths receive – The Smiths have had at least 10 consecutive chart hits and we still can't get on Radio 1's A list. Is that not a conspiracy? The last LP ended up at number two and we were still told by radio that nobody wanted to listen to The Smiths in the daytime. Is that not a conspiracy? I do get the scent of a conspiracy.

'And, anyway, the entire syndrome has one tune and surely that's enough to condemn the entire thing.'

People say that about The Smiths. And it seems to me that you're foregrounding something that isn't necessarily relevant to a lot of black music, especially hip-hop. It's like me saying that I don't like The Smiths because they don't use a beatbox.

'The lack of melody is not the only reason that I find it entirely unlistenable. The lyrical content is merely lists.'

Do you dislike the macho masculinity of many of the records?

'No. I don't find it very masculine.'

Well, a lot of it is about . . .

'What? Chicks?' he sniggers.

No. One upmanship. Having the best, the biggest.

'Mmmm. It's just not the world I live in and, similarly, I'm sure they wouldn't care that much for The Smiths. I don't want to feel in the dock because these are some things I dislike. Having said that, my favourite record of all time is "Third Finger, Left Hand" by Martha And The Vandellas which can lift me from the most doom-laden depression.'

Why is that people like yourself can eulogise Sixties black pop and yet be so antagonistic towards present-day black pop? Nostalgia?

'No. It was made in the Sixties but I don't listen to the record now and say "Well, I must remember this is a Sixties record and it's 1986 now so let's put it all into perspective." It has as much value now as ever. We shouldn't really talk in terms of decades.'

It seems to me that nostalgia is something that afflicts the whole indie scene. They can't face up to the fact that pop music is no longer created; it's assembled, quoted and collated. That's why so many indie bands are caught in a timewarp with 'real' musicians playing 'real' music on 'real' instruments. Isn't that the reason for The Smiths' much vaunted Luddite tendencies? Can't hi-tech have a liberating aspect, enabling non-musicians to construct music? And isn't this well in tune with the punk ethic that the indie scene is supposed to draw its inspiration from?

'I hate the idea of having to learn to play the instruments, too. But it makes it so easy. It means that anyone with no arms, no legs nor a head can suddenly make a superb LP which will obviously go platinum. I can't help it. I love Wigan, I love George Formby, I love bicycles. I love Wigan's Ovation.

'Hi-tech can't be liberating. It'll kill us all. You'll be strangulated by the cords of your compact disc.'

Suddenly Morrissey breaks off and stares at me as I munch my way through the giant bowl of crisps on his hotel room table. 'Why are you eating all those stale crisps?' he asks. 'You'll regret it in the morning.'

There's a knock at the door. 'Shall we see who it is?' I suggest.

'No. It's probably a cockroach,' he replies. Such is the Morrissey interview experience.

In every home a heartache

'And someone falls in love,
And someone is beaten up,
and the senses being dulled are mine.' 'Rusholme Ruffians'.

Legend has it that sometime in the late Seventies, somewhere in the north-west of England, there existed a mythical city called Manchester. To the north of the city lay the infamous Collyhurst Perrys – a vicious cult of midgets dedicated to Jumbo cords, wedge haircuts, Fred Perry tee-shirts and easy violence. Morrissey remembers them well. So do I, especially the night my skull cracked open under the weight of a specially sharpened heavyweight Perry belt-buckle (Perrys were always good at CSE metalwork).

'They're still there. Trouble is, now they're all 33 and they're still doing the same thing. The memories I have of being trapped in Piccadilly Bus Station while waiting for the all night bus or being chased across Piccadilly Gardens by some 13-year-old Perry from Collyhurst wielding a Stanley Knife. Even when I was on the bus I would be petrified because I would always be accosted. They were the most vicious people. They would smack you in the mouth and ask you what you were looking at after.'

They were all so small, as if suffering from sort of genetic defect.

'Hence "City Hobgoblins" by The Fall. What's the line? . . . "Half my height, three times my age".'

They always used to hang around the Arndale Shopping Centre.

'I know. On "The Queen Is Dead", "Never Had No-one Never", there's a line that goes "When you walk without ease/ on these/the very streets where you were raised/I had a really bad dream/it lasted 20 years, seven months and 27 days/Never had no-one never". It was the frustration that I felt at the age of 20 when I still didn't feel easy walking around the streets on which I'd been born, where all my family had lived – they're originally from Ireland but had been here since the Fifties. It was a constant confusion to me why I never really felt this is my patch. This is my home. I know these people. I can do what I like, because this is mine. It never was. I could never walk easily.'

I know what you mean. In one way I despise Manchester and yet I still have a deep affection for the place.

'That's because we're in Cleveland not in Manchester,' he laughs.

If the Perrys didn't get you, then the beer monsters were waiting around the corner. I still remember studying the football results to see if City or United had lost, in order to judge the level of violence to be expected in the city centre that night.

I can remember the worst night of my life with a friend of mine, James Maker, who is the lead singer in Raymonde now. We were heading for Devilles (a gay club). We began at the Thompson's Arms (a gay pub), we left and walked around the corner where there was a car park, just past Chorlton Street Bus Station. Walking through the car park, I turned around and, suddenly, there was a gang of 30 beer monsters all in their late twenties, all creeping around us. So we ran. We bolted. Unfortunately, they caught James and kicked him to death but somehow he managed to stand up and start running. So James and I met in the middle of Piccadilly Bus Station and tried to get on a bus that would go back to Stretford because they were chasing us and they were really hefty beer monsters.

'We jumped onto the bus and thought "Saved!" and turned around and saw it was completely empty, no driver. We thought "My God! We're trapped on the bus!" They were standing at the door shouting "Get out, get out!" We had all these coins and we just threw them in their faces and flew out of the bus. We ran across the road to a bus going to God knows where. We slammed four fares down and ran to the back seat. Suddenly the emergency doors swing open and these tattooed arms fly in – it was like "Clockwork Orange". The bus is packed, nobody gives a damn. So we run upstairs and the bus begins to move and we end up in Lower Broughton. For some reason we get out and we're in the middle of nowhere – just hills.

'On top of this hill we could see a light from this manor house. We went up these dark lanes to the manor house and knocked on the door. It was opened by this old senile, decrepit Teddy Boy, no younger than 63, with blue suede shoes on. "Do you have a telephone?" "No."

'We had to walk back to Manchester. It took us seven days. We came back home to my place, finally, at something like five a.m. and listened to "Horses" by Patti Smith and wept on the bed. That's my youth for you in a nutshell.'

Life for the would-be Bohemian in Manchester was always hard. Pre-punk, those seeking sanctuary from the patrolling behemoths covered in vomit, had little alternative but to take refuge in the gay clubs, like Dickens (a sleaze pit where your feet stuck to the floor when you walked in), or the gay pubs, like the Thompson's Arms, the Rembrandt or the Union (the hippest spot of degeneracy in town – full of trannies with plastic legs).

'The gay scene in Manchester,' says Morrissey, 'was a little bit heavy for me. I was a delicate bloom. Do you remember the Union? Too heavy for me, as was Dickens. The Rembrandt I could take. It was a bit kind of craggy. There was no place, at that time, in Manchester, in the very early stages, that one could be surrounded by fascinating, healthy people' (pause) 'fascinating, healthy bikers for example. It was always like the cross-eyed, club-footed, one-armed, whatever!

'The gay scene in Manchester was always atrocious. Do you remember Bernard's Bar, now Stuffed Olives?'

I do indeed. I particularly remember the endless stream of ageing music hall acts that Bernard booked (Mr Memory men, jugglers, etc) in order to create what he thought was an upmarket ambience. Perhaps that's where the inspiration for 'Frankly, Mr Shankly' came from? I also remember that you were kicked out if you dared so much as snigger at the appalling turns.

'If one wanted peace and to sit without being called a parade of names then that was the only hope. Bernard's Bar was fine for a while but what I was really into was the music.' That's where punk fitted in.

'Nineteen seventy-five was the worst year in social history. I blame "Young Americans" entirely. I hated that period – Disco Tex and the Sex-o-lettes, Limmy and Family Cooking. So when punk came along, I breathed a sigh of relief. I met people. I'd never done that before.'

Punk changed everything. The Manchester Scene was born. Sweaty nights at the Electric Circus watching The Sex Pistols, The Buzzcocks, Blondie, Television et al and sordid nights at The Ranch, a one-time gay club run by female impersonator Foo Foo Lamar.

'I never liked The Ranch. I have a very early memory of it and it was very, very heavy. I never liked Dale Street. There was something about that area of Manchester that was too dangerous.'

You big jessy, you big girl's blouse, Morrissey. But he's right. It was dangerous and, with the increased media visibility of punk, the violence got worse. You see, punks were not only faggots, they were uppity faggots as well. They made music, they wrote poetry, and, of course, they dressed up. It was as if they were protesting against the limits of prole Northern experience: 'There must be more to life than *this*,' they said. Something more than the endless round of beer-swilling and snogging at Tiffanys followed by a boring day on the factory floor or in the office.

At the heart of the scene was an understanding by the people involved that they were destined for something other than exploitation. The Manchester scene wasn't a product of Manchester but a triumph over it. It was a battle against some of the longest odds possible to be something other than dull prole pond-life. So what happened? Fame, success, a little bit of money – and the cries of 'Sellout' – the usual story. So was it that special?

Morrissey thinks it was: 'It was a breed of people. It was like the wartime scarcity crowd who have gone now. Compared to what we have now, good heavens, we *had* something then. We have nothing now. It was a very creative time.'

Do you think it was something to do with the water?

'It definitely began with the water. It must also have something to do with Central Library. I was born in Central Library – in the crime section.'

If any Manchester bohemian worth his salt spent his nights at The Electric Circus and The Ranch then his days were spent at Central Library. There you could spend hours searching through their extensive collection of fiction from all corners of the globe and, at lunch, you could hang out with the older bohemian set in the basement cafe. And what about the toilets? I remember it well.

'I used to love it at Central Library. The smell and the sound. How, when you dropped a book, the sound would echo around the place. Musical, musical! The toilets were guarded by uniformed gorillas. It was like guerilla warfare going on in there – an awful, frightening place.'

What about Whitworth Street toilets (an infamous cottage)?

'Ahh, yes, Whitworth Street toilets. I never knew Bert Tilsley. But let's steer away from public toilets.'

Shall we leave Manchester now?

'Da dee-dee. Do we have to? We still haven't discussed the hours and days I queued up outside Coronation Street waiting to get Minnie Cauldwell's autograph.'

I was never a large Coro fan.

'A severe large gap in your cultural capabilities.'

Ah, Manchester – the music, the clothes, the violence, the grace, the sex . . .'

'I don't remember any sex,' says Morrissey coyly.

Which is where we came in.

POOR BOY, RICH BOY GEORGE

Culture Club by Mick Brown

From the moment the Culture Club star had begun to rise, George was an incessant presence at the offices of his record-label, Virgin, gee-ing up record 'pluggers', arranging video sessions and superintending the fan-mail. Gone was the frenetic nightclubbing; in its place, chastening pronouncements on the decadence of a previous generation of rock stars, and an anti-drug regimen which promised immediate dismissal for anyone in the group who might indulge.

It was a professionalism that withstood even the tempestuousness of his relationship with Moss. On tour, the pair would squabble incessantly in a fashion that would drive fellow travellers to distraction. 'God knows what they got from each other,' says one who toured with them. 'They were like children.'

'The whole Culture Club thing of going from nothing to mass popularity was George's dream,' says another associate of the time. 'He always wanted to be recognised as a songwriter, but he loved being a media celebrity, and from day one the press was always the most important thing. George was completely hungry for fame, and once it arrived he became addicted to it.'

As the Culture Club phenomenon grew, George took to ringing up the press office from all over the world, demanding that his press-clippings be read over to him. It was a time-consuming task, for the lessons learned in the early days – his innate understanding of the media's appetite for 'news' – had stood him in good stead. 'I knew that if I walked into the ladies' toilet that it would make the *Sun* – so I did it.'

The sheer volume of press first astonished then alarmed his publicity handlers at Virgin. George wilfully made himself as available as possible, to the point of telephoning journalists to dispense titbits. Matters came to a head in Japan, on the group's first world tour in 1983, when Ronnie Gurr, Virgin's press officer, attempted to keep the accompanying press corps at bay and was berated by Tony Gordon for being 'rude to Fleet Street'. Gurr resigned. George, he now says, was blind to a fundamental truth of celebrity; that it depends on the maintenance of mystique.

George began to discover that fame is an entity dangerously susceptible to the laws of gravity. For a group so dependent on the oxygen of publicity the growing indifference of newspapers to his activities was a serious danger. There were signs, too, that the group was becoming complacent. The third album, *Waking Up the House on Fire*, was written and recorded in haste after nine months' solid touring. The lack of strong songs told and the 'Medal Song', released for Christmas 1984, became the first Culture Club single since 'Do You Really Want to Hurt Me?' two years before not to reach the top 20. The seemingly indefatigable ardour of the fans was beginning to wear thin.

George's personal life was also beginning to fall apart. The relationship with Moss had finally exploded into anger, recrimination and then bitter silence over Moss's relationship with a girl. George, according to friends, was 'devastated'. Without Moss's moderating influence, the old hedonistic George began to re-emerge.

In Paris, George, now world famous, was the centre of attention among models, photographers and hangers-on, all of them sharing cocaine. At a nightclub, a photographer palmed him a packet of heroin, which he snorted for the first time. He was violently sick, but not discouraged. Within a month he was taking up to a gramme a week. Soon it would be more.

Having time on his hands did not help. 'I began to realise that all the time I was successful, I had never thought about *why* I was being successful, or what it meant. And I suddenly realised that it wasn't what I wanted; that it wasn't enough, if you like.' The momentum of Culture Club was running down. The row between George and Jon Moss had affected everybody, and the prospect of continued touring was more than anyone could face. Two years at the top had, anyway, brought the group an embarrassment of riches. Their tax advisers counselled exile. The manager Tony Gordon, and Roy Hay, the guitarist, moved to Marbella; bass-player Mikey to Paris. In a bid to repair their relationship, George pleaded with Jon to go with him to New York. Moss refused, and George set off alone.

The seeds of dissolution sown over the last few months in London and Paris found fertile ground in New York. His old friend Marilyn was along for the ride, and life became an endless round of nightclubs and parties, with a growing circle of new acquaintances: 'trashy coke dealers,' George now remembers, 'disgusting people, and dregs'. John Maybury, his old friend from Warren Street, turned up in New York and was shocked at George's condition, and the way he had become a caricature of everything he had once professed to despise.

'Everything about him had become scary. He was overweight, over-made-up, grotesque. But on the club scene there was this sycophantic thing that because he was Boy George whatever he did was OK.'

For George the pretence of being 'a bright young thing, going out to clubs', was becoming inescapable. 'I began to realise,' he says, 'that I was killing myself.' A doctor confirmed his diagnosis. 'He said I could catch Aids from the way I was behaving. That frightened me. I stopped, left New York and went home. And carried on doing heroin.'

The London club world where George had disported himself three years before had changed; the extremities of style which he had helped to pioneer had been eclipsed by even further excesses of self-invention. At the once-weekly Taboo Club, held in a tawdry Leicester Square disco called Circus Maximus, Leigh Bowery, a fashion designer and exhibitionist, held court over a menagerie of exotica drawn from the fashion and art-student worlds.

Yet the old mood of carefree exhilaration had gone. While the good times of three years before had run on natural energy, now they ran on drugs: heroin, barbiturates and the 'designer' drug Ecstasy. 'The whole scene,' Maybury remembers, 'was haywire and mad. Everything was available, and everybody was taking it. Trojan and I would sit at home saying someone is going to die. It never occurred to us that it would be one of us.'

George, too, was mindful of the dangers. 'Every time I took heroin I would think, is this it? Am I going to die? I was always afraid.' He had begun reading Freud, 'wondering whether I was behaving like this because I'd had an unhappy childhood; or was I sexually insecure? Then I realised it was both.'

Throughout 1985, Culture Club had continued to perform to ecstatic response in America and Japan. But George's erratic behaviour was having a progressively debilitating effect on the group's activities. There was growing anxiety at Virgin Records. George and Virgin's chairman Richard Branson had met only briefly before, but in April 1986 Branson wrote to his artist, who was staying with Marilyn in Jamaica. It was becoming plain to everyone, Branson asserted, that George had a problem which he was not willing to acknowledge – 'So clear that one newspaper is now offering £50,000 to anyone who can prove it. You believe you have this problem under control, but it's patently not true.' George, he said, should 'acknowledge the problem, and let us help you . . . before it's too late'.

Branson offered to put George in touch with Meg Paterson, a doctor whose 'black box' treatment had cured Eric Clapton of heroin addiction. It would be three months before George would accept Branson's offer. But the warning about Fleet Street was real enough. In its role as arbiter of private morality, the press's interest was no longer in praising George, but in burying him.

The first blow was struck on June 10, 1986, when the *Daily Mirror* ran a story alleging that George had taken cocaine. The source was a rock photographer named David Levine, who was alleged to have received a fee of £15,000 for his story. In the pop music world word continued to circulate that richer pickings were still to be had. What nobody could have anticipated was that the real story would be had for nothing.

The first intimation that Gerry O'Dowd had of his son's drug problem came in October 1985, in Montreux, where Culture Club was completing recording of its fourth album, *From Luxury to Heartache*. Relaxing in George's rented villa on the shores of Lake Geneva, Gerry O'Dowd was alarmed to note that, for the first time, people connected with the group were taking drugs. George poured balm on his fears; the most he had had was 'the odd smoke' of cannabis.

But at a party on Boxing Day 1985 at George's Hampstead mansion, his worst fears were confirmed. 'I realised then there were people around George who were not his friends. They were a cancer.

'The one thing that was very hurtful was that George shut us out,' says O'Dowd. 'We became his enemies.'

For six months, the situation deteriorated. Gerry O'Dowd began a remarkable vigil, monitoring the comings and goings at George's home, accumulating a dossier on all his son's drugs contacts. On one occasion he trailed a 'courier' carrying £800 of George's money to buy drugs to a house in North London. He telephoned the police to tip them off, but nothing happened.

Convinced now that his son would die unless something was done, Gerry O'Dowd went to George's St John's Wood mews house for a final confrontation. George had locked himself in the bathroom and refused to come out, answering his father's pleas with a torrent of abuse. 'Do you want to die?' Gerry O'Dowd shouted. 'I'll see if you want to die.' O'Dowd told his son he would burn the house down. 'I lit some paper, put it out and held the smoke to the door. George opened the door and came running down the stairs. I said, "See George, you don't want to die." '

That evening, sitting with his youngest son David, Gerry O'Dowd broke down and said he could take no more. 'Don't worry, Dad,' said David. 'I'll do something.' The next day Nick

Ferrari, a showbusiness reporter on the *Sun*, received a telephone call from David O'Dowd offering something which Ferrari remembers would 'absolutely stagger' him: the 'full story' of George's heroin habit. And it would cost the *Sun* nothing. The story which appeared on the front page two days later, 'Junkie George has eight weeks to live', was emblazoned in letters two inches high. George, it claimed, was smoking up to nine grammes of heroin a day, at a cost of £800 – a quantity which doctors had said would almost certainly kill him.

O'Dowd would later explain that he had broken the story in a desperate bid to jolt George to his senses. 'I'd run out of all ideas; the family had run out of ideas; there was nothing more we could do.' While the essence of what the *Sun* printed was true, it was embroidered by what O'Dowd would subsequently claim was a heavy veil of fiction.

'I said my brother was a drug addict. The rest, how long he had to live and all that, is a complete load of crap. All I said to them was that it might be soon that he drops down dead. That was why I did it.'

Whatever the truth, the prospects of reclaiming it were lost in an avalanche of sensationalism. It was a story that had everything: fame, drugs, weird sex; squandered wealth; grace bestowed and scorned. 'George,' says John Maybury, 'had always been a subversive – a drag queen welcomed into the bosom of England. When he was successful he was untouchable. But when it was discovered he was a junkie it was a chance for Fleet Street to take revenge.'

For George, events now began to move at a bewildering pace. On the day on which the *Sun* story was published, he appeared on the *News at Ten* in an attempt to deny it. At his mews house reporters camped on the doorstep and eavesdropped at the windows. For four days, George dodged and ducked to no avail. On the fifth day he vanished.

On Saturday morning, Richard Branson received a telephone call from George's boyfriend, Michael, asking whether Branson could arrange a meeting with Meg Paterson. That same night, under a blanket of secrecy, Branson drove George, Michael and

Paterson to his house in Oxfordshire. 'The idea was that nobody would know where he was,' says Branson.

In the press, the hue and cry for George had also become a clamour for retribution, with Monday's *Daily Mirror* leading the call for 'action' from the police. In the early hours of the following day a squad of detectives, engaged in Operation Culture, raided George's St John's Wood house, and a flat in nearby Westbourne Terrace. No illegal substances were found at George's house, but a number of people, including his brother Kevin and Marilyn, were charged.

Following the raids, the police announced that they were now looking for George himself. Branson immediately told them 'in confidence' that George was under medical supervision. 'I said I would appreciate it if the police did not tell anybody where he was. Since he had done nothing illegal, there was no reason why they should be involved.'

The police initially agreed to Branson's request, but within four days they were informing him that they had changed their minds, and that a warrant was out for George's arrest. By that time George had been moved to the house of Roy Hay, the Culture Club guitarist, in Billericay, Essex. George was nearing the end of the prescribed length of Meg Paterson's 'black box' treatment when police arrested him at Hay's home. Shaking with the tremors of withdrawal, he was taken to Harrow Road police station. 'I gave one statement where I lied, said nothing. They were asking me all those questions about people I knew – did I know that Marilyn took cocaine? I said I couldn't care less whether he shags chandeliers, mate. Then I thought, they're never going to let me out of here. I became terrified and just kept talking.'

It was largely on the basis of his confession that George was charged with possession of heroin. Two weeks later, on the advice of his lawyers, George pleaded guilty to the charge at Marylebone Magistrates Court and was fined £250.

Richard Branson, among others, was perturbed at the conduct of the police. 'You had someone who had gone, voluntarily, for treatment. If every addict thought the police were going to arrest them after they'd gone for care, none of them would. And I think the press were very much responsible. George was being penalised for who he was.'

The chaotic circumstances of his treatment, the interruption by his arrest and continued harassment had all exacted their toll. George was, by his own definition, 'a nervous wreck'.

His pronouncements that the worst was behind him and that he would now embark on a 'crusade' against drugs were well intentioned, but essentially illusory. The next four months would see him wavering between fighting his dependence and succumbing to it. With the failure of Paterson's treatment, George began to take prescribed valium, and then fell back on heroin. Depressed, fearful, 'convinced I was going to die', he began to take methadone – a legally prescribed heroin substitute.

What was clear was that he now needed to set about repairing the damage to his career. He would make a solo album. To help, he called on the services of Michael Rudetsky, a musician and arranger he had befriended in New York.

Rudetsky arrived in Britain on August 4, 1986, carrying with him a card confirming that he had recently completed a drugs detoxification course in America. Customs officials at Gatwick strip-searched him but found no drugs.

The next day, Rudetsky arrived at the offices of Virgin for a meeting with George and the Virgin A&R (artists and repertoire) department. George was 'groggy' from his prescribed drugs, but lucid in discussing ideas for songs. Only Rudetsky, leaving the room to throw up, cast a shadow over the afternoon.

His behaviour the following day was to give more cause for concern. In rehearsals at a studio in Brixton he began drinking heavily and passed out. George poured a carton of orange juice over him to revive him. They returned to George's Hampstead house. At midnight, George left to go to his other home in St John's Wood, leaving Rudetsky with brother Kevin. Later Kevin, too, left. He returned at 4.45 a.m., drunk, to find Rudetsky's corpse in the lounge.

The inquest recorded death by misadventure, after his body

had been found to contain a fatal level of morphine. No explanation was given about where he had acquired it. Speculation that he had smuggled cocaine into Britain in a swallowed condom, which had burst in his stomach, was never confirmed.

Rudetsky's death plunged George into a deeper trough of depression, but he was still determined to work.

At the end of August, George, his boyfriend Michael and the producer Stewart Levine flew out to Montserrat to begin recording. Within a fortnight there were eight songs in the can. 'George was feeding off the situation,' says Ronnie Gurr. 'He felt he couldn't let anybody down.' Back in London, however, to complete recording, the diligence began to evaporate. George had begun to supplement his prescribed drugs with other illegal drugs, and his behaviour was again becoming erratic. Stewart Levine noted that the difference between George in Montserrat and George in London as like 'Jekyll and Hyde'. On one occasion in the studio, Levine confronted George over drugs, challenging him not to disappear to the toilets to take them, but to do it in front of him. After a stern talking to, Levine was able to report that George was 'in fine shape'.

But the respite, such as it was, was only temporary. It would take another three months, and the death of Mark Golding, to persuade Boy George that his own life was worth saving.

At Christmas 1986, Dinah O'Dowd arrived at George's Hampstead mansion to find a newspaper photographer loitering outside the gate. 'What do you want?' she demanded. He replied that he was 'waiting for George to die'.

The power of Fleet Street as executioner, as well as king-maker, was to prove crucial in the story of Boy George. Yet, incredibly, throughout the period of his travails with drugs, George continued to maintain a pact with the press, which, in itself, seemed a measure of his dependence on publicity as a tool to vindicate as well as destroy him.

Throughout the latter part of 1986, he gave a series of interviews which attempted to belie the truth of the drugs problem he continued to suffer. This reached its apotheosis in November 1986 in a front-page interview with the *Sun* headlined 'My Junkie Lies by George', in which the repentant star admitted he had lied in the past about having put drugs behind him. The accompanying photographs, taken by his brother David, strongly suggested he was still not being altogether truthful.

Within a month, as the photographers hovered at the gates, his parents were once again desperately petitioning to have him admitted to a clinic. Maybury's advice was to 'be with him, cuddle him, and don't let him out of your sight'.

That Christmas, George says, was the worst time of his life: heavily sedated by non-addictive drugs, agitated, tearful. 'What I went through was terrible: physical fits, being jerked about and having no control over my body; screaming at people and throwing things. To want to go through that again, you would have to be crazy.'

By New Year's Eve he was through the worst. His doctor, who by chance is also a Buddhist, and had visited each day, introduced him to chanting. George re-emerged into the outside world through the decompression chamber of Buddhist meetings, lectures, and a pantomime version of *Alice in Wonderland*, staged by the Buddhist group in London. It was, he said, the best show he had ever seen in his life. Nobody would suggest that the music was ever going to rival Culture Club, but there was a line from one of the songs that kept running through his head, and runs there still. 'People who live in glasshouses,' it goes, 'shouldn't . . .' Just shouldn't.

MADONNA: THE PROS & CONS

The Material Girl by The Tatler

First there was a midget DJ boyfriend called Jellybean, a prancing disco routine and a look that verged on the putrid One ny buzz. Then she said that losing her virginity was a career move and laughed. One Rolling Stone cover. Then she farmed the fat, did the movie and paid the 22-carat producer. Thirteen million copies of Like a Virgin sold. She had, they said, a shameless elan so she nursed it, rehearsed it, married it and invested it. One sell-out world tour. She was the subject of our random calls: they loved her (loquaciously) and hated her (monosyllabically)

And she don't give a damn.

PRO

EDNA O'BRIEN 'Madonna is terrific: she has an icy aura and a warm heart.'

ALLEN JONES 'I don't have her on file. The person seems delectable and the image seems collectable.'

RALPH STEADMAN 'Da Vinci would have liked to have known her; Rembrandt too.'

MARINA WARNER 'When I first saw her I was fascinated by the way she played with sexual blasphemy. That was a very Italian sense of humour, rather like Cicciolina's election. I liked her best with longer, darker hair, when she looked closer to her Italian roots. Now she's Marilyn Monroe-like, which is a man-made icon of self-sacrifice. I was gripped when I saw her in her underwear. It was very much in place as an outrage.'

GEORGE MELLY 'I think she is tremendously sexy, because of that look of sluttish availability. She's not a great beauty. It's that look of sensuality: not, like Marilyn Monroe, a love object; she's a free spirit.'

JOHN GALLIANO/JASPER CONRAN

JG: Madonna, I just love her. In fact I was the first person in London to get into her.

JC: No you weren't, I was.

JG: Shut up. Even when everybody said she was just a slag I knew she was a star.

JC: I knew it first.

JULIE BURCHILL 'I like Madonna because she looks like a slag and acts like a man – which, as everybody knows, is the best sort of girl. I liked her best a couple of years ago before she started refining herself. Someone must be giving her bad advice or no advice because that marriage, that film, and that last single are not the by-products of a sentient being. I do not think she will get any bigger and I don't know if she is a good actress or singer. She is just very good at being a star: the same way a dwarf is good at being small.'

MARGI CLARKE 'I bet she always attended her history classes at school because IN THE PAST is the message of the Eighties stardom. She is called the modern Monroe but she is actually much more Carole Lombard. She can turn base metal into gold.'

MALCOLM MCLAREN 'I did like her better before she turned into a housewife – the last single was just the sort of stuff housewives like. The most wonderful thing was that crucifix that swung across her navel and the way you would see ten-year-old girls in New York and LA being sexually provocative in imitation of her. But the very best thing about her is that that is her real name.'

ANNAJOY DAVID 'She has set the terms of debate for her career. She chose what she wanted to be and became it: she is honest, she is confident, she is FAB.'

PETER YORK 'Like her or dislike her, she is a force of nature and infinitely improves the quality of my life each time I gaze at that sepia album cover. I particularly liked her subtle and emotive cover version of Jonathan King's "Una Paloma Blanca".'
ANTONY PRICE 'She is the modern Alexis. Millions of people in the world can look good, sing and dance but to push your business package that far almost indicates a Mrs Mafia.'

CON

NICKY HASLAM 'Not really the immaculate conception, is she?'
LADY ANTONIA FRASER 'I never think about Madonna at all.'
VICTORIA GILLICK 'I know nothing about the poor little thing. I only recognise one Madonna.'
WILLIE DONALDSON 'I think she is disgusting. I am 52 you understand, so I don't think she is meant for me.'
MAGENTA DE VINE 'She's an immaterial girl.'
GAVIN STAMP 'I have not knowingly heard her sing. She looks repulsive. I do dislike people with single names.'
GEORGE GALE 'From what I have read about her she seems to be a rather tiresome female.'
STEPHEN FRY 'Definitely a case of hand ball. It is a great injustice that so vain an individual has acquired the reputation for being the best in the world. She does a disservice to womankind. Gary Lineker is much better.'
MICHAEL HEATH 'I thought she was finished, old hat. I do not believe in Madonna, I am an agonistic.'
GLYNN BOYD HARTE 'I have never heard of *it*.'
KATHY ACKER 'She is an image, an image which seems rather in keeping with the times. These days images have power, but you never know who really wields it, who is behind it – a bit like Ronald Reagan.'
WHITNEY HOUSTON (From the *Sun*) 'I would kill my children if they looked like her. Madonna says nasty horrible things like "Go to bed with anyone you want." In the long term I am sure she will just be forgotten. I don't know what she has but I don't like it.' (For the *Tatler*) 'I have never said anything bad about Madonna. She is OK. She has her audience, I have mine.'

NED SHERRIN 'I appear to be the only man in the world she leaves cold.'

THE SUN & THE STAR

Elton John by John Sweeney

Sleazy? Sleazy is not the word. Sleazy comes nowhere near to conveying the full ripeness of the Apollo Club (Members Only), perched in a Soho attic. There has just been a fight outside on the street. The loser, a fresh-faced lad breathing fast, pleads for admission: 'There are bottles out there.' But the pig-necked bouncer is having none of it: 'You are not coming here and getting lairy with me, son.'

Inside, the ambience owes something to a motorway service station urinal. No women are in sight. No one comes to the Apollo for a chat – or indeed the view, a side-on glimpse of the squeaky-clean Swiss Centre through matt-black window blinds and grubbier windows. Elderly businessmen tinker with their gins and tonics. Smut-moustached young men look on, waiting to be picked up, as bored as Tesco check-out girls. They drink, smile queasily and then hit the streets.

It was at the Apollo in early 1987 that the story of Britain's biggest libel action began when the *Sun* newspaper got in touch with a rent-boy turned pimp, 'Graham X', who frequented the club. There followed a series of stories about the rock singer Elton John. The stories, based on Graham X's souped-up confessions, were as untrue as they were nasty. The first, ELTON IN VICE BOYS SCANDAL, published on Wednesday 25 February 1987, contained the gist of all that was to come. Graham X 'confessed' to supplying Elton John and Billy Gaff, a pop manager, with 'at least 10 youngsters, who were each paid a minimum of £100, plus all the cocaine they could stand'.

Elton sued. The *Sun* printed more, and nastier, stories. Elton sued again and again, issuing in all 17 writs against the *Sun* from February to September 1987. The writs led, last Christmas, to a grovelling front-page apology by the *Sun*. It is a grisly and sorry tale, from the rent-boys who lied for the *Sun*'s money to an incredulous RSPCA inspector who was asked to investigate the case of The Dogs That Didn't Bark.

It started with a tip-off. At the beginning of the year, the *Sun* was told by one of its regular sneaks, paid on a story-by-story basis, that a good-looking teenage rent-boy with an angelic face could be sitting on a cracker of a story. The sneak pocketed his money and disappeared from view.

The *Sun* left word at the Apollo that it wanted to get in touch with the rent-boy, later to be called Graham X, but who was known 'up West', that is, in the West End, as 'Barry Alexander' or 'American Barry'. (It is a peculiarly common feature of young people who have broken from their families to claim that they are American or that their family has moved to America.) His real name is Stephen Hardy.

No one should be in the least bit surprised that the *Sun* was interested in the kiss-and-tell stories of a male prostitute. Britain's most profitable newspaper has built its massive sales – at roughly four and a quarter million, more than 10 times as many as those of the *Independent* – on a diet of virulent xenophobia and soft pornography, all streaked with a slickness which is the hallmark of its editor, Kelvin Mackenzie. Mackenzie comes from a family of journalists in south London. On his first paper, as a cub reporter, he was sick over the editor's suede shoes. Such stories have lent weight to the cartoon view of Mackenzie, that he is just a sewer-mouthed yobbo. But Mackenzie is a brilliant tabloid editor, and perhaps the most powerful journalist in the country. Under his stewardship, the *Sun* is dispassionately admired in Fleet Street as a well-made thing. It makes for a repulsive but fascinating read, pored over by 13 million Britons a day.

Stephen Hardy, of course, was and is a regular *Sun* reader. 'Everybody who reads it hasn't got a GCE between them,' he told me, unfairly rubbishing at least one reader – the *Sun*'s editor, who has one GCE, an O-level in art.

Hardy existed – and, to an extent, still does – in a world of rapidly shifting loyalties and fuzzily transmitted reality. In 1987, when he was not quite 20, he was living in Twyford, Berkshire, but making frequent trips 'up West'. Hardy is a blond, slightly built sharp-dresser whose surfeit of identities comes in handy in his line of business. He often speaks with an American accent, although, prosaically, he originally came from a small village somewhere off the M1 near Nottingham. An adopted child, he says that he had been expelled from four schools before posing naked in a male porn magazine. He was paid £100 for this first nude modelling job in 1983, when he was a baby-faced 16. 'I was on the streets with nowhere to go,' he says. 'It was either that or sleeping with people.' Nothing Hardy says should be taken as gospel, but clearly his childhood could hardly be described as conventionally happy.

Suspecting that there might be money in it, Hardy followed up the *Sun*'s approach and phoned Craig Mackenzie on the paper's bizarre column, which features pop gossip and singles charts. Craig Mackenzie, who lives in the shadow of his editor brother, has since left the *Sun* to join the *Daily Express*.

In 1987, Craig, whose *Sun* nickname was the 'Bouncing Bog-Brush', was in a hurry, anxious to prove himself his own man. The old nursery competitiveness between the brothers Mackenzie partly explains why neither of them ever dared get off the ruinous track they were on. It was to cost the *Sun*'s proprietor, Rupert Murdoch, £1 million in damages and, probably, half as much again in costs.

What Hardy told Craig Mackenzie on the phone was sufficiently promising for a *Sun* team to roar into the forecourt of Twyford railway station in Berkshire in a black Porsche. Hardy was impressed, as the journalists had intended. At the time,

Hardy was working as a laundry-presser in the village, earning £120 a week, and living in a council house with his then girlfriend and their baby son.

Hardy told Craig Mackenzie that he had been to several parties thrown by Rod Stewart's former manager, Billy Gaff, at his Great-Gatsby-in-the-Home-Counties kitsch mansion in Finchampstead, near to Elton John's Windsor home and not far from Hardy's Twyford council house. Hardy also told a lurid story about the supplying of other rent-boys, an expenses-paid trip to New York and vast cocaine consumption. Gaff's name cropped up a number of times, but Elton John's name was only mentioned as someone who was on the fringe of the scene.

Billy Gaff is one of the great Seventies rock managers, embodying all the vivid, platform-soled excesses of that era before the greyer Eighties. An interesting, somewhat hyperactive mixture of voluble Irishman and Hollywood camp, he made his first fortune managing Rod Stewart. Gaff went on to repeat his success by managing John Cougar Mellencamp, a hugely popular American singer in the Bruce Springsteen mould. Although Gaff and Elton John know each other, Gaff is a great deal closer to Elton's manager, a Scottish terrier of a man called John Reid. Both men are gay. A friend of mine went to a couple of Billy Gaff's parties at roughly the same time as Hardy. One of the features of both parties was the presence of a knot of effete, sweet-faced young men looking lost.

A story linking rent-boys with Billy Gaff – whether true or untrue – would not cut much ice with the *Sun*'s readers, to whom Gaff was hardly a household name. It was the name 'Elton John' which crackled in the *Sun* journalists' ears. 'Elton John' was what Hardy's new customers wanted to hear, so that was what they got. Hardy was sent a rail ticket and invited down to Wapping to meet the editor.

Hardy has a good recollection of the fateful meeting. He had to brave the NGA pickets, still screaming 'Scab!' after almost a year standing outside the Nato-issue razor wire of Murdoch's massive print plant. In the room were the brothers Mackenzie and the paper's then deputy editor, Dave Shapland, who has since left to run a sports features agency. Hardy got on all right with Craig Mackenzie and Shapland, but he did not warm to the editor: 'I didn't like his attitude. One minute he was a semi-Australian hard-talking guy, the next he was like a puppy.'

To help Craig Mackenzie, who had the responsibility of turning out the Bizarre column, *Sun* writer Neil Wallis was drafted into the Elton John investigation. Wallis had previously worked on the *Sun*'s gutter rival, the *Daily Star*, where he was billed with becoming modesty as 'The World's Greatest Reporter'. Fleet Street legend has it that Wallis, a jovial Mancunian nicknamed 'Wolfman' because of a lupine beard, is something of a 'chancer'. As far as the Press Council goes, the mythology does not bear close examination. According to the council, Wallis is cited in only one adjudication in recent years, for a story entitled THIS CHILD WAS TOLD CHRISTMAS JOY IS EVIL, a minor classic of the genre. As it happens, the Press Council rejected the complaint against Wallis and the paper he then worked for.

A mole at the *Sun* takes up the story:

'After two weeks of investigation, Wallis and Craig Mackenzie felt they were 90 per cent sure that something untoward had gone on at Billy Gaff's house and that drugs were in abundance. Kelvin nagged them for a date. They had rough dates, but nothing specific. Eventually they settled on a specific date, which proved to be a big mistake. Needless to say, there was no discussion whether it was a just story to run. No one at the *Sun* discusses morality.'

On the eve of publication Mackenzie had an intimation of disaster. The front-page splash had been made up: ELTON IN VICE BOYS SCANDAL. He stood in front of it, admiring his handiwork. 'Right then,' he said. 'Let's fackin' go for it. Elton John! We're all going down the pan.' And with that he held his beaky nose and mimicked the pulling of a lavatory chain. The gesture was to prove prophetic.

The story, dated Wednesday 25 February 1987, carried the by-lines Craig Mackenzie and Neil Wallis and was in traditional *Sun* style. The singer, the *Sun* alleged, had snorted cocaine while begging tattooed skinheads to indulge in bondage.

Everything was based on the uncorroborated evidence of a rent-boy – and rent-boys are notoriously bad witnesses – who now says '97 per cent of it was untrue'. According to Hardy, 'I would give them a line and they would write it all up. It was a manufactured story.'

The final paragraph of the front-page story put the usual gutter-tabloid po-faced sanctimony in the mouth of Graham X: 'I am ashamed of what I did. I am speaking out to show how widespread this sort of thing is and to warn other gullible young kids to steer clear of people like these.' The story failed to add that the *Sun* had paid Graham X £2,000 for his altruism, and was to pay him £250 a week most weeks, for the next few months.

For people of my generation, in their thirties, Elton Hercules John is the Vera Lynn *de nos jours*. Songs like 'Goodbye Yellow Brick Road' and 'Saturday Night's Alright (For Fighting)' provided the noise wallpaper at our first parties and teenage discos. More than that, Elton – born Reginald Kenneth Dwight – did not, as Jagger and Lennon did, become a tax exile and disappear off into megastardom. He therefore occupies a homely, warm place in our affections. He was judged ideologically cuddly enough to be the first Western rock star to play the Soviet Union and to visit China. And although he had pink hair long before Johnny Rotten gobbed at 'shocked' journalists, Elton was a friend of Prince Andrew and would willingly fly 12,000 miles to see his beloved Watford, the football club he owns, achieve a goalless draw against Charlton Athletic.

Elton's essential homeliness wasn't in the least compromised by his admission, in 1976, that he was a bisexual: 'There's nothing wrong with going to bed with somebody of your own sex.' Such honesty by a public figure marked a departure from the traditional closet mentality which imprisoned many showbiz homosexuals. It was rewarded by mass chantings of 'Elton John's a poof!' by opposing football fans, chants he braved. Facing up to his potentially destructive experience had a lot to do with the robustness with which he took the *Sun* head on, a decade later.

He is not, however, an angel. His lifestyle in the early Seventies, when he was at the peak of his success, might well have excited the moral seraphim at the *Sun* if they had been minded to paw over it in any great detail. Rumours about him even reached the ears of the Royal Family. According to a recent biography of him, at a concert at The Rainbow in north London in aid of the Queen's Silver Jubilee Trust in 1977, Elton was asked by Princess Alexandra in a backstage conversation: 'Do you take cocaine?' The princess later apologised for the indiscretion.

But when the *Sun* struck in 1987 Elton had been married to recording engineer Renate Blauer for more than three years. It was well-known that the marriage – which was to end effectively that spring – was in trouble, but he had more than his own reputation to protect. Moreover, he was completely innocent of the charges Hardy made. The police later looked into the allegations, but no action was taken. No one who came into regular contact with rent-boys, such as the charities who look after them, or the vice squad, had ever heard of Elton John being talked about as a punter by the boys on the streets. Elton was a wronged man.

When the story broke, the rock star was in Australia, recovering from an operation on a growth in his throat which, at one time, was feared to be cancerous. Friends, including, it is said, Mick Jagger, advised him to ride the storm. If he were to sue, the *Sun* might go looking for dirt. It is a nasty consideration which keeps many public figures at bay.

Nevertheless, the sort of mud the *Sun* was flinging has a habit of sticking. The first to dump Elton were Cadbury's, who had bought him up to front a major promotional campaign for their chunky-bar Dairy Milk, Whole Nut, and Fruit and Nut chocolate. Minutes before the ads were due to be aired, Cadbury's scrapped them.

Elton was to prove to be chunkier than the chunky-bar menu. The pop star was no stranger to the High Court, having the year before won almost £5 million after suing his first music publisher, Dick James, over song rights. The *Sun* was totally unprepared for the force of Elton's counter-attack. Elton later told the *Daily Express*: 'They can say I'm a fat old sod, they can say I'm an untalented bastard, they can call me a poof, but they mustn't lie about me.' The first writ from Elton's solicitor, Frank Presland, of solicitors Frere Cholmeley, was issued so fast that the second Graham X story, on Thursday 26 February, was printed with the caption: 'The story they're all suing over.'

Schadenfreude is nowhere indulged in with more glee than in Fleet Street. On the same day the *Sun* published its second story, the *Daily Mirror*'s almighty four-letter front-page headline screamed LIES, with the sub-headline: 'I was in New York and I can prove it, says pop super-star.' The *Mirror* story, by John Blake, showed that on the only specific date mentioned in the *Sun*'s original Graham X story linking Elton with rent-boys – 30 April 1986 – Elton was in New York, being whisked about in a limousine. The *Mirror* had receipts.

More intriguing still was a vanishing story trailed in the *Sun*. At the bottom of the first orgy story published on the 25th was a white-on-black block sign-posting the next day's scoop: 'TOMORROW: Elton's pink tu-tu party.' The story never appeared. It probably fell victim to the large holes which were beginning to appear in Graham X's evidence. Witnesses were piling up to say they had never seen Elton John at Billy Gaff's parties; never, in fact, seen him at Billy Gaff's house. But the *Sun*'s game-plan was to keep on hitting Elton so hard that he would give up long before a judge heard the matter.

The second front-page splash, on Thursday 26 February, was headlined ELTON'S KINKY KINKS, followed on pages 4 and 5 by ELTON'S DRUG CAPERS. The *Sun* was claiming, among other things, that Elton 'demanded that the young male prostitutes found for him should be drugged with vast amounts of coke before they were brought to his bed'. Elton sued. The following day, Friday 27 February, the *Sun* printed YOU'RE A LIAR ELTON. Elton sued again.

One man who was concerned about the story was Rupert Murdoch. According to a *Sun* mole, Murdoch treats Mackenzie with the affection shown by the teacher to the naughtiest boy in the class, whom he has to punish but secretly admires the most.

He has been known to call Mackenzie 'My Little Hitler'. But when the writs started to fly, there were worries that Elton would boycott Murdoch-owned television outlets. *Sun* reporters were soon trading versions of a phone call described by Mackenzie in his booming voice. The story is that Mackenzie was woken at home in the wee hours of the night by a familiar Australian voice, calling from one of the five continents where News International owns things:

MURDOCH: Kelvin, are we all right on this Elton John business?

MACKENZIE: Yes, boss.

MURDOCH: All right. [*Click*]

The brevity of the phone call, it is said, left Kelvin twitching with worry.

Another man who lost sleep over ELTON IN VICE BOYS SCANDAL was John Boyce. Boyce is a Scottish conman, homosexual pimp and former rent-boy who went to the same school as John Reid, Elton's manager. Asked about his criminal record, Boyce told a Thames Television journalist: 'The largest amount of convictions I've got is for fraud. I've got nine convictions for fraud, and I've got one for attempted murder.' This was the saviour the *Sun* turned to in its hour of need.

Boyce had been toying with the idea of flogging a rent-boy story to the tabloids and was horrified to see the prospect of good money slipping into someone else's hands. When the first Graham X story broke, he phoned up the *Sun* immediately, offering his services as a go-between. Boyce was willing to hunt down rent-boys and secure affidavits from them which would support the thrust of the *Sun*'s allegations – for a price.

Boyce, who works out of a gay pub in Manchester, has been bought up by a former *People* journalist called Terry Lovell. Lovell is writing a book about the affair, so Boyce was unavailable for an interview with the *Independent Magazine*. (Lovell, who broke the Harvey Proctor spanking story and many other sordid revelations with rent-boy sources, has junked his £37,000-a-year job at the *People* after having found God. He now works for the *Christian Bookseller Review*. Lovell told the *UK Press*

Gazette: 'I honestly could take no more. The cheating, the lying, the conniving and the utter pointlessness of many of the stories I was no longer able to justify.')

Being born again did not prevent Lovell from taking a modest fee for introducing Boyce to Thames Television's *This Week*. The uncut interview at the Apollo Club between granite-jawed Thames reporter Lindsay Charlton and John Boyce is a model of its kind, as this section shows:

BOYCE: Basically, the whole idea at the beginning of it was to get people to dig dirt against Elton John, and . . .

CHARLTON: What sort of statement did they want?

BOYCE: Basically, they wanted to crown the guy, and he was in the Honours List at the time . . . So they [the *Sun*] turned round and says to me, they says, by the way, can you dig up any kind of crap on the guy . . . And we used to bring people to hotel rooms and they would tell us that they had an affair with Elton John and you know – I mean it was all pure crap.

Boyce's attitude to his work was that it was a 'nice little earner'. He was paid £1,750 for each affidavit, passing on about £500 to each rent-boy who signed up. Not all rent-boys got the full £500 promised by Boyce, not all signatories had ever been rent-boys and, it transpired, none of them had ever done anything they told Boyce they had done with Elton John. After a couple of weeks, the *Sun* realised it had been had, and stopped paying Boyce. He told *This Week*: 'If Mr Murdoch is there, by any chance, I would appreciate a cheque tomorrow morning.'

Having cut its losses with Boyce, the paper redoubled its efforts to get the 'dirt' on Elton, as Mick Jagger had predicted. The *Sun*'s Elton John squad included Wallis and its Midlands reporter, Andrew Parker. According to the *Sun* mole, 'they scoured the planet'. Elton's solicitor started to get reports from places as far apart as Melbourne, Manchester, Los Angeles, Scotland and London that strangers were making inquiries about the star's sexual history and habits.

Meanwhile, in Twyford, all was not well at the Hardy household. It had taken the rest of Fleet Street about 24 hours to trace

American Barry to his council house, but, as yet, no one had got a picture of him. The *Sun* had blanked out his face in ELTON'S KINKY KINKS to preserve his anonymity. It is part of the Samurai code of honour among the tabloids that when one paper buys up a contact and keeps his identity secret, all the others must do their damnedest to find out who he is and print the worst.

The siege moved *en bloc* to the house of Hardy's girlfriend's parents, in a cul-de-sac just off the A4. The *Sun* decided to get Hardy, girlfriend and baby out of the country before he was questioned too closely by the opposition, with the *Daily Mirror* at the head of the pack.

The *Sun*'s Thames Valley reporter, John Askill, a large man nicknamed 'The Jolly Green Giant', was detailed to babysit the Hardys. But first the *Sun* had to get them out of the cul-de-sac and off to the airport. The Fleet Street pack had parked outside the house, hoping to take snatch pics as Hardy was moved out. The Jolly Green Giant rose to the occasion. Hardy, always acutely conscious of how he dresses, recalls this episode with genuine hurt: 'Askill wrapped me up in a balaclava and a scarf, and put a blanket over my head. When we came out of the house Askill left me standing there with this blanket over my head looking stupid as he said "Hello!" to all his mates from the other papers.'

Next, four taxis hired by the *Sun* arrived and blocked off the cul-de-sac, parting like the Red Sea to let the *Sun*'s car out but closing again to stop the pack from following. However, one of the opposition reporters had parked his car on the A4, so an epic car chase across the Home Counties followed. The chase meant that when the *Sun* car finally lost the opposition, its passengers had missed their flight to Spain. Hardy, girlfriend, baby and Askill flew to Paris instead.

They spent four days in the Hotel Sofitel at Charles de Gaulle airport near Paris. Then they flew, first-class, to Malaga, before driving to the five-star Melia Don Pepe in Marbella. Hardy was greatly chuffed: 'It really was high living.' But after a while, the foreign lifestyle lost its appeal. The girlfriend didn't want to feed her baby on Spanish baby food, so a woman *Sun* reporter flew out with fresh stocks bought from a proper British supermarket.

Before returning, the exiles spent a couple of days in Gibraltar, where Hardy took the *Sun* man's picture framed against the Rock. In all, Hardy spent a month abroad at the *Sun*'s expense.

Back in Britain, the trawl for filth on Elton John had finally come up with something. Tom Petrie, the *Sun*'s news editor, had to get a thick wad of used readies for an exchange which was like something out of Le Carré novel. The trade-off took place underneath the stark searchlights outside the *Sun*'s Wapping fortress, because the mystery supplier refused point-blank to enter the plant. What the *Sun* got for its money were three Polaroid photographs, depicting Elton John in, first, a full-frontal nude shot, second, warmly cuddling another man and, third, the man and Elton in a compromising position. Dave Shapland, the paper's deputy editor, was heard to say: 'I've got a lot of Elton John tapes in my Porsche, but now I can't bear to listen to them.'

The Polaroids were deeply embarrassing for Elton – who had never lived a life of monastic sobriety – but they were not supporting evidence for the original Graham X story that Elton used rent-boys. The man in the photographs was a consenting adult, not a rent-boy. The pictures were taken in the late Seventies or very early Eighties, long before Elton was married.

The *Sun* made sure Elton saw the Polaroids before they were published. It was, the paper thought, the knock-out punch. Kelvin Mackenzie was convinced that Elton would fold. Someone who was close to Elton at the time told me: 'Elton realised that those photographs looked pretty bad for him, but they didn't have anything to do with Graham X. There was a lot of pressure on Elton to settle with the *Sun*, but he said no. Elton showed tremendous guts.'

ELTON PORN PHOTO SHAME by Neil Wallis flopped on to the streets on Thursday 16 April 1987, with a cropped shot of Elton's full-frontal on page one. As to the third Polaroid, the *Sun* adopted its most priggish tone: 'The Polaroid photograph is simply too disgusting to print in a family newspaper.' No mention of the fact that the same family newspaper had bought the set for £10,000.

The *Sun*'s readers hated it. They had always quite liked Elton John, and were beginning to suspect that what was amiss had nothing to do with Elton John, but with the *Sun*. The paper was sounding like a bully.

Elton went on a chat show hosted by his old chum Michael Parkinson, and told his side of the story. Although he looked haggard and at the end of his tether, Elton was warmly applauded. He managed to get in a crack at the paper, which, he said, had tried to approach his wife's doctor: 'They probably want to examine my sperm. You would have thought they'd have buckets of the stuff.' The telly audience loved it.

Worse for Mackenzie, on days when the rent-boy story was on the front page, internal News International circulation figures showed alarming falls. The depressed editor was heard to moan that the *Sun* had lost 200,000 sales on one issue. The rent-boy effect was even starker because the readers came back whenever a 'normal' *Sun* story went on page one.

While Mackenzie worried in London, Hardy returned from Spain to Twyford to find that he had lost his job, his photograph had been printed in the *Daily Mirror* and the vice squad wanted to talk to him. The regular money from the *Sun*, handed over by Askill in a Thomas Cook holiday wallet, was beginning to dry up. It was not the best of homecomings.

The police inquiries culminated in what the *Sun* called on Wednesday 1 July a BIG GAY VICE SWOOP. Hardy was taken away for questioning in a police car, leaving his girlfriend, in tears, holding the baby. He was later charged with living off the immoral earnings of male prostitutes.

The stakes in the game were upped in July when a jury awarded Jeffrey Archer half a million pounds against the *Daily Star*, then the biggest libel settlement ever made. In the light of the Archer case, the *Sun*'s final attack on Elton John in 1987 could only be described as barking mad.

MYSTERY OF ELTON'S SILENT DOGS, by-lined John Askill, printed on Monday 28 September 1987, alleged that Elton had his 'vicious Rottweiler dogs . . . silenced by a horrific operation'. Askill quoted RSPCA inspector John Hutchinson to support the story about Elton's 'silent assassins'. Hutchinson disowns the story: 'I was appalled by it.'

But what was most peculiar was that the *Sun* ought to have suspected it was nonsense all along. Askill filed the story with a disclaimer stressing it was not copper-bottomed. Elton's dogs are Alsatians. They bark. Elton sued for the 17th time.

By late autumn Hardy – newly married and waiting for his court hearing to come up – was no longer being wooed by the *Sun*. With memories of the Spanish trip fading fast, his next move was inevitable. On Friday 6 November 1987, the *Daily Mirror*'s front page splash – MY SEX LIES OVER ELTON – quoted Hardy as saying: 'It's all a pack of lies. I made it all up. I only did it for the money and the *Sun* was easy to con. I've never even met Elton John . . . I've never been to one of his concerts or bought one of his records. In fact, I hate his music.'

If Hardy had stuck with the *Daily Mirror* version of events, he might have found it easier to deny the pimping charges against him. But he changed his story yet again: by the time his case was heard in mid-January 1988, he was on good terms with the *Sun* once more. Hardy pleaded guilty to pimping, and was sentenced to 240 hours of community service. Of course, the *Sun* would clearly have difficulty making out a case that Hardy was a reliable witness when the first Graham X libel came to court. The *Sun* mole's view is that Mackenzie may have realised there was a possibility that he was going to lose, but had decided that the paper would go down 'with guns blazing'. 'There would be at least two weeks when we could report the dirt on Elton John,' the mole said. 'We would bring him down with us.'

Unfortunately for the *Sun*, at this stage Elton's lawyers managed to bring the barking dogs case – writ 17 – to court before the rent-boy allegations, despite the fact that the story had been printed months after the others. For Elton, the move was a major tactical victory.

The effect of the switch was to take the pressure off Elton, who had prepared himself for some unpleasant hours in the witness box, and put the squeeze on the *Sun*. The paper had to face the hopeless task of defending the Dogs That Didn't Bark story or giving in. There would be no dividend in fighting the case. Elton would come out as the Great British Dog-Lover; the paper would look deeply foolish and lose the first battle of the campaign. The earth started to shift even further under Mackenzie's feet, it is said, when Murdoch realised how much the lawyers' fees might add up to if all the cases were fought. The *Sun* went into reverse, fast.

On Monday 12 December 1988 the dog story was due to be heard in front of Mr Justice Michael Davies at the High court. Fleet Street was slavering for the juicy details, confident that the *Sun* was in for a whipping. Instead, that morning the paper carried a massive, two-word headline, SORRY ELTON, followed by a lickspittle apology approved by the rock star, covering the whole saga, from Graham X to the dogs.

A press statement released the same morning admitted in wheedling terms that Kelvin Mackenzie personally associated himself with the climbdown. Although the paper had recently apologised to the Queen on its front page, this was the first libel apology ever to lead the paper. The story quoted a *Sun* spokesman: 'We are delighted that the *Sun* and Elton have become friends again and we are sorry that we were lied to by a teenager living in a world of fantasy.'

More surprisingly, Elton was quoted as saying: 'This is the best Christmas present I could wish for. Life is too short to bear grudges and I don't bear the *Sun* any malice.' In the centre pages, the paper carried an astonishing tribute to Elton's diet: 'The 41-year-old rock singer has shed an amazing TWO STONES in less than two months.' Elton had been badly mauled by the *Sun*'s claws; now he was being licked to death.

The million-pound settlement – double the Archer award – clearly suited both parties. The *Sun* was spared a drubbing by a jury; Elton was spared the dredging-up of old lies about his private life. Others were less happy. The judge, who had been told about the settlement as soon as it was made the previous afternoon, appeared piqued at the matiness of the two parties, and attacked them for forming 'a mutual admiration society'. 'The Queen's courts are provided for the trial and resolution of disputes,' he said, 'not as a supine adjunct to the publicity machine of pop stars and newspaper proprietors.'

According to a leading QC who followed the Elton John case closely, 'It just exposed the nonsense of agreed statements made in open court. The statements are fashioned according to the bargaining positions of the parties and the game of bluff and counter-bluff which libel proceedings increasingly are. You can't necessarily believe anything that is read in open court. It is not the truth as if it had emerged from contested proceedings, but a privately agreed version. Many feel that there ought to be some form of investigation by the court before it allows a statement to be made in its name. The judge was upset that the parties seemed to be exploiting the rules, but the answer is to change the rules. The parties did nothing wrong.'

The force of the judge's remarks was to take some of the gloss from Elton's victory. This was perhaps a little unfair. Elton had not invited the *Sun*'s Uriah Heepery, but desired an 'apology that matched the smear'. He wanted all 13 million *Sun* readers to know the paper had got it wrong; more, he wanted them to know that the paper had paid him a million. The *Sun* has a way of burying apologies written in legalese in the inside pages, so the front-page SORRY ELTON, written in the *Sun*'s style, was part of a strategy to get the maximum possible publicity for the settlement.

The judge appeared to misunderstand this. He had also attacked the announcement of the amount of damages. Living in a wider world, Elton wanted something more specific than 'substantial'. As to the tone of the apology, a regular reader of the *Sun* might have realised that when the paper says sorry, it does so with the same salivating frenzy with which it goes about the rest of its business.

And what now of our cast? Elton John saw his marriage break up and went through a crisis of depression which blighted his life for months. He tried to sell Watford, then changed his mind, but did sell many of his rock memorabilia. He came out of his ordeal a thinner, richer man, and is about to go on a world tour with a new album.

John Boyce was last heard of in a court, after being involved in a fight in a hotel. No doubt he is conjuring some new 'nice little earners'. Stephen Hardy told me: 'I lost my job, my marriage and my self-respect over this. I've got no friends left. I still get very badly depressed about it.' His ex-wife is perhaps the saddest victim of the affair. At the age of 20, she has had a child by a man who is notorious in the small community where she lived.

And what about Kelvin Mackenzie? According to the *Sun* mole, 'Kelvin's self-confidence took a massive knock over the Elton John story. He's a better editor now and the *Sun*'s a better paper.' For even Rupert Murdoch cannot afford to write off £1 million as loose change. In the week before Christmas Mackenzie invited his staff into his office. They expected a pep talk, a few words of congratulation about the best sales figures in the Western world and a Yuletide drink. They got a nasty shock. The *Sun* mole said: 'It was a foul-mouthed abuse session. He warned that the next reporter who got a writ would be out. He said: "It's got to stop. If I go, I'm going to take you bastards with me." There was no mention of Merry Christmas.

Nevertheless, Mackenzie is still there. After all, Mackenzie's *Sun* makes Murdoch more than a million pounds a week profit. While the balance sheet is still in Mackenzie's favour, neither a huge libel bill nor a stack of privacy acts nor an ombudsman will change the tenor of the *Sun*. Mackenzie may well end up the same way his predecessor did. He was knighted, for services to journalism.

WHAT MAKES MALCOLM RUN

Malcolm McLaren by Alix Sharkey

One of the following statements about Malcolm McLaren is completely untrue. Which one?

a) He once threatened Richard Branson with a baseball bat.

b) He started the Sex Pistols to sell more trousers.

c) He has a platinum Excess credit card which bears the legend 'The Fat Guy With The Cigar Will Pay'.

Got it? That's right! It was in fact a *cricket* bat.

For a man so consistently ahead of his time Malcolm McLaren is rotten at keeping appointments. Twice jilted, I await his presence at a Soho restaurant. Forty minutes later he finally arrives, but not before I reflect that since I'm paying, at least he won't be able to spring his most endearing party trick on me. One of the things that gets Malcolm off, see, is running out of restaurants just after the coffee, and just before the bill. He can't explain it. Call it mischief, call it restaurant anarchy, call it staying in touch with the street, man, but the fact remains: every once in a while Malcolm likes to do a runner.

Like the time he took a group of friends to a renowned Chinese establishment in Covent Garden, and ordered 'flied lice and Ho Chi Minh' all round, and dallied until closing time before asking the head waiter to nip out and get a pack of cigarettes, giving him a tenner and telling him to keep the change. As soon as the man was out of sight Malcolm jumped to his feet and shouted

'Run!' His startled guests didn't even make it to the door, but McLaren was gone, laughing hysterically as he legged it through the Piazza.

Or the time in Berlin with former girlfriend Andrea, who wore the black mink jacket Malcolm had bought her the week before. The romantic mood of the evening – candlelight, wine, good food – was rent asunder when, without a word, he leapt up and bolted. Andrea caught up several blocks later and proceeded to pummel McLaren, who was helpless with mirth; in the panic she had left her mink. His response: 'It's very simple. Leave it, or go back and pay the bill.'

'But the best one was at La Coupole,' says Malcolm, warming to the theme. His voice is thin, high-pitched, middle-class, with streaks of pre-war Cockney slang and mid-Atlantic phrasing. 'Me and the New York Dolls and four or five French guys, record company people. It was a fabulous dinner, and the bill came to what, 600 quid. So I looked at it and I nodded to the others. And we were *off!*' Unfortunately, a nod is not as good as a wink to a drunk Frenchman. 'Poor old Albert. He was there all night, phoning people to come down with the money,' he chortles, wiping tears from his eyes.

Ah, Malcolm. Still crazy after all these years.

When it comes to the lunatic, the perverse, the antic, the howling-at-the-moon beserk notion that gnaws at even the most liberal and sophisticated sensibility, Malcolm has long since cornered the market. It is worth noting that even his failures have never faltered through lack of panache. Who else would have put the draggy, druggy, dreggy New York Dolls into red patent leather and had them spout cod-Communist slogans as they teetered on platforms, stoned to the eyeteeth? Or the rumoured musical drama about the IRA? And 'She-Sheriff', a punky, spunky update on the Dolly Parton theme? And the original Pistols' film script, 'Who Shot Bambi?', which was to be directed by mammary mogul Russ Meyer? Should we count Bow Wow Wow, a one-hit wonder featuring a 14-year-old schoolgirl shouting gimcrack Rousseau as her pubescent nipples peeped out of her blouse? And what about the kiddy porn magazine *Chicken*, named after the paedophile slang for jailbait, which had the blessing of both the BBC and EMI before someone realised what kind of cock it involved?

What about it, Malcolm? Did you chicken out?

'No! I would've done it. But Fred Vermorel, an old art-school associate, got scared. Not me, I was thrilled by it. Using £20,000 of EMI's money to fund a chicken magazine? It was brilliant! I even went to the extent of involving the BBC in recording the making of it. And that archival material lurks in the bowels of the BBC, protected by Alan Yentob. Robin Denselow was the director! No, Fred Vermorel hid all the photos, wouldn't answer the phone, he was terrified. But it didn't really get me off. It couldn't. You just couldn't ever get it up like that again. People see you coming.'

Couldn't get it *up* like that again? Clearly, a question of the chicken and the ego.

It's a Friday night in the West End and we're standing at the bar of the Mudd Club, Philip Sallon's teeny night at Busby's, when Malcolm wafts in, wearing a beautifully cut dark wool suit, white silk shirt, tasteful tie, his crown of ginger curls bobbing up and down, framing a pale, freckly face with birdlike features. His eyes are hard and clear like bits of broken green glass. He has pink eyelashes.

He is here to promote his new single, 'Deep In Vogue', with the help of one Willie Ninja, a black dancer from New York. He's a little worried that nobody will show up, but people reassure him that it's still early and besides, everyone has been talking about the event all week. He wasn't sure about this, he says, but Sallon – an old friend – talked him into it. His record company, CBS, weren't interested at all. 'They keep saying to me, "Malcolm, Malcolm, forget about dance music. Forget about young kids, forget about nightclubs. Leave that to the Rhythm Kings of this world. Just get the CD out, get the ten quid across the counter." They keep telling me that's my market, and I suppose they're right.'

Malcolm McLaren, doyen of CD suburbia? CBS think so, and have lined up a series of interviews that might suit Anne Diamond better than the Clown Prince of Punk: there's *Woman's*

Own, Woman's Realm, Marie Claire and *Options.*

'Well, this new LP is very romantic, very lush, very opulent. I wanted to take the best of European culture and mix it with the best of American culture. So you've got that grand, splendid, eighteenth-century middle-European waltz thing, being supported by the vibrancy and urgency of black American R&B. It's a peculiar marriage, but perfectly complementary. Perfect car music, big, full of colour.'

Such perfect car music, in fact, that it features in the TV commercial for the new Renault 19, the one with the car being sketched and erased, and re-drawn as it tours the countryside.

Vogueing, a camp stylised form of body-popping that originated in New York's black gay clubs, is 'a little dance craze I picked up, a kind of bookend. Just a nice way of finishing off the LP.' The crowds arrive in force, Malcolm introduces his record, and Willie Ninja struts his Vogueing stuff. A lot of fresh kids and a lot of old faces have come to watch. The evening is a success.

Later, I mention the recent *Tatler* cover that featured Vivienne Westwood made up to look like Margaret Thatcher. Malcolm bristles; he *hated* it. He tried calling Vivienne to tell her, he says, 'But she won't talk to me anymore. I think she's gone mad.'

What was it that upset him so much?

'It was just such an . . . *acceptance.* It was finally saying, "All right, you've won." '

Back in the restaurant, conversation turns towards the inevitable. 'I love jokes,' says McLaren, 'I like to upset the apple cart.' And his greatest joke, predictably, was the Sex Pistols.

'That was my moment, and I was ready for it. *Go*! They'd say calm down, let's retreat, take stock – not me, man. Over the hill. No fear! I wanted to go into that darkness, right through that forest, I don't care what's lurking, go right in there, all the way.

'My lawyers were always running 100 yards behind me, trying to catch me up,' he laughs, as his voice takes on a strident nasal tone, like a horse-racing commentator. 'One o'clock in the morning, trundling on to meet A&M's lawyers, catching a taxi at one-thirty with a 75 grand cheque in my back pocket, there we'd see the president of EMI walking past Selfridges, I hail him and my lawyer says "Put your hand down!" and I say "Maybe we can give him a lift!" and of course we'd just come out of EMI six weeks earlier with *another* 50 grand!

'You know, for me, it was like the streets were *mine*. It was great. You were news all over, you radiated, people recognised you, it was major. Fleet Street phoned me up, said: "We just sold more papers with the Sex Pistols on the cover than we did on Armistice Day." That was the editor of the *Daily Mirror*. He said, "You're a genius. You've got a story, Malcolm, we'll print it." Yeah! the media was my lover, all the sex was coming out, spraying everywhere. All those dog-collars and everything, that was just theatrics. But the big, *big* gesture with the establishment, that was the real hard-on, that was the crack. All the other stuff was just foreplay, all the stuff with the group.

'My lawyers could never understand it,' he says, still chuckling, 'why I didn't wanna just get down to the business of making records. I wasn't *interested*. Absolutely of no consequence to me whatsoever. But it had to be done to keep everyone in tow. I would never have signed to Virgin otherwise. I just so *adored* having this guy Richard Branson call me up every ten minutes. And I said "You call me again, I'm gonna come round with a fucking cricket bat. You understand that, boy? Don't call me, 'cause I don't like you, I don't like the sweaters you wear, I don't like what you represent. I can't stand your fucking logo and I don't go to the Portobello Road. I *hate* it. So don't call me." Ten minutes, 15 minutes later, the secretary would call me. They . . . never . . . stopped!'

The race won yet again, Malcolm's pitch sinks, as he gazes into his plate and considers his finest hour. Talking to McLaren without mentioning the Punk saga is impossible, but there is an unavoidable prickly feeling that he could go on eating free meals forever, could live comfortably and never lift a finger except to raise a glass to his lips, on the strength of that brief episode.

But then, why not? He's a better raconteur than most, and certainly well qualified to recount those events. He's even smart enough to employ a shade of modesty: 'If it hadn't erupted in that form, it would have erupted in some other way. It just happened that at the time I was on my horse, poised, ready. It just came to me, that's what happened. I could see it clearly, and *I could see how to make my world*. And I was never going to miss that opportunity.'

Malcolm McLaren was born in London on January 22 1946, the second son of Emily Isaacs and Peter McLaren. Almost immediately, he says, he was 'torn away' from his mother by his maternal grandmother, Rose Corré, whom he describes as 'a troublemaker, incredibly anti-establishment, amazingly spoilt, and a woman who had no sense of the real world, only what she could get from it.' This action must have traumatised McLaren, but the expected sense of outrage fails to materialise. In fact, he is full of praise for his grandmother, and is still, at the age of 42, in awe of the woman.

'She was a very competitive spirit, she didn't really like the husbands she married. She came from an incredibly wealthy diamond-dealing family, Portuguese-Dutch Jews. She was a fancy girl, she wanted to be in the theatre world.' McLaren is almost boastful about her, telling how 'She would never wear a copy. That's an old phrase meaning she only wore *couture*.'

McLaren lived his life through his grandmother's eyes, to the extent that she had him removed from school almost before he had started, to be taught at home until he was nine years old. They were unusually close – he slept with her until he was 13. 'She gave me an open book, but she always wanted me to be bad,' he says. 'I was lucky in some ways, having such a focused and cosseted environment – I was never made to love anything until I left. I was prime, virgin soil, man. And I *was* a virgin when I met Vivienne. And it was upon sleeping with her after two weeks that I got her pregnant.' At the age of 21 McLaren was faced with fatherhood, having just left home and lost his virginity.

But this peculiar upbringing is made doubly strange by the events surrounding his father, who disappeared soon after Malcolm's birth. McLaren is troubled by the coincidence of his father's uninterest and his grandmother's possessiveness. Or, as he puts it, 'It was in the war, and I'm sure a lot of things happened. My grandmother couldn't have been more than 35, my mother was about 16. And if you don't like, y'know, like your husband that much, you might cavort with this person or that, who knows? Who knows whether my mother is my mother? Who knows whether your grandmother's not your mother?' His mother, whom he recently saw for the first time in 23 years, is unable or unwilling to resolve the question for him. 'She's sort of tired, and a little old and, y'know, people don't really *want* all that part of their lives opened up again.'

To get to the truth McLaren has hired a private detective to try and trace his father, although he accepts that there's little hope now, nearly half a century after the event. Add to this the chaotic state of public records just after the war, when refugees poured into the country and many people had good reason to change their names and disappear, and the odds stack up very high indeed.

What did he expect, if by some chance he found his father? McLaren suddenly looks vulnerable, like a small boy who realises he is lost. 'I don't know. My mother says he was a brilliant artist. Not in a professional sense; a characteristic. I don't know much else, man. He stole a lot of cars in the war, that's all I know.'

The waitress approaches tentatively, sensing the poignancy of the moment. Malcolm looks directly at her, but without seeing her, and slowly, very slowly, starts to giggle, then guffaw, until his laugh rises to a seriously embarrassing volume as he manages to squeeze out the words: 'Did a lovely spray job . . . and used to sell 'em!' His face is creased with laughter, the words hissing from his teeth, '*Ran a wonderful business . . . until he got caught . . . and served time!*'

Some people say 'Like Father, Like Son' and Malcolm McLaren has been called many things, including a charlatan, a rogue, and a con-man. But this is the pop industry we're talking about, not the medical profession. And while Peter McLaren willed himself into oblivion, his son revels in the celebrity he has achieved here, and more recently, in the USA. His relationship with actress

Lauren Hutton may be over ('I sincerely loved her, I still do in a way, but it was becoming a bit like running on the spot,' says McLaren) but it helped him carve a niche in Hollywood. There are his various movie deals, including the musical film with Steven Spielberg; the treatment of 'Fans' that he recently completed with Barrie Keefe for director Richard Donner and the latest, a film about Vogueing that he's working on with Richard Price, who wrote 'The Color of Money' and 'The Wanderers'.

And then there is the small industry surrounding his life, the most bizarre product of which is 'The Wicked Ways of Malcolm McLaren', an inverted hagiography by an American journalist that would seem to cast him as a cross between Errol Flynn and Rasputin, and which is due out later this year. One of the more reputable Malcolm-watchers says that he has talked incessantly about his parents and grandmother for most of the year. 'Yeah, that's his riff at the moment, the family. Of course, he's sincere, but it doesn't come across that way. The other riff is his *badness*. That's one of the things about Malcolm. He's so . . . self-evident. All that stuff about him being an evil man, it's complete nonsense.'

Malcolm McLaren is no Machiavelli or Svengali. He is, by his own admission, 'a spoilt, snobby art student', a savvy shopkeeper who started the Sex Pistols because, he says, it seemed like 'a good way to sell more trousers. And they did, believe me!'

Who could deny it? We are all wearing Malcolm's trousers. We are all carrying Malcolm's cultural baggage. He is the spiritual Baden-Powell of the past decade-and-a-half, a cheery chicken-loving scoutmaster, showing us how to put half-hitches in reality, how to whittle away at logic, how to start a blaze in a damp forest using only rotting timber; pointing with salacious glee to the patch of high ground where we'll make our aesthetic camp tonight.

His secret love's no secret anymore, it's the creed of a whole generation of media brats and fashion hacks. Quite simply, he never pays the bill. Sometimes he'll do a runner, sometimes he actually picks up the tab. But whether it's now or further down the line, someone else will always pay. Usually The Fat Guy With The Cigar.

AGEING SMOOTHIE

Robert Palmer by Tony Parsons

Little Bobby Palmer. You can see why they used to beat him up all the time.

His family move to the small Yorkshire town of Batley when Robert is nine and the kid is definitely odd. At home, if his mother gives him a white school shirt that is less than pristine clean and pressed, he gives it back to her to wash and iron again. And at school, among all these gritty northern kids with skin the colour of a dead goldfish, dapper Bob is very different. He is suntanned from a childhood spent in Malta, he is short for his age and – among the local foghorn tones of the Yorkshire playground – the clipped bray of his Oxbridge accent sounds like a siren. And he is over dressed. At breaktime the mob gathers around him, baying for his blood.

'In Malta we had no school in the summer months and only half days in winter because it was so hot,' he tells me 30 years later. The Oxbridge accent is long gone and the voice is now a kind of Bahaman Yorkshire cool. 'There were children from all over the free world down in the Mediterranean and life was very open. I came back to one of the most provincial spots imaginable, somewhere that totally ignored the existence of the outside world, and I had a dreadful time. I found it very difficult to adjust. Every day they descended on me.' He sips a cocktail so elaborate that he had to write down its ingredients for the bartender. 'I lived in England for nine years of my life. The most miserable years of my life.'

The blood on the lips of Batley's Little Lord Fauntleroy clearly left a lasting impression. He never gets over it and is condemned to go to his grave pining for his early life by the Med, destined to spend his time trying to get back to his sweet lost Malta, those soft summers and big blue days on some idyllic beach, fated to have a career that is spent in pursuit of some warped idea of the good life.

Talk to him about sun, sea and coconuts, about women and swimming pools under cloudless skies, and Robert Palmer acts dumb. 'Image? What image?' he says. 'That's the way I live.'

On record and in the toasted flesh, Robert Palmer is the ageing smoothie incarnate. Casual sexism and smug, menopausal good taste abound. His solo albums are into double figures now but he has not changed that much from the early days of Little Feat licks and willing chicks. Even more than Bryan Ferry in his capped teeth, white tux and gossip column period, even more than The World's Forgotten Lad Rod Stewart in his straw boater, Art Deco lamps and Swedish blow job phase, Robert Palmer has presented himself as the playboy of the western world, a smirking rake, a wolf in tropical weight clothing, frolicking as only a fancy man can by floodlit pools and on moonlit lawns.

If the music he's made has been all over the show (covering the waterfront from funk to metal with scatterbrained eclecticism, what Palmer himself refers to disarmingly as 'the K-Tel effect'), then the vision has at least remained constant. On his album covers bikinis are cast off, exotic barefoot girls lose at strip poker and naked girls in high heels are activated by pressing a button on your TV's remote control.

His most typical song is 'I Didn't Mean To Turn You On'. In this tune Robert's sexual magnetism is accidentally unleashed with disastrous consequences. He takes a girl out and though he doesn't mean to, he accidentally turns her on. Her head turned, the young thing runs emotionally amok. Palmer apologizes for inflaming her desires.

He has knocked out enough popular melodies over the years

to keep his career extant (the posturing 'Sneaking Sally Through The Alley', the insinuating 'Johnny And Mary', the touching 'Some Guys Have All The Luck', which was wonderfully covered by Rod) but it was 'Addicted To Love' that turned it all around for him, the single starting an avalanche of success that resulted in an American number one, four Grammy nominations and a new recording contract with EMI (moving on from Chris Blackwell's Island). Amazing what you can do with a catchy riff and a sperm-brained video.

'That success took me out of the red for the first time in my life,' he says. 'I was in the black for 18 months. Then I spent all the money in the bank making a new record.'

The new record is 'Heavy Nova' (Robert rubbing your nose in his K-Tel consciousness with this title, a hybrid of heavy metal and bossa nova), an album that charts Palmer's usual romp across all the musical borders – at one point the man yodels – though, as befits the Bing Crosby of the Club Med set, he is at his best when he is crooning. There are two concessions to his entré into Grammyland – the opening track 'Simply Irresistible', which is a brain dead ringer for 'Addicted To Love', matching the earlier song's tongue lolling bombast, though not its crunching charm, and the Terence Donovan photograph on the cover which sets Palmer's moody and slightly saggy good looks against the same black and red flaming inferno that served as the backdrop in Donovan's 'Addicted To Love' video, a subtle little reminder to the record buying public that Robert Palmer has already been advertised on TV.

He swaggers into the twilight gloom of the bar at the St James Club, shorter than you would expect – just above Amis height – as edgy as he is cocky inside his boxy suit, a Cagney for the cocktail lounge. He is tanned and testy, this ageing smoothie, resenting the need to sell his wares, and this lack of the rakes's easy charms is a disappointment. At least you could always count on Ferry being polite to the waiters.

'I am a very private person,' he says in his Yorkshire drawl. 'Look at this place.'

We look at the opulent darkness of the private club. Some rich tourists are being loud at the bar. 'It's a hideaway,' Palmer claims. 'I used to stay at Blake's but it got too rock and roll.'

Blake's is where George Michael does his thing, I remark conversationally. What about that 'Explore Monogamy' number? Where does Robert Palmer stand in the sex death debate? If you did some of those old album covers now, would you have a packet of Mates sticking out of your pocket?

'I imagine George Michael sits down and thinks very carefully about this *shit,*' Robert says rather rudely. 'I bet he tries it on in the mirror and adjusts his earring. I personally avoid like the plague anything to do with politics or religion.'

Wondering if Palmer thinks rubbers come under the heading of spiritual or ideological, I change the subject. Knowing that the subject of his raffish, roué public persona makes him even more tetchy than he is normally, I attack the topic from behind – is he a feminist?

'I enjoy the company of women,' he murmurs suavely. It is a line that comes up again and again throughout our little chat, a constant corny refrain echoing through the conversation. 'I enjoy the company of women . . .' It begins to sound like an endlessly repeated after shave commercial. I enjoy the company of women. That's why I wear . . . Roué. *Roué* New from YSL. For men who enjoy women.

'I have no particular stance on feminism,' he says. 'But I enjoy the company of women. As far as I am concerned, feminism is just female chauvinism. Half my band is female these days. It makes life so much nicer on the road – it cuts down on the cussing.'

Yes, I saw your band on the 'Addicted To Love' video.

'No, no, no,' he smiles, a lovely big ultrabright smile he has, full of bashful arrogance. 'Those women are not my band. And they are not my speed.'

In fact, Palmer, despite all those sun drenched stud cavortings that he has tried on since leaving Vinegar Joe in 1974, is very much an old fashioned guy. He has been married to the same woman, Sue the painter, for nearly 20 years. Strange to think that popular music's most brazen ageing smoothie, far from growing old disgracefully, will probably be the first chart act to celebrate a silver wedding anniversary.

'If I have a business lunch or something I have to do I always insist the other guys bring their wives or their girlfriends.'

Big of you.

'It is not that I spend my time flirting and chasing after women – not at all. Sue and I have been married for 18 years and we have two children. I don't enjoy the exclusive company of the lads and I get on with women very well. Men are just more civilized when there are women around. I personally enjoy women as companions and for their sense of humour and the shit they have to put up with. I can find glamour in the image of a woman shaving her legs.'

I bet you sometimes wish you had been born a woman, right?

'When it comes down to it, I'm a chauvinist,' Palmer says. 'I like the way things are. More and more I suspect that my attitude to women is the same as my father's.'

The quickest way to get Palmer irascible (and it is never hard) is to bring up these accusations of sex war crimes. He sees himself as a red blooded, gallant, wrongly accused gentleman. If I was him, I would tell me about the other pencil dick men of music – from Adidas heeled hip-hoppers to heavy metal hairies – who even more obviously see women as slabs of meat there for turning into steak tartar.

But Palmer does not do that. Instead he acts innocently and tatty in turn (someone stayed married to this guy for 18 years?), eventually pleading guilty to the lesser crime of being just like his father.

'The music business is not a place you can be subtle in,' he says, snapping my head off.

Personally I found those undead painted strumpets in the 'Addicted To Love' video pretty funny, but maybe what truly offends so many people about so much of Palmer's work – from the early album covers like 'Pressure Drop' and 'Some People Can Do What They Like' through to the more recent collaborations with Terence Donovan – is not that women are your common or garden sex objects, but that they invariably seem to have a frontal lobotomy. It is almost as if, in sunny Palmerland, you can have a brain or you can have a fanny but you can't have both. He sees women literally as objects – symptoms of the good life, like swimming pools or fancy clothes or drinks with fruit floating about in them: conclusive proof that at long last here is success, he has finally made it back to his lost beach.

'My father said the old thing – "I kept expecting him to get a proper job". You know when he stopped expecting me to get a proper job?' Palmer's smile lights up the gloomy bar. 'When he jumped in my swimming pool.'

One of Robert's distinguishing features, part of the glossy Palmer facade, was that he lived in the Bahamas. In Palmerland – the nearest his neglected England ever got to the Brian Wilson myth – it was always summer, always a short walk to the beach where there were girls who were always wet (I think you know what I'm talking about). The Bahamas were very important to all that. But now Robert Palmer is living in Lugano, a Swiss citizen.

'The first four or five years in the Bahamas were idyllic, then they built the recording studio directly opposite me. But you can't really impose a rock and roll lifestyle on the place so it never got out of hand. But in the last 18 months there everything went downhill very quickly. It got to the stage where I was more relaxed in New York than I was in the Bahamas. I had been planning on moving out and the violence sped it all up.'

What violence is this?

'The cocaine wars. It happened because the cocaine trade into America was getting out of hand, so outrageous, that right wing pressure in America said to the authorities – look, if you don't cool it down there we are going to pull all the money out. The authorities had to make a show of cooling it, so instead of cocaine going through the Bahamas, it was staying there. And within six months the population was completely fucked up.

'I was sitting at home watching television at midnight and suddenly there was all this uproar outside. The house is right on the sea and I open the curtains . . . there's a helicopter out there, a couple of guys with machine guns, a bunch of cigarette boats. All outside your window. Burglars broke in and shot my dog, man. A load of guys were cracking up. It was unbelievable! So I got out in June last year. I had been trying for two years to get Swiss citizenship and when it finally came through I was able to buy a house there.'

The Palmer family has been relocated in the clean and frosty heart of Europe for nearly a year now. The kids – a boy of ten and a girl of eight – apparently miss their Bahaman home and it can only be surmised what their old man has to say to them about their homesickness. You can just hear his droll Yorkshire tones telling them how lucky they are to have moved to Lugano instead of Leeds. Or maybe the guy is more understanding than that, maybe he understands totally how keenly his children feel the loss of their sandy paradise. His early years in Malta, before that dreaded move to Yorkshire, is the only subject that gets him truly misty-eyed.

'There was this bunch of expatriate English people doing this job down in the Mediterranean,' he says wistfully. 'It was like South Pacific. *South Pacific*, the movie. Most of my time was spent at the beach with adults. When we went to formal affairs there would be navy people from all over the world there. I always thought the Italians looked the best. Italian sailors, man. I just don't have the same icons as everybody else . . .'

So your father was in the navy? Did being a military brat give you something to kick against?

'Well, my father was attached to the navy,' Palmer says coyly. 'He wasn't exactly military. His job, uh, his gig, uh, was listening to the movement of, uh, foreign war things. He was a spy.' He stares past me into time, fingering his empty glass. 'England was never my home. Malta was my home.'

Palmer wants another drink. The waiter still has his written instructions of how to make up his special cocktail and that is good. Robert Palmer feels on top of things, in control, as though there are light years between this suntanned 40 year old Swiss citizen and that scared little kid, the one in the grey hateful playground with snot on his chin, a sob in his heart and blood on his freshly ironed clean white shirt.

AXL GRINDING

Guns N' Roses by Georgina Howell

Dublin, Friday, May 15

Flowering chestnuts along the Lansdowne Road, bathed in late afternoon sunshine, over-top the hotel railings where little girls hang like bats, screaming at anything that moves on the upper floors. In the metal-frame windows at the top, thick drapes obscure the nameless activities of Guns N' Roses, the world's most dangerous heavy rock band. The reclusive Axl Rose has not been glimpsed since his brief transit of the lobby from stretch limo to lift, head down and flanked by bodyguards, two days previously. The rest of the band, at an hour way in advance of their regular wake-up time, are giving interviews. Their beringed right hands wrapped round tumblers of Jack Daniels, they move restlessly between cameras and notebooks, dazed but happy. They're once more where they love to be, on the road, on the European tour for their new albums *Use Your Illusion 1* and 2.

Duff McKagan, bass, is holed up in an airless room with Italian journalists and is looking for something to drink. He wears a gauzy blouse of black and white spots, a tattered denim jerkin, a ring through his nose and two pounds of metal jewellery. His lifeless hair, white and red in parts, resembles the remnants of a bleached J-cloth caught for years on a telegraph wire. Plagued by a lack of synchronisation in his movements, he makes a couple of attempts to place a high-heeled black crocodile chain-stirruped boot on the edge of the coffee table. Asked how the band amused themselves the previous night, he plays for time while trying to locate the answer.

'See, I'm jetlagged.'

His voice, like a rusty chainsaw, jumps 500 watts. 'CAN ANYONE GET A F***ING DRINK ROUND HERE?' Earl, Axl Rose's 6ft 5in black minder, lolls on the bed. Rolling over, he dials room service, and Duff's wide, candid face brightens. Memory comes flooding back. 'Oh yeah! I've got relations here, in Cork, and they showed up. So I hang out with them for a bit and then I ring my mom in Seattle. I say, "Hey Mom, I'm with our Irish cousins"; and she yells at me, "Do you know what time it is? It's four in the morning!" '

He is asked what kind of a show it will be tomorrow, when Guns N' Roses play Slane Castle. A large pink vodka, placed in front of him, has a beneficial effect. 'Bright and colourful show,' he produces triumphantly. 'It's got anarchy. It's not sloppy.'

Duff is currently being sued by a man he beat up in a bar 'for staring at me'. He has £15 million, three houses, a Ferrari and an ex-wife. He wants a big family but sighs, 'In LA it's real hard to find a wife,' and moodily watches a journalist type this into a laptop computer.

The waiter has left the door open and an inner draught suddenly slams it shut. This is too much for Duff, who nearly spills his drink and looks badly shaken. 'Scared the *shit* out of me,' he mutters, glaring over his shoulder.

Along the corridor in suite 636, Slash, lead guitar, is being questioned by RTE about his past heroin habit. He sits sideways on a double bed, chain-smoking, and says he has it beat. 'I was in rehab for three days and I thought f*** this and I quit. But I did it on my own in Hawaii and it's been three years now.' His voice is quiet and smoky. Now and then he gives vent to a sinister 'heh heh' laugh. Bushy curtains of black ringlets close over his sun spectacles so that only his large lips are visible.

'It was success that screwed us up. We were miles apart. That's why we went with the Stones gig in '89, just to get back to working together.'

They were an LA club band until they signed with Geffen Records and their first album, *Appetite for Destruction*, went to number one and stayed there. One year later they became the only band of the Eighties to have two albums simultaneously in the top five.

'We were two years on the road,' he murmurs. 'When they finally dropped me off at the airport I had no place to go.'

Suddenly richer than they had ever been, the band fell apart. They saw all that they had won slipping out of their grasp, and painfully hauled themselves back together. They reluctantly fired former drummer Steven Adler, and rhythm guitarist Izzy Stradlin resigned of his own accord. 'Kicking Steve out was hard. We tried for a year to clean him out. He lied about his situation and the band was going stir-crazy.'

Slash gets to his feet, stretches and excuses himself. Outside the door he starts to run, accelerating down the corridor to the room where Duff leans groggily against the wall. Slash bursts in, seizes him by the leg and tries to wrestle him to the floor. Duff, spilling his drink, resists with surprising vigour. Slash abandons the project and returns to his room.

The press bus, heading out of Dublin a couple of hours later for the sound checks at Slane Castle, is rapidly passed by the band's long gunmetal Mercedes.

This rural venue, possibly the most beautiful in Europe, is a natural bowl of wood and pasture dropping from the great grey castellated house down to the banks of the River Boyne, where a stage of roughly equivalent size disperses its thunder across the landscape. Sixty people have laboured for four days to erect this 160ft spread of scaffolding and plastic, where distant figures from support band Faith No More now struts their stuff. Crescents of safety barricades front the stage and will divide tomorrow's crowd of 50,000 from the circus ring of trucks and trailers at the back.

Slane Castle belongs to the Earl of Mount Charles, a worried looking young man to be found rootling among piles of papers in a chaotic office in the old stable yard. He is dealing with helicopter shuttles, local health authority queries, catering and the licensing authorities. Henry is wild about bands. Since 1981 he has hosted Thin Lizzy, the Stones, Bob Dylan, Bruce Springsteen and Queen.

He rests his leg, encased in plaster, on the desk. A crutch leans against the wall. Skiing accident? His secretary shakes her head. 'He did it dancing a jig in the Castle nightclub on St Patrick's Day.'

A sound of greater than usual ferocity bursts on the summer air.

'Ah,' he beams. 'The dulcet tones of Guns N' Roses.'

A quarter of a mile away, down among the trailers, the band's personal manager Doug Goldstein has just traded his laminate for a Muddy Waters guitar pick. Duff McKagan suddenly abandons the sound test and can be seen making his way down the back of the stage and between the Transam Trucking Vans to the limo where he stands alone, moping.

Doug calls over: 'You sick, Duff?'

He nods, forlorn.

'Wanna hug?'

Duff's bottom lip trembles. He nods.

They hold each other tight.

Saturday, May 16

For the last mile before Slane, the coaches and mobile homes and cars are parked bumper to bumper. Women are selling Cokes and lemonades, as many cans as they could pack into the boots of their cars, from prams or garden tables. Helicopters come and go above a sea of young people, many in Axl's wide headband, moving eight abreast towards the gates, filling the hedgerows with cans and bottles as they go. Alcohol will be confiscated at the gate: there's a lot of drinking to be done in the last 300 yards.

By 4 p.m. Faith No More are playing their hearts out with *Epic*, their final number. The minute the band is off the stage, big John Reese bodyguards me through to the mixing riser, province of sound engineer David Kehrer, to begin the long wait for Guns N' Roses.

By five the crowd begins to build human pyramids. One boy stands triumphantly aloft, holding a pose, then lowers his pants and presents his naked butt to the wind. It's 6.15 when ever-heavier levels of sound start to roll in on us like giant breakers. Someone throws up a flattened red cardboard Coke cup, and the next minute everyone is doing the same and the air is filled with a scarlet blizzard.

There is a tidal wave of noise and Guns N' Roses' first expletive of the evening hits the airwaves at a quarter of a million watts. 'Get ready to rock, you Irish mother-f*****s!' screams Matt Sorum, springing up like a jack-in-the-box from behind the drums. On come the wall of sound and the banks of lights. Axl Rose streaks across the stage, head down, hair streaming behind him like a cloak, arms horizontal behind him, a human Concorde at take-off. He leaps 5ft high into kick splits, bare legs bent. His screech and Slash's chord enter the bloodstream together, and 48,000 people join their war dance. Throughout *You Could Be Mine* Axl tears up and down the ramps, pirouetting, progressing backwards with a malignant hop, thrashing the air with a mike stand as Slash gallops to each end of the runway, black hair flying like a banner.

'Here's a nice priddy song,' rants Axl. 'It's dedicated to all those . . . you know the kind, they want you to be as unhappy as they are! Call them up tonight. Tell them to go to hell, they're double-talkin' . . .' The crowd has identified the song and roars the first line with him: '*Found a head and an arm in da garbage can . . .*'

'*In the ring*!' thunders the crowd. 'Sing *In the Ring*!'

'I think we're already in the ring,' he hurls back. 'You know what? I think we're already in the ring, motherf*****s, and I think we're winning!' and screams fit to frazzle your mastoids 'WAKE UP! Time to GOOOO!'

Up rises the rape monster from the boycotted album cover of *Appetite for Destruction*, a balloon the size of a bungalow, a red toady thing with four tendrilly hands and a belt of silver knives above a waving, phallic tongue.

'I'm a cold heart-breaker

Fit ta burn and I'll rip your heart in two
An I'll leave you lyin' on the bed
I'll be out the door before ya wake.'

When Axl's on stage it's only Axl you see. There seem to be three of him, all on stage simultaneously in different jackets.

With baroque sound effects, pyrotechnics and flickering screens pulsing out 'Guns N' Roses', they launch into *Paradise City* and *Knockin' On Heaven's Door*. They've given generous value but the crowd want more. A tattooed Apache in a black leather kilt, Axl runs offstage, hurling 30 bouquets of red roses at them.

The last few of us climb aboard a coach long after midnight. Winding back to Dublin, we stare out of the windows at the litter. The young are still marching home. Their faces shine up at us in the moonlight and the creeping cold cannot disperse their expressions of happiness.

Sunday, May 17, 8.30 p.m.

Slash lies full length on the sofa of his private suite, smoking, but rises courteously to shake hands. Guitar cases big as children's coffins lie strewn around the floor. He tours with a fraction of his 67 guitars: two Gibson Les Pauls, a BC Rich and a Travis Bean for slide.

'It's like cars,' he says quietly. 'You can't drive all of 'em. I kick the shit out of my guitars and some things are too valuable for that.'

Born Saul Hudson in Stoke-on-Trent, son of a graphic designer in the music business, Slash moved to California at 12. What he knows about drugs he partly learned at his mother's knee: a costume designer on *The Man Who Fell to Earth*, for a while she dated David Bowie. If adorable Duff is the band's mascot, Slash is Axl Rose's closest friend and his co-strategist.

He's still in a state of some shock from having been asked to perform at 5.45 p.m. at Slane Castle. 'It's the first time in my life I've played a show in daylight.'

What did he think of the venue?

'It was f***in' gorgeous. But it was the first show of the tour and we were all just worrying about remembering the songs.'

We talk about the bad press Guns N' Roses have had. 'We're on such a high profile, big status rock thing the press is looking at us with a microscope.'

They always have. Slash's adopted name particularly appeals to journalists, who call him Slosh, or fondly recall the old story. After a historic punch-up that started when a business man called Axl Rose 'a Bon Jovi lookalike' in a Chicago hotel bar, Axl went to jail and Slash ordered another bottle of Jack Daniels. When Doug Goldstein picked him off the floor and threw him over his shoulder, Slash showed his gratitude by urinating.

At one point Guns N' Roses told the press that if they wanted interviews they would have to sign contracts with stipulations giving the band copy approval. 'We did that just to scare the crap out of them. They'd told so many lies about us.'

So the stories I've been reading aren't all true? Did Axl, for instance, beat up a parking lot attendant in Philadelphia?

'Well, that happened.'

Didn't you say 'f***' on live television at the American Music Awards?

'Yeah, that went down.'

The riot at the show in St Louis? You walking into a vintage guitar shop in London and passing out on the floor? Duff and Izzy beating up the drummer of Faster Pussycat in Hamburg?

'Yip.' A rueful smile crosses his dark face. 'Heh heh.'

So, what isn't true?

'I didn't f*** a girl in a bar in New York like it said across a whole page in *People* magazine. My *Mom* rang me that time. She said, "You have your pants down in a bar on a Saturday night?" I said, "No, hey, you know me. I'd have gone to the bathroom if I'd been going to do that." Then there's a lot of shit about me and Axl fighting. That's not true. Axl and me have a serious personal relationship. And there's assumptions about why Izzy left.'

Rhythm guitarist Izzy Stradlin resigned in 1991 following the first Guns N' Roses world tour, having made a habit of staying at separate hotels, apparently in disgust at the life they were leading. Each member of the band was fighting his own private battle with hard drugs.

'We all had our ways of getting clean. Axl's always been pretty much OK. Izzy took the route of disassociating himself completely from that lifestyle. He just couldn't be around us. With me, it's around all the time but I just figured it out. That's not what I want to do.

'I was a major heroin addict. Got to the point where I was shooting anything up. Finally I got into trouble in a hotel and I nearly went to prison. That's when I took a plane out and kicked.'

Naked and hallucinating, he wrecked much of the ground floor of a golf resort hotel before they tackled him.

Slash owns eight cars, an alligator and 30 snakes, but he still grieves for Clyde, who used to sleep under his pillow.

'He was, like, the rock n' roll snake. He was on the road more'n I was. He'd stay anywhere. He was cool with me but he bit everyone else.' Once Clyde was found in the electrical system of the trash compactor, fully connected and smoking. 'Another time he poked one of his eyes out. Finally the whole thing got the better of him and I buried him in the back yard next to my old 260lb anaconda.'

On this tour, at least three members of the band are at another turning point. 'We've been through drugs and trying to figure out if you want to have one woman or you want to f*** everything that walks. I'm very much in love with a girl I've been with for the last two years. The first year was fine. I was home recording stuff. The next year I went back on the road and reverted to my bad old ways.'

The band sits round at three and four in the morning, griping about money.

'Some shows don't make enough to buy a candy bar. We go over time and it costs $5000 a minute. We *care* about the music. We do it when we want and for however long we want. It's the two or three hours on stage that make it all worth-while – the hotel rooms, not being able to go where we want, the business end, trying to renegotiate a record deal.'

Slash leans forward and picks up a stack of paper. 'It's not like it used to be,' he mourns. 'I used to be able to hang out at a bar all day and not be noticed.'

'What happens now?'

'Oh, I hang out at a bar all day and get hassled. Heh heh.'

Very late in my room the phone rings. An extremely together voice says, 'This is Axl'.

'Can we talk?

'I've got stuff to do tonight. We can talk tomorrow. I'll ring you.'

Monday, May 18

The day and much of the night pass in waiting for Axl Rose. Closeted in his room, he is said to be sleeping or with his doctor, talking to his shrink, consuming a milkshake; frequently on the telephone to his girlfriend, American supermodel Stephanie Seymour.

I received counselling from his PR in the States, Bryn Bridensall. 'He's a wild animal,' she told me. 'Deal with him like that, like there's no zoo keeper around. You can't schedule him to a time.'

The call comes through at 1.20 a.m.

'Now.'

But when Amy Bailey, Axl's beautiful and astonishingly serene sister, brings me to his shadowy suite, there's no one at home. When he arrives, he backs into the room, talking to someone in the passage. Introduced, he nods without smiling. Wearing a nondescript T-shirt and Spandex shorts printed with roses, he initially projects none of the electric presence that held thousands in thrall two nights previously. Round-shouldered, thin, he plods over to the bar in his big white customised Converse Allstars and crashes about with cans and glasses. He sits down, knees far apart, a veil of sandy hair over his shoulders. He has a Celtic king's reddish Saxon moustache and trimmed beard: a white, hard face and colourless eyes.

About Saturday he says, 'We're more of a night-time thing. If we had our way we would not go on until after midnight.'

His talking voice, forged in Lafayette, Indiana, is slow and deep, hypnotic and full of dramatic pauses and turns. Below its velvety surface you can hear some of the strata of its phenomenal range, suggesting the mighty metallic power he keeps hidden in his larynx.

From years on the road, his sleep pattern is shot. He packs sleepless hours with vibrational medicine, cranial adjustments and vocal exercises. Anyone who's with him – and there are 46 plus 40 perpetually moving on ahead of the band – is on call 24 hours a day. That includes Suzy, his therapist, and 'the witchdoctor', the bearded, long-haired chiropractor, Dr Stephen Thaxton. Surrounding Axl Rose is a lot of awe and downright fear: which is not to say his team don't worship him. The mixture of love and fear produces the charisma he turns on at will. His word in his world is absolute law.

'I hate daylight and stuff. I'm told that's a classic symptom of all kinds of abuse.'

When bestowed, Axl's interviews turn into marathons of self-exposure. Twenty-nine and at a turning point in his life, he's ready to make revelations, just as he will rant on to audiences of 50,000 people as if his problems and theirs were the same. His songs are abusive and brutal, but they are credible because they are almost all about his own experiences. Mick Jagger projected sex; Axl Rose projects retaliation.

'I got suspicious first of all because of certain ways people where I came from would talk about my father.'

A few weeks ago he decided to talk for the first time about the sexual abuse he says he suffered as a child. At 17 he discovered that his stepfather was not his real father, whose name was Rose. Through therapy, he says, he has discovered that his father kidnapped him when he was two, injected him with something and then sexually abused him in his cot. 'There's physical damage to prove it.' He says his stepfather molested Amy and repeatedly and brutally beat him and his brother. When I had asked her about it, his sister Amy had told me, 'Yes. It happened.'

Rolling Stone, the American music magazine where he first

made these allegations in April, could not trace Axl Rose's natural father and believes him to be dead. Axl Rose's brother and a family friend corroborated to the magazine his revelations concerning his stepfather. Axl's mother and stepfather declined to comment.

At 16 and 17 Axl Rose was one of Indiana's most troublesome delinquents. Despite his high IQ he was arrested over 20 times and imprisoned for a total of three months on an assortment of charges ranging from drug-possession to brawling and under-age drinking. The hair-trigger temperament, bar-wrecking angers and the demonic binges he is now struggling to bring under control.

'I do therapy as often as it can be. I've done 10 or 20 years of work in about a year and I can't stop. I've got to the point where I don't have a choice. I do the work or I go down the tubes. It's my destiny to be dealing with this crap. I have to do it in order to pull off this tour.'

As he talks his face changes. Sometimes he looks vulnerable and ordinary, sometimes handsome as a young Red Indian, but now and occasionally over the next four-and-a-half hours he will withdraw to the back of the sofa where his face settles into an eerie paralysis and he regards you unblinking, glassy-eyed.

'I came with a nice big package of defects. So I do past-life regression therapy and work with a homeopathic doctor.' He indicates a leather pouch on a side table, brimming with bottles.

In Guns N' Roses' transformation from Hollywood club band to international stadium band, Axl's ability to turn himself into the superhuman figure he projects on stage is crucial – whatever it takes.

'On stage I have to rise above it all. This tour, I'm just hoping I don't die. I almost passed out at Slane. At the end I was too tired even to cry. Luckily my movements are so unorthodox no one can tell when something weird is happening.'

He suddenly gets up, closes the door and cracks open a bottle of champagne.

'When we started we wanted to be the coolest, sexiest, meanest, nastiest, loudest, funnest band. There was a group consciousness of rape, pillage, search and destroy! There's a lot of things that helped us get where we are. People talk about how wrong it was doing drugs. Maybe they were the only tools I could find then; but I've got better tools now.

'For a while I wanted to go back to those days so bad. When we were done touring I would go out and try and raise the same hell, but I could only do it once every three weeks or it would have killed me. I was 27 and an old man.'

The low point came the night of the first Stones date, when he went on stage and said drugs were destroying Guns N' Roses. Later, he announced he was leaving.

'Everyone was wiped out. I was fat and lethargic and had no energy. We did those four shows and I was drained. It's pretty gnarly to have to go out in front of 100,000 people on video screens and act like you are on top of it. Sometimes I tell Slash, "I hate you for this. I gotta go out and fight Mike Tyson tonight."

The shows are triggered and fuelled by Axl's aggression. Anything can happen, although these days, since Castle Donington, since Rio and since St Louis, they try to keep the lid on.

'We like them being as crazy as possible but we've had people crushed to death at our shows and for the sake of the crowd you sometimes turn it down a bit.'

The St Louis riot started when Axl took a flying leap off the stage and closed with a man he had been trying to point out to the security guards.

'When people are obnoxious sometimes it's like no, no, I'm going to deal with you personally. You're leaving.'

He fixes a Dunhill in a white cigarette holder.

'About St Louis. Right now we're negotiating with the prosecutor on resolving the situation. They want me to be on probation. I'm not prepared to do that.'

He is always working out strategies in his head. He has to be the one in control. 'If something's going wrong on stage and I feel like cancelling the show I'm going, "Get Dougie. How much will it cost to refund the tickets?"

'If it takes $1.6 million of the money off this record to make the video, because the record company won't pay, we'll do it.' He turns on the sofa and salutes the empty chair. 'Thanks for the help, guys.'

The woman's part in the band's long-form video is played by Stephanie Seymour, although the story was originally based on Axl and Erin, his ex-wife, and their volatile relationship. Axl, who first saw Stephanie in a magazine picture, planned it that way for a couple of years before he asked her. 'It took me all that time to create the situation and for my life to evolve to the point where it was proper for me to call her.'

Stephanie has become so important to him that in his relationship with her he follows a precise and self-imposed etiquette, unable to believe, perhaps, that she would take him as he is. He evidently wants a 'nice' relationship with a woman, but he feels he has nothing to build on.

'Two years ago I wouldn't have had the opportunity to meet Stephanie and I wouldn't have known how to function. I didn't have certain graces or communication skills. I haven't any experience of independent, career-minded women. I was raised in a family where if a woman wore pants she was going to hell!'

He says he would have married Stephanie already but for the sake of Stephanie's son Dylan they didn't want to rush things and make a mistake. Dylan is two, an age with horrifying associations for Axl Rose.

'I have a little house, but it's pretty much a one-person dwelling.' He recently sold his condominium to MTV, who ran a national competition to give it away. 'It was our way of beating the market.'

He is a consummate tactician. But, I wondered, is it smart to be so consistently late for his shows? Because of the promoter's fines, doesn't it mean that he loses money?

'I'm the way I am on stage because it's what the songs require. People say, "Leave your personal life out of this, get on stage and just do it." I've tried that and it's shit. Generally, if I'm late I'm suicidal, because I don't like letting anyone down and the pressure is insane.'

Before the show on Saturday the tape that supports his

weak ankles ran out. His watch was set wrong, making him think he had an extra hour. His vocal exercises and muscle-testing programme took longer than expected.

Once on stage he holds all the cards. 'I'm negotiating all the time. We ask if we can go beyond the curfew time, because if not the crowd are *not* going to be happy. Then there's the fact that if we don't do *Heaven's Door* and *Paradise City* they're going to tear the town apart.

It is 5.30 a.m. when we say goodnight. I leave his room and so does he. I go to the lift. He pads down the corridor and knocks at a door. He's ready for therapy or muscle testing or vibrational medicine.

Tuesday, May 19

Mammoth executive effort assembles the team in the hotel foyer at 4.30 p.m. sharp for the flight to Prague on Guns N' Roses' private plane, on loan from MGM.

Rhythm guitar Gilby Clarke and keyboard Dizzy Reed are approached by the father of a pale teenage girl who sits in a corner of the lobby in a wheelchair; they make much of her. Drummer Matt Sorum cruises the room expressionlessly. Some of Duff McKagan is visible in an armchair in the corner, but most is obscured by a high-heeled brunette in a printed catsuit. Piling into coaches or limos, we meet up in the VIP lounge at Dublin airport.

A canyon of disapproval divides the lounge in two, isolating the Guns N' Roses team from the rest of the VIPs. Slash lies face down and motionless across a sofa. Behind him, Matt an' Earl tussle amiably. Earl get up, heaves Duff up on to his shoulder, twirls him round and tips him face down on to the carpet. Wiping his hands, he strolls away through the glass doors into the sunshine on the balls of his feet. Duff gets to his feet and creeps after him. Just when Earl seems most nonchalant, Duff springs. Reeling, wrapped around each other, they rebound with a shattering noise off the plate-glass doors, stagger across the room and crash back on to the sofa.

Ladies' man Slash carries my case on to the MGM special, a normal-sized 727. Inside the plane, drawing-rooms, bars and staterooms are redolent with the scent of properly cooked hot food. Bags are thrown down anywhere, huge comfy armchairs tip back, legs stretch out, vodkas and fizzy drinks come round at once served by a team of crisp, laughing American girls in fitted black waistcoats and bandsman's pants. Backing vocalist Roberta Freeman lies flat out on the carpet being stroked, presumably in a chiropractic way, by Dr Thaxton.

Dizzy Reed sits cross-legged on the floor talking about his home state, Colorado. We eat and drowse, but not Axl. He is suddenly beside me, electrically awake, hunkered down on the floor in a Very Good Mood. 'When we hired the plane, Slash was having trouble justifying our spending that much money. I said, "But dude, you're a rock n' roll star!" He looked at me and he said, "You almost made me throw up"!'

On the first Guns N' Roses trip to New York, everyone worked. 'There were tables flipped down, laptops out, we had accounting going, one of the staterooms was a video preview booth, another had a meeting, another was the obligatory drug den for those that just couldn't handle it. It was awesome! It was like Air Force One.'

The arrival in Prague at 2.30 a.m. local time wipes the smiles off everyone's face. Passport and customs control come boot-faced on board so the band can get straight into their cars, but the rest of us are lined up to be scrutinised by surly people in military uniform, and then spend an hour unattended, waiting for our baggage. Finally, big Ronnie Stalnaker, Slash's troll-like security man, lets out a roar of rage, stomps along the moving but barren carousel and ducks under the rubber apron to unload the plane single-handed.

The hotel that had been booked for us cancelled at the last moment when its management realised that this particular group of musicians was not in Prague for the international violin competition. We went instead to the Panorama Hotel, a brown cement block in a vast construction site where the staff took one look at us and closed ranks. Room-cruncher John Reese was the first to do battle, but over the next 24 hours each of us would fight our own separate war.

Prague, Wednesday, May 20

Hatred of the hotel has succeeded where every other strategy has failed. Axl is at the venue early, even before twilight.

The Strahov Stadium, 20 miles outside Prague, is insanely big, a dusty 250,000-seater divided in half for Guns N' Roses. On the far perimeter, Czech soldiers down beers at bars in a M*A*S*H-type encampment of old military tents; the band's valiant catering corps are providing a choice of four hot dishes under canvas. Behind the stage in the late afternoon sunshine technicians wearing T-shirts printed 'F***ing hostile' and 'Just don't bite it' amble over lanes and motorways of cable.

At 8.15 the stage floods with GNR technicians. Pretty soon the flying fingers of David Kehrer on the consoles open up the support band's mere 40 channels to 100 and the ears of 40,000 Czechs are assailed by a masterpiece of courtesy and tact:

'You ex-Commie bastards, prepare to rock!'

Hair and kilt flying, whirling like a fan, Axl burns straight into the rabble-raiser *It's So Easy*. His voice maintains the pitch of iron girders thrown on top of each other from a tall building. From the quavering beginning of *Live and Let Die* he seems powered by pure electricity, feeding glorious noise and anarchy into ravenous minds and souls. Slash coaxes raw and raucous sound out of his Travis Bean for *Bad Obsession*.

Here on the far edge of Europe, where the band could blow it and it wouldn't matter, they get down to playing great dirty rock n' roll. Out there under the eerie stadium lights, in front of an audience that understands maybe one word in 20, they are jamming for the love of it.

After Guns N' Roses' final departure from the stage, the aching void is filled by a piece of obnoxious cartoon animation. The crowd begins to make its way out of the distant gate.

'Axl wants to talk with you.'

His private army marches me the quarter-mile to the back of

the stadium and up cement stairs, where I enter a hot and smoky room packed with people and tables of food and drink. Duff, with three girls on his lap, is struggling to make room for a fourth. Behind a half-open door Slash is changing. At the head of the room, with the usual distance between him and everyone else, Axl stands in red bandana and grey towelling robe, drinking vegetable juice. He says, 'We'll go to my dressing-room.'

We walk across a covered bridge to a narrow room, all metal-framed windows and nylon-covered armchairs. He throws off his robe in the adjoining shower and comes back still in the fishnet top he wore for *Heaven's Door*. His tattoos and metal nipple studs are visible through the coarse netting. He sits on the floor to remove his shoes and the shields and supports inside. He pads around bare-foot, helping himself to crisps.

'Want a drink?' He's offering Coke or Dom Pérignon. 'We label them Prague, Budapest, Vienna, then we taken 'em home and sit around saying "Great vintage, that Prague '92".'

Within three days he has two more shows.

'I've had to learn about my voice. Like smoking Dunhills instead of Marlboros,' he says, 'I've got to sing on top of Slash. I checked the other day. I said, "You're playing at 140 decibels. That's a 747 at take off."'

'Come and see this,' he says, leading the way down the steps to the lower level. 'You'll like this.'

The well of a room is occupied from side to side by his newest toy, a gleaming chrome and black leather machine like an abstract motorbike, high as a horse, long as a stretched out man.

'It gives you a complete workout in four minutes. It cost 10.'

For the next 60 minutes, Axl talks quietly and at random about past-life regression theory, about people who are trying to get some measure of power over him, about the effort it takes to get everything under control, about Stephanie and about his plan to take the band to Africa next year.

Hanging loose, every antenna aquiver, strange things seem significant to him. Czech hedgerows, for instance, are filled with the exact same white-flowering bush that used to separate his family's backyard from the neighbours. 'It divided the Baileys from the Dalys.'

In the old city of Prague yesterday he saw a statue of a king on horseback. He was told it commemorated a Czech king killed by his brother after taking sanctuary in a church. Why can't he get that out of his mind? He goes over and over the things that didn't go right tonight. The pyros were wimpy. Something made him trip. That made him angry, so he kicked one of the monitors into the pit.

'We've as good a stage show as any band ever had,' he says once. 'I'll say that' and 'We *are* the f***ing band of the Nineties.'

Slash, in black and silver, joins him for a meeting, sitting cross-legged on the floor while Axl lies apparently half-asleep, propped up against the legs of the table. The subject under discussion is the Paris show on June 6, which will be beamed through 400 international carriers and shown from Kuala Lumpur to Sun City.

The head of the video team reveals problems with personnel. Axl displays about these an ice-cold rage. 'Why didn't we see this coming? Why wasn't I told about this?'

At about 3 a.m. Axl laces up his white Converse Allstars and shrugs on a wide black leather jacket, the back hand-painted with a life-size portrait of Madonna. Axl's chauffeur has been waiting four hours. Shadowed by Earl, he walks back along the bridgeway. Profiled against the moonlight, he straightens up, sandy hair flying, looking with his headband and white shorts like a young tennis star minus racquets.

Purring back along the road into Prague, Axl snaps on the radio and listens for two seconds to a woman singing 'Baby, it's over'. 'Eeeach!' he spits, punching the off button and throwing himself back in his seat. 'If it's over, don't pussy around, wimp. F***in' tell it!'

It's 3.30 when the car enters the old city and comes to rest by the statue he has been remembering all day. Blocking the quiet moonlit street, left wide open, the silver limousine presents as inappropriate a sight in the dignified antique avenue as if it were a flying saucer. PA Blake and Earl look up and down the street while Axl circles the massive base of the statue with its allegorical figures at each corner.

Back at the Panorama we pack into a tiny bedroom with Wendy Laister, head of GNR European press, and Doug and Jenny Goldstein. Axl slumps against the wardrobe door in the narrow passage outside the bathroom, knees bent. We talk, about anything and everything, and notably about the British press. Axl is funny and vicious and magic company until 5 a.m., when he suddenly get up and leaves, possibly even to sleep. Tomorrow, Hungary, then Austria, Germany, Paris and the UK. Two cities done, 17 to go.

And so Guns N' Roses rampage on through Europe, ranting, taunting, drinking, screwing, talking dirty, their very existence an affront to decent society. So long as they don't mess up along the way, so long as Axl keeps control, they reach Wembley on Saturday, leaving behind them such a wake of happiness as could unify the young of all nations. They are massive and getting bigger. To miss them is to join the grey gunge at the bottom of your locker, the fluff in your pocket seams and the hairy stuff in the plughole of the bath.

Manchester, June 9. Wembley, June 13. Gateshead, June 16.

Just be there.

Rock n' Roll.

WHO THE HELL DOES RINGO STARR THINK HE IS?

The Singing Drummer by Tom Hibbert

Ringo, why do you wear two rings on each hand?

'Because I can't fit them through my nose.'

Beethoven figures in one of your songs. What do you think of Beethoven?

'He's great. Especially his poetry.'

How did you find America?

'We went to Greenland and made a left turn.'

But that was nearly 30 years ago, innocent times when the small one – Ringo, how tall are you? 'Two-feet, nine inches' – with the extended nose sat with the other three before the press of the world and cracked his mop-top jokes, playing the clown and acting the goat, The Lovable One, the one you could take home to meet yer mum and yer dad. In The Great Throne Room at Buckingham Palace, October 26, 1965, the Queen asked the 'Fabs' how long they had been together and, quick as a flash, came Starkey's reply. '40 years!' The wag.

It is now much later, April 1992, but the 'natural' Scouse 'wit' of olden times remains intact: The Lovable One clambers aboard a podium at London's Dorchester Hotel and drily announces: 'My name is Ringo Starr.' The assembled members of the press laugh loudly at the pithy sally; a female reporter from Belgium, in the excitement of the moment, squeaks 'Yah!' It is quite like old times . . .

We are gathered here today to hear exciting news. Ringo is about to release a new LP and it is called Time Takes Time. Furthermore, his new amusingly-named All-Starr Band – featuring Dave Edmunds and Joe Walsh and Todd Rundgren and diminutive trampoline champion Nils Lofgren – is touring Europe in the summer. Cameras clack and the PR woman sternly warns us to limit our questions to 'the present and the future' (ie nothing about *them* – The Beatles – and nothing about alcoholism, if you please). And so the problem begins as a girl from Sweden asks the occasional drummer why he is starting his tour in Sweden: 'Why not?' Uproarious laughter. And a girl from Italy asks him why he is finishing his tour in Italy: 'Crazy question. It may be a surprise to you, lady, but I am a musician.' Hoots. And a girl from somewhere equally foreign asks him if he is 'reaching out to the new generation' – 'You had zis Thomas Ze Tank Engine, no?' – and he says he's just playing his kit now because he is a musician and he likes to feel the 'love' flowing from an audience because it's in his blood. Somewhere along the way we learn that Ringo has absolutely no intention whatsoever of playing with George Harrison at tonight's Albert Hall concert in aid of The Natural Law Party because what Ringo's doing now is promoting his album which is really jolly good and everything so everybody should buy it . . .

Two hours later, upstairs in a hotel suite, Ringo Starr is staring at me through his darkened spectacles. The expression on his somewhat wizened face is somewhat sour. 'This record deserves to be a Number 1,' he is saying. 'It's a fine album.' The ready quips are not dropping from the lips of The Lovable One this afternoon. His impressive nose is twitching in irritation. I have made a dreadful mistake. I have dared to ask him about . . . them.

He had entered the room in seemingly stony mood. He had thrust himself down upon a sofa and had glowered. 'Is this yer first time?' he had muttered. 'Er, come again, Mr Starkey? 'Is this yer first time?' My first time what? My first time in a posh suite at The Dorchester Hotel or what? 'Just joking,' he had muttered bemusingly. My opening question had been designed to be one of the most psychologically challenging – nay, disturbing – ever to be posed within the context of a rock interview. It was this: Have you, Mr Starr, or have you not, felt a twinge of pity ever for Pete Best (The Good-Looking One who was booted out in favour of Ringo, of whom John Lennon was once heard to remark, 'When I feel my head start to swell, I look at Ringo and know perfectly well we're not supermen')? There was a pause containing the faintest twist of menace. 'Crazy question,' The Nice One murmured, adding a withering stare for good measure.

'Did. I. Ever. Feel. Sorry. For. Pete. Best?' Yes, that was the enquiry. 'No. Why should I? I was a better player than him. That's how I got the job. It wasn't on no personality. It was that I was a better drummer and I got the phone call. I never felt sorry for him. A lot of people have made careers out of knowing, er . . . The Beatles.'

He has said it. He has uttered that word, that thing that we are not supposed to mention because Ringo has 'moved on' and is living for today and for tomorrow and not for, in the word of his old mucker in the rhythm section, yesterday. He has said 'Beatles'. So can we talk about The Beatles, then? Ringo shrugs his shoulders. 'Sure,' he grunts. So tell me about your image. You were The Goofy One. Was this an imposed personality or was it the real Starkey or what?

'That's not how I am. That was how we were in the movie, in Help! and A Hard Day's Night. That was what people felt we were like.'

But didn't you mind always being given the goony songs to sing, Octopus's Garden and Yellow Submarine and that awful one about 'the greatest fool who ever made the big time'?

'They were writing a lot heavier songs than I was and the ones they wrote for me were never that heavy, either. That's what made the combination that we were. All completely different but together we were a mighty force.'

Presumably this 'difference' in personalities was what made the break-up of The Beatles particularly acrimonious and acid. Discuss.

'That's stupid. We'd changed. We didn't have the time to put in all that energy. We were all married then. Most of us were married. I had children. John had a kid. George got married. So it was a natural end to it. We finished. That's it.'

At the morning's press conference, Ringo had been banging on about how you can't beat the feeling of playing live, of how he's 'addicted' to it, the love teeming from the audience, the 'buzz', the 'vibe' etcetera. But if we examine the history (and leave out the Ringo Starr and his All-Star Band jaunt of '89), we see that since '66, he has played on stage hardly at all. This is not a criticism, I was just wondering whether . . .

'Look, playing live is how I started,' he snaps. 'That's where my blood is. We played live for four years as The Beatles but in the end it was impossible because the reaction we used to get was so loud that I was turning into a bad musician because I could only keep the off-beat, so we were deteriorating. How often do you want to play stadiums? We as The Beatles lost the contact. I want to feel the love from the audience and you don't get that in a stadium. Bruce Springsteen loses the love and the audience contact and Guns N' Roses and the Stones and Paul McCartney, they all lose the love and the contact. They just forget that it's a great privilege to play to an audience, so on my tour I'm playing Liverpool and I'm playing Hammersmith and . . .'

And so he goes on for several weeks about all the intimate sheds he's going to bash his drums and sing that one about 'You're sixteen and you're beautiful and your mii-iine', or whatever it is, in.

So stadiums are useless. I had always imagined, in my simplicity, that The Beatles at Shea Stadium was just one of the most thrilling moments in all of popular music history. Am I entirely incorrect?

Ringo tuts and he crosses his arms, a huff-orientated posture.

'Shea Stadium was *brilliant,*' he goes. 'We were breaking new ground. Of course it was brilliant. But if you see the video on Shea Stadium, you see how crazy we all were, anyway. John wasn't playing it note-for-note. John went mad. It was a thrill.'

Did Ringo go mad all those years ago, what with all those American girls saying he should be President and swooning at his shaking fringe?

'It wasn't only American girls, you know,' he points out, helpfully. 'It was English girls and Swedish girls. So, yeah, I went absolutely mad round about 1964. My head was just so swollen. I thought I was a God, a living God. And the other three looked at me and said, Excuse me, *I* am the God. We all went through a period of going mad.'

Presumably drugs made a major contribution to the mental mayhem.

'The drugs came later. Well, there was always some element of alcohol and amphetamine and then several other substances came into play and then The Beatles was over.'

And in '68 you all went to India to 'groove' with Mr Maharishi Mahesh Yogi. That was mad . . .

'Well, I was in hospital with my ex-wife (Maureen) delivering Jason, my second son, and I got back and there was two messages on the answerphone, a message from John and a message from George, and they were saying, We've been to see this Maharishi guy. So I said, What's that all about? So they told me how great it all was and I met Maharishi and I fell in love with Transcendental Meditation and I got to India and I took two suitcases, one full of clothes and one full of baked beans because I don't eat curry, and it was a high for a while and then I thought, That's the end of it for me, thank you very much . . .'

By this time, the drummer of the Perky Personality had embarked upon his unlikely career as a screen actor, playing a gardener who has love on billiard tables in the hippy sex romp Candy (which featured Marlon Brando as a guru personage not a billion miles removed from Mr Maharishi), and then a foil for Peter Sellers in the simply awful The Magic Christian (and then being actually quite good as a teddy boy drummer in That'll Be The Day). Ringo doesn't think that talking about his Thespian pursuits is very interesting at all because he's moved on and music's the thing, like . . .

'We just decided we wanted to be an actor. I'm not interested in that acting any more . . .'

In the mid '70s, Starr made (along with some really dud LPs) a couple of splendid pop singles: Photograph and It Don't Come

Easy. The man who, in 1963, said 'whenever I hear another drummer I know I'm no good' (and who sits here today peering at me with a certain chill and insisting 'I am the best rock drummer on earth and it's not just me saying that, many fine musicians say that' when I have never even questioned his capabilities) comes over refreshingly modest for once when I say I liked those tunes.

'Well, I just decided to make some singles because The Beatles always took so long to make albums and so I started to write but I could never finish a song. I was great for two verses and a chorus but I could never finish a song so I'd have to ask George to finish it and we'd just have rows because George would always put in the 'God verse' and I don't sing about God, so after a few smashes it all went downhill because, er, well, yer know...'

I do know. It all went downhill because Ringo was hitting the sauce with alarming abandon.

'It was my addictive personality. Suddenly you're starting to drink at nine in the morning and I was procrastinating me balls off and I was just trapped as an alcoholic, a drunk.'

He was too drunk even to pay any great attention to the shooting of John Lennon, he says.

'I wasn't well when he got murdered and I wasn't well after it. I was in such great pain that I hardly noticed...'

The voice of Thomas The Tank Engine and The Fat Controller was killing itself with booze. But then – hey presto! – Ringo booked into De-Tox Mansions, USA, and everything was all right again.

'One day I had a second, maybe half-a-second, of clarity and I was in so much pain and I knew that Barbara (Bach, second wife whom he met on the set of the dismal Caveman film in '81) had mentioned a sort of re-hab situation. She had a problem, too. She found this place in Arizona. I haven't had a drink or a drug since and that was October '88 and I've given up smoking cigarettes, too.'

Ringo was cured of his urges by the power of love.

'It was love. It's love. And the proof of the difference in my lifestyle is that I've put a band together, I've made this album and...'

Ringo takes this opportunity to tell me what a great musician he is and how his new LP is really jolly good and everything until

I interrupt to suggest that however good his new LP is, it can hardly hope to top Abbey Road, can it? He looks at me as if I am deranged:

'What, as an album? My album can't beat the Abbey Road album as an album?' That is, in a nutshell, what I was driving at.

'Well, the so-called B-side of Abbey Road is one of my favourite sides, the one with Bathroom Window and Polythene Pam, but just by chance I was re-listening to Sgt Pepper the other day and that's a fine album too and it's a bloody marvellous album, it's a bloody fine album and The White Album was great because we were like a band after Pepper and all the craziness and Rubber Soul was great and the first album which took 12 hours to put down was an achievement . . . So I don't know what you're talking about. That was 30 years ago man. I'm still making records and you can hear that I'm a great musician on the new record, Time Takes Time, if you can ever be bothered to mention it. This is an actual bloody *legend* in front of you. I'm not expecting you to comb the bloody legend's hair but you could mention the new LP and these other fine musicians I'm still playing with.'

Ringo Starr is close to rage and I don't know quite why. I decide to placate him by talking about his All-Starr Band. This ploy is not a success. What is it like working with Todd Rundgren, I enquire? Todd Rundgren's a bit mad, isn't he?

Ringo lunges forward in the sofa, almost doing himself a mischief.

'What? *What*? Have you met him? Why would you say shit like that? You don't even know the man. How dare you say shit like that about a friend?'

I meant 'mad' as in 'genius'. It is a compliment.

'You're talking shit. That's like saying Frank Zappa's mad. Frank Zappa's probably the nicest man I ever met in this business. I've been in the game too long for this shit! I've done my bit. I've made a record, I've made the thing and I hope it's a Number 1 because I've done my bit, I'm promoting the thing . . . or I'm trying to promote the thing . . .'

What manner of umbrage is this? Ringo Starr seems to feel –

and strongly – that my failure to spend this interview discussing his new LP and the brilliance of Tom Petty and Jeff 'Skunk' Baxter and Harry 'Schmilsson' Nilsson and everybody else who played on it – is impudence of the first order. But wouldn't such an interview be a trifle limiting and boring and . . . ? I am unable to make this suggestion because The Clown, The Lovable One, seen here in his updated role of Pop's Mister Crosspatch, continues to rant away . . .

'If you bothered to listen to the single Weight Of The World you'd hear this line in it which goes . . . er, er . . .well, it says that you can't live in the past and that sums it up. Because you're living in the *past*. As far as this interview has been going on, it's *shit* because it's been The Beatles interview and you haven't even mentioned Time Takes Time or Weight Of The World. But that's OK. You've got the time. That's what you asked. I've answered your questions. And . . .' Ringo rises from the sofa, two feet nine inches of unbridled anger . . . 'That is *it*!' And it is. He flounces from the room, a cry of 'Thanks a lot!' that oozes with sarcasm, his cheery farewell. What this man needs, in my estimation, is a stiff drink, or a cig, or both.

That night, on stage at the Albert Hall, George Harrison played Taxman and a lot of other aged songs and then announced 'a blast from all our pasts' and on bounded Ringo. How could this be? Had not the man assured us earlier in the day that he would most definitely not be gracing this political rally thing with his presence? Well, there he was, anyway, and he played drums on While My Guitar Gently Weeps and Roll Over Beethoven, no doubt feeling all the love wafting up from the auditorium. Then, at the conclusion of this horrid old rock'n'roll novelty, up strode some representatives of the peculiar Natural Law Party to talk embarrassingly about this 'night of magic' that the crowd had been privileged to witness. And as the spiritual oration continued, a lone cry of protest rang out from the back of the stage, a bellow of annoyance, a sharp 'Shut up!' The culprit of this ill-mannered intrusion was identified only as a man with drumsticks and a great big nose . . .

SEX AND DRUGS AND ROCK'N'ROLL, ESPECIALLY SEX

Chuck Berry by Mike Sager

On a humid day in an office on Main Street, an attorney and his private eye draw the window shades, ready to run some videos for a journalist. It is home stuff, a well-known celebrity. How they were obtained, no one's explaining just now. Suffice it to say there are 20 tapes in all, and that up until this moment, no member of the press or general public has looked at this strange, dark cache. It is ghastly, it is compelling, it is exclusive, and the lawyer and the detective are looking to sell.

'I have to tell you: What you're going to see will make you sick,' says Vincent Huck, the P.I, a self-described hillbilly, former Special Forces black belt, sometime DEA informant and, until recently, a handyman in the celebrity's employ. The attorney is Ron Boggs. He's a former elected prosecutor in St Charles, Missouri, a preciously restored cobblestoned olde towne by the banks of the Missouri. Boggs scratches his head through the netting of his carefully mussed toupee, twists his leathered face into a frown. He hits PLAY.

A hotel suite, Lake Tahoe, five New Year's Eves ago. A circular bath-tub, an attractive blond white woman. A black man steps naked into the tub, stands tall over the woman luxuriating in the suds. He has high cheekbones and dimples, sideburns past his earlobes, a bit of a bulb at the end of his nose. His hair is processed into a pompadour, combed straight back. He is sinewy and muscular, but there is weather on the bark. Look closer, he could be 60. Well preserved, you might say. He takes his penis in his hand. 'See this here?' he asks the woman.

'Yes,' she says, a little breathless, kind of coy.

'This is what you're gonna bathe in.'

'It is?'

'Kiss it,' he says. She does.

'You really love me?' he asks.

He begins to urinate. She raises her hands, trying to block the stream, and says, 'I really love you.'

'Put your hands down!' he orders. He lets fly again. 'Take it! Take it! Open your mouth.'

She holds her long hair back off her face and complies. He passes a long, low blast of gas. He finishes, one last spurt.

Now the man closes his eyes. He sighs. She begins to cry.

'How's that piss taste?' he asks. 'Salty, ain't it? Did I piss in your eyes?'

'Yes.'

'I pissed all over your neck and your hair,' he says as he swabs her face with a towel. 'But you love me.'

'I love you.'

'I won't betray you. I won't betray you ever.'

She reaches up for a kiss.

'Baby, I can't kiss you, you smell like piss. Stand up and take a shower.'

Now Charles Edward Anderson Berry disappears from the frame, and she rises to shower. She puts on a little show for her date, the author of 'Johnny B. Goode' and 'Maybellene' (and its flip side, 'Wee Wee Hours').

She finishes, turns off the water, begins a little dance with the towel. From behind the camera, Berry's voice is heard: 'Now it's time for my breakfast.'

They go back to the tub. He lies down. She straddles his face. She defecates. He grunts like a wild animal.

They call this coprophilia in the research, fetish on the streets and in bookstores where you can buy magazines with titles like *Shit*

Eaters. Formerly it was part of the secret life of the loose-limbed, duck-walking hipster with the low-slung guitar, the happenin' threads and the wicked gleam in his eyes, one of the first inductees into the Rock and Roll Hall of Fame. For most people who have heard about Chuck Berry's recent legal troubles, a pot charge – criminal possession, a guilty plea, a sentence of probation and a $5,000 donation to local rehab programs – was the first and last of it, an unremarkable two- or three-column-inch wire-service report. But Berry's more elaborate, more exceptional means of self-gratification remain the focus of at least seven civil suits, some in which he is the plaintiff, some in which he is defendant, including a class action involving 200 women all over the country.

Berry was born in St Louis, largest city in the Show Me State, on October 18, 1926, the descendant of slaves, masters and Indians, according to his plainly unghostwritten autobiography, an eight-year project that began in earnest with a typing course he took while serving four months in federal prison for tax evasion. It was his third time in the pen. Two indictments for violating the Mann Act – bringing a minor across state lines for purposes of sex – got him one dismissal and one guilty verdict, for which he served two years.

Published in 1987, *Chuck Berry: The Autobiography* serves in hindsight as a particular chronicle of one man's sexual psyche. Early on, a full page is devoted to two stories, one about a chicken his daddy rescued from the outhouse, the other about his first solo attempt on the indoor 'slop jar'. A long passage is devoted to 'the white nurse lady in the navy-blue-and-white uniform' who came on house calls after his bout with pneumonia. 'She chastised me whenever I would mess with gadgets in her nurse bag. Mother supported her in paddling me when I was into any mischief and I grew to fear [her] . . . I became determined to satisfy the nurse's instructions, and it wasn't long before the noticeable change in my mischievous nature brought a hug and a kiss from the nurse. The feeling of her lips, the same lips that forgave me after once punishing, has yet to leave my memory.'

Miss Walker, his fourth-grade teacher, 'had an enormous bottom that shifted when she stepped and rolled when she walked. Her threats were taken seriously by all not wanting to fall victim beneath her huge bottom, breathless.' Harry, a high school friend, 'fused the rocket that launched my... love of science and photography, which has cost me over three quarters of a million dollars in electronic equipment... To see a picture fade into view beneath the dark red light, especially of a nude, was amazing.'

Soon came his first spell in prison, formative too: the young, handsome felon carrying on a flirtation with the white wife of the assistant warden. When he got out he married a girl named Themetta Suggs. Eventually they would have four children. (They have remained married, leading separate lives, to this day.) Working two jobs, the young Berry found time to form a band, and in 1955, at age 28, a chance meeting with Muddy Waters in Chicago gave him entrée into Waters's recording company, where Berry soon taped 'Maybellene.' It would be the first of 14 Top Forty hits. Generally regarded as rock's most influential guitarist and songwriter, Berry became the musical godfather to bands as diverse as the Beatles, the Beach Boys, the Rolling Stones and U2.

In time, Berry would buy up large amounts of real estate in Wentzville, about 30 minutes west of St Louis on I-70, a major east-west artery across the lower 48. He bought houses, trailer homes and commercial buildings and, in April 1957, 30 acres where he set about realizing his lifelong dream to build a country club. Berry Park Country Club was to be an interracial haven, a reminder of the pleasant days he'd spent as a boy working around the all-white Glencrest Country Club with his dad. (A place, his autobiography tells us, where he once stumbled upon a white couple making love The woman teased him, and had him rub and kiss her feet.)

When Berry Park opened in August 1960, it averaged more than 1,000 customers a week. For a small admission price, guests could swim in the guitar-shaped swimming pool. There was hunting, fishing, dancing, a lodge with bedrooms. But by the end of the decade Berry Park had become a rough scene, beset by drugs and rowdiness. Eventually it was forced to close. Berry appeared in a few movies in Hollywood, continued touring, worked around his properties. His hobby, his relentless pursuit, was women. His book mentions dozens – a Texas millionairess, naughty nurses, a French sex bomb, a Native American girl, waitresses, stewardesses, hotel workers, on and on.

Nearing the conclusion of his 327-page memoir, the grandfather of 13 wrote the words that would become the preface to the current, messy phase of his life: 'Now that I know much more about the writing of a book, strangely enough I intend to go for another. One that I will enjoy, the true story of my sex life. It shall not infringe on anyone or thing but me and my excessive desire to continue melting the ice of American hypocrisy regarding behavior and beliefs that are now "in the closet" and only surface in court, crime, or comical conversation.'

On December 27, 1989, it first became clear that something strange and unthinkable was going on in Wentzville. An article on page 4 of the *St Louis Post-Dispatch* reported that a civil suit for invasion of privacy had been filed in St Charles County Circuit Court by Hosana A. Huck, a former cook at Southern Air, a Wentzville restaurant Berry brought in 1987. Huck alleged that Berry had secretly installed video cameras in the women's restrooms and dressing rooms at the restaurant. The tapes, made over a one-year period, 'were created for the improper purpose of the entertainment and gratification of the abnormal urination and coprophagous sexual fetishes and sexual predilections of Defendant Chuck Berry,' the suit charged. The newspaper provided no further details.

In the coming months, two more suits would be filed against Berry, one a class action that lawyers say could involve as many as 200 women who'd visited the restaurant and Berry Park. Besides a number of tapes similar to the Lake Tahoe video – chronicling private assignations between Berry and various busty blond white women – the controversy focused on what Boggs would call 'the toilet tapes'. There were two, which Berry denied owning, showing hundreds of women, all shapes and ages, all white, in the act of relieving themselves. One of the cameras was evidently behind the toilet seat: The videos feature anatomical close-ups of girls and women at the moment of urination or defecation. The overhead cameras allowed for aerial views – aerial views of the toilets' contents during the seconds after the women stood but before they flushed.

Edited painstakingly into quick cuts – allegedly in Berry's well-equipped video workshop – the tapes amount to 'highlight' films, showing only the actual flow of excreta. Sometimes the frame is frozen for a few seconds. Lingering on moments that must have been considered particularly moving. Most of the females pictured appear to be of age. Some, however, appear to be as young as six, according to documents filed in connection with the cases.

How the tapes surfaced remains a point of contention. According to an affidavit filed by Vincent Huck, he had been working for Berry for about three years when, one day a little more than three years ago, he 'received an anonymous telephone tip telling him that something of interest to him might be found in the trash dumpster located on public property . . . in Wentzville.' In this scenario, according to sworn documents, Huck went to the Dumpster, looked inside and found, right on top, a cardboard box containing about 20 videos and about a dozen Polaroids. Fortuitously, his moment of discovering Berry's property in a public place was witnessed by local police. An anonymous caller had tipped them as well. And since he'd merely *found* the tapes and pictures, and had the police to vouch for him, Huck had an alibi if Berry ever accused him of stealing the tapes himself.

Huck went home, he says, and looked at the tapes. There suddenly appeared onscreen some parts of a woman he recognized. It was Hosana, his wife. 'My first inclination was to go after Berry with a baseball bat,' he says. Instead he went to Boggs, the lawyer and former DA for whom he sometimes worked as an investigator.

According to some sources close to the case, however, the scenario may have played a bit differently. Some say an unhappy former girlfriend of Berry's led Huck to the tapes. Berry contends in a lawsuit that Huck found them on his own while spiriting around the Berry home one day in his capacity as handyman. And, some sources say, he found tape of his wife having sex with the father of rock'n'roll.

A suit filed by Berry's attorneys in federal court claims that Vincent Huck, Boggs, Hosana Huck, her attorney, Tom Jones, and several others 'entered into illicit negotiations with video distributors . . . to capitalize upon Mr Berry's status as a world class performer.' Berry's suit, the second of several he would bring, was filed shortly after Vincent Huck sold eight full-frontal nude stills of Berry and various dates to *High Society* magazine. Berry's attorneys further allege that the Hucks, their attorneys and several others conspired to deprive Berry of his civil rights and to 'blackmail [Berry] under threat of filing lawsuits and seeking his criminal prosecution' and asked Berry for $10 million for the return of the tapes.

In any event, the discovery of the tapes, and Berry's apparent resistance to alleged blackmail attempts, set off further action. According to an affidavit filed by an agent of the so-called Multijurisdictional Enforcement Group, Huck had also been working at the time as an informant for the DEA and told them that Berry was a major trafficker in cocaine, carrying 25 kilos at a time into Wentzville in his guitar case. His drug business had netted him more than $9 million over the years, according to the MEG affidavit.

Berry Park was raided one summer morning in 1990 at 5:00 a.m. by St Charles County authorities. More than a dozen officers, some wearing ski masks, participated in the raid. Berry was away in Massachusetts. One of the things police were looking for, according to the search warrant, was 'large quantities of cocaine' in a safe.

In the end, they seized three firearms, two plastic bags containing a 'green plant material,' some 'hard dark brown material' in aluminum foil, seven trays of pornographic slides, 59 VHS videotapes, three paperback books and four newspapers described as 'sexual in nature,' and $122,501 in cash. Although

Berry's alleged coke dealing seemed to be the cops' overriding interest, police found no evidence of cocaine.

Nevertheless, county prosecutor William J. Hannah – Boggs's successor – promptly held a press conference and, according to a Berry lawsuit, declared that 'Berry is involved in cocaine trafficking, earning millions a year.' Three weeks later, after an editorial in the *Post-Dispatch* accused the elected prosecutor of 'showboating' and of working with 'bungled information,' Berry was charged with one count of possession of marijuana and three counts of child abuse. Under Missouri law the appearance of young people naked in videos constitutes child abuse. Berry, who had been on tour in Sweden when the charges were filed, turned himself in when he returned home. He denied making the tapes and using cocaine.

Now everyone got busy.

One of the lawyers moved to recruit toilet-tape victims for the class-action suit. There was talk of broadcasting a TV commercial to alert cross-country travellers who may have been caught unawares. Berry, meanwhile, hired an associate of Melvin Belli's. He sued for the return of his tapes. He sued lawyers and plantiffs. He sued *High Society*.

Huck accused one of Berry's attorneys (who denies it) of hitting him in a brawl at Crow's Sports Bar in nearby St Charles. And women came out everywhere with testimonials, ready to tell about 'Charles.'

Sharissa Kistner was one. She and her mom had lived with her sister in one of the trailers at Berry Park for a while. 'It wasn't until he told me one day that he could see into my bedroom from his mansion that I began to wonder,' says Kistner, who appears in the toilet tapes and is named as a plaintiff in the class-action suit. 'Then came a real shock. He said, "I was thinking of you yesterday while I was playing with myself." Chuck wanted me to be his mistress. He begged me, offering a mink coat and a new car. He said, "People will call you Mrs Berry. All you have to do is come up to the big house and entertain me." ' Later, Kistner found a tiny video camera in the air-conditioning vent above her bed, she says.

Chuck Berry's wife of 42 years professes obliviousness. 'I never read the papers,' Themetta Berry says, 'and most of the time I don't know what's going on in Chuck's life. I've heard he's in trouble, and he knows I'll stand by him.'

Three months after the raid, the US Attorney's office in St Louis, without explanation, returned Berry's seized money. And then, on November 3, 1990, three days before the local elections, Berry sued the prosecutor, Bill Hannah, describing the criminal charges brought against him as 'maliciously baseless' and politically motivated. 'Hannah is basically trying to run for reelection at Chuck Berry's expense,' said one of Berry's attorneys.

Hannah lost the election and, three weeks later, after extensive plea negotiations, dropped the criminal child-abuse charges; Berry dropped his suit against Hannah and agreed to two years' probation for a misdemeanor marijuana charge and to make a $5,000 contribution to local substance-abuse programs.

Today at least seven suits by and against Berry are still pending. A visit around Thanksgiving to the rolling Mississippi River valley countryside that was once Berry Park finds the people's country club in a state of decay. The black oaks and cottonwoods have dropped their leaves across the brown expanse of grass where bikers and hippies once romped at three-day rock concerts. The lodge is boarded up, the bridge across the man-made lake has gone to peeling paint and splinters, a small set of bleachers lie tossed to the side. The gate is padlocked. There are no cars parked next to the double-wide trailer houses scattered across the property, no signs of life at the jumble of the main complex. Friends say Berry is touring in Europe.

'Look at all the guys who suddenly get rich and famous, and you understand why Charles lives out there like a recluse,' says one of Berry's lawyers, who agrees, like many Berry friends, that the troubles and the suits against him amount to an 'economic lynching' of another uppity black man.

'I mean, it's incredible, he can't go anywhere without people pestering him, and it's not even fun. He's got all this money, and all these women dying to fuck him, and all the time on his hands because being a rock star isn't a real time-consuming job, and you know, your imagination runs away with you. You could walk around Wentzville and ask people if they've ever imagined doing any of this stuff and they'd all tell you no. But if we could hook them up to a machine and their heads exploded if they lied, there'd be brains everywhere. There's a guy in a major law firm in St Louis who won the 'Mr Leather of America' contest. He's got three rings through his nipple. It's in us. It's in everybody.'

THE MAN WHO FELL TO EARTH?

David Bowie by Charles Shaar Murray

The Man Who Fell To Earth? You're not kidding. When David Bowie toppled from the height of mass acclaim he achieved with 1983s *Let's Dance* album and Serious Moonlight tour, the crash reverberated throughout Planet Pop. It seemed as if everybody, including some of his previously most fervent admirers, had been eagerly waiting to see him fail.

The problem with Bowie – as far as trad-rock orthodoxy is concerned – is that, despite his charter membership of the Big Rock Survivors' Chums League, he is not trusted. He doesn't Mean It. He is neither a Clapton, scarred by a lifetime of traumatic losses and seeking solace in the eternal stoic verities of the blues; nor is he a swaggering buccaneer like Keith Richards, grizzled and seamed but essentially unbowed; and he certainly isn't a Phil Collins-style suburban everyman. Bowie is a trickster, a chameleon on a tightrope; his ability to survive and create perpetually dependent on his capacity for constant reinvention and redefinition of self, for the absorption and manipulation of new ideas. As with Dylan and The Beatles before him (and Prince and Madonna after), one of the core pleasures of Seventies Bowie-watching was the suspense of waiting to see what kind of wild mutation he would become with each new album; what guise he would adopt for each new tour. In rock and roll's uneasy trek into the future, Bowie was the point man, the scout.

What Bowie did today, be it high-camp lite-metal glam-rock, stylised white soul, or synthesiser alienation, there were regiments of wannabees – from The Sweet to Gary Numan to Spandau Ballet – ready to follow.

Until *Let's Dance*, that is. *Let's Dance* was both Bowie's triumph and his undoing. Its four-million-or-so sales figure may seem less than overwhelming when compared to the megasquillions routinely racked up by Michael Jackson, Pink Floyd or, f'Chrissakes, New Kids On The Block, but it was enough to paste his phiz on the cover of *Time* and to make him a mass-market artist for the first time in his life. As such, Bowie no longer presented a moving target, and he thus became vulnerable in a way that he had never been before; no longer the brilliant magpie on pop's cutting edge. Prince managed to take over Bowie's point-man position whilst selling larger quantities of records than Bowie ever did, but the problem was that, unlike Prince, Bowie was uncertain about how to cater for that new mass audience. This mature success – more than a decade after Ziggy Stardust – had 'fixed' him, just as the 'large cult' following of his previous career had freed him. *Let's Dance* had simply been the album that he wanted to make; and its immediate sequels, *Tonight* – an album of classy filler without any real centre, and *Never Let Me Down*, possibly the worst album of his post-'Space Oddity' career – were the work of a man who'd lost the plot.

And then there was Tin Machine. Avant-metal in suits – the brainiest, funkiest hard rock since Living Colour – complete with roughneck rhythm section and mad-professor guitarist. No-one knew quite how to take T.M.: What was Bowie *doing*? Answer the first: he was Bloking Out: being a Bloke with a bunch of other Blokes. I'll spare you the detailed disquisition on why Blokes are neither Lads nor New Men (though *Arena* could probably parlay the concept into a double-page spread which would then be picked up in the nationals), but the notoriously arty side of Bowie's personality is balanced by a decidedly Blokey aspect, which mainly emerges with appreciable quantities of lager on board. I'm sure that he's a reformed character now, *heh heh*, but I remember a moderately riotous night in '84 at Gaz's Rockin'

Blues club in London, during which Bowie spent most of the evening swapping estoteric black-music trivia with his party and scheming to entice Gaz's devastatingly gorgeous black receptionist into letting him have his wicked way. He claimed to have been going to the club for several months not just to enjoy Gaz's impeccable taste in music, but because of unrequited lust for this awesome specimen of Afro-Caribbean womanhood. As far as I know, he never succeeded, but doubtless that first shock of disappointment has long since receded.

It's therefore not overly surprising that, after the massive raspberry handed out to the overblown Glass Spider tour – during which Bowie took on so much organisational responsibility that he was generally exhausted by showtime – the idea of dissolving into a mutually supportive quartet of Blokes, willing to spread the weight of creative and organisational responsibility, must have seemed intensely appealing. Answer the second: Tin Machine enabled him to indulge a taste for guitar-strangling hard rock which had remained semi-dormant since the days of the Spiders From Mars. And answer the third: since Tin Machine's music was emphatically not aimed at mass tastes, he was able to retreat from the mainstream in which he is clearly so uncomfortable. Bowie has enjoyed playing the star far more than he ever enjoyed being one.

The first Bowie fan I ever met was Richard Neville, at the time editor of the famed hippie irritant magazine *OZ*. Richard was vastly intrigued by 'Space Oddity' and took me to the Roundhouse in the autumn of 1970 to see him perform it. This particular Bowie was an earnest, reedy youth with a blond bubble-cut, a 3-button granddad T-shirt, a 12-string acoustic guitar and a harness-mounted harmonica which, as these things often do, displayed an alarming tendency to bang him in the teeth when he was trying to sing and to slip away when in actual use. When he sang Van Morrison's 'Madame George', the song seemed too big for him, but 'Space Oddity' was utterly spellbinding. When he brought on an electric band – featuring a guitarist whom I later discovered was Mick Ronson – Neville walked out; he'd only come to hear 'Space Oddity'.

The first Bowie I ever met face-to-face was Ziggy Stardust, two years later. I was on my first-ever assignment for *NME*, which suited the strategy adopted by Bowie's then manager, Tony DeFries of MainMan, of keeping his boy away from journalists who'd known him in any of his previous incarnations. The interview took place at the Dorchester Hotel, not a hangout for hippies other than exceptionally wealthy ones, and Lou Reed and Iggy Pop, the prime source-points of Bowie's Ziggy persona and at that time fellow MainMan clients, were deployed as exotic human decor (eventually they realised this and left MainMan). Gone was the nervous hippie, and in his place was the ultimate future-rock star: jumpsuited, spike-haired, languorously arrogant. The curls-and-granddad-vest Bowie was someone very much like my hometown drug buddies, albeit more creative and more successful: this one was like no-one I'd ever met in my life.

The first question I ever asked David Bowie was something along the lines of 'The most commonly used words in current rock writing are "punk", "funk" and "camp". How much do you think you've contributed to bringing this about?' Bowie seemed intrigued by the question – presumably it made a change from 'Why is your hair that colour?' and 'How does your wife feel about you being bisexual?' – and he denied any connections with funkiness, sidestepped 'punk', and suggested that there was something camp about anyone who felt more at home on a stage than off it. 'No-one ever called Jerry Garcia camp,' I replied. 'Ah,' said Bowie, 'but he's a musician, and I'm not.' And we were away. My path and Bowie's crossed fairly frequently after that: since the *NME* always wanted Bowie stories and Bowie liked doing interviews where he could discuss a few of his more esoteric preoccupations, it seemed a mutually agreeable arrangement. When Bowie 'retired' Ziggy at Hammersmith Odeon in the summer of '73, I was the one who got the tip-off thereby enabling *NME* to have its 'Bowie: That's It, I Quit' cover story rolling off the presses even before Bowie had made the onstage announcement.

A few other Bowie memories: prolonging what was supposed

to be an extremely brief 1973 interview during the *Pin Ups* sessions at the Chateau d'Herouville in France by having photographer Joseph Stevens feed our reluctant subject an endless succession of spliffs. During the taping of 'The 1980 Floor Show' at the Marquee later that year, marvelling at Bowie's ability to switch his charisma on and off: he could enter a crowded room, full of people for whom he was the focus of attention, and not be noticed until he was ready to be noticed. Attending an industry lunch at which Bowie was being presented with about a zillion gold and silver discs, and ending up at a house he was then renting in Cheyne Walk (a few doors down from Mick Jagger's place) to hear extracts from the current work-in-progress, which turned out to be *Diamond Dogs*. I was wearing a promo T-shirt for one of Bowie's contemporaries, and Bowie was mildly offended. 'He's a real cunt,' Bowie said, 'and one day I'll tell you why.' He never did, which was just as well, since that contemporary is a leading Rock Chum, and they'll probably meet again at the next Big Benefit. They might even sing a duet.

I didn't see Bowie for another few years, missing out the Los Angeles and Berlin periods, which was just as well, because that was the time when Bowie was at his craziest. When we next met, in 1977, Bowie had terminated a fairly intense relationship with white powders (as indeed had I), and had just released *'Heroes'*, one of his enduring masterpieces. With his relaxed demeanour, untinted hair and 'normal' clothes, this Bowie was, notionally at least, 'unmasked': a Bowie who saved the extravagant role-playing for studio and stage. The '80s introduced the Serious Moonlight Bowie: a dashing-English-gentleman-about-the-arts seen in the Serious Moonlight rockumentary footage, shot in Singapore, as a sort of Prince Charles with Diana's hairdo. In private, though, he was a South London Bloke, albeit with highly arty tendencies, and that's about as close to the 'Real Bowie' as any of us are going to get.

Two more Bowie memories: at the climax of that night at Gaz's (the aftermath of a gruelling editing session for the 'Blue Jean' vid), Bowie, Julian Temple, your humble servant and one other were stumbling around Wardour Street in an advanced state of disrepair in search of taxis. A passing car screeched to a rubber-burning halt, and an incredulous face popped out of the window, ''Ere,' said the face, 'you're David Bowie, aintcha?' 'Wooaaarrgghhhh!' whooped Bowie. 'Everybody says that. Wish I 'ad 'is fakkin' money!' And finally, during a break in a Tin Machine rehearsal in Dublin, Bowie recounting how he and his son Joey went to a PiL gig in Switzerland, and the former Ziggy Stardust found himself confronted with his awful legacy: a son with red and green hair. '*You*,' said Bowie, in stern-paterfamilias mode, 'are not coming out with *me* looking like *that*.' And Joey put his head on one side and said, '*Daaaad* . . .' They went out.

Bowie has a new record, cut with Nile Rodgers, who also has something to prove. At the time of writing I haven't heard it, but all I can say is this: if it's been made to please Bowie and Nile, it'll probably be well worth hearing. If it's been made to please a notional mass audience, it probably won't. For many people, Bowie is still paying for the early Seventies: those who loved him then for his vaulting imagination and mercurial shifts demand the same thing from the forty-something Bowie as they got from his twenty-something self. And those who distrusted him then – for being contrived or derivative – are convinced that his adult self is similarly untrustworthy. And those who weren't around at the time simply don't understand what the fuss was about. Mick Jagger faces some of the same problems, but then Jagger has Keith Richards to keep the authenticists happy, while Bowie has only himself. For the man who single-handedly championed the power of the imagination in Seventies rock, respect is due. May he regain it in the Nineties.

THE DEVIL IN U2

Bono by Sean O'Hagan

'Some days are dry, some days are leaky
Some days come clean, others are sneaky
Some days take less, but most days take more
Some days slip through your fingers and on to the floor
. . . Some days are better than others'
(U2: 'Some Days Are Better Than Others')

It is late October and the four members of U2 are holed up in a rehearsal studio in Dublin, surrounded by a slimmed down retinue, trying in vain to keep the outside world at bay. In a few weeks, they will depart for Australia and the final leg of a ZOO TV world tour that has lasted over two years and traversed America and Europe twice. There is a palpable degree of pre-tour tension in the air, a sense of there being too many loose ends needing to be tied up in too short a space of time. Which is indeed the case. Before they depart, there is a video to shoot in Berlin with Wim Wenders and then Bono has to hightail it to the States for a solo video rendezvous with Frank Sinatra. And today, which was meant to have been a rehearsal day – like yesterday and the day before – an Australian TV crew is in attendance plus at least three other journalists, all waiting for an audience with Dublin's Fab Four.

Today, the U2 rehearsal room is sparsely populated with a few sound engineers and technicians who all share that stoical air that is particular to people who spend a lot of their time waiting around for something to happen. There is an eerie quality to the place that, as Joan Didion once pointed out with her usual insight, emanates from 'the masses of wires and blinking electronic circuitry with which musicians live so easily'. But, today, there are no musicians. In the far corner, atop a humming speaker stack, a computerized sign flashes a continuous message that may or may not have some deeper meaning pertinent to the moment. 'ANOTHER FINE DAY IN GOTHAM CITY...' it reads, 'OR IS IT?'

A few doors away, however, in a makeshift management inner sanctum, with cables and lights and metal flight cases littering the already overcrowded floorspace, things are as normal. Or as normal as it gets around U2. In one corner, Naomi Campbell, supermodel *extraordinaire*, is emptying the contents of her designer handbag on to the floor trying to find a wayward plane ticket to Cologne. Also present are a make-up girl and a wardrobe man, a press officer and a management woman. And a receptionist who remains remarkably calm despite a relentless influx of faxes and memos and a phone that just won't stop ringing. Right now, it's ringing for Bono.

'Is Bono still here?' the receptionist asks no-one in particular. 'Can someone tell him I have Chuck D holding.' Bono, it turns out, is in an adjacent room being asked awkward unscheduled questions by a brusque Australian TV anchorwoman about the role that ego plays in his performance. As the Public Enemy rapper is put on hold, the door opens and The Edge enters, looking more than ever like the epitome of Afghan rebel chic. Before he has time to take off his coat he is caught in a pincer movement by the charming, but resolute, make-up girl who dusts his face with powder, and the equally charming and resolute press officer who talks him through the latest requests for interviews, quotes and sound bytes. Soon after, Larry Mullen arrives, suntanned and, like Bono, sporting a beard. He is not in a good mood. A recent back injury is acting up and, lately, he says, there have been too many distractions and not enough band rehearsals. 'At the moment,' he tells me, 'we spend two hours a day playing and ten hours a day organizing.' On cue, the phone rings yet again. This time it rings for The Edge. The voice on the other end belongs to William Gibson, contemporary fiction's reigning techno-punk, who wants to talk about a possible collaboration on some as yet unspecified ZOO TV media project.

A few minutes later, I am ushered into a quiet room where Adam Clayton is relaxing, seemingly immune to the buzz of activity outside. He looks fit and healthy and, on the surface at least, remarkably unscathed by his recent and ongoing brush with tabloid infamy. (NAOMI'S U2 LOVER AND 5 HOOKERS ran the News of The World's tantalising headline a few weeks earlier.) As we exchange greetings, Bono emerges from his Australian TV interview, looking like someone who's just been put through the mill. 'Why are we doing this?' he asks a passing management woman, 'Just run it past me again. Are we not selling tickets in Australia? Is that it?' He laughs, shaking his head. The management woman laughs too, then says, 'Bono, we have to talk about who's gonna direct the Sinatra video. Like, now.' So, they talk about who's going to direct the Sinatra video (Bono and Frank singing 'I've Got You Under My Skin'). They reel off a list of names: Scorsese – would love to but can't; Coppola – would Frank see the funny side?' Clint Eastwood – a definite maybe. Then Bono says, 'Ring Winona. Winona would definitely know who'd be up for it.'

These days, even by rock star standards, U2 keep some seriously stellar company. Then again, since they hit the big time, they always have done. It's just that now it's more upfront, more visible, more in your face. Mind you, these days, so are U2. Recently, their workload has been phenomenal, their media presence ubiquitous. In the last two years, they have released two critically acclaimed albums that have placed them, for the first time in their career – and at a moment when most mega-rock bands descend into formula – at the very cutting edge of contemporary music.

They have also skirted the globe with a multi-media live show that redefined the term state-of-the-art and offended as many people as it enthralled with its wilfully overloaded melange of video imagery, subliminal sloganeering and general techno-artiness. Along the way, they helped Bill Clinton get elected, introduced Salman Rushdie to a Wembley Stadium audience, appeared on the cover of *Vogue*, made the dance charts and, in no particular order of importance, discovered irony, post-modernism and designer wear.

Then, as if the once fixed boundaries between their pop life and their pop art weren't blurred enough already, Adam and Naomi become an item. The item of the year.

'I suppose to a lot of people it might look like U2 have become the classic rock group cliché, hanging out with supermodels and all the rest,' Bono tells me, when I finally pin him down the following day, 'but, y'know, there are a million clichés to be exploded and we're having a lot of fun exploding them. The whole ZOO TV philosophy was about standing the perceived image of U2 on its head 'cos, really, it's all surface. Everything, except the actual music, is pure surface.'

The fact that you are reading this article in ARENA is probably further proof, if needed, that they have certainly succeeded in 'standing the perceived image of U2 on its head'. There was a time, not that long ago, when ARENA – and, indeed *Vogue* – would not have touched U2 with a bargepole much less considered putting them on the cover. And, to be fair, the feeling would probably have been mutual. Back then, U2 were famous for simply standing on a stage and playing music. They were so good at it that, after some years working the American circuit, they became as big as any band who simply stood on a stage and played music could possibly become. In the process, they were perceived as the ultimate caring rock band, writers of soaring rock anthems like 'Gloria' and 'I Will Follow' that often carried a message of spiritual uplift. Over five albums, they grew and grew until, with 1987s 'The Joshua Tree', which sold over 13 million, they finally entered the rarefied stratosphere of mega-rock stardom.

'The Joshua Tree' was a masterpiece of sorts. By then, the U2 sound had been honed down to a set of composite signatures – thudding drum and bass, chiming, spiralling guitar and emotive, self-questioning vocals. The whole, however, transcended the sum of its parts. On record, with the help of production alchemists, Brian Eno and Daniel Lanois, U2's best music emerged as both ambient and anthemic. In live performance, they created a big music that actually made sense in a stadium environment, that managed, against both the odds and the environment, to be both stirring and strangely intimate.

In retrospect, 'The Joshua Tree' was also a culmination of sorts, both the pinnacle and swan song of The Big Music that U2 had first created on songs like 1981's 'Gloria'. The follow-up, 'Rattle And Hum', an uneven double set, part live film soundtrack, part studio album, was a rag-bag affair. It showed a band, originally conceived in the white heat of the post-punk purge, trying, belatedly, to fit into an older lineage. Dues were paid to source music like blues, soul, gospel and primal rock and roll in a definite, some might say, desperate, attempt to belong. 'One of the hardest things about this U2 thing,' Bono would tell me, much later, 'is that we don't belong in any tradition. We've definitely gone looking for a place to belong in the past, wanted to fit into that great rock and roll tradition but it's not something we worry about anymore.' Bono now regards 'Rattle & Hum' as 'a glorious failure'. Larry Mullen Junior, as ever, is less self-forgiving. 'It was a mistake albeit one that maybe had to be made.'

In retrospect, the album is an intriguing exorcism of some of the old U2 baggage: a final failed attempt at embracing ideas of authenticity, traditionalism and belonging before abandoning all those aspirations for an emphatically post-modernist reinvention . . . 'Back there, we were lost,' admits Larry Mullen. 'We were mega-rock gods in America but we had lost touch with what was happening in Europe. We'd been away too long and, in our absence, the soundtrack had changed.'

Then U2 did what most mega-rock monsters do when the world moves on and leaves them behind – they disappeared from view for longer than usual. It was during this time that they began to look closely not just at where their music was going but at their 'perceived image' as mediated in the rock press and beyond. In some vociferous media quarters, they were fixed, unfairly and squarely, as lumbering stadium rockers with a semi-spiritual message hopelessly at odds with the still prevailing ideology of sex and drugs and rock 'n' roll. They even made it on to *Spitting Image,* cruelly lampooned in a parody of 'I Still Haven't Found What I'm Looking For' entitled 'Nobody Knows What I'm On About'. If that wasn't bad enough, along came the Pet Shop Boys with their pop-tart thrashing of 'Where The Streets Have No Name', a high-camp disco deconstruction that U2 may have abhorred but which nonetheless brought them to a new audience. Neither jibes were that funny, but they hurt all the same. 'When you make it on to *Spitting Image,*' Adam Clayton once remarked, 'you've become part of the establishment whether you like it or not. Believe me, that was not a comfortable feeling.'

'The media,' says Bono, 'does have an ability to cartoon you that you simply can't get around. I used to try to put out information all the time to try to explain where we were coming from, that it was the music that was important not the clothes of morality the media dressed us up in. I thought if we could only explain it, people would get it. Not true. We've learnt that lesson. Now we put out disinformation.'

The ZOO TV process of disinformation began in 1991 with a single called 'The Fly'. 'Some people thought of me simply as this rock star jerk so I thought I'd have fun with that – invent the rock star jerk supremo,' laughs Bono, who has spent a great proportion of the last two years as his alter-ego, method acting for the media behind wraparound Fly shades. 'The Fly' was the first clue that U2 had rewritten their own script. From the opening chords, it was clear something strange and altogether unexpected had occurred, a creative reinvention whose opening statement of intent had rendered U2 almost unrecognizable. Gone were the musical signatures of old, replaced by a charged-up, edgy noise that was taut, muscular, rhythmic and surged along on the electricity of the unfamiliar. This quantum leap into alien territory continued apace with 'Achtung Baby', an album full of dark, obsessive and insular love songs propelled by post-industrial rhythms and jagged dissonant soundscapes. The album was recorded in Hansa Studios in Berlin just after the Wall came tumbling down. In the ultra-contemporary cut-and thrust of songs like 'Zoo Station' and 'The Fly', one could hear the ghosts of other, older Hansa albums like Bowie's 'Heroes', Iggy's 'Lust For Life' and Lou's 'Berlin'. 'I need a location as a writer,' attests Bono, 'but really the location of "Achtung Baby" is not so much Berlin as the heart. It's really a landscape of the heart – love, lies, sex deceit, doubt, trust. It's about the other side of love, the dark side, love stripped of the fairy dust. In truth, it's twelve versions of the one song, twelve angles on an obsession.' There was something else going on here too, though; a sense of renewed purpose, of revitalization, of a band gleefully stomping all over its own mythology. 'We've always had this idea that you could tear away the flesh of the group but the spirit would still remain intact,' elaborates Bono. 'We wanted to see how far we could go in defacing the idea of U2 that was out there, the media-mediated idea of U2 that had grown up around us and was now perceived as the truth. "Achtung Baby" is the sound of four guys chopping down "The Joshua Tree".'

Significantly, 'Achtung Baby' was the most difficult U2 album. 'At the start of recording, we were totally out of sync with each other like never before,' Larry Mullen recalls. 'There was a constant sense of waiting for an explosion. It was like a marriage that had turned sour. I remember thinking, "What's happened to us?" It was literally sink or swim time and, in a strange way, that galvanized us – we *had* to do something radical.' The radicalization of U2 continued apace with the groundbreaking, globe-skirting ZOO TV live multi-media overload, a show that literally redefined the term state-of-the-art.

Then, with a creative momentum that surprised even their record company, they released another album. 'Zooropa' is probably the most accurate gauge yet of the lunar distances U2 have travelled since 'The Joshua Tree'. It contains a multiplicity of voices where there once was only one voice; a slippery, shifting point of view where there was once only the first-person singular. There was a time, not that long ago, when U2 songs had titles like 'War'. Now, they have titles like 'Lemon'.

The irony is that U2 have always been looser, quirkier, funnier than their music might have suggested. 'We used to think,' Bono told me after 'Achtung Baby' came out, 'that irony was the enemy of soul.' Though, in retrospect, he may already have been talking in ZOO TV soundbite-speak, that statement nevertheless encapsulated the shift in emphasis between the old and new U2. Certainly, in the old days, Bono always came across as a strangely flattened-out character in interview and performance. 'There was too much emphasis placed on the people, particularly myself. It was something to do with the kind of rock singer the audience wanted at the time, but I was never really that comfortable in the role. I guess you inevitably become imbued, in the public perception, with the tone of your music – and that's definitely what happened to me in the Eighties.'

Perhaps, I suggest, for a long time there was only one U2 tone. 'Maybe,' he reflects, 'maybe. Other sides of our personality definitely get a look in now, some darker and more decadent, some lighter and more upful. I think sometimes that's what infuriates a lot of critics who think, hang on, you're *this* band so you can't be *that* band.'

When ZOO TV touched down at Wembley Stadium for four dates in August, some nights were better than others but the opening night definitely the least best of all. 'There was,' Bono remembers ruefully, 'definitely something in the air.' That something was the inevitable critical backlash. It centred on a controversial segment of the show that featured a live satellite link with residents of the besieged city of Sarajevo. Here was all the evidence some critics needed that, beneath the new postmodern, ultra-ironic veneer, lurked the same old bunch of caring, campaigning rockers with a conscience. 'The problem with U2,' one critic concluded, 'is that they may have changed their image but not their habit of addressing social issues. They want to be ironically cool but still caring.' That in-built air of superiority that so defines and constricts 'highbrow' English culture is often unwittingly echoed in the Brit-pop critical establishment where there is a definite sense that, whatever U2 do, the arbiters of pop taste will never forgive them for being an Irish band. And, an Irish band who had the cheek to become the biggest group in the world without their approval. When I remind Bono of the chorus of disdain that greeted the ZOO TV Sarajevo section, his combative tone suggests that the scars of that particular critical mauling are still unhealed. 'First up, there are no rules governing what a rock 'n' roll show should and shouldn't be. Who says a rock show can't have uncomfortable moments? When's the last time you stared at your boots in a rock show? Secondly, those people in Sarajevo were being bombed to shit and picked off by snipers in the hills every time they left their shelters. The voice of the Sarajevo girl on the first night was totally accusatory – "You will do nothing. You will leave us to die." It was a voice that was live and unedited and it was uncomfortable but it wasn't exploitative.

'English critics found it uncomfortable but, let's face it, the English and French were the ones who slowed down the whole intervention process against what was essentially a bunch of fascists and maybe they didn't like being reminded of that. Ultimately, I think *so what* if we offended a lot of middle-class English critical sensibilities. Tough shit. It meant a great deal to the people in Sarajevo.' In this instance, perhaps that's all that ultimately mattered.

ZOO TV, according to Bono, 'was a three-act show that moved from irony to soul to cabaret.' The 'ironic' section included the immediate pre-show fanfare where martial music and cut-up images from Leni Riefenstahl's long-suppressed Nazi epic, *Triumph Of The Will*, were employed to draw some tenuous parallels between stadium rock and Aryan rallies. Leaving aside the moot point of just how ironic it is to critique a stadium rock show 'within' a stadium rock show, the intro immediately raised the question of how far U2 were prepared to go in the deconstruction of their previous mythology. At times, ZOO TV moved uneasily between sincerity and irony, seriousness and serious piss-taking, while giving the distinct impression that everything under the sun – from appropriated Nazi propaganda footage to Jenny Holzer-style slogan art to traditional greatest-hits interludes – was grist to the ZOO TV mill; that somehow, the nature of the entertainment, particularly the idea of jump-cutting from hard to soft images, was its own justification.

Predictably, but not justifiably, the critics accused U2 of having their cake and eating it. That, according to Bono, was the whole point. 'There was an element of taking all the strands of rock performance and somehow stringing them together, highlighting and demystifying the whole rock 'n' roll process. I do think that there is now a subtle difference in the way our audience approach a U2 show. There's a degree of surrender involved in their response that perhaps wasn't there before. For some people, what has happened since "Achtung Baby" is that they have to ask themselves, "Can I give myself to this the way I used to?" It's all a bit more knowing and, yes, *ironic*. At its extremes, watching ZOO TV is a bit like standing in front of a piece of Jeff Koons art. I mean, he's asking you to make a different sort of leap. Some people might think that leap is not worth making and that's fair enough.'

The final ZOO TV leap – into total parody – features another Bono alter-ego, MacPhisto, who operates way out in some camp cabaret zone that is the polar extreme to the perceived image of Bono, the crusading rock singer. MacPhisto has pancake make-up, horns and a gold lamé suit. He sings 'Desire' with the thespian lisp, like a Luvvie Elvis exhumed. Here, Bono seems to be saying, is the final irrefutable evidence to back up the ZOO TV 'philosophy' that EVERYTHING YOU KNOW ABOUT U2 IS WRONG.

There is no doubt that U2 now operate in a different, more complex media environment. Ironically enough, this has precious little to do with them reinventing themselves creatively and loads to do with them being relocated by the media in terms of celebrity. 'It's the difference between being famous for being a good musician and being famous simply for being a celebrity,' confesses Larry Mullen, who seems to be the U2 member least enamoured of this shift in emphasis. 'When I signed up for this job I wanted to be famous for being a good musician. Full stop. That still applies.'

Unfortunately, with rock megastardom, what you want and what you get are often as far apart as where you think you are and where your audience perceives you to be. 'Sometimes, particularly over the last year,' The Edge will admit, over the inevitable pint of Guinness in a nearby Dublin pub, 'I feel like we inhabit two parallel universes. We've definitely gone somewhere else in terms of fame or celebrity or whatever you want to call it. People see us now in a more glamorous light – hanging out with supermodels and what have you. That affects the way you live and I think we're all having to deal with that in our own separate ways.'

The person at the epicentre of the recent upsurge in media interest is Adam Clayton who, as Bono quips, 'has become a media celebrity by osmosis'. It has not been an easy ride. His engagement to Naomi Campbell has meant that his world has shifted suddenly out of kilter. 'It's a bit strange seeing yourself in the papers on an almost daily basis,' he winces, 'and if you're trying to be taken seriously from that position, you're in the wrong gig. Basically, you have to use all the ironic tools at your disposal to be able to be present in that context.'

A few weeks prior to our meeting, the *News Of The World* had run a sex and drugs and rock 'n' roll cover story on Adam and a bevy of escort girls. Many of us thought this was taking the philosophy of 'standing the perceived image of U2 on its head' a little too far. But this was a tabloid baptism of fire that definitely wasn't part of any ironic ZOO TV agenda and it has left the wayward Adam chastened but philosophical. 'I've gotten into trouble one way or another over the years through dealing with the pressures of this particular lifestyle in certain ways that were a bit self-destructive. Maybe I was living in an unreal world and I have a face up to that now.' Maybe, I venture, you're just about to find out how unreal things can really become? 'I do seem to spend an awful lot of the day making plans,' he laughs. 'It's no longer a case of going to the movies in a pair of jeans. I'm suddenly realizing that just going out anywhere is a media event for certain sections of the press. I have to take that on board. I can't run away from it because that's the life I live now.'

The next day, I am having lunch with Bono in the Tea Rooms of the Clarence Hotel in Dublin's increasingly trendy Temple Bar area. The Clarence is U2's latest acquisition and it is in the throes of being turned into, in Bono's words, 'the kind of hotel Sam Beckett would have liked to stay in'. Three floors below us, the basement is being transformed into a dance club as we speak. I am not sure Sam Beckett would approve but, if he were around, maybe Bono could indeed convince him that his perceived image needs standing on its head. We are talking about glamour, fame and, yes, supermodels.

'There's only one thing we weren't banking on and that was Adam falling in love with Naomi,' he grins, munching on a mixed grill, 'who brings this whole fanfare with her. That's interesting. When it happened, I thought, "Oh shit, this is where it really becomes interesting." On a purely creative level, as a writer, I'm not going to run away from new experiences and Naomi and her friends are a whole new world for me, but it's a world that's very familiar. They're performers, too. People forget that. I see them as being like silent movie stars from the Thirties. There's that sort of mystery. I have a total respect for them as performers which is nothing to do with the fact that they operate in a business that's often as shallow as the rock business.

'I think it's kinda funny that the media suddenly sees us in a different light. U2 are hip and trendy all of a sudden. We're on the cover of *Vogue* and one of us is in the papers every day in association with a supermodel. But that's not where we live as a band. Nor, indeed, where Naomi lives as a woman.'

This is all undoubtedly true, but it does beg the question, where exactly do U2 live as a band these days? And that, perhaps, is the crux of the matter. Funnily enough, I remember asking Bono a similar question during 'The Joshua Tree' tour. Back then, he said, 'I feel more of an affinity with country music and even folk than with the posing of Eighties rock 'n' roll *à la Vogue, à la Cosmopolitan*. Rock 'n' roll with a wink has taken over in England.' Some people might say, with some justification, that U2 have become part of the rock-'n'-roll-with-a-wink brigade.

'Well, that was before I discovered that irony wasn't the enemy of soul,' he laughs. 'I was the one who was up for the *Vogue* cover because, among other things, it was a laugh. But, the thing you've got to be aware of is that we're playing around with personas here. The reason we tried to kill off the perceived idea of U2 is ultimately to give the music more breathing space, to let it stand on its own without the old baggage. The music's still the core of what we do, just like it was in the Eighties when U2 would never have got near *Vogue* or ARENA. Anyway, no matter how much we strip away the mythology, the spirit of U2 remains constant. Hopefully what's happened is that our audience don't expect so much from us as people but they still expect an awful lot from the music. That suits me fine. I never wanted to be seen as a righteous person.

'I've found that there's a great freedom when you have your feet in two so-called mutually exclusive worlds – the world of irony and the world of soul, the world of flesh and the world of the spirit, the world of surface and the world of depth. That's where most people live. That's where U2 live. Then again,' he grins, 'maybe it's just a phase we're going through.'

A CRISIS OF FAITH

George Michael by Robert Sandall

George Michael's 30th birthday party ought to have been a blast, and for most of the 200 guests who attended, it was. The only person who appeared to be having trouble enjoying himself at this minutely organised, lavishly catered event was the host.

To anybody who did not know better – did not know that he was locked into an attritional battle with his record company, had not been able to complete a song for the best part of a year and had recently borne the death of a close friend – Michael looked fine. The elegantly cut Versace clothes and neatly groomed micro-beard proclaimed the familiar Mediterranean-styled figure whose name has for years been inextricably linked with the 'designer' prefix, from suits to stubble. He had lost weight since the Wham! days, when he used to stay up all night drinking, dancing and fooling around in clubs, but that had just given his features a less rounded, more sculpted look, and made his dark eyes more prominent.

In keeping with the mood of London clubland in the summer of 1992, the party had a 1970s kitsch theme, with plenty of flares and fake Afros. When Michael put on a curly wig and jumped on stage to perform a spoof version of the old disco classic Carwash, the general feeling among the partygoers was that, yes, George was finally starting to unwind. 'I think he had fun on the night,' said one old friend. 'But it took several hours before he seemed to be really enjoying himself. He's not as uptight as he was a couple of years ago but it's noticeable that he's a lot more careful now about who he talks to.'

The venue for the party was a marquee in the grounds of a stud farm in Hertfordshire, a gift to Michael's Greek Cypriot father from his son, the joint 113th richest man in Britain. Earlier in the day, a select band of close friends, mainly family, had travelled up to the Newmarket races; by night the rest of the guests arrived for a sit-down dinner and all-night disco. Many of them had been bussed in and scarcely knew where they were. The night before the party, they had received instructions to report on the Saturday evening to a spot in Watford, from where they would be transported to a final, unnamed destination. Such is the meticulousness, and some might say secretiveness, of Georgios Kyriacos Panayiotou, the person who 11 years ago chose to introduce himself to the world as George Michael.

Because his private life is just that – extremely private – it has always fascinated the press, and all night on June 26 there were bouncers in position down the Hertfordshire lane and out in the surrounding fields, specifically to discourage photographers. Had any managed to penetrate this burly cordon they would have found little to fill the gossip pages.

While the party's guest list acknowledged Michael's superstar status, it actually said more for his reputation as a generous and loyal friend. He had gone out of his way to invite the people who had known him as a young gun about town, if not before he became famous then at least before he was canonised as a household name and Spitting Image puppet. There were some well-known figures from the pop world, mainly representing the camp fringe of clubland – Neil Tennant and Chris Lowe of the Pet Shop Boys, Elton John's manager John Reid, and Paul Rutherford of Frankie Goes To Hollywood. The one notable absentee was Andrew Ridgeley, once the other half of Wham! and now resident in Los Angeles. But celebrity accounting was not really the point: this was more a friendly party than a starry one.

The paparazzi might also have been disappointed, though probably not surprised, by the party's lack of romantic intrigue. Since he stopped seeing Kathy Jeung, the Japanese make-up artist with whom he writhed erotically in a video for his song I Want Your Sex in 1987, Michael has not had an identifiable girlfriend. Even in the Wham! days, when tabloid tales of the duo's promiscuity were a daily diversion, he never quite came across in real life as the ladykiller he seemed to be in his profession as a teen idol. The notorious shuttlecock-down-the-shorts episode – a teen-pleasing climax to a game of badminton that Michael and Ridgeley pantomimed on stage in 1983 – implied a man with a degree of ironic distance from the mechanics of sexual attraction, as well as a wicked sense of humour. He claimed he lost interest in one-night stands as soon as he felt that it was himself as the star, rather than the girl, who had become the target and the prize. But no significant other has arrived to fill the romantic void. 'Obviously the thing that's missing from my life is a stable relationship,' he admitted in 1990, in his authorised biography, Bare. 'But I don't wake up wishing I shared my life with somebody.' And that was, and still is, that.

To many of those throwing shapes in the birthday marquee three years later, Michael seemed to be his usual charming self. He chatted and danced with female friends such as Wham!'s old backing singer Pepsi de Marque, and left in the fairly early hours to sleep alone in one of the stud farm's outlying bungalows.

Whether it was specific anxieties that sent Michael to bed before many of the party guests, or just incipient middle age, he certainly had plenty on his mind. The year had started tragically, with the sudden death in Rio of his Brazilian friend Anselmo Feleppa. Michael never alluded to their friendship in public and little is known about it, but Feleppa himself was less reticent, boasting to friends and the Brazilian media about the gold Cartier jewellery and the Mercedes his pop-star buddy had given him, and the holidays they enjoyed together. To Michael's inner circle Anselmo became a well-known name and, when the pair hit the clubs in New York or London, a familiar face.

The two met after Michael headlined the Rock In Rio II concert in the giant Maracana football stadium in January 1991. For the next two years, a period during which Michael opted to spend less time performing and recording than he had at any previous point in his career, he and Anselmo seemed to develop an almost brotherly closeness. Because the 32-year-old Brazilian was homosexual, rumours inevitably circulated; but Michael has a history of non-sexual male bonding, notably with his schoolfriend Andrew Ridgeley and his second cousin Andros Georgious, both heterosexual. And whatever affection he felt for this flamboyant son of a well-to-do Catholic manufacturing family, Michael must have been devastated when, in March of this year, his friend collapsed and died of a brain haemorrhage. Only weeks before, Anselmo had been boasting to friends in Rio about the New Year break the two of them had enjoyed in the Caribbean. Michael, wary as ever about his privacy, did not attend the funeral. According to Anselmo's mother, he paid a discreet visit to the grave later in the spring.

This unexpected trauma in his private life came at the worst possible time, because by now he was also facing the biggest crisis so far in his professional life, one that threatened to end his recording career, at least until the year 2003. He had decided to sue his record label, Sony, repudiating his contract on the grounds of restraint of trade. Win or lose, he said, he would not record for the company again. Although Michael had gone into the studio a couple of times since issuing the writ in November 1992, nothing happened.

Amid all the excitement in the record industry surrounding his unprecedented attack on what was, give or take a percentage point or two, a standard recording agreement, the curious wording of George Michael's public statement attracted little attention. In it he referred to his relationship with CBS/Sony as a formerly 'successful affair' that had turned into an 'arranged marriage' from which he now wanted a 'divorce'. He seemed to be talking less like a righteous litigant than a disappointed lover. Whatever the legal grounds for this mighty contest between superstar and multinational company, his motives sounded strangely personal.

* * * *

The High Court is not the kind of place you would normally go to glimpse off-duty pop stars, but this autumn the camera crews and photographers were out in force in the Strand, jostling for position behind the metal barriers on the pavement as the limousines pulled up and the bodyguards swept past. Inside the gothic warren, showbiz reporters were in hog heaven. In one court Boy George was fighting a paternity suit on the grounds that he had 'never penetrated a woman' in his life. In another, Elton John was successfully suing the Sunday Mirror for a libellous allegation that he once suffered from a bizarre eating disorder. And next door, in Court 39, George Michael was patiently and politely explaining his dissatisfaction with Sony Music Entertainment to a number of older men in black gowns and white horsehair wigs. Here, Old England, with all its legal pomp and circumlocutions, was grappling with suited but tieless New England – and doing so diligently, never asking who a person called Madonna might be, though occasionally consulting a bright pink volume of The Guinness Book Of Hit Singles.

As the arguments grind endlessly on, the dusty complexities of this action have discouraged even the most devoted George Michael fans. In the public gallery upstairs, the band of largely female supporters who restlessly hugged the rails for his three-day witness statement in October have gradually melted away. To anybody with the patience to endure it, the case now seems to hinge as much on ancient precedents in contract law as it does on Michael's assertion that Sony, and in particular the American end of the company, is deliberately trying to sabotage his career. The legal issues at stake here have often seemed to be something of a shadowplay. There has been talk about money, royalty shares and packaging costs, but Michael admitted at the outset that he has more money than he knows what to do with. Million-dollar deals escaped his notice at the time, he testified, or have slipped his memory since. When Sony's counsel, Gordon Pollock QC, put it to him 'that the real reasons for this action have little to do with the legal pleadings; you just don't get on with Sony / CBS any more, do you, Mr Michael?', the plaintiff did not try to deny it.

But while the proceedings in Court 39 have shed little new light on the intricate plot of the George Michael story, it has been a good place to spy on some of its key characters, such as his manager and friend Rob Kahane, loyally sporting the Michael facial stubble, and the ebullient record plugger Gary Farrow, one of whose children is Michael's goddaughter. At the back, on most days, sit Michael's parents: his neatly groomed mother Lesley, a British woman who married a young Cypriot immigrant called Jack Panayiotou, then an impoverished waiter, now a successful and distinguished-looking restaurateur with a shorter name, Panos, a grey pinstripe suit and glasses.

If George Michael has shown himself to be a tough and ambitious high-flyer, he is no more than his father's son in a different key. In fact, had young Georgios not made such a flying start, achieving pop stardom while still a teenager, he would probably, as the sole male heir, be running the family restaurant in Hertfordshire today.

When he was born in 1963 there were no such secure prospects. The Panayiotous' third child and only son spent six years living in a flat above a launderette in Finchley, north London. Through Jack's hard work and enterprise the family moved out and up, first to Edgeware and then to a large house in the countrified Hertfordshire town of Radlett. The demands of the restaurant meant that George saw little of his father, spending more time with his mother and two sisters. Life at home, as he has described it, sounds more materially comfortable than emotionally warm. 'There were things going on when I was growing up that I never understood,' he said later. 'Things that make me really admire my mum. If there's anything I've got from her, it's that she's like a rock. I've got that stability from her.' He has never, he said, felt any affinity with his father's Greekness, 'other than how hairy I am.'

In 1975 a precociously hirsute and rather plump G Panos turned down his parents' offer of a private education and enrolled instead at Bushey Meads comprehensive. His father was severely disappointed; he became even more so when 'Yog' (his schoolboy nickname) started hanging out with the son of another first-generation immigrant, a high-spirited Egyptian/Italian Jew called Andrew Ridgeley. By the age of 15 they were skipping classes to busk in Green Park Underground station in London. In 1979, entranced by the disco movie Saturday Night Fever, they formed their first band, The Executive. Although George somehow scraped through a couple of A-levels – English literature and art – it was clear he preferred music to studying. It was equally clear that his father would not stand for it.

In the summer of 1981, Jack gave him six months to get his career as a musician on the road, before he invoked family duty and hauled him off to the restaurant. Just before the six-month exeat ran out, 'Yog' and Ridgeley signed their first recording contract, with Innervision. A year after that, Wham! was the hottest group in the world and Georgios Panos had transformed himself into a star called George Michael.

That first contract, by all accounts a punitive document, might have been his last had it not been for Dick Leahy, who normally sits just in front of Mr and Mrs Panos in court. Leahy, tanned and skinny with a shock of straight silver hair, looks more like a healthier version of Jeffrey Bernard than the protective godfather of George Michael's career. Although he describes himself as a song publisher (the person who collects the songwriter's royalty when tunes are played or performed) he has often acted more like a manager. 'I use publishing as another way of working with artists,' he says. 'But if an artist doesn't know who he is and why he is doing it, you're wasting your time. And with George that was always there from day one.'

George knew a lot for one so young. According to Shirlie Holliman, Ridgeley's girlfriend in the pre-Wham! days and a dancer on the duo's videos, 'George has always had an older mind; he always seemed too mature for his age.' He certainly knew how to write snappy, sound-of-the-moment pop songs such as Wham Rap, and cool, timeless classics like the sax-driven ballad Careless Whisper. He also knew how to hang on to himself when the craziness of success took hold: amid all the hysteria of Wham!'s Club Fantastic tour in 1983, his sisters Melanie and Yioda were around to help with his hair and make-up, and his second cousin Andros was just around.

The following year, with Leahy's help, Michael fought to get out of his record contract and, after gambling all of his £100,000 earnings with Wham! on the action, won. The American label CBS bought off its small subsidiary, Innervision, and signed the group direct on much better terms. 'I'm not an arrogant person,' Michael said later, 'but I have a real inner confidence. I never let situations get on top of me for any length of time. I really am an optimist.'

He needed to be for what he pulled off next. In 1985, largely at Michael's instigation, Wham! announced that it had decided to split. The singer with the tandoori tan and the Lady Di haircut wanted to relaunch himself as a serious solo artist. So, less believably, did Ridgeley. So do most musicians who start out at the nursery end of a pop market, a career cul-de-sac which allows its stars roughly a three-year tenure. The big difference in George Michael's case was that within two years he had successfully reinvented himself. 'I believed in Wham! as a great way to entertain people, but when I walked into a room full of people they had a totally wrong idea of what I was about,' he said. And he proceeded to demonstrate the fact beyond anybody's wildest expectations.

Faith, his first solo album, released at the end of 1987 and featuring songs written, arranged and mainly performed by himself, was to become one of the most fêted albums of the decade. In 1988 in America, it outsold Michael Jackson's Bad and won a Grammy award (a music industry Oscar) for album of the year, a prize that rarely goes to a non-American performer. More remarkable still, the boy from Bushey, whose name was still a byword for inauthentic pop posturing among snobbish rock critics back home, found himself on the receiving end of one of the most coveted accolades in America: the black urban stations played Faith to death. At the American Music Awards – an event that chiefly celebrates black R&B artists – he won in the 'male vocalist' and 'soul/R&B album' categories. In Britain, meanwhile, he was elected songwriter of the year for the second time. As Faith went from being a hit album to a commercial phenomenon, with sales in excess of 15m worldwide (it continues to sell at the rate of about 1m per year), Michael went on an exhausting two-year world tour. And then, in 1989, at the height of his fame and with millions piling up around him, he started having another lot of second thoughts.

What was bothering the star most now, he said, was his image. Surveys carried out by his record company showed that his appeal was strongest among single white women. This was hardly surprising. The stubbly, bare-chested figure burrowing around in his leather jacket on the sleeve of Faith did not look as if he was searching for a plectrum. Nor did images such as those in the I Want Your Sex video, portraying him writing the word EXPLORE on a naked girl's rump, discourage the everywoman view of George Michael as macho Latin lover numero uno.

Suddenly, he started reversing away from this style of presentation. Of course he was aware of the sexuality in his music, he said, but the image had happened by accident. That was the way he had felt then, and now he did not feel like that any more. 'I'm going to kind of disappear,' he told various interviewers, adding that he would not be appearing in any more videos because they made him unhappy. At the time, the reason he gave for this was that he wanted 'people to like my music for what it is', and that he had grown tired of all the marketing hype. In court three years later he alluded more guardedly to 'personal reasons'.

One widely touted explanation for his retreat from handsome-hunkdom holds that by the end of the Faith tour, Michael had come to the conclusion that he might be bisexual. Michael has neither confirmed nor denied this. When asked in 1989 whether he had ever had a homosexual experience, he laughed, blushed and said: 'I wouldn't tell you even if I had.' Whenever he has talked in public about his personal relationships – which is not often – he rarely names names.

What does seem clear is that openness and intimacy, whatever their sexual connotation, are not Michael's usual style. Simon Napier-Bell, Wham!' manager, has said publicly that 'George is not demonstrative of anything he feels'. Shirlie Holliman, his friend from the Bushey days, has gone even further: 'George is one of the most secretive people I know. I am not sure how he feels most of the time. He is one of those people you have to push to get anything out of, otherwise he will just carry on playing "I'm okay, I'm coping".'

Visitors to Michael's Hampstead home, which he shares with a golden labrador called Hippy, have confirmed this impression of a man who seems almost a stranger to himself. He apparently lives without the customary personal mess and clutter of bachelor life. 'Considering how much time he spends in that house, it feels quite unlived-in', says one of the singer's acquaintances. 'It's all very stark and modern, with cream carpets, glass and metal tables, a couple of huge leather sofas, and a big jukebox on its own in a room upstairs. The overall feel is of a very expensive airport lounge, or of that mid-1980s "spartan wealth" thing.'

Michael's own accounts of his life have sounded equally distant and austere. 'I can't imagine living with someone,' he has said. 'I have a horrible feeling that part of my pleasure of living on my own is that my need for privacy is so much greater than other people's.' He concluded: 'I feel a very great need to be away from George Michael most of the time.'

Unluckily for him, this attempt to repudiate his former sexy persona coincided with an enormous shake-up in the senior management of his American record company. Following the takeover of CBS Records by Sony in 1988, a new triumvirate was installed in the label's Manhattan headquarters.

Michael later tried to claim, in his evasive way, that it was the new Japanese ownership that had caused the souring of his relations with CBS/Sony, but that was only part of the story. There was also his dealings with the Americans who now ran the company in the states, and in particular Tommy Mottola and Don Ienner.

* * * *

'Kick-ass' is a term often mentioned in connection with Tommy Mottola, a man who began his career as a singer signed to the CBS label and, 15 years later, found himself in charge of it. According to a former colleague, 'He's a street Italian, and if there's anything this industry worships it's the macho, street, kick-ass personality.' Mottola's boss, Don Ienner, a tall, thickset character in his late 30s, is another hard-headed music mogul, with a string of past successes at the Arista label.

Like any incoming management, this pair had something to prove. They wanted to break new acts, create new stars and report some booming sales figures. Mottola had his eye on a young white soul singer called Mariah Carey. Ienner was keen on an up-and-coming dance act, C&C Music Factory. Neither of the go-getting new brooms could have been too thrilled when George Michael explained to them in the summer of 1990 that his follow-up to the blockbuster Faith would be coming without the support of a video, and bearing a black and white sleeve that did not feature his alluring mug at all. Even his name and the album's lumpy title – Listen Without Prejudice Volume 1 – were to be relegated to a corner of the Cellophane wrapper.

By the time that Michael set out on a tour six months later, he and CBS/Sony were busy bickering by phone and fax. The fact that the Cover To Cover tour deliberately avoided the songs on his new album – comprising instead a selection of other people's material, mostly tunes that Michael grew up listening to – hardly helped to resolve an increasingly bitter row about exactly who was trying to sabotage the commercial chances of Listen Without Prejudice. By the end of spring 1991 it had achieved less than a third of the sales of Faith and was considered by the company to be 'dead'. When Mottola and Ienner flew to one of the Cover To Cover shows and rather insensitively left during the interval, taking Michael's manager Rob Kahane with them in their private jet, Michael's trust in his record company finally expired.

For the next year-and-a-half, until the writ last autumn, it was pretty well all over between them bar an Aids charity album and a great deal of shouting. George Michael is a determined and, understandably, proud man. He had fought his way out of one record contract and managed a brilliant career relaunch as a solo artist. He had gone on to become the only British superstar that CBS/Sony had ever produced.

The discovery that his second solo album was being given no more of a promotional push by the American company than the debut offering by the then unknown Mariah Carey inevitably offended him, not least because Carey was by then well on the way to becoming Mrs Tommy Mottola. Ienner touched a nerve, too, when he suggested that a track of Michael's called Too Funky might benefit from a club remix by his highly successful protégés, C&C Music Factory.

There has plainly been some nasty name-calling in both directions. Whatever the company felt about the economics of his decision last year to donate three tracks to the Aids charity album Red Hot And Dance (and another story tells of Ienner responding to the news by protesting that he had 3000 people in his New York office to feed, for Chrissakes), they must have worried about its effects on his female fan base.

In conservative, straight Middle America, Aids is still seen as a gay issue. George Michael performing at a memorial concert for Freddie Mercury and duetting with Elton John on his song Don't Let The Sun Go Down On Me are not the sorts of career moves that any big record company is likely to prescribe for one of the great male heterosexual icons of the past decade. Even Elton John, an altogether less romantically inspiring figure, suffered a dip in sales that coincided with his public admission that he was bisexual.

However, Michael is nothing if not tenacious, and some might call him headstrong. 'The record industry is a bunch of headless chickens,' he once declared. 'They can't tell me what to do because they don't know themselves. After I realised that, it was easy, because then I knew I had to do it all myself.' The role of Aids crusader is one he clearly believes in, and only last week he was again doing something about it, starring at a benefit concert at Wembley Arena alongside k d lang and Mick Hucknall of Simply Red. He has also been busying himself with other projects recently, notably writing a film script which Touchstone

Pictures has paid to go into development.

What he has not done is get down to finishing Volume 2 of Listen Without Prejudice, the album he promised to deliver in 1991. Three years ago, on a South Bank Show devoted entirely to himself, Michael explained that it was as a songwriter that he wanted to be remembered; but this songwriter has enjoyed his greatest recent successes as a covers artist, in the company of Elton John and the surviving members of Queen.

'If I step outside the promotion and marketing of George Michael,' the singer intimated before the release of Listen Without Prejudice Volume 1, 'then I think I have every chance of surviving as a successful musician and a balanced human being. I've achieved every other goal – I've done just about everything that I could – and that's my goal now.'

Brave words these, but perhaps not as wise as some others he uttered around the same time; words that might return to haunt him as he shuttles between the High Court and his elegant, empty house on Hampstead Heath: 'It's not commonplace for people to get to the top of this profession when they're very young, and then to live happily ever after.'

A DEATH IN THE FAMILY

Kurt Cobain by Steve Dougherty, Johnny Dodd, Bill Donahue & Craig Tomashoff

Shortly before sunset on April 9, Courtney Love, wearing one of her dead husband's trademark cardigan sweaters and accompanied by a small group of friends, wheeled her 20-month-old daughter Frances Bean's baby carriage into a beach-front park. On the shores of Seattle's Lake Washington, the park was just a short walk from the grey-shingled $1.1 million home she and Kurt Cobain had moved into three months before. For a few moments, Love, 28, paced the pebbled beach, then she wept and hugged a comforting friend. 'Why?' she sobbed quietly. 'Why?'

It was a mantra much repeated last week as fans, in shock, outrage and sorrow, tried to understand why Cobain, the gifted yet chronically unhappy rocker, had gone alone to a small room above his garage in Seattle's quiet Madrona neighborhood and ended his life with a single shotgun blast. 'I came here looking for answers,' said one grieving 20-year-old who had kept a vigil outside the house since morning. 'But I don't think there really are any. I was hoping it was a dream. Ever since I heard the news, I wanted to wake up.'

Cobain's last nightmarish act was born of the same explosive anguish that fired the music of his band, Nirvana, and made it world famous. In the end, the humour that tempered the fury of Cobain's art, and the newfound happiness brought by the birth of the baby he adored, somehow deserted him. Pain, it seemed, was all that remained.

News of Cobain's death spread quickly on the morning of April 8 after Gary Smith, 50, an electrician contracted to install a burglar alarm, discovered his body sprawled on the bare floor of the garage apartment. 'Now he's gone and joined that stupid club,' said Cobain's mother, Wendy O'Connor, alluding to the pantheon of rockers who died in their prime – among them Janis Joplin, Jim Morrison and Jimi Hendrix, whose grave is 15 miles south of Cobain's home. All had died, like Cobain, at 27.

Though widely believed to be winning his long struggle with heroin addiction, Cobain had backslid into old drug habits in the five weeks since his return from Rome, where on March 4 he had sunk into a coma after overdosing on a mixture of tranquilizers and champagne. (Despite rumours of a suicide note, Italian authorities remain convinced that the overdose was accidental.) Haunted by the incident, Love feared a suicide attempt and called police March 18 when Cobain locked himself in a room during a domestic quarrel. Police, who had responded to a similar call from Love last June, confiscated three handguns, a semiautomatic rifle and 25 boxes of ammunition for safekeeping. Afterward, Courtney agreed to a so-called tough-love intervention and, with several friends, confronted Cobain on March 25 about his drug use. 'I told him,' she said. ' "You've got to be a good daddy. We've got to be good parents".'

But the intervention backfired March 28 when Cobain bolted 36 hours after checking in to the Exodus Recovery Center, a drug-treatment facility in Marina Del Rey, Calif. His mother reported him missing after five days, but Seattle police, informed that Cobain had purchased a shotgun, were unable to locate him. Nor could a private investigator hired by Love. Cobain apparently spent one or two nights in a country house he and Courtney owned near Carnation, 40 miles northeast of Seattle. Days before his death, Cobain, looking ill and wearing a heavy coat on a warm day, was reportedly seen by neighbours in Madrona.

Then on Thursday morning, April 7, Courtney was arrested in

Beverly Hills for drug possession and taken to Century City Hospital for treatment of a suspected overdose. She was released by police that same day after posting $10,000 bail. That night, authorities believe, Cobain locked himself in the room above his garage and composed a note to his wife, friends and fans. Writing in a tight, left-handed scrawl with a red ballpoint pen, Cobain alluded to the chronic, undiagnosed pains in his 'burning, nauseous' stomach that had plagued him for years and had often made him consider suicide before. Heroin, he told Michael Azerrad, author of 1993's *Come As You Are: The Story of Nirvana,* was the only drug that quenched the fire in his gut. Cobain agonized, too, about his music. 'I don't have the passion anymore,' he wrote.

In a phone interview with MTV's Kurt Loder on April 9, Love quoted Cobain's final missive: 'It's not fun for me anymore. I can't live this life.' So fearsome was the blast that he fired to his head, authorities had to use fingerprints to identify the body. The next day, Love said, she clipped a lock of Cobain's blond hair. Later that night, she washed it, remembering how he hated to shampoo. She even wore some of Cobain's clothes in order, she hoped, to come to terms with the fact that she and Frances would never see him again. Suicide, she added, was the 'Cobain curse.'

A sense of fatal despair has, in fact, run in the family. Two of Kurt's father's uncles committed suicide in the late '70s, according to cousin Bev Cobain, a registered nurse specializing in mental health. Alcoholism and dysfunctional marriages plagued the clan, she says, adding with a weak smile, 'I don't think there was much functional stuff going on in the whole family.'

Yet the pain that led Cobain to kill himself was not evident in early childhood. Born in 1967 in Aberdeen, a depressed logging town on the Washington coast 108 miles south-west of Seattle, he was the first of two children of homemaker Wendy Fradenburg and auto mechanic Donald Cobain. A precocious, energetic child who loved to draw and to sing Beatles tunes, Cobain was diagnosed as a hyperactive preschooler. Doctors prescribed Ritalin, an amphetamine-based drug that often kept him awake until 4 a.m. To counter the drug's side effects, he was also given sedatives. Yet Kurt remembered those days as 'blissful times . . . I was constantly screaming and singing.'

His world collapsed in 1975 when his parents divorced. They later conceded that their children, especially 8-year-old Kurt, had been seriously wounded by the legal and emotional battles that followed. 'It just destroyed his life,' said Wendy. 'He changed completely.' Retaliating for his unhappiness, Kurt sketched rude caricatures of his parents on his bedroom walls, captioning them 'Dad sucks' and 'Mom sucks.'

Growing more angry and difficult to control, Kurt was sent from Wendy's house, where she raised daughter Kim, now 24, to live with Don, whose interest in hunting and sports Kurt despised. Urged by his father to join his junior-high wrestling team, Kurt once blew a big match by allowing his opponent to pin him without offering any resistance. Don, watching from the stands, walked out in disgust.

When Don couldn't control his son, Kurt moved in with various relatives, including his paternal grandparents, Iris and Leland Cobain. His grandmother, says cousin Bev Cobain, 'was the only person who gave him unconditional love.'

By his freshman year in high school, Kurt was smoking marijuana on an almost daily basis. Alienated from most of his classmates, especially jock types, whom he would taunt and spit at – and sometimes get beaten up by – Kurt grew his hair long and dyed it wild colors. 'He stood out,' says childhood friend Cameron Ross, 22, 'like a turd in a punch bowl.'

Cobain, meanwhile, had begun playing guitar. 'His main goal,' says Warren Mason, an Aberdeen musician who gave him lessons in 1981, 'was to learn "Stairway to Heaven",' the then-ubiquitous Led Zeppelin anthem. Music, Mason saw, transformed Cobain. 'He wasn't the moody guy you read about,' says Mason. 'He was a happy, responsive little kid.'

After turning on to the Sex Pistols and other punk groups, Cobain began to meld Zeppelin's heavy-metal power chords with the Pistols' punk iconoclasm. The result would, within a few years, help Nirvana become the avatar of Seattle's neopunk grunge sound.

But his rebellion was more than just musical, and Cobain dropped out of Aberdeen High School a few weeks before he was supposed to graduate in 1985. Though the otherwise poor student had won two state art scholarships, he decided to skip college and live instead what he called the 'Aberdeen fantasy version of being a punk rocker.' Working part-time as a janitor at his old high school, he crashed where he could, living at one point under a bridge. Days were spent drinking and doing drugs. At night he vandalized cars and defaced buildings.

Kurt's pained, haunting voice and his talent as a guitarist saved him from a life of petty crime. 'You always went away hearing Kurt's voice,' says Jack Endino, 36, who later produced Nirvana's first album, *Bleach*. 'It stuck in everyone's mind.'

In 1987, Cobain, along with a high school friend, bassist Krist Novoselic, now 28, and a succession of drummers – Dave Grohl, 25, signed on in 1990 – began performing his songs around Aberdeen and, later, in Olympia and Seattle. Taking the name Nirvana in 1987, the group released *Bleach,* which cost only $606.17 to record in 1989. Geffen Records signed the group two years later, and Cobain never fully recovered from the shock when Nirvana's next album, *Nevermind,* sold more than 10 million copies worldwide and gave his generation an anthem, 'Smells Like Teen Spirit.' The song, full of verbal twists ('I feel stupid and contagious / Here we are now, entertain us'), startling guitar passages and Cobain's primal screams, made him a superstar overnight.

As poster boy for today's lost generation, Kurt turned his torn jeans and grungy T-shirts into an anti-fashion statement of punk alienation. His hacked blond hair, sometimes bleached or dyed pink, hung over his eyes, obscuring surprisingly sensitive good looks. In front of cameras, he mugged with a madhouse gleam in his eye, acting as if only a demented world would declare him 'the voice of a generation.' 'Kurt was a poet,' says Ray Manzarek, 59, the ex-Doors keyboardist who had watched Jim Morrison self-destruct 23 years earlier. 'Kurt didn't speak for his generation. He spoke for himself. That's what poets do.'

In performance, Cobain would jerk around the stage as if

being electrocuted, attack the amps to create ear-splitting feedback and howl his sometimes disturbing anthems – 'I was drawn into your magnet tar pit trap,' he sings in 'Heart Shaped Box,' 'I wish I could eat your cancer when you turn black' – into the microphone. But for all his onstage bravado, Cobain, who could laugh at his own ambivalence – 'Teenage angst has paid off well,' he sang in the opening cut of Nirvana's last album, *In Utero* – felt isolated and misunderstood. Early last month, when he was on tour in Germany, he telephoned his 52-year-old cousin Art Cobain in the middle of the night. 'He said he was getting really fed up with his way of life,' says Art, who hadn't seen Kurt since the singer was a child. 'He really seemed to be reaching out. I invited him to our family reunion, but he never showed up.'

In the end, not even Love, who had become the dominant person in his life, could reach out to Cobain. A child of divorce himself – her mom, Linda Carroll, is a well-known psychologist; she lost track of her father, Hank Harrison, who once published a book about the Grateful Dead – Love had formed her own punk band, Hole, by 1991 when she and Cobain began their cyclonic courtship. A former actress who used to dance in strip joints to make ends meet, Love, who has said 'we bonded over pharmaceuticals,' was pregnant by the end of the year. The couple wed in early 1992. Six months later Frances Bean was born, and Cobain appeared to have found an anchor. But in the end, neither the daughter he doted on nor even the numbness provided by heroin could help Cobain cope. And when the poet of pain became a suicide, it left family and fans grappling with troubling emotions of their own.

During an outdoor candlelight vigil held in Seattle two days after Cobain's death, thousands of fans listened as organizers played a tape recording of Courtney's angry reading of her husband's suicide note. One depressed 28-year-old fan in the crowd went home afterward and, like the rock idol he had gone to mourn, killed himself with a shotgun.

For Cobain's widow, despair turned to rage. Breaking down on the tape-recorded message, Courtney interrupted her reading and cursed herself for submitting Cobain to the 'tough-love bulls--t.' In a cracking voice she said, 'He always said he was going to outlive everybody and live to be 120 . . . He's such an asshole. I want all of you to yell "asshole" really loud.' Toward the end of the reading, she asked the assembled fans to chant. 'Say "You're a f--ker." And then say that you love him.'

While fans listened, Love herself was attending a memorial service for Cobain a few blocks away at the Unity Church of Truth. Hurriedly organized for family and friends, the service was attended by about 100 people, including Kurt's sister Kim, Don Cobain and Don's father, Leland. Heart-broken that she had been too ill to attend, Kurt's grandmother Iris told Bev Cobain, 'Now I have no way of saying goodbye.'

Dressed in black, Love read passages from the Bible and a portion of Cobain's suicide note. A message from R.E.M. lead singer Michael Stipe, a friend of Cobain's, was also read. Following the two-hour service, as a tape of songs by Cobain, the Beatles, Leadbelly and Iggy Pop played in the background, friends lingered and talked quietly among themselves, wondering aloud, as so many others were, 'Why?'

'It's complicated and hard to figure out,' says producer Endino, who attended the service. 'Basically he was just a nice guy who didn't like fame. He was not your typical rockstar exhibitionist. The complete antithesis of David Lee Roth. He was happy to be making music and to get the hell out of Aberdeen. But how many rock icons blow themselves away at the height of their fame?'

But on April 9, as she cradled Frances Bean in her arms during her walk by Lake Washington, Courtney couldn't consider such questions. Struggling to hold back her tears, she pointed to some birds swooping overhead. 'The birds, Frances, look at the birds,' Courtney said softly, her voice cracking. 'Do you want to fly like the birds?'

DON'T DO THAT ON STAGE ANYMORE

Frank Zappa by Ian Penman

For the pop life of me, I cannot see why anyone past the age of 17 would want to listen to Frank Zappa again, never mind revere him as a deep and important artist, never mind worship at the tottering edifice of his recollected, remastered and repackaged works. Surely the only pertinent use for Zappa was as an interim stage for young lads – scared witless by what they suddenly perceive as the transience or hollowness of popular culture – for whom Zappa represents a gi-normous prefab *sneer* of self-importance behind which they can shelter for a while. (And, lest we forget in the pre-*Viz*, pre-Mayall and Edmondson 1970s, he was the only legitimate supplier of fart and bum and willy jokes.)

When you're a Zappa fan, you're supplied with a number of get-out clauses from the idea of simple plain fun most of us plain simple folks get from popular culture. If you're still slightly nervous about the idea of worshipping some geeky, greasy-hair, guitar-stranglin' guy, there is Zappa's obeisance to notions of Western cultural fidelity (as witness his attempts at More Serious Works) to buoy up your sense of *engagement* with something bigger, something . . . Beyond. If you're just an average Bill 'n' Ted kinda guy, looking to gross out on guitars 'n' guffaws, then there is Zappa's blanket cynicism, misogyny, *Catch* 22 smutty humour (supposedly a parody of smutty attitudes – yeah, and

Are You Being Served is Hegel in hiding). And finally – and perhaps most important for all for Frank's fan-boy club – is the fact that all this would-be cultural iconoclasm is served up with its outsize Guitar Worship intact. So Frank's boys can genuflect at the feet of a Real Musician; they can collate and collect and fanzine-date each and every guitar solo into hermetic, cultural, slo-death oblivion – while simultaneously pretending it's all being held suspended daintily between gilded quotation marks. Just like Frank did for most of his life. Instead of having to come out and face the difficult adult world of belief, lust, dirt, pain, you can instead strike ironic poses about belief, lust, dirt, pain; you can string ironic distancing effects like so many fairy lights, finally, around everything you do. Even unto your own aspirations.

At the beginning of his career, Zappa may have perceived one or two truths, whose pure toxicity proved too much for him. Not being someone whose genius was innately, genetically wild and crazy (no Beefheart, Iggy or Reed / Cale he), but who still wanted to be somehow, someway centre stage all the same (and all the time), he cast around. Could he be a leading edge satirist like Lenny Bruce say? (No, because he wasn't innately . . . etc) Could he be another Dylan, an irritant, generational Voice? No, because the economic veracity of the Song never was (and never would be) his forte. Then, why not just jack in all this rock culture bullshit he had such obvious contempt for from the very off, and stick to the Berlioz / Varèse beat, where he could carve out a respectable career as a 'modern composer'? Well, no, he wasn't quite good or brave enough for that, either. So, let's recap: can't sing, can't dance, not a pretty-boy or an intellectual, contemptuous of both the academy and the Street . . .

Welcome to Zappaland! A strange world of negative values and funhouse mirrors where acolytes spread out across the world, a demented glare in the eye, determined to persuade us non-believers of things that are manifestly not so. Just like Scientologists, who will earnestly tell you what a rocket scientist type guy L Ron really was (or *still* is), so the Zappoids buttonhole you with what a political giant he was, what a musicological genie, what a wit and a wag. But just because a few poor East Europeans deprived of guitar solos and anti-consumerist humour for a few decades made him Trade Minister Without Portfolio or something this does not a Noam Chomsky make of the man who inflicted *200 Motels* on the world.

Zappalytes say things like 'OK, by this point the humour was getting a little oafish, and the endless tales of groupies and on the road life a little stale, and yes, perhaps we can even detect a mouse-peep of misogyny here and there, but – Wowee Zowee! – check out the modal declension in the five minute solo on "Limburger Corporation Wowser"; it's about the third best version on record so far! Hot Poop!' No, they *really do* say things like that. Even (or especially) the intelligent, grown-up ones. Even the ones who have an otherwise coherent grasp of the adult world and all its politics and evasions and lies claim him to be the author of some kind of on-going modern Leviathan – a splenetic contemporary satire, withering in its attack, all-encompassing in its range. Then you (and they) search for the actual targets of this piercing worldview, and what do they (and you) find? Satires on porn, wanking, dope, more porn, cocktail jazz, teenage girls, disco music, more porn, TV evangelists (always a favourite stop-off for the more *intellectual* rock star), um . . . session musicians . . . um, hello?

I've been saying some of this stuff about Zappa for years, so when the staff here at *The Ire* (*sic*) sat me down with the first batch of Frank releases from the first stage of Rykodisc's all-embracing reissue programme (there are, naturally, lots of double and triple CD treats herein), I thought what a great chance to fire poison darts at the Emperor's pimply bod. I really would like to present you with a monumental, work-by-work deconstruction of the Zappa canon (I even started to write one: honest), but all those 'pressing' questions about matrix numbers and matching edits and how they differ from semi-legal bootlegs and so on, crumble into dust when confronted with just a few seconds of the globe-encircling smugness, of that Zappa-knows-best voice intoning 'Stinkfoot' or 'Dinah Moe Hum'. I mean, this is the sort of stuff you play real quiet so the neighbours don't think you're the sort of person who listens to this sort of stuff.

The classical pieces? About as desiccated as bourgeois formalism gets. (The only time I got a *genuine* laugh out of these reissues was reading an exasperated Zappa-penned sleeve note about how one of his 'ground-breaking' pop/classical crossover performances had to be curtailed when the LSO went off to the pub to get drunk halfway through and never returned: *Y-e-s!* Let's hear it for that Dunkirk spirit!)

Doesn't even that supposed split between serious and workaday popular idioms tell us something about him? You can tell a lot by a person's language, and Zappa's – both musicological and critical – is split between two poles: smut and seriousness, both of which carry an overwhelming aura of anal retentiveness, of shoring yourself up against an unmanageable world. The 'serious' Zappa ultimately operates on the same double-level as the scabrous stuff. It's so laced with his flashily dissimulated self-doubt and Other-hatred that it points continually to itself as a parody of its form, so that if the world catches on to what a big con trick is being pulled, he can then turn around and say: 'It's all just a parody.' Or: 'You either get it or you don't.'

Zappa albums valorise the idea of virtuoso instrumentalists and guitar heroes (or rather, Jean Luc Ponty, Terry Bozzio and Steve Vai) to a point which is beyond parody, however. We were always meant to *worship* these people, make no mistake about it. (You can never get through any piece on Zappa without certain giveaway buzz phrases cropping up: 'chops', 'seamless virtuosity', 'modal run', 'great studio sound', etc.) This is, in essence, as un-rock or un-subversive as music can get, in a way that Terry Riley or Morton Feldman or John Cage, say, never were: this is all about how fast your fingers can go . . .

. . . And how low your sarcasm can dredge. Zappa takes the piss out of some of the best things in the modern world (girls, drugs, discos, S&M) without offering anything better in their place. (Except colour-coded Boy's Own Record Collecting.) He took the piss out of – or hitched a ride on (as with doowop) – the transient world of Pop, but tell me this: if you were stuck on the proverbial desert island, which disc(s) would you rather have – one solitary song by Brian Wilson or the entire Zappa back catalogue?

He had long hair but sneered at longhairs; he made a long and lucrative career out of endless guitar solos but sneered at other rock musicians; he constantly bumped his little tugboatful of 'compositions' up against the prows of the classical establishment, but he lambasted that, too. In stuff like 'The Torture Never Stops' and 'Dancing Fool' he got some of his biggest audiences by exploiting the very idea of exploitation he was supposedly upbraiding. He sneered at people who took drugs; he sneered at their parents who didn't. Most of all, he sneered at women; girls trying to get by in a world full of hateful, mastery-obsessed fools like himself. He sneered at anything which represented the mess and fun and confusion of life. He sneered, in short, at anything/everything that wasn't Frank Zappa.

And all through his long, lonely night of merciless Reason, the only people who thought they weren't being sneered at were the fans. Well, how deluded can you get? Go ahead – you buy something called 'Titties And Beer' and persuade yourself you're not the asshole and butt of the joke; and that not only are you *not* being sneered at but you're participating in a revolutionary act. That takes some kinda tortuous contortion of logic, beyond most pop fans, so I guess maybe in the final analysis Zappa fans *are* smarter than the rest of us poor schlobs, at least as far as advanced sophistry goes.

As for the looming, monolithic, Mad King Ludwig shadow of this reissue programme – think about it: there really isn't any equivalent of this sort of monomaniacal, anally-retentive, self-congratulatory madness in cinema or literature. (There is, of course, in music: Zappa is nothing if not a kind of weird 'n' whacky Wagner for junior *Ring*-spotters.) This is not because Zappa's career in popular music represents some kind of brave singularity – it's because elsewhere is real culture and (t)his is ersatz. Compare him with anyone from George Clinton to Can to Sun Ra to Miles Davis (some of whom have their own reissue programmes underway) – genuine breakthrough artists who didn't just reshuffle the given forms – and realise that although Zappa built a career on purporting to despise the facades of Western consumer culture, he could never actually tear himself away from its value system (he just recycled it, reflected it back in myriad 'negative' forms); he could never step out of his circus-master role and plunge into the world of the Other.

The strangest feeling I got from listening to all this back-to-back, hyper-clean, remastered stuff is that Zappa – supposedly the great arch-modernist, the man who lived inside a studio console – was actually on some level scared witless of technology, or that he could only approach it (like everything else) as something to be mastered, a kind of aural vacuum cleaner for his archives, and that any real mind-scrambling interface with music-as-techne or techne-as-music was quite beyond his scope; that any rending of the veil of the future and away from his beloved twin antiquarian unreconstructed poles of Guitar and Symphony would have sent him gibbering into a permanent yesteryear.

Modern composer? *Please*. Like those poor fools who early on in their careers get stuck in one pose of drug-taking Wild Man or buffoon, Zappa early on got saddled with a job description of iconoclast, and there is nothing more wearing than nearly 30 years of neat, tidy, conscientious, sniping iconoclasm. The only way Zappa could ever wow anyone, finally, was through quantity not quality. He was a jack-off of all trades, and master of none.

CHARMED ROBBERY

Shaun Ryder by James Brown

The interview, a stop start conversation between three people catching up, re-assured, relaxed, confiding, is controlled by the eyes. Every three or four minutes as we go deeper into our conversation Shaun Ryder casts his eyes down at the tape recorder and I will reluctantly press PAUSE. At first it made sense, stories about old mates getting rich illegally, but pretty soon each and every Ryder anecdote would have the over-worked **loaded** legal commandos wishing they were dealing with yachting problems.

'Fucking hell Shaun,' I protest, 'I was only just thinking that time and distance will allow me to tell some real stories from before and here it is happening again . . .'

Shooting at cars in anger, freebasing whilst driving, being a pop star in that Mad bad rush around the beginning of the '90s certainly had its moments. Still the names can be changed . . .

'No, I know what you're talking about,' he says, like it's been at the back of his mind for some time as well. 'You're talking about the prostitute in the hotel in Brazil aren't you.' Indeed I am. The most outlandish case of give and take I've ever come across, when 'Our kid,' the likeable Paul Ryder, managed to shock his elder brother, who if the rumours at the time were to be believed, slept in a coffin eating white pussy all night. We may be here to talk about the return of Shaun Ryder, and his new band Black Grape which he's put together with old mate Bez and Ruthless Rap Assassin Kermit, but there's some history to catch up on first. Some baggage to check in. One or two things to declare.

'I know exactly which story you're on about . . . our kid drugging that prostitute and robbing her. Fucking hell!! She was supposed to do that to him, not the other way round. Took all her money, her drugs and her clothes, and checked out of the room. She'd already been out to fetch us all weed and then he goes and does that to her. I had to pay her and give her me tracksuit bottoms not to come up with her brothers. Fucking mad bastard.'

I once went on holiday with Happy Mondays. A fantastically sordid and shocking Coca-Cola sponsored week-long riot of fantasy, fame and drug greed. You can forget your Readings, your T's In The Park, your local crustie fest. This was the last big rock and roll corporate crap out. Exotic, untouchable and outrageously indulgent. Rock In Rio, where the modern world's music scene preened itself gluttonously on adoration like some free fat Nazi sunning himself on a distant beach.

This wasn't the height of the narcotic lunacy for Happy Mondays, it was the height of their success. Playing in a thunderstorm to 120,000 people who started out chucking rubbish at the band and ended up going carnival crazy to 'Wrote For Luck' in the torrential rain. Just to be at such altitude amongst MTV generated millionaires and artist-rockracy indicated how far the Mondays had come from doing the Boardwalk in Manchester.

Whilst everyone else played rockstar, the Mondays did what they did best, lap it all up like criminal street scum having the time of their lives. Pouring into the whore infested discos like sailors on leave, ending up in an estate with two gaunt Polacks chipping away at a brick of rock cocaine the size of a television set. And coming away with goldfish bags full at 50p a gramme. Barbecue at Ronnie Biggs with *The Sun* was the nearest anyone came to sightseeing. The rest of the time it was one long drug induced stretch by the pool under the watchful eyes of the armed hotel guards, the vultures in the sky, and the starving peasants down from the favellas to observe people in malls buying things. The tramps had been cleared off the streets and never reappeared. The papers insisted the Mondays were bringing 10,000 Ecstasy tablets with them so the festival organisers rushed them through the airport's diplomatic corridor, and children were cutting open the shirts of fully grown men to get at their money belts.

It's no wonder it's strange to meet up with Shaun and Bez again now. This was when things were going well, but at the time it was hard to decide which was more unspeakable. The things that were done to lure the world's rock barons to Rio, or the behaviour of the Mondays once they arrived.

Times change, drugs don't. A new generation of pop stars won't go anywhere without their airtight bags of charlie, and others are fracturing because of smack. You want a real barometer for what's changed whilst Shaun's been out of circulation? Glastonbury, luxury tour buses, guns, pushers and healing fields have never mixed so conveniently. Almost a decade on from first meeting him in The Ellesmere Pub, north Manchester, Shaun pimp rolls into a fancy Hampstead cafe, looking stocky and old style rough – just like he had the first time I met him – talking with comeback confidence. This is a better comeback than Mike Tyson's though. Both of them have found religion, but Shaun's using his to musical and comic effect. The new single out this month is called 'Reverend Black Grape', the album (out August) is titled *It's Great When You're Straight . . . Yeah.*

'You see that woman behind the bar, Jim,' he says, by way of explanation as to just how he's been playing everything down. 'Well, I've been coming in here for about two months and I've been out with her in a big group of us and I've chatted to her loads and she just said to me then . . . "Oh Shaun, I never knew you were the singer in the Happy Mondays. I always thought you were a drug dealer." Heh heh heh.'

And you check the glimpse of gold around his wrist and fingers. The expensive clothes worn so casually, and the fresh convict crop, and you realise it's a mistake you can easily make because Shaun Ryder's one of the few singers in England who veer towards the American rappers' association with gangster chic. With Shaun it goes deeper than image; if he wasn't capable of spewing out the lyrics to songs he can never remember the name of, the woman's observation would probably be a hundred per cent right.

Since the Mondays split acrimoniously three years ago – 'they were throwing darts at pictures of me and Bez, they wanted to get another singer. They're all telling me I'd fucked it, but, fuck me. They're stark raving bonkers, do you know what I mean?' – Shaun's evaded the spotlight, not wanting to become another spare part on the party scene. He's got himself a band, a record deal, he's relatively cleaned up – where some men smell of after-shave Black Grape smell of skunk – and he seems mellower. In between recording the brilliant debut album he's been travelling around specifically to Ireland, Israel and a return to Morocco where Bez once lived, chiliba an all.

'We went to stay in the north with these people Oriole's dad knew from the '60s. Up in the hills where they grow all the kif and everyone's walking round with guns. The bloke who looked after us had had something to do with Brian Jones so we were in good hands. Getting there the army didn't want to let us through because they thought we were going to trade. They had us out of the car asking us all about our families and our jobs and everything, the bloke driving the car was going fuckin' bananas screaming at this cop.'

Being away, all concerned agree, has been the best thing for Ryder. Last year Black Grape hung out with the Roses in Wales, Shaun listened to Snoop Doggy Dog, Dr Dre, Scarface and turned Kermit on to classic Rod Stewart. After a holiday in Israel Shaun returned and spent a week in Bez's loft smoking dope and listening to the Beatles in the countryside round Glossop. Slowly they've been adjusting themselves to re-entry.

'Two and a half years off and it's all started again now. It's gonna go exactly the fucking same man I'm tellin ya. We had a really good time doing the album, it's like "fuckin' hell, I'll start again". Then I'll have another few years chillin' out. It's been fuckin mad. Really cheeky. I'm off the rock, the brown, I'm not into coke or Prozac and I'm not going anywhere near E's. I'm watching all this lot and thinking "I used to do worse than that." Came out of the clinic and went straight back onto it. Fucking crashed into that vicar. That was just before the group split. Downed a bottle of vodka, going out to score and smashed straight into a fucking vicar in a Lada. That's the scar in me fuckin' head. Vicar jumps out and he's all right. He's fucked off, and says "I'm calling the police". So I leg it, police show up at mine and say "Shaun you daft bastard, your number plate fell off."

'There's been some shit gong down the last two and a half years. Someone's been signing on as me in Manchester, and someone else bumped into some people pretending to be me and Bez to get into clubs and get drinks. But it's getting sorted out.'

Shaun's headline grabbing shock quotes of old about 'crack, fags, and rent boys' have gone some way towards painting him as a thick vicious hooligan but any cross examination of his lyrics suggests otherwise. The music he's put together is a quality return to form. Now joined on vocals by rapper Kermit, Shaun has a certain way of catching things. He has a detached vision that allows him to lift from advertising jingle and Bible alike without any break in continuity. As before there's a heavy reliance on the Stones for inspiration but now, more than ever, Shaun sounds like Bob Dylan singing the script for *Miami Vice*. Since the first Mondays album it's also been a Ryder kick to bring Beatles lyrics up to date: 'You paid a debt today, oh boy/one thousand packages in a courtroom to destroy'.

'The main musical ingredient is me, Kermit and Danny Sabre who produced Cypress Hill. Then there's Jed who did the percussion and Wags from Paris Angels on guitar and he's got no ego problems so it was really good fun. I can't play instruments so when we were getting it together I'd be sampling the bass lines and tunes I wanted and giving it to Danny and he'd take it a bit further. Kermit's really good. I never wrote with someone before, but it was good for me getting into the music side and production. It's a lot better this stuff, big heavy bass we've paid attention to that. We've been lashing the songs out, we've already got the next album ready we've done so many songs.'

At the end of 'Shake Your Money Maker', one of Black Grape's premier songs, you can hear Shaun shouting like a madman in the background, 'yer fuckin' cunt'. It's another little tale of bagging up coke, making deals, and being addicted to greed. Like the previous track on the album, 'Submarine' – presumably titled because the snoop the song's about, Sherlock, is soon going down. Most of the songs have little story lines chopped up and infiltrated by bizarre references like the Cresta Bear line 'It's frothy man' or a sample from the legendary Troggs tape, where you hear them struggling to record a follow up to 'Wild Thing'.

There's a surprising depth and variety to the songs, that make the influences less immediately obvious than say Oasis or the Roses. Shaun says that they went out of their way to find and make and record as many interesting details and noises as possible; letting the production team of Danny Sabre and Stephen Lironi, formerly of Altered Images, bring the Ryder gang out of themselves just like the Dust Brothers did for the Beastie Boys on their comeback album *Paul's Boutique*.

From rappers like the Bhutu Clan and TLC through to sharp talking drug action films like *Bad Lieutenant* and *Pulp Fiction*, Black Grape have spread a fine selection of influences onto their music. In particular Shaun got into classic French songwriter Serge Gainsbourg after video director Wizz, who did Flowered Up's *Weekender* rave film, passed him on a video tape. Most of all though, there's character in the grooves.

'What we did on the tracks right, there was "fucking cunt" on every track, wasn't there, we had to get it down and then take all the cunting and fucking out of it all.' Kermit sees their style as being the same as 'freestyle rappers. We have conversations, that's how we do it. It's different working with this band, white guys are funny. There's more freedom you don't have to stick to one genre.'

Shaun's known Kermit since his days using smack. He started hanging out with him pretty much as soon as the Mondays had split, a good combination considering Kermit's psychology degree. Bez on the other hand, Shaun's known since school where Bez had the fastest sending off ever in a football match. Loitering between Hampstead and Glossop Bez has been getting 'Bohemian'd up'. At the height of the madness Bez never considered he might die or anything.

'Never say die! No surrender! No rest for the wicked! Even at its worse,' remembers Bez, 'it wasn't really chaos, we knew what we were doing when it was out of control, we knew what we were doing with the drugs because we've been doing them for years. We just let it happen. OK, it was pretty stupid when I broke my arm, it wasn't a planned accident or anything. With the Mondays it was just shit in the end. The break was needed, we'd kinda got overkill of everything.'

Shaun readily admits now that if the Mondays hadn't broken up Black Grape wouldn't have existed. Which brings us back to the Rise and Fall of The Mancunian Empire. Just as the good times for the Mondays appeared all over the music press so the bad times, the outrage, and the law breaking screamed in bold headlines from the tabloids. What made the band, broke the band and eventually came crashing down around them. Packed off to Barbados, with Chris Franz and Tina Weymouth of The Tom Tom Club, with the aim of turning hip credibility into something as hugely successful and accessible worldwide as the producers themselves had experienced with Talking Heads. Instead Shaun and co found the island's crack houses.

Months in the sun wrecking cars, water skiing and breaking limbs produced an emaciated version of what they were after. Squabbling over money and commitment, and sick of each other, it wasn't long before the Mondays imploded. After the mediocre sales of the album, *Yes Please*, one last substantial offer was made by EMI's Clive Black, son of *The Italian Job* lyricist Don Black, but by the time it was tabled Shaun had left the building. In more ways than one.

* * * *

Like the Smiths and The Clash they were dead before their time. Other frontline bands were either hibernating, trying to catch up with the Mondays' smack habits, or had lost their creativity. A scene had been confined to history. Just as the Stones, Rod Stewart, The Beatles and the Small Faces came out of rhythm and blues, and punk went hand in hand with reggae, so rave – that combination of drugs and house music – created great rock and roll bands. Council estates and training shoes replaced art schools and Chelsea boots. Hooded tops, Kickers, football fashions and sports labels became the look. Across Amsterdam, Ibiza, Iceland, Spain, New York and the UK a heady combination of drugs, travel, festivals, nightclubs, World Cup and sex inspired a memorable soundtrack. Along with the Stone Roses, the Farm and the Primals, the Mondays stimulated a scene that would eventually help create **loaded**.

Perhaps the best post-script to the scene is the healthy return of the Roses and Shaun and Bez. And it's a wonder the Self Destruct Twins crawled from the wreckage. People definitely had Shaun written off and Bez, well, few people had him written on in the first place. But here they sit, mooching about, going with the flow in lush north London settings, drinking Guinness and rolling up.

'Bombing seems to be getting really popular,' says Shaun, lifting his head out of the paper. 'That happened to us once, they cordoned off the whole of Manchester a few years ago and I had to get into the centre to score. I was desperate to get in there and then I remembered this snide little route and I was sure the police would have forgotten about it and so I got in the car and went over. And sure enough this route, this little back alley, they'd forgotten about it. I drove right into the centre where it was all going off, no one about, everyone gone, and I just ran into the house, got me stuff and fucked off back the way I'd came.'

Shaun Ryder. Charmed robber.

TOP BREEDERS RECOMMEND IT

Rod Stewart by Adrian Deevoy

'Who's in here?' as Nigel Tufnel once demanded of an under-stuffed olive. 'No-one.'

Casting a nosy eye around this empty and exquisitely characterless Dorchester suite, we are offered just three clues as to who its present occupier might be: a discarded necktie, Ralph Lauren, gold silk; one pair of stylish Mizuno football boots, brand new, size eight and a half; an abandoned handkerchief, white linen, extra large.

Here to solve our mini-mystery comes the owner of these identity parading artefacts, his high-pitched, soothingly serrated voice entering the room before even his celebrated conk. He speaks in the cockles 'n' pears mockney of a North Londoner who has spent half his life in Los Angeles. His actual greeting is, 'All right my old cocker? How ya doin', mate?'

The shirt and trousers are virgin white. The boots are of cricketing lineage. The hair is streaked and magnificently erect. The teeth are expensive and expressly non-NHS. The tan is more tikka than tandoori. The eyes are a-twinkle with middle-aged mischief. The flies are undone.

'Fuck me,' declares Rod Stewart, zipping up carefully. 'I've been walking around with the old block and tackle out.'

Ask Rod, Mod God, ace face, tartan tart, disco jock, lad of lads, soul singer supreme, if he'd mind talking about live performance and he responds with a helpful 'bollocks'. Wonder, alternatively, if he would prefer to answer 60 cheeky questions in one hour and he pauses pensively before returning his considered verdict. 'Bollocks.'

Rod, you rapidly realise, doesn't give a monkey's nut-sack. He cancelled his appointment with The Guardian this morning, preferring instead to view some mansion-like properties in Oxford. He delighted in discussing football minutiae in order to brighten up a lifeless encounter with 'some boring bird' from a listings magazine.

Much later this evening, he intends to visit a continental restaurant with a complicated name where he'll guzzle chilled Chardonnay, get cheeky with the ladies and behave just like any other 50-year-old teenager would. Tomorrow, he's off flogging his crop of summer concerts, talking up his new LP, pressing the press flesh and, once again, applying that substantial nose to the commercial grindstone.

But before that, why not charge your glass, slip into something a little more comfortable and cuddle up on the sofa with a gent who, to many, is a living legend and, to many more, a singing bog-brush. Because tonight, and you may wish to take precautions, he's yours.

What is the most memorable live performance you've ever witnessed?

Apart from my own? (*Laughs*) Otis Redding at Hammersmith Odeon. Late '60s. Booker T. And The MGs. Carla Thomas. That was the best. I was 17 or 18. It made me cry. I had a little tear in my eye when he did These Arms Of Mine. Missed the fucking tube home as well.

What's the smallest audience you've played to in your career?

Smallest crowd? First Faces gig where we called ourselves Quiet Melon. We was all about 21 and we played this airforce base up North somewhere. Terrible. Must have been 20 people there. By the time we'd done our stuff, all the GIs had fucked off.

Have you had a fight on stage?

Let me see. Close to it, yeah. I've nearly had punch-ups with band members. I threw a bottle of wine at Carmine Appice, my old drummer. I was singing I Don't Want To Talk About It and I turned around and he was doing all this flailing stuff. In the middle of the number. So I lobbed a convenient bottle. Nearly connected as well. Scared the living shit out of me. Don't know what it did to him.

Ever left the stage for a wee?

Oh many times. Not so much now, but in the old days, when I was singing with Long John Baldry over at Eel Pie Island because I'd get stuck into the Newcastle Brown. As you get older, you can tolerate the volume of beer better. But I'd have three pints of Newcastle then chase that down with a Scotch and I'd find that halfway through Hoochie Coochie Man I'd be busting for a pee. I remember once I was on the stage and I ran upstairs for a pee and I'm too late for the bog so I'm peeing in a beer mug, right, and you know sometimes when you're peeing in a glass and it's filling up and you know you can't stop? Well, it's overflowing over the fucking top and I can't stop and it starts going all over the floor but I've got to get back downstairs to finish the song. So I get down there and it's only dribbling through the ceiling. My own piss is coming down on my head. Long John went mad. He was going, You dirty bastard! Nearly fired me on the spot.

It's odd that no-one has followed The Faces' example of giving out bottles of drink in the audience before they came on.

Yeah, get 'em drunk and they love you. Someone should do it. I can't really do that any more. Be too fucking expensive. I kick out footballs now.

What were the benefits of growing up above a sweet shop?

Well, I could always have a Flake when I came in pissed.

How old were you when you were doing that?

You'd be surprised how old I was. It was after my beatnik phase when I'd gone over to France and Spain busking. I'd come back and I didn't know what to do. I hadn't really locked into music, so I went back to live with my mum and dad. They were running a tobacconist shop on Archway Road. So I would have been, believe it or not, 18. And I was doing a paper round. Dad used to get me up if one of the paper boys didn't come in. He'd get me by the ear 'ole and drag me out of bed. Very humiliating, doing a fucking paper round at that age. But he used to say, Come on, you're not working, so you have to earn your keep.

What did you really want to do?

No idea. All I knew was that I really loved playing guitar. I just wanted to be like Bob Dylan. This was before I started listening to rhythm & blues. Bob Dylan's first album had just come out and I knew every track on that. But I really didn't know what I wanted to do, so I was sponging off my parents.

So what would occupy you during the day?

Nothing really. Practise guitar, and if me dad went out, I had to look after the shop.

Could you run a tobacconist's at 10 minutes' notice now?

Yeah. Piece of piss.

Is it true that your colleagues once locked you in a coffin when you were a grave digger?

It was like an initiation. It was pretty scary because I didn't think they were going to open it for a couple of hours. Actually, that happened after I was a grave digger. I went and worked up in North Finchley for a guy that ran a funeral parlour and that's when I sat in my first coffin, not, funnily enough, when I was working at Highgate Cemetery.

Did being buried alive eradicate your fear of death?

Course. Forever.

There is no record of Rod Stewart ever signing to Brentford FC. Discuss.

I know there isn't, but it's true that I went for trials there. They sent four of us down from Finchley. I was never really an apprentice but I used to go down there early mornings in the summer and help mark out the pitch. But I was never signed as an apprentice.

When did you first hear Sam Cooke?

When I was working at a wallpaper factory in Kentish Town. I was on silk screens. You had to copy the wallpaper with this ink, then the ink would burn through the silk screen. And it was there I first heard, 'Cupid, draw back your bow.' And Chain Gang. That was it. Real turning point.

Was there a record playing when you lost your virginity?

I was in a tent. There was music playing, probably Kenny Ball or Ken Collier's Jazzmen. It was at the Keighley Jazz Festival just after I'd left school. Went down there and got shagged. I only got it in for about a second and I come me bolt.

Was Maggie May really recorded in two takes?

The backing track was done in two takes. I wouldn't have done many vocal takes. I don't really do many now. If I do six takes now, that's a lot. Ask anyone I work with. But with Maggie, two, three takes. It was unheard of to do anymore than that in those days.

Is that song a load of sexist twaddle?

I suppose you can look at it like that, yeah. Funnily enough, it was about the time I lost my virginity.

Could Stay With Me be considered even more sexist?

Oh, I think so, don't you? (*Laughs*)

Would you say you were a PC bloke?

PC? What's that?

Politically Correct.

(*Laughs*) Is that what they call it now? PC. No, I don't think I'm a particularly PC bloke. It's never bothered me at all. (*Laughs*)

Did you deliberately contrive a vocal style or is that your natural singing voice?

I used to sing in one key above what was natural for me to try and force it a little bit. I remember Sam Cooke did that. So naturally anything Sam did I would do . . . apart from getting shot in a hotel room by a hooker.

Did you listen to rap?

I have to because my kids listen to it all the time. I like 2 Pac, a lot of the stuff he does. But there's so much of it, I can't keep up. It's like the bloody music scene here. You just can't keep pace.

Fucking bands put an album out, they're on MTV then they break up. There's one rap thing I really like. It's about the act of dying. Remarkable. It goes, 'You've never seen a man cry / Till you've seen a man die.'

Sounds like Ice Cube.

Don't think it's Ice Cube. It might be Ice Bucket! I really get my son going with that. He's got the fucking hat on back to front and the trousers down there and the underpants up here and I say to him, Yeah, I really like that House of Paint record. He goes mad. Dad! You know it's House Of Pain! I try and explain some of the samples to him, where they come from. Because you'll often hear Sly And The Family Stone samples, so I'll tell him about that, because I think it's important that he understands the roots of what he's listening to. My daughter, who's 15, has completely blown out the whole rap thing now and she's listening to Cat Stevens.

What would you do if a bloke who was like the young you turned up to take her out?

I wouldn't mind at all. If it makes her happy, and it's legal, then that's fine. I wouldn't mind her going out with a rascal.

The blues – it's a bit miserable, isn't it?

I just come back to the blues again and again. Why do I always put on Muddy Waters when I'm having a bath? I just love those guys. I met Muddy and you couldn't have wanted to meet a nicer gentleman. I get so fucking tongue-tied when I meet someone like that. I met Denis Law the other day. Now here's someone I've idolised all my life. I check into hotels under the name Denis Law. I use his name. I've known him off and on but I haven't seen him for 10 years. But I meet him and I can't speak. I've got loads of things in my head I want to ask him and then I walk away and think, What was wrong with me? Why couldn't

I just talk to him normally? But what a player. Do you know, he's two pounds lighter now than when he was playing. And he smokes and drinks. I'd gone up to Maine Road in Manchester to promote my concert and we had a little kick about: Denis was there and Mike Summerbee and Frannie Lee – he can't do much now his knees have gone, but he's still got his bog roll factory – and you pass the ball to Denis and he never does anything standard with it. He'll always flick it somewhere you don't expect it to go.

What position do you play in now?

Full back. Any further back than that and I'll be doing the St John's Ambulance behind the goal.

Are you hard?

I don't think so. I can tackle hard but I'm not dirty or niggly. I don't think there's any need for that. But I give it a lot of shouting. I like to shout at my boys. That's always been part of the game.

You've got a reputation for choosing clever cover versions. What's the worst one you've done?

Oh, there's been some dodgy ones. I did All Right Now by Free which I should never, ever have touched. It was a fucking electric drum version too. Dreadful.

Is it fair to say you've nicked lines off Bob Dylan?

No, it isn't. Like what?

Like your song called Forever Young?

We settled with him for that. The melody was different. There have been eight songs called Forever Young. Bob's wasn't the first. I could aim the same things at Bob Dylan. Scarborough Fair. And I heard a line the other night – 'My father's house has many mansions' – and he nicked that from the Bible. But how can I not be influenced by someone I hold in such high esteem? There's another bloke I've only met twice in my entire life, and both in bizarre circumstances. First time, I was in The Faces and I'd just met Britt Ekland and Bob said, Do you want to come back to so-and-so's house and have a play? And I was like, I've just met Britt Ekland, fuck off, Bob! And that's something I've regretted all my life. Then just two years ago I was rushing out the door of Madison Square Garden and he was just standing there by the limousine, and I said, Bob! I gave him a big hug and said, Hope you got a good seat, and off I went. And I'm kicking myself thinking, Why didn't you invite him back for a drink? That was Bob Dylan!

Who said this: 'Rod is as tight as two coats of paint and a right cunt'?

Could be anyone really, couldn't it? A right cunt. Mmm. Dunno. Who said that?

Ronnie Wood.

Ronnie? Oh, that's great. Anyone else and I would have been offended.

Is it true that you have techniques for avoiding paying for rounds in pubs?

Oh, I've got loads. Open someone's car door for them in the car park then they have to go into the pub before you. And this one (*stands up*), I do this one after football. Go into the pub first, What do you all want, lads? Come on, my shout! Then as they all rush to the bar, I'm (*bends down, ties shoelaces*) and suddenly you're at the back. It's a good one, that.

What was the attraction of leopardskin print?

I think I'd seen it in some old movie book. I'm sure that I wasn't the first person to ever have a leopardskin suit.

What are the tightest trousers you've ever worn?

Tightest? Must've been those leotard things. (*Puts head in hands*) Fucking hell, why was I fucking wearing those fucking things? What was I thinking of? (*Composes himself*) Yes, my tightest trousers were probably during my Da Ya Think I'm Sexy period. To show off one's . . . toolbag.

I've heard that you're not very well endowed.

No, I'm not actually well endowed. I'm not, you know . . . fucking hell what are we getting into here? Here we go, what's the last thing you want to hear in a gents' toilet? Nice cock! (*Laughs*) But no, I'm just average. Happy enough with it, though.

At the time the Smiler LP came out, you described it as 'shit'. Do you stand by that?

Yep. Was and still is a piece of shit. It didn't sell. I was just doing the same as I'd done on the previous two albums. Instead of trying something new, I just did the same formula again but the magic wasn't there. I deserve a smack around the head for that one.

Were you proud that The First Cut Is The Deepest kept the Sex Pistols' God Save The Queen from the Number 1 spot?

Do you know, I wasn't even aware of that at the time.

Is it fair to say that by 1978 – the winter of our discothèque – you had become kitsch?

I think kitsch would be a wonderful word to use. Silly cunt is another word you could use. God, I'd lost the plot. Actually it was more '79. In 1978 I released Footloose And Fancy Free with Da Ya Think I'm Sexy on it. That was a good album. But Blondes Have More Fun with Alannah on the back cover of it . . . I don't know what I was doing. That sold six and a half million and there isn't a decent track on it. No-one ever asks for any track off that album. I think my fans were embarrassed by it.

And what happened to the visor?

Oh, stop! This is fucking cruel! Actually, Woody started off wearing those, so I must give him credit for that.

What part did you play in Elton John's drug downfall?

I didn't play any part at all. I was very supportive. I've been with him and seen everything he's done. I've been there. I thought at the time that he was a happy person and it turned out he wasn't. I mean, I can drink and do my drugs but he could go all night, 24 hours, and I'd be like, Fuck, Elton, I'm going to bed, and he's going, No you're not, you're coming to Watford with me, we're playing Liverpool. He'd go and have a shower, change and come out as Mr Director. I had an early warning system and he didn't. Woody's like that. He can go two or three days. He had a medical recently and he had a clean bill of health and the doctor told him to keep on doing what he's doing.

When was your coke period?

Round '79 until about '85, '86. But I get depressed, irritable. My nose gets fucking blocked up and I don't want to do it for another month. But, you know, if someone has a little bit . . . It's a good social drug for me. But the stuff you get now is horrible. You get nose bleeds, all sorts. In the old days it was pure. Are you the bloke who asked Elton if he'd put coke on his knob?

Yes.

That was very funny. I've never done that . . . I've put it up my bum though! Me and Woody in The Faces, when we couldn't get it up our noses, because they'd got so bad, we used to put it in fucking cold capsules. People have asked me if I've put it on my knob. What a waste. Errol Flynn used to do it, apparently, but in those days it was pure cocaine. We used to be able to get that pharmaceutical cocaine. Skull and crossbones on the bottle. Wonderful.

Have you really got a football pitch in your back garden in Epping?

Full size. One hundred and eighteen yards long, nearly 80 yards wide. In fact, I made it four foot wider today. Bigger than Ibrox. It's not as big as Villa Park but it's bigger than most Premier Division grounds. Two groundsmen.

What did you make of Nick Hornby's book, Fever Pitch?

Brilliant. Loved it. I'd like to get to meet Nick. He wrote in an article that he'd like to meet me and talk about music. I'd like to meet him and talk about football.

Do you have football dreams?

Oh, millions. I'm always in the blue of Scotland scoring the winning goal at Hampden in the last minute.

You're in a nightclub and Hotlegs comes on. What do you do?

It sounds good now. Robert Palmer once told me that Addicted To Love was influenced by Hotlegs. I wouldn't dance to it, though. I can't dance in clubs. On stage I'm fine but I'm too self-conscious of people watching me in a club, even if I've had a skinful. I used to be able to with the help of (*taps nose*) a bit of that in Tramp. But I'm getting old.

How much is a pint of lager?

Funny you should say that because my local publican hasn't made me pay for a drink in the 10 years I've been living near his pub, bless him. But I would say, let me take a guess. A pint of lager? About a pound and 10 pence.

Miles out. In London you're looking at two quid.

Faaaacking hell! Two quid! How much is a pint of Toby? That's what I drink.

Pound seventy.

Fuck. Still, at least I didn't say 35p or something, did I?

Have you ever lost your self-confidence?

Every time I go to write a set of lyrics. I don't consider myself a songwriter.

What's your best lyric?

Killing Of Georgie. That was a difficult subject to tackle at the time. This new song I've written called Muddy, Sam And Otis, I'm really proud of that. It's the best song I've written in 10 years. Mandolin Wind was bloody good for someone living in the Archway Road to conjure up all that American stuff.

When did you last hit someone?

Phew. I don't think I can remember. I'm not sure I would hit anybody any more unless I was provoked. I used to be able to handle myself back then. Oh, I know. A photographer in Australia. I knocked him back into a flowerbed and he sued me and won. Before that, I hit a geezer that owned a restaurant because he was pushing us out. He asked us to leave and I said,

I think we've spent enough money to be treated a bit civil. And he tried to get hold of me by the jacket. It was the last thing he did. He got an elbow. That's a fucking good question, though. Do you know, no-one has ever asked me that and I had to really think. I mean, it's nothing to be proud of but it really got me digging around in the old memory box.

What are you most likely to complain about in a hotel?

The smell of smoke in a room. Or mushrooms growing in the bed. But smoke can drive me mad. Otherwise, it's not getting things you've paid for. That's why we used to smash up hotels, not because we had nothing better to do but because you were paying top money and you weren't getting any respect.

What does it feel like to smash up a hotel room?

(*Whispers*) It's *great!*

If you were to do it now, in here, where would you start?

Usually there's a few guys sitting on the sofa and a couple of others come in, tip it over and they all fall off the back. Then it all kicks off. But we don't wreck rooms now mainly because it's so bloody expensive. It's funny, my eldest sister, Mary, she's nearly 63 and she loves it. She comes on tour with me sometimes in Europe and what we do is clear every stick of furniture out of one of the band's rooms. Curtains, pictures, the lot. Put it all in the elevator or the storage room. So he walks in, pissed, with a bird and turns the lights on – make yourself at home, darling – and there's nothing. Imagine that after a skinful. Brilliant.

Have you ever kissed a man with tongues and everything?

I've kissed a man . . . but let me finish. I want to get this in context! Guys kiss each other on New Year's Eve and such occasions. Or when one of the chaps scores a goal. But not what you're saying, not in a sexual context.

What would you cook me if I came round your house?

The best I could manage for you is eggs anyway you want them. Boiled, fried, poached. I'm not much of a cook.

How much do you weigh?

Hundred and seventy five, which is about five pounds too much right now.

What's in your pockets?

Nothing. Nothing at all.

Could you empty them?

OK. (*Turns out trouser pockets*) Oh, here's a phone number of an old mate I want to get in touch with. Bloke I used to knock about with in 1963. Apparently, he's lost the barnet and put on a right load of old suet.

What physical feature do you most dislike about yourself?

The nose. It ruins pictures. I can only be photographed from one side, otherwise it looks like a fucking huge banana. I'd change it if I could but it would ruin my voice.

Are you a good swimmer?

Totally useless. Owned a load of swimming pools and can't swim. They're for the children really, aren't they, swimming pools?

What do you wear in bed?

Nothing.

Do you have sensitive teeth?

No.

Can you whistle using your fingers.

No. (*Laughs*)

Are you any good at rolling cigarettes?

(*Laughs*) Fucking hell! No.

Do you go into the barber's and ask for 'a Rod'?

Oh, I'd love to! I'd fucking love to. I must do that. (*Ruffles hair*) It just does its own thing now. About four years ago I brushed it all back and I got loads of letters complaining, so up it went again. I started this hairstyle and I'll end it.

Your plane is going down. What is the last thing you do?

If I was suitably drunk I probably wouldn't give a shit.

What is the greatest song ever written?

The Flower of Scotland.

How would you stop Demi Moore harassing you in the work place?

I certainly wouldn't. I'd love it.

What's your most memorable sexual experience?

Oh, so many. I think sex in unusual places is always the most erotic. I'm very good in the back of limousines. Elevators I've had a go at but it's all over too quickly. I've shagged on balconies of hotels. As long as there's an element of danger. But, by and large, I'm a bed man.

Anything to declare?

I think that we've covered a very wide range of subjects. Good questions. But I hope this isn't a family magazine. You see, I'm just not PC, dear.

Before Rod takes his leave, he has a question of his own: why do British men always take their trousers down when they're drunk?

'Funny, innit?' he puzzles. 'I did it the other night in a nightclub in Monte Carlo. Few drinks and woof, fucking strides down, arse out.' A sudden thought grabs him. 'Hold on, I've got some photos.'

So he has. Lurid gloss-finish holiday prints that come with a free film and a running commentary: '. . . that's me well pissed' (shirt asunder, Oliver Reed-like state of advanced refreshment) '. . . one of me in my undies. What a slut!' (posing saucily in bedroom doorway wearing microscopic undertrousers) '. . . my old arse' (Rod's tanned buttocks on public display in busy nitespot) '. . . me in the electrical closet of this club with a saucepan thing on my head' (crammed into electrical closet of club with saucepan thing on head) '. . . my mate's bollocks' (outsized testicles at horrifically close quarters) '. . . this was Elton's birthday. I got him one of those old women's '70s hairdryers' (Elton beaming beneath head-encasing salon blower) '. . . and, oh, no I'm not showing you that one.' With minimal persuasion, Rod reveals the censored shot. It is a snap of his fragrant wife sitting on the lavatory, a lacy suspension bridge of knicker beneath her knees, an 'Aw-Rod-you-got-me-again' expression of patient resignation across her face.

'That's the missus on the kharzi,' announces Rod, brimming with artistic pride. He studies the portrait and, for a few moments, a mist of reflection, introspection even, clouds his brow. 'Hang on,' he frowns, 'I don't remember taking that one.'

HE GETS ALL THESE SEX STARVED YOUNG GIRLS WITH BIG BREASTS . . .

Oasis by Miranda Sawyer

'Arrogant. Big-mouthed. Self-centred. Rude. Crude. Sexist. And sickeningly talented.' Speak of the devil. Noel Gallagher, soft-spoken, hard-headed *überführer* of Britain's foremost rock 'n'roll band, Oasis, is slyly itemising what some see as his group's better points when his little brother Liam comes bowling into the bar, all mouth and trousers and slump-shouldered swagger. Everyone looks up, Liam, like all great lead singers, has a discernible notice-me aura – a baleful, chaotic, surly hurly-burliness that makes you stare at him; but not straight in the eye. He is very beautiful, despite his Play-Doh hairdo (short, but long *before* the ears). He shoots Noel an unreadable look and sits down at a separate table.

It's three o'clock in the morning. Four hours ago, in a tent on a wind-battered beach in Irvine, Strathclyde, Oasis were drawing a 6,000-strong gig to a triumphant close. Now, the bar of their hotel a few miles away is doing brisk, convivial business. As well as the band entourage – Noel and his contingent living large around one small table – there's a well-laced stag party whose groom-to-be has just finished eating a cigarette. 'For 1967,' he explains.

Noel is holding court. There are six music journalists here – representatives from Smash Hits, NME and Melody Maker – and there's nothing Mr Gallagher likes more than muso-chat. A genial, talkative 28-year-old, with terrible teeth, terrifying eyebrows and eyes that squidge into curved slits when he smiles, he is getting cheerfully worked up over Mojo magazine's '100 Greatest Albums Ever Made'.

'The Beach Boys! Fucking hippy California surf beach bollocks,' reasons Noel, a man whose musical allegiances become clearer when he tell you that he can't end a day without uttering the words 'The' and 'Beatles'.

A joshing, train-spottery discussion follows until suddenly, at the other end of the room, Liam lurches savagely to his feet. He growls something incomprehensible, hurls a half-full beer bottle at the ceiling, and stalks out. As an exit, it makes Cantona's Crystal Palace two-footer seem underplayed. He silences the room. But Noel doesn't even turn his head, doesn't skip a beat. 'And Stevie Wonder's only at Number 20,' he continues, as his fellow revellers goggle and gawp at the still-swinging foyer door.

When Oasis smashed their way into the nation's pop consciousness in April of last year with their cocksure debut single, *Supersonic,* much was made of Liam and Noel's brotherly unlove. The media portrayed them as constantly a-bicker; interviews would regularly end with the pair in hand-to-hand combat. Their difference? Noel thought Liam had some growing up to do; Liam viewed Noel as an overbearing know-all. The brothers' splutter and spleen kept the rest of the band – rhythm guitarist Paul 'Bonehead' Arthurs; bassist Paul 'Guigsy' McGuigan; with Tony McCarroll on drums, now replaced by Alan White – well back in the shadows, where they have stolidly remained.

After a platinum LP, *Definitely Maybe,* which sold three million worldwide, and seven Top 40 hits (including five Top 10s and one Number One, *Some Might Say*), the duo are keeping their fights private. The stereophonic media view of Oasis has gradually faded into one man yapping: Liam has been sidelined. Though the tabloids scream about who he supposedly spends his leisure hours with (Paula Yates; Helena Christensen), Liam doesn't get to talk about work these days. That's left to Noel. And the on-record squabblings are no longer in-house; instead, Oasis gripe about Blur.

Oasis versus Blur. Blur versus Oasis. You would have to have been living with your head in a bucket of custard for six months to have avoided such a Great Pop Tiff. Who do you support? Oasis: northern, no-nonsense rock blusterers with instant tunes and rent-a-lad demeanour? Or Blur: pouting southern art-ponces of crafted, crafty pop? The crucial colours-mast-nail interface occurred in the week beginning 7 August, with the simultaneous release of the singles *Roll With It* (Oasis) and *Country House* (Blur). After a week of breathless pan-media speculation, the 13 August chart revealed a fop-pop victory: Blur at Number One, Oasis Number Two. *Country House* sold 280,000 in its first week, rising to 400,000 in the second; *Roll With It* shifted 250,000 in its first week and about 350,000 overall.

Privately, Blur's people admit it was they who altered the release date of *Country House* to coincide with the Oasis single, though publicly they intimated exactly the opposite. But there was no way that the two bands' LPs would come out at the same time – far too much money at stake. So Blur's fourth album, *The Great Escape*, is already in the shops and universally lauded. Will the Oasis offering *(What's The Story) Morning Glory* do as well when it arrives in just over a week's time? *Definitely Maybe* earned them a Brit (for Best Newcomers) and a Mercury Prize nomination.

Noel calls *Morning Glory* '*Definitely Maybe*'s big brother' – as he would. If you press him further, he reveals that it sounds like 'half of it is sat in a hammock smoking a massive spiff and the other half is walking round the streets of England with a petrol bomb in its hand'.

More precisely, it's another supremely assured, rapid-fire, tune-packed rock album for boys, recorded in 15 days (*Roll With It* was laid down in one take). So far, Oasis songs are of two types: the elbows-out, balls-out R&B anthem of Friday-night urban masculinity (*Rock N Roll Star, Cigarettes And Alcohol; Hello* and *Roll With It* on the new album), and the slower, sleepily wistful, not-quite-love-song (*Slide Away* and now *Don't Look Back In Anger*). This time around, though, Noel's Beatles obsession has made things a touch more psychedelic: strings and swirls, songs occasionally extending into twiddly fuzz-guitar workouts.

Once again, his big tunes nestle immediately in the sing-along section of your memory; and his words are as vague, as hit and miss, as ever ('roll with it', 'feel no shame'; erm, 'caught beneath the landslide in a champagne supernova in the sky'). Oasis lyrics revolve around an unspecified 'me' and 'you', though 'you' occasionally has a girl's name. They're slack, occasionally ridiculous, often rabble-rousing, and sometimes – as in *Don't Look Back In Anger* – they can be gorgeous.

This last is the stand-out track on the LP, not least because of the vocals. It's Noel, not Liam, who's flexing his tonsils. The songwriter likes to warble a bit at gigs during his acoustic set, but *Don't Look Back* comes with full band backing, and when Oasis play it live Liam walks off stage.

'Yeah, well, that's his fault,' claims Noel, post performance, pre hotel, in a chilly little Portakabin set up outside the gig marquee. Noel pulls on a Benson and Hedges, hacks like Steptoe the Elder, and continues.

'I'd written these two songs for the LP, right?' he drawls in his Mancunian whine. 'One was *Don't Look Back In Anger*, and one was called *Wonderwall*. I wanted to sing *Wonderwall* because the guitars are acoustic, but our kid insisted that he wanted to sing it. So I said, all right, but I'm gonna do *Don't Look Back In Anger* then, and I have to play that with the band, and it's going to be a single at Christmas, and you won't be singing on it . . . I think,' grins Noel, a little nastily, 'he thought I was bluffing.'

Poor muddle-headed Liam. At a time when attention is being focused more and more on Noel, not only is the baby of the family missing out on interviews, he's also talked himself out of vocal glory. Don't you feel sorry for him? 'No, I do not,' sniffs his elder brother. 'He made his choice, simple as that. I'm 28, he's 23. I don't want to argue with him no more. I don't feel sorry for anyone. No. Why should I? It's not as though he's got a bad life, is it?'

Liam's life would surely have been very different if it hadn't begun five years after Noel's, in a small house in Burnage, south Manchester. The two shared a room: the root of all their problems, according to Noel. He can get on perfectly well with his older brother Paul (an unemployed labourer, easily recognisable at Oasis gigs from his Gallagher hedgerow eyebrows and his habit of wearing a Manchester City FC top with the club sponsor, 'Brother', emblazoned across it), but, he says, he will never forgive Liam for invading his space – ie, for being born – and also ' 'cos he wasn't a bird. At least then I could have gone out with his mates'.

By the time Noel and Liam were in their teens, their room was jammed with musical equipment: stereo, guitars, amps, microphones, bits of four-track recording machines – all Noel's. The posters – of the Jam, the Smiths, the Beatles, the Who – were his too. What did Liam have? Noel looks at me blankly.

'Nothing,' he says, eventually. 'Himself. And that was enough. Oh, and a Bananarama poster.'

Mrs Margaret 'Peggy' Gallagher, now a 'hardcore gardener' according to her middle son, then worked in the local McVitie's factory, pulling all the defective biscuits off the conveyor belt. 'That's what you used to get fed,' remembers Noel, unfondly. 'Come home from school and you'd have two ham sandwiches, a tiny little bottle of milk and about 60 Penguins and 70 Jaffa Cakes. Made you dead popular at school, though: "Here comes Gallagher The Biscuit".'

Mr Gallagher ('What's his name? Twat. No, Thomas') was, and still is, a Country & Western DJ who plays local Irish social clubs and weddings. Liam, reckons Noel, has his dad's temperament: 'a short fuse, a bad temper'. Noel resembles open, happy-go lucky Patty – though he doesn't sound too easygoing when he tell you that he hasn't seen his dad for 10 years, 'and it's not a big deal, but I don't want to, either'.

Still, it was his dad's guitar that Noel Thomas David Gallagher first plucked at the age of eight. A tiddler as a child (both he and Liam are slight now, a pocket-sized 5ft 7in), little Noel couldn't see over the top of the instrument, so he played it flat, on his knee, like a slide guitar. Left-handed, he taught himself to strum right-handedly. Then 'someone showed me *The House Of The Rising Sun* and I never looked back.'

He wrote his first song at 13. It was called *Badge* and it was about people wearing badges. 'The best line,' recalls the man now heralded as a living, in-one Lennon-and-McCartney, 'was: "And on your badge it says, Wear A Badge." Heheh.'

Soon after, the two other incidents occurred which were to radically alter the course of his young life. He went to see his first gig – the Damned at Manchester Apollo: 'it blew me head off' – and he lost his virginity. The latter sounds like quite an event.

'We were at the girl's house – she was bunking off school. And as we were upstairs, having it, we heard this almighty commotion and there's this knocking on the front door,' Noel recalls. 'So we thought, sod that, and carried on. When we finished, we looked out of the window and there was an ambulance. It turns out the dustman had had a heart attack and dropped down dead on the front doorstep! He'd been knocking to try and get us to call a doctor . . .'

In eerie synchronicity, there's a banging at the Portakabin door. It's Robbo, the tour manager, wanting Noel to sign autographs for the marrow-chilled fans waiting outside. Noel's good about things like that, possibly because Oasis is his first band. He writes his name quickly and easily on the proffered photographs.

Noel and Liam attract different types of appreciators. 'He gets all these sex-starved young girls with big breasts, right. I get all the psychopaths.' One thinks she has written every Oasis song before Noel did, in her dreams. And after *Supersonic*, which includes the memorable couplet 'I know a girl named Elsa / She's into Alka Seltzer', it seems to Noel as though every Elsa in the land has claimed the right to his innermosts. 'I'd just like to clear that one up. Elsa was a dog, right. A rottweiler.'

Noel finds lyric-writing tricky at best. Usually he just sings nonsense until he arrives at the first line and takes it from there. He steals phrases from all over. For instance, 'Stand up by the fireplace / Take that look from off your face', from *Don't Look Back*, is what his mum used to say to him as a kid, when she lined up the three boys for their annual Christmas photo to send to their granny in Ireland.

She must be very proud of you and Liam.

'She is. She's funny, though. When she sees you on the telly all she's arsed about is, do you think you could bloody smile? And, do you have to always go on about drugs?'

It could be argued that it was drugs that brought the band together ('Mind you, if we hadn't been tripping all the time maybe we'd have had that music conversation 10 years earlier,' comments Noel, dryly). He, Bonehead, Guigsy and Tony all met in the local park at Urwood Road, where a gang of about 40 kids would play football and gobble down the abundant magic mushrooms. Parklife indeed.

They would come back after a night's clubbing, nick a fleet of milk-floats from the local dairy and take them for a drive across the golf course: 'We were out of it. We'd think we were Robin Hood. You know, "Forsooth, you brigand, I shall take your truncheon for the people of Nottingham . . ." OK Sarge, I think we've got a live one here.'

It wasn't long before Noel was on first-name terms with the local constabulary. He advanced from shoplifting to swiping car stereos to burglary. So he turned his light fingers to more legitimate ways of making a living: bakery, sign-painting, fish-tank-making. Then, at 20, he wangled his way into a roadying job for bowlhead Mancunian then-contenders the Inspiral Carpets. Noel was a guitar technician for five years, touring the world, showing it the crack of his bottom, learning about the business.

What did you learn? 'I learnt that you don't make money unless you're as big as U2. I learnt that you'll get ripped off unless you're very careful. And I learnt that all record company people are twats, bar none.'

In 1992, he returned to find his kid brother Liam had set up Oasis. Noel said he'd join, but only if they all did exactly as he said, ' 'cos if you do, we'll be on *Top Of The Pops* in a matter of months. And we were . . .

'All I ever wanted to do was make a record. Here's what you do: you pick up your guitar, you rip a few people's tunes off, you swap them round a bit, get your brother in the band, punch his head in every now and again and it sells. I'm a lucky bastard. I'm probably the single most lucky man in the world – apart from our Liam.'

The band hierarchy remains unaltered from its original despottery. When Creation Records supremo Alan McGhee offered Oasis a deal on the strength of one performance (in Glasgow's King Tut's on Noel's 26th birthday, 29 May 1993: the band had bullied, blagged and bundled their way on to the bill), it was Noel who got them a manager.

Noel writes all the songs, Noel owns all the equipment, Noel makes all the decisions as to how the record sounds, what the artwork looks like, who does what, when, how and in which pair of trousers. Though Noel says that if anyone left, Oasis would no longer exist, this is not Liam's band, nor is it any of the others'. Nothing gets done here without Noel's say-so.

Doesn't that irritate the other members? 'They throw their toys out their prams sometimes, yeah.'

And wouldn't you? It must be unbelievably frustrating, especially when your boss is such a hard task master. Especially when he's just your mate – or even worse, your older brother. Especially when he's always right.

'The thing is, it's been two years now, and I'm still on a roll. And you have to keep busy when it's like that, because one day you're not going to be able to write anything,' Noel points out. 'But while it's happening, then these records are coming out whether anybody likes it or not.'

In those two years, Noel has met and made friends with the posters on his wall – Paul Weller, Johnny Marr, even Paul McCartney. He's not met and made enemies with the New Seekers (they sued him for nicking 'I'd Like To Teach The World To Sing' in *Shakermaker*) and Neil Innes from the Bonzo Dog Doo-Dah Band (over *Whatever*). He's split up with his long-term girlfriend Louise Jones, moving to London with just his guitar: 'People say I'll never find a girl like that again, but I'd rather be lonely and live like this.'

Also in those two years, Oasis have toured Britain four times, plus Japan, the United States, Canada and Europe, been deported from Sweden and Holland and banned from two hotel chains – giving hope, in the process, to a generation of unreconstructed, unironic lads who'd always had a suspicion that they were just the butt of Blur's joke. Two years ago, Noel Gallagher only wanted to release a record. Now he'd like to play Maine Road, and he's the star attraction on the Warchild charity record *Help*, released earlier this month to raise funds for Bosnian children.

The only bleak moments in their careers have been their failure to win the Mercury Music Prize this week and not beating Blur to the chart top slot. 'Look, they knew that if they put their single out the same day as us they'd go in at Number One. We're only concerned about being the best in our own eyes and we are and we always will be.' And can you remain friendly with them? 'The guitarist I've got a lot of time for. The drummer I've never met – I hear he's a nice guy. The bass player and the singer – I hope the pair of them catch Aids and die because I fucking hate them two.'

Oasis are at a strange and crucial point in their career. *Morning Glory* will establish their superstardom in this country and could well break the unbreakable America. But will the group shatter first?

Noel's ruthless work ethic and unrelenting restlessness – 'I'm bored all the time. And boredom's my greatest fear' – plus the band's runaway success and capacious capacity for recreational delights – 'I'm on a line of coke every 40 minutes,' confesses their leader easily – must eventually take their toll. As Oasis become more and more famous, more and more people want a piece of them. As a band they are slightly less reliable than previously (most of their UK tour has been cancelled because Guigsy is suffering from nervous exhaustion); slightly more paranoid. Noel has already started to make rumblings about their record company: 'A bunch of indie kids, man. They're too narrow-minded . . . they are not in the big league,' he huffs. 'It's not their job to be chaotic, that's my job.'

Still, Gallagher is clearly happier than he's ever been: 'To be acknowledged as a songwriter has definitely made me more content,' he beams. 'I know I will leave my mark. Even if I never write another song I've written enough now.'

And he remains ludicrously jovial about his future prospects: 'I've been a punter, a roadie, a pop star. Next? Junkie and ex-pop star, I'd say.' Even then it should be all right for Noel. He's even got a ready-made fairy mod-godfather in Paul Weller, with whom he duetted for the *Help* LP.

'He told me: "When you get to the point where you have lost it and you think you are never going to get it back, then I will be there for you. Because I've been there and I know what it's like and I came out of it and I'll make sure you do too." I was really touched. 'Cos he's right, I will lose it.'

So while Noel is floundering, what will happen to his band? How will volatile, thwarted Liam keep his jut-chinned head above water? Noel has not come this far for his feet to get chilly: 'Yeah, I stare at hotel walls and worry,' he grins, wolfishly, self-assuredly, unworriedly. 'I stare at them and wonder. "Where did it all go right?" '

WHITE, SOUTHERN & MIDDLE CLASS

Blur by Jessica Berens

The Devil's Music has taken a strange turn of late. It's become chipper; it's become cheeky-chappy, cockney-sparrer, fan-Phil Daniels-tastic. It is telling us of Mother's Pride and bingo and bank holidays and bringing itself on shamelessly with Solina organ and Wurlitzer arrangements that recall skating rinks and seaside amusement arcades. It is at its best when, with a small sneer, it steals a Syd Barrett lick and describes the tragedies of those who are doing what they feel they should rather than what they would like. We have heard about them before, these very British people, for their little lives have appeared in songs by The Kinks, Madness and Squeeze.

Now, somewhere along the line, the rebel yell has turned into a rowdy song in the back of the school bus and announced that it will never carry a piece or go out in a body bag. It is very white and it doesn't smell like teen spirit – it smells like Tommy Steele. You have seen the future of rock 'n' roll: its cultural gamut stretches from *Quadrophenia* to The Smiths to skatewear shops in Camden. It does not want to see any more Barratt homes or polluted rivers. It does not wish to be a mad axe hero. It is wearing black-framed spectacles and living next door.

Today, at a photographer's studio in north London, some members of Blur are taking their clothes off. If you were one of the 205,000 teenage girls who read *Sugar* magazine you would have to be taken away by St John's Ambulance at this point, because, if you were a reader of *Sugar* magazine, you would have been told, somewhere between page twenty ('the latest word on matt lippie') and page 78 ('my boyfriend gave me HIV') that Damon Albarn is 'The Lushest Lad Alive'. The Lushest Lad Alive is, of course, a most subjective view – convulsion is not compulsory – one might prefer the Even Lusher Ryan Giggs ('Sagittarius'). Nevertheless, the undressing of Blur is a most refreshing sight to a woman whose tired eyes are suffering from hysterical blindness due to the relentless trauma of watching *ER*.

Some of them are slouching in Barbours, smoking Camel Light, reading *Colette*, doing the *Times* crossword, and coughing in a slightly alarming way. Alex James, bassist, is tall and beautiful. 'What do I do to relax? Well, I drink quite heavily.' Graham Coxon, lead guitarist, wears a checked shirt and a badge saying 'Pontins'. He polishes his glasses. 'I'm astigmatic.' Dave Rowntree, drummer, is the oldest at 31. 'I'm married.' Damon Albarn is the singer. 'This shirt is too big.' He has a hairy chest and the love beads his mum gave him and jeans that fall down at the back because he is thin. Of the four he is the most disconnected, possibly because he has the most reason to protect himself. Certainly, at the moment, everyone wants a piece of him so he observes people before he makes friends with them.

'This shirt is too big.' Why this should be no one knows. He went into Ralph Lauren and chose it himself: neck size 16½. But it is too big and it has to go back. 'A cup of tea would be nice,' he shouts to no one in particular and puts on a tape of The Kinks. 'Waterloo Sunset' is followed by a recording of a message left on the answering service at his record company's office. A teenage girl lisps: 'This is just to say Damon I think you are fantastic . . .'

'Do you get a lot of that?' asks Rankin, the photographer. Everyone laughs. Damon laughs the loudest and leaps around, eyes rolling.

'Damon,' James explains, 'has got an incredibly big gob.'

James has a fanzine devoted to him called *Alexzine. A Damonzine* is also in the offing. Does this surprise them? 'Not really,' says James. 'We're all reasonably good-looking lads.'

'It's not that I'm God's gift to women,' says Damon later, 'but I have always been quite popular. I'm not one of these people who has gone from being utterly ignored to being utterly adored.'

A man in a green suit arrives with a bag and disappears into the make-up room in which Justine, the girlfriend of James, is working. Damon also has a girlfriend called Justine: Justine Frischmann, the lead singer of Elastica. This is muddling to the visitor but they have doubtless sorted it out amongst themselves and know which Justine is which.

'He has come to check my willy,' says James of the man in the green suit. 'It went black. I thought it might drop off. Over-indulgence or something.' The doctor, you will be glad to hear, gives the all clear. Appendage is destined to remain attached to pop person. Justine, the James girlfriend not the Damon girlfriend, gives a nervous giggle and a lot of thumbs up signs with both hands.

'Right everybody,' says Rankin, who has had an idea, 'go geek.' This is not a problem. Coxon combs his hair into a ludicrous pointy fringe; Rowntree mugs in a train-spotter hood; Damon puts on specs; they all hold hands, pull faces and become hideous. This is the most telling moment; the moment that reveals why they deserve the love of the universe. They have enough self-confidence to make themselves look ridiculous and this is the sexiest thing of all.

Blur formed in 1990, but last year they connected with the zeitgeist and won the pop lottery. Their third album, *Parklife*, sold over a million copies and spawned four top twenty singles, including the memorable 'Girls and Boys'. Their live show at Alexandra Palace slotted in between the Criminal Justice Bill and the World Cup as *Melody Maker's* fifth most important event of the year and the rest of the polls saw them jostling with the Manic Street Preachers and Oasis for various top positions. This year they won four Brit awards, appeared on the cover of innumerable magazines, and, in April, it was announced that their manager, Chris Morrison, had negotiated a publishing deal with EMI estimated to be worth between £2 million and £4 million. In June, they headlined to a crowd of 25,000 people at the

Mile End stadium. 'Wear a condom,' Damon told his audience. 'All right Granddad,' they shrieked back. This month, the release of Blur's fourth album, *The Great Escape,* sees them at their most British and most endearing, blessed, as they are, with an uncanny ability to make you laugh for no apparent reason.

Damon Albarn could be a hundred blokes. He could be you. That is what strikes one at Blur's party thrown in a Bethnal Green sports hall after the Mile End show. The party, for fans and family, was characterised by the slickest mod gear, mod hair, mod dancing with a lot of fancy leg-work, T. Rex songs and Blur mingling with autograph seekers. He did a royal round, Damon, in his Adidas jacket, for he is keen that pop music should be for everybody and Blur should not be cordoned off by celebrity. One little girl waited patiently for her autograph, only to be passed by unnoticed, for ordinary though he appears, and certainly more accessible than many musicians, there is a minder ushering him about: Smog. From Wolverhampton. Chosen, according to James, 'Cos 'e's big 'n' placid and fuckin' bastard 'ard.' Sometimes, when you are surrounded by Smog, it must be difficult to see out.

The Lushest Lad Alive is late – to Mike's Café in Blenheim Crescent, a place near west London's Portobello Road where it is possible to buy boiled bacon and two veg for £3.80. It is in the heart of Ladbroke Grove and round the corner from the big house where he has, according to one newspaper, a 'live-in leg-over arrangement', with 'Blur Indoors'. Her family come from Transylvania; his come from Lincolnshire. Her father is an architect; his wrote a book entitled *The Language of Pattern; an Enquiry Inspired by Islamic Decoration.* Justine Frischmann – stylish, strong, androgyne – writes short punky songs, one of which is about impotence but not about Damon. She bought Martin Amis' *London Fields* for him, which inspired some of the mad urban tribespeople who pop up in *Parklife;* he encouraged her to start a band. It was a good idea. This year Elastica's debut album went in at number one.

Sonny and Cher. Maurice Gibb and Lulu. Justine and Damon.

They are the new pop monarchs. He, sensitive, could be Queen; she, ballsy, could be King. Perfect. Will they marry? 'I don't think marriage is important,' he says. Does he want children? 'I think so but I don't know what the sequence of events should be these days. I get very confused. I think you should adopt, really.'

They have just returned from Glastonbury; Elastica played, Blur did not. On the way Damon read *The Story of Mr Sommer* by Patrick Süskind. It is about a man so debilitated by claustrophobia that he has to tie his legs to the bedpost in order to stop himself running about. 'My mum always gives me these books to make me feel better about m'self,' he says. 'That's the only bad thing that has happened to me over the last year – I developed claustrophobia just before *Parklife* came out, when 'Girls and Boys' was doing really well.' There is the theory that claustrophobia can be connected with fear of the mother's death. He is silent for a minute and nods. 'That is one of the only things that fills me with utter fear.'

The hangovers did not help; neither did the coke, though he says he was 'comically sparse' in his use of it. Once, when he was very young, he saw a friend of his parents, in a terrible mess, jacking up, and now he says 'I can't be positive about drugs,' almost as if he was ashamed of such a thing. 'My parents were very straight, although my mother hates me saying that in interviews.'

Nowadays, Damon is playing with those who totter at the top of the heap. He has sung with Ray Davies ('There are few people who can measure up to him – he's as good as Cole Porter'); hung out with Damien Hirst ('Buy one of his things? Nah, he'd give me one. I ain't paying for his two-bob tat . . .') and been courted by Tony Blair. A meeting at the House of Commons produced an affable conversation and the conviction that 'there is definitely a will to make amends for the damage that the Conservatives have done.'

He has very blue eyes, wonderful eyes, but his charisma lies in his detachment. It has been a conscious decision, this detachment. He is driven, he says, by a self-constructed urban mysticism which protects him, creates a distance, and gives him a life-support system in the absence of a religion. He sees himself as part Indian holy man, part lager lout, and, although the former is a reckless claim, there is something about his personal presence that corroborates it. In a crowd he is, as James puts it, 'an incredible show off – the natural-born front man'. On his own, he is different. Calmer. He drinks a cup of tea. Conscious that there are some who think he is pretending to be something he is not, that he is wearing a street cred to which he is not entitled, he is keen to explain why he is 'a fucked-up middle-class cockney who sings about the new Britain'.

Damon Albarn, son of Keith, was born in London's Whitechapel Road in 1968. Keith Albarn was a beatnik who liked jazz, was interested in Sufism, and designed light shows for the Soft Machine, a legendary but short-lived Sixties outfit known for one album and a series of 'happenings'. 'In the South of France they once set a whole coast alight,' Damon says proudly. His dad is a good bloke. 'He hasn't got the killer instinct that I have, or that obscene craving to be loved by everyone.'

Keith Albarn married Hazel, a set designer, and they bought a house for £3,000 in Leytonstone. 'Outside it was a Victorian terrace house; inside it was very strange. The front room was silver . . .' In 1977, the Albarns sold the house, silver and all, and moved to Colchester where they bought a fifteenth-century bakery. There wasn't much money but it didn't matter. 'It was made apparent to me at a very early age that you can be very happy and have a high quality of life without a great deal of money,' says Damon. 'I'm not motivated by money really.' He smiles. 'I met this man called Grub. He told me where to put it . . .'

Keith Albarn became principal of the local art college – making ever-dwindling funds go as far as he could. His son, meanwhile, developed 'several accents', a 'split personality', and a weird affection for Terry Hall.

'I was very much a Londoner,' says Damon. 'We lived in a dominantly West Indian and Pakistani community; then I was suddenly put into this new Britain where there were no blacks, no Indians, no Jews, and I was officially an outsider. I was strange. And I was in this environment where all the energy was chanelled into decimating the countryside and building Barratt homes. I saw it happen, from 1979 until I left. When I moved to Colchester the River Colne had hundreds of trout in it; when I left there were hardly any. I saw the destruction of rural Britain and I think this is absolutely integral to what I do.'

When he was twelve, Damon met a very small, very shy boy called Graham Coxon who had been born in Germany because his dad was in the army. Coxon taught himself to play lead guitar by listening to The Jam and later became fixated by My Bloody Valentine and The Pixies but, at that point, he was playing the sax. 'Damon was making a demo round at Michael Morris' house,' he says. 'Some soppy thing about beautiful ladies. I put a sax solo on it and we became friends.' They both attended Stanway, a comprehensive where some boys were skinheads, a lot of boys were in love with Morrissey, and where, according to Coxon, 'Damon would stare at people and check them out. People didn't like it. They used to hit him and I used to scarper.'

They separated when Damon went to East 15, a drama school in London, and Coxon, having compiled a portfolio of pictures painted in 'plastic paint stuff', was granted a place at Goldsmith's College, whose art department has recently launched a new race of conceptual artists. Exiled by the gravity of his peers, Coxon made few friends. He could not like people who didn't think *Blue Velvet* was funny. He once put a telephone into a bowl of soapy water and entitled it 'Dirty Phone Call'. No one laughed. So he made friends with Damien Hirst, who was older but understood, and with Alex James, who was doing French and lived in the room below.

'Graham was the first person I saw when I arrived,' says James. 'I was getting out of my parents' car and he was getting out of his. I remember looking at him very carefully, I thought he was dead 'andsome – I thought "shit – he's better looking than me . . ." ' James, who had left his Bournemouth grammar school with thirteen O-levels and three A-levels, remembers that Coxon's room was full of suits with moth holes, hundreds of pairs of second-hand shoes and a huge extractor fan. 'They were always collecting things from skips and making art out of it. He threw the fan out of the window one night. The bursar drove his VW camper van into it.'

They sat up all night talking about the meaning of things and the meaning of the meaning of things. 'If there is a genius in the band,' says James, 'it is Graham.' Coxon introduced him to Damon, who had the key to a recording studio because he was working there as a tea-boy. 'Damon was making really drossy, happy-time pop music,' says James. 'He was being so arrogant and boastful. I completely ripped him to pieces and he asked me to join the band. Damon always respects people who disagree with him.'

Dave Rowntree was recruited by Coxon, everyone dropped out of college, a record deal was negotiated with a small label named Food, and as they attracted the Indie crowd that still forms their fan base, the relationship evolved that has bound them together for six years. They have a 'scene'; hanging out in the Mars Bar, a restaurant in Covent Garden; in the Good Mixer in Camden; and at a drinking club named The Soho House.

'I do take the brunt of everything,' says Damon, 'but for taking the brunt I have more say. I think I have made it clear what everyone's roles are – any band that lasts a long time relies on each other in strange ways. I do have a lot more control but if I even sensed that I wasn't making the right decision they would be the ones who would sort of control me. I can't really pin it down. It must have something to do with the fact that we all have one sister and no brothers. We are quite fraternal. We don't have fights but we do shout a lot. Well, I shout a lot and they just laugh at me.'

The cementing of Blur is linked, like most friendship, to the test of crises. In 1992, they spent eight weeks touring America. 'We were all drinking very badly,' says James. 'Nobody was the least bit interested in us; Nirvana's *Nevermind* had come out and it was the beginning of grunge. Then we got back to England. We weren't famous any more and Suede were.' This must have been particularly pleasant for Brett Anderson, with whom Justine

Frischmann had been living before she fell in love with Damon. Blur drank more, slagged off Suede and fought with Food who rejected some of the material for their second album, *Modern Life is Rubbish*.

'We have been as low as it gets,' says Damon. 'We could have gone bankrupt two or three times easily.'

Blur's chosen apparel – sneakers, jeans, acrylic sportswear, aertex shirts, golfing hats that defy belief – hints at asexuality and reflects their non-materialism. Their look – naturally, ironically, inevitably – recently went down the catwalk in the form of Dolce & Gabbana Lycra T-shirts and Versace-clad dorks in drip-dry nylon. The man of the moment is Joe 90 in a designer shell-suit; understated to the point of invisibility. One wonders if, on some level, he has surrendered; the victim-imagery is underpinned by statistics that say, in Britain, more young men are committing suicide and less are passing exams.

Damon says that he writes 'inoffensive little songs' and 'makes a prat of m'self on stage', but, as a writer, he was also the child who saw the trout die in the River Colne and the worried teenager who believed the prophecy of Orwell's *1984* when he read it in 1982. For him and for those to whom he speaks, it is not death that represents the great unknown, but the future. In some ways, both dark intangibles have melded into one abyss where the apocalypse is a pretty sure thing. In his songs he relays comedy cameos about made-up people named Ernold Same and Colin Zeal, but he also knows that the real joke is that nothing is certain, that 'tomorrow I could just disappear'. Like the trout.

WHAT'S LOVE GOT TO DO WITH IT?

Ike Turner by Robert Chalmers

On Ike Turner's dressing table, half-concealed under 14 pairs of sunglasses and several videotapes of himself, there is a Bible kept open at Psalm 22. 'My God,' it begins, 'why hast thou forsaken me? I am a worm, and no man; a reproach of men, and despised of the people. All they that see me laugh me to scorn; they shoot out the lip, they shake the head.'

Other readers may be more pious, more learned or more conscientious, but few can be so well placed to empathise with these Old Testament verses as Turner. His public reputation – tarnished even before he shot his paper boy in the early 1980s – was finally obliterated by *I, Tina,* his former spouse's autobiography, which revealed him to be a cocaine addict and wife-beater. In the 1993 film version, *What's Love Got To Do With It,* his character is dominated by those rarely complementary traits, sadism and buffoonery.

In the early 1950s, Ike Turner discovered and encouraged such prodigious blues talents as Howling Wolf and Elmore James. An inspired producer, he was the creative force behind *Rocket 88* – widely regarded as the first rock and roll record – and Ike and Tina Turner hits such as *Fool In Love* and *Nutbush City Limits*. One of the crucial figures in the history of popular music, Ike has spent the past few years living on a housing estate in southern California, watching as his ex-wife's success and the ruin of his own career conspired to make him, to borrow a Les Dawson phrase, 'about as famous as Lord Godiva'.

My attempts to set up a meeting with Turner began 18 months ago. The first time I called him at home, the background noise was such that you could have been forgiven for assuming he was listening to a BBC Sound Effects record entitled *US Orgy*. He broke off at one stage to shout: '*Give me my wallet.*' Our subsequent discussions repeatedly foundered when he demanded large cash payments. This time, he agreed, he would be available at no charge, and even offered to meet me at his local station – Oceanside, near San Diego – and put me up for the night.

I took a late afternoon train down from Los Angeles anticipating a lively evening, bearing in mind Ike's best-publicised recreations: crack cocaine and firearms. A contributor to the American magazine Spin had told me that she once declined a similar invitation. 'Of course you should be OK – you're a guy,' she said, adding: 'but even guys can get shot.'

He was waiting on the platform, an unmistakable figure with his goatee, red and black hooped T-shirt and black shorts: Mephistopheles dressed as Dennis The Menace. Ike Turner is 64 this year, but looks at least 10 years younger; proof that the old maxim of rock 'n' roll's being 'good for the body, good for the soul' is probably half right.

We set off in Turner's gold Mercedes with Twana, his daughter, and Jeanette, whom he had married three weeks earlier. A white woman from Saint Louis, exactly half his age, her previous boyfriends include his son, Ike Junior. A degree of doubt surrounds the exact number of Jeanette's predecessors, but the consensus places her at number 13. Heather, Twana's three-year-old, slept peacefully as the man she calls 'Grandpa' cranked the stereo up to ear-splitting volume and grooved frantically to one of his own records. In a leather pouch behind the driver's seat was a photograph of Ike, autographed in gold. 'What's love got to do with it?' the inscription read. 'Not a damn thing.'

One the front door of his three-bedroom bungalow – mindful, no doubt, of his chequered history with commercial callers – Ike has hung a sign which reads: 'No soliciting'. In matters of home furnishings, his boldness is legendary: it was the understated nautical feel of his lounge in the 1970s (television in the shape of a whale, couch with tentacles, waterfall) that moved record executive Bob Krasnow to remark: 'Hey – so you really can spend $70,000 at Woolworth's.' His creative instincts are now sadly constrained by considerations of price, but Ike's house still includes a number of novel features, such as an air-freshner in the shape of a cello. His bathroom is so mercilessly colour-coordinated in pale orange that you become aware, on exit, of how a fly feels when it struggles free from a pot of full-cream apricot yoghurt.

Turner made a cup of tea, watched a film of himself performing and announced he was going to bed. Since he came out of jail in 1991, after serving two years for possession of crack, those who know him insist he has not touched drugs. Abstinence has not diminished his stamina: I was woken at 7.30 a.m. by the unnerving sight of Ike's face peering down at me, enquiring if I was 'ready to start now'.

As we sat down on the back porch in the early morning sunlight, his thoughts turned, as they often do, to *What's Love Got To Do With It*. 'The way they projected me in that movie, man,' said Turner, who has remarkably firm opinions about a film he claims he has never seen, 'they thought it was going to kill me. At the time I was doing drugs. Walt Disney gave me a lousy $45,000 – I didn't know, until I was sober and in jail, that I had signed away my rights if they portrayed me in a bad light. They murdered me in that movie.'

Turner is ill at ease giving interviews, and confides to friends that he feels his lack of eloquence leads him into trouble. His use of language is sometimes childlike, and rather endearing: you may hear new adjectives like 'flusterated', or 'orgy' as a verb. He stammers when excited, which is most of the time. Every so often he issued an impromptu embargo – warning that he would not talk about 'the Tina stuff', or 'the drugs', but moments later would be discussing the proscribed topic with passion and tenacity.

With his scorpion medallion, huge ice-diamond rings and the malevolent cackle of pantomime demon, there is much in Ike Turner that indicates conscious self-parody. Though he is eager to stress his complete reform, aligning himself with badness is an instinct which he cannot always stifle. 'That movie reversed on them,' he said. 'Kids come up to me today and say: "Ike – we ain't mad at you man. *Put that bitch in check.*" But some women look at it and say: "Hey, he's a monster." Overall, man, when she did that movie, she took my name away.'

Absurdly exaggerated though the film may be, the central allegations of violence are clearly proven in Tina Turner's book. There are simply too many sources, including a nurse from the local hospital, who confirm that he inflicted injuries on Tina and other women with implements including telephones, shoes and coat-hangers. He says he has never read *I, Tina,* though the collection of two dozen paperbacks on his bookshelf includes two copies.

Ike, in any case, has never been much of a one for books. Although he does seem always to have had Bibles around, he does not claim to be religious. His father was a Baptist minister in Clarksdale, Mississippi, but he, like his son, tended to find ecclesiastical ideals compromised by his secular interests. One of Turner's earliest memories is of the arrival of a posse led by the white lover of one of his father's girlfriends.

'They kicked our door down,' he said. 'There was a truckload of white guys in khaki pants. I think I was four. I know I was small, because when they pushed my mother over I was in her arms; I remember that. She tried to hold on to my daddy but they pulled him away and put him in the back of the truck and left. When they came back I heard the lady next door screaming.'

His father was dumped on the step – 'he had holes in his stomach from being kicked and stomped and stuff like that' – and subsequently refused admission to Clarksdale's white hospital. 'In those days in the South,' Ike said, 'being a black person was like being a cockroach or something. The health department put up a canvas tent for him outside our house. There was a little window with a drawstring: Daddy would spit into paper cups then pass them out, and I would take the cup and throw it away.' His one memory of the time before the beating is of seeing his father blow a cat to pieces with a shotgun. What was his reaction to this first encounter with sudden death? 'I was excited,' Ike said. 'Excited at what a gun could do.'

His father died of his injuries when Ike was about seven. His mother, a seamstress, remarried; at the age of nine he remembers being whipped with barbed wire by his stepfather, and responding by knocking him unconscious with a pole. His recollections of family life recall the ménage presided over by Mr Punch: a world of random brutality whose message to the young Ike could, you imagine, be summarised by the puppeteer's traditional refrain: 'That's the way to do it.'

'My stepfather would come home drunk,' he continued. 'One time he grabbed this material my mother was sewing. She took a hot skillet and went right upside his head with it. I saw that. But,' Turner added – suddenly aware that this account could help explain where he got the idea that GBH might be an appropriate response to domestic difficulty – 'I don't think that's got nothing to do with nothing in my life.'

He had piano lessons from Pinetop Perkins, Sonny Boy Williamson's accompanist, and evolved a repertoire which included Dr Clayton's *Cheating And Lying Blues*, better known for its refrain: 'I'm gonna murder my baby.' In 1951 the Kings of Rhythm, his first group, recorded *Rocket 88* – a celebration of the merits of the Oldsmobile 'Rocket' Hydra-Matic 88 – on which Ike (then travelling by pedal cycle) pioneered the frenetic piano style later espoused by Little Richard. He switched to guitar and recorded ground-breaking rhythm and blues records for labels including Sun, Chess and Modern.

Turner established a parallel reputation as an extraordinarily gifted talent scout. Hired in 1952 by the Bihari brothers, owners of Modern Records, he was given a Buick and $150 a week to tour the South. He returned with makeshift recordings of some of the greatest names in electric blues. 'I travelled round Mississippi with a tape machine in the trunk of my car,' he said, 'stopping at pool halls and saloons. I found Howling Wolf in one of them bars. Junior Parker, Rosco Gordon, Elmore James: I recorded all those people.'

Ike met Annie Mae Bullock in a Saint Louis nightclub in 1957. As Tina Turner, she became his vocalist, then his lover: a development that prompted Lorraine, his previous girlfriend, to shoot herself through the heart in Ike's bathroom. He had discovered his greatest protégée; an instinctive performer capable of realising his musical and erotic fantasies simultaneously. While Turner lurked upstage, with the sly panache and malevolent leer of a seasoned procurer, the Ikettes – backing singers whose obvious wigs, short skirts and sleazy *hauteur* perfectly embodied their employer's idea of a quality night out – accompanied Tina's frenzied rendition of songs like *Hurt Is All You Give Me* and *I Idolise You*.

These titles, like most of Ike and Tina's lyrics, have acquired a certain irony. At his own estimation, the instances of Ike's infidelity while he was with Tina run into three figures. His Saint Louis residence had been known as The House of Many Thrills; by the time he was running his own LA studio, Bolik Sound, in the early 1970s, even this feeble innuendo was superfluous; his private suite was known simply as 'the whorehouse'.

All the time you talk to Ike – about his session work for B B King, say, or the recording of *River Deep Mountain High*, during which producer Phil Spector paid him to stay out of the studio – 'the Tina stuff' hangs over your head. The unfortunate truth is that interviewing Ike Turner, before you broach the subject of marital cruelty, is like talking to Professor Barnes Wallis without either of you mentioning the bouncing bomb.

One of the best-known allegations is that, when Ike and Tina's first single *Fool In Love* was released in 1960, with Tina pregnant, jaundiced and in hospital, he forced her to discharge herself prematurely in order to perform. Tina left voluntarily, Ike argues, knowing that he was desperate to pay a lawyer following his alleged involvement in what he calls 'a scheme on paper' – or, as you and I call it, cheque fraud – a charge on which he was eventually acquitted. 'I got $167,000 out of a bank in Saint Louis,' he recalled. 'They indicted me. This guy that did it with me turned evidence against me and confessed. I couldn't touch the money, because I didn't know if the notes were marked.'

Before one show in Los Angeles, Tina swallowed 50 sleeping pills. In Ike's loose-leaf history books, such incidents become modern miracles in which his involvement is a benign encouragement to 'take up thy bed and walk'. 'She was lying on the hospital table,' he told me, 'with this bag for when she breathed. Suddenly it stopped moving. I said: "You're trying to take the chickenshit way out, and leave me with all these fucking bills." Tina and I,' he explained, 'had a sister-brother relationship. I said: "If you was going to commit suicide, why didn't you go to a god-damn overpass and jump in front of an 18-wheeler?" The moment I said that, the bag started moving. So whatever I said was the right fucking words because she's here today.'

Ike and Tina's memories of their wedding day – in keeping with their recollections of most things that happened during their 18-year relationship – are not entirely consistent. Speaking to Rolling Stone in 1971, Tina said the ceremony was 'one of those house things, little preacher things, sort of quiet'. Ike remembers their marriage certificate as a novelty item dispensed by a photographer in a Tijuana *cantina*. Whatever the true circumstances, there are not many interviewees, as someone once noted, who give you a better opportunity to use the line: 'When did you stop beating your wife?'

'I did no more to Tina that I would have someone do to my mother in the same circumstances,' Ike said. It is a response which he repeats like a credo. 'And I love my mother.' Could I take it that he would have no objections if I beat his mother senseless? I could not, Ike said, amiably. 'Not in this lifetime.' He has perfected his defence – he may have struck Tina, but never beat her up – to the point where he is, if not credible, then at least consistent in his own terms. Every blow of their last fight, in a limousine in Dallas in 1976, has been scrutinised with an attention to detail befitting the critical round in a world heavyweight contest. Tina's account has her fleeing, penniless and bloodstained, to a nearby hotel. Ike says that she kneed him in the chest and he hit her open-handed.

'I like Ike,' said one friend and long-standing collaborator of Turner's. 'He is funny, he can be generous and he is an unusually talented musician. But he is in denial. One thing I would say is that you should remember we came from a violent society. This is not an excuse, but I find it quite easy to see why people like Ike – and he wasn't the only one – behaved as they did. Everybody was beating the shit out of everybody. Sometimes,' he went on, 'I would be driving and they would be fighting in the back. Ninety per cent of the time I remember him starting it. She banged him once or twice. It wasn't pleasant. It never is.' Had he ever attempted to intervene? 'I tried. Nobody,' he added, 'could control Ike.'

When Ike and Tina separated, she renounced all financial claims on condition that she could keep her stage name. 'Other than that,' he boasted, 'I could have just grabbed me another Tina Turner and kept going.' Another Tina Turner? 'I know 1,000 girls,' Ike said, 'that can do what she did. In other words, man, there ain't no Tina Turner in reality. There is no Tina.'

Such grandiose assertions have hardly been confirmed by experience. In the first 15 years following their separation, Ike lost all his assets, saw his recording studio burn down and was sent to prison. Around the time that 150,000 people gathered to watch his nonexistent ex-wife at the Maracana stadium in Rio de Janeiro, Ike was going from door to door, staying with friends in LA. 'I didn't have 100 dollars,' he said. 'I didn't have a bicycle.'

In the early 1970s, he recorded a song which contained the line: 'Things go better with cocaine', a view he has since had cause to revise. He began to use the drug heavily in 1968, when somebody told him it enhanced sexual performance. A few minutes after warning me that 'I'm not even going to *talk* about that stuff', Turner gave a detailed and celebratory account of how he once drove through Los Angeles impersonating a police officer in order to confiscate crack.

The worst thing about the drugs, Ike believes, was that they made him 'procrastinate and philosoph-eye. I was always going to start work tomorrow,' he told me. 'Tomorrow never came.' His friends point out that Ike has not only stopped taking drugs, but rarely drinks, gave up cigarettes in 1992, and has managed to content himself with what, by his previous standards, are humble surroundings – at the same time coping, albeit splenetically, with his portrayal in a multi-million-dollar film where the only things missing were his tights and trident.

Public admission of fallibility, however, is still not Ike's forte. Taken at his own estimation, you might conclude that, as Watson said of Holmes: 'Other than cocaine, he has no other vices.' Concerning his arrest, he maintains that 'they never caught me with drugs. I *had* drugs but they never caught me with none. I had them in the gas tank of the car.'

Press reports in 1981 revealed that newspaper delivery staff in Ike's area, already struggling against such traditional impediments as dogs, inclement weather and tightly-sprung letter-boxes, now faced a new hazard: gunfire. What chapter of accidents could possibly have concluded with him shooting his paper boy? 'It wasn't an accident,' said Turner. 'I shot him purposely. He said: "Shut up, bitch" to the girl I was married to. I wasn't at home. Three weeks later, I asked him why. He said: "Go ask the bitch." '

In the face of this provocation, Ike's response was much as you might expect. 'I said: "Peace, brother. I will go and ask her." My bodyguard,' he went on, 'said: "Man – that guy has to have a piece, talking like that." ' Ike, who had already acquired two gunshot wounds and the sobriquet 'Pistol-Whippin' Turner' by the time he was 18, went on: 'I didn't know what "piece" meant.' He paused, like a colonial governor pondering some obscure tribal vernacular. 'It means . . . "gun".'

'So I reached up,' Turner went on, 'and got a .38. He said: "What are you going to do? Shoot me?" I said: "What do you think?" Pow! And I fired in the air.' Events took a turn for the worse, Ike explained, when he thought he observed a suspicious movement and shot his visitor through the leg. 'He sued,' Turner added. 'He got a million-dollar judgment against me. That paper boy was 49 years old and 6ft 7in,' he grumbled. 'That was the paper boy.'

How many guns did he have to choose from at the time? 'Fifteen or 20,' Ike said 'There wasn't no problem with guns.' Why did he maintain such a substantial arsenal? 'I don't know,' he said. 'I just *had* them. The machine guns went when my studio burned down.' 'Who . . .' I began. 'What do you mean *who*? Why does it have to be a *who*?' snapped Turner, who has been irked by unproven gossip about arson. 'It was an electrical fault.'

Such costly misadventure is a thing of the past, says the musician, who has become an enthusiastic supporter of Neighbourhood Watch – a development which cannot have passed unnoticed by those on the San Marcos estate for whom Ike Turner is now the contiguous link in the human chain protecting their life possessions. Eager to offer evidence of his rehabilitation, Ike showed me the running machine he keeps in his bedroom and the large tubs of Royal Jelly and vitamin tablets which, he says, account for his remarkable state of preservation. On subjects other than his past misdeeds, he can be humorous, engaging – almost *nice*.

'Ike,' one of his close friends said, 'once told me that there are two people in his head. There is Ike Turner, and another guy he calls Willy. Willy is the decent, sensitive person whose feelings are right there on the edge of his sleeve, who can be very easily hurt. And when Willy is in danger of being hurt, that's when Ike comes out, to take care of business.'

When Turner was released from prison, he stayed with his daughter Twana, an officer with the California Highway Patrol, whose mother had been one of the occasional visitors to the House Of Many Thrills. 'Very apprehensive' when she first made herself known to her father in the late 1980s, shortly before he was arrested, she says she has been surprised by the determination with which he has remained clean since. 'When he came out he was pretty much broke,' she said, 'but prison was the best thing that ever happened to him. I watch him now, taking my three-year-old daughter out for the day, and I think: "Well – this is the cracked-out coke-head Ike Turner. This is a man who, a few years ago, didn't know what it was to go to a beach, or walk in a public park." I'm very proud of him for what he has accomplished.'

Later that morning we drove down to the beach at Oceanside. In the car, Ike sang *Old MacDonald* for his granddaughter, chattered amiably about how he used to rub cocaine into his in-growing toenails, and described, in some detail, the sinus problems he has encountered since the drug perforated the septum dividing his nostrils.

Whooping with delight as he spotted a handicapped parking place ('We won't pay shit!'), Ike led the way to the beach bar where he ordered root beers and hamburgers. There was an indication that his re-education still has some way to go, when a jeep drove past carrying four young women in bathing costumes. Ike threw back his head and with his wife of three weeks at his side, began barking like a dog. 'Don't put that in,' said Twana. 'Women,' Ike mused. 'They have short pants – they cover them up. They have mini-skirts – they're always stretching them down. The next day they go out and buy a bikini.' 'Only you,' his daughter said, 'would think of that.'

As we walked along the sand, Ike talked about the difficulties of remaining faithful. A few weeks before he married Jeanette, he announced that 'I've had 12 wives, and I'm never going to marry again.' Watching his unambiguous greeting to a beach party of girls almost half a century his junior, it was difficult to be confident that he will stick on 13. 'The day I stop looking, man,' he said, 'that's the day I'm dead.' Monogamy must be harder, I suggested, for a touring rock singer than, for instance, an office worker. 'Yeah,' said Ike. 'Mind you – I'm pretty dangerous in an office.'

Unburdened of a cocaine habit that cost $300,000 a year, Turner says he is gradually restoring a degree of order to his finances. Interest in his back catalogue still generates substantial royalties: an early Ike and Tina track, *I'm Blue*, for instance, was sampled on *Shoop* from Salt 'N' Pepa's 1993 album *Very Necessary*. In Britain, Ace Records has just released *Rhythm Rockin' Blues*, a collection of his early recordings. He is currently preparing to tour with the Ike Turner Review, a nostalgic recreation of his lowlife stage act from the 1970s, which includes Jeanette as a backing singer. With the help of an English admirer, he has completed his own book, entitled *Takin' Back My Name*. In a typically Ike-esque development, the British publishers have had to delay distribution because another company claims he previously sold the rights to them.

A thoroughly candid account of Turner's life, rigorously researched, might just have been the rock publishing event of the decade. Early indications, however, suggest that objectivity, penitence and trenchant self-analysis will not constitute the keynotes of *Takin' Back My Name*. Neutral observers will hope that he manages to avoid the sometimes unchivalrous tone of a series of articles in the Sun in 1987, in which he and others accused Tina Turner of lesbianism, baldness, masochism, having varicose veins and keeping 'enough firepower to kill 10 men stuffed between her boobs'. For those unwilling to wait for publication, Ike recently inaugurated a special telephone line which gives a brief summary of his views on what he considers the major questions.

For a charge of a dollar a minute, callers to 1-900-990-IKE-1 are greeted by a tape-recorded female voice with the vacant civility of an American car-rental agent. 'Hello,' it says, 'if you would like to know if Ike feels he was used by Tina to launch her career, press one. If you want to know whether Ike was a wife-beater or Tina was a masochist, press two. If you would like to know if Tina was ever pregnant by a band member, press three . . .'

It is the source of some consolation to Ike Turner's admirers that, when the history of popular music is written, his pioneering work with Howlin' Wolf, B B King and the Kings of Rhythm is likely to be celebrated more keenly than his former wife's MTV anthems such as *Private Dancer*. Where his own history is concerned, Ike's continuing reluctance to articulate remorse condemns him to the rank of disgruntled outcast – a position he may occupy forever, unless Willy masters the art of public speaking.

Permissions

For permission to reprint copyright material the publishers gratefully acknowledge the following: ELVIS PRESLEY CALLS HIS MOTHER AFTER THE ED SULLIVAN SHOW by Samuel Charters (Coffee House Press 1994). © Coffee House Press 1994. THE BEATLES IN YORK AND LONDON from *'Love Me Do!'* by Michael Braun (Penguin 1964). © Michael Braun 1964, reprinted by kind permission of Jonathan Clowes Ltd. THE FIRST TYCOON OF TEEN by Tom Wolfe first appeared in *The New York Herald Tribune* in February 1965 and later anthologised in *The Kandy Kolored Tangerine Flake Streamline Baby* (Farrer, Straus & Giroux 1965). © Thomas K. Wolfe, Jr. 1965. DIRTY BLUE SUEDE SHOES by Michael Lydon first appeared in *Rolling Stone* on December 7, 1968. © Straight Arrow Publishers Inc., 1968. All rights reserved. Reprinted by permission. MISSIONARIES OF APOCALYPTIC SEX from *The White Album* by Joan Didion (Harper Collins 1979). © Joan Didion 1979. Reprinted by permission of the author. THE YEAR OF THE SHARK from *Hammer Of The Gods* by Stephen Davis (Sidgwick & Jackson 1985). © Stephen Davis 1985. THE TRUE ADVENTURES OF THE ROLLING STONES by Stanley Booth (Heinemann 1985). © Stanley Booth 1985. I NEED MORE by Iggy Pop (Karz-Cohl Publishing 1982). © Iggy Pop 1982. THE LEGENDARY TROGGS TAPES by Mat Snow first appeared in Q in May 1991. © Mat Snow 1991. KEITH

MOON: THE ROLLING STONE INTERVIEW by Jerry Hopkins first appeared in *Rolling Stone* on December 21, 1972. © Straight Arrow Publishers Inc., 1972. All rights reserved. Reprinted by permission. MAMA'S DREAMAWAY LOUNGE from *The Rolling Thunder Logbook* by Sam Shepard (Viking Penguin 1977). © Sam Shepard 1977. Used by permission of Viking Penguin, a division of Penguin Books USA Inc. A DAY ON THE RIVER from *Style Wars* by Peter York (Sidgwick & Jackson 1980). © Peter York 1980. RETURN TO SENDER by Albert Goldman first appeared in *Arena* in 1991. © Albert Goldman/Shpritzgun Productions Inc 1991. SCUM ALSO RISES by Nick Kent first appeared in *The Face* in August 1986. © Nick Kent 1986. WHEN WE WERE GLASS by Adair Nye and David Quantick first appeared in *Arena* in March 1989. © David Quantick & Adair Nye 1989. THE GREAT GREENLAND MYSTERY by Danny Baker first appeared in the *NME* on April 4, 1981. © Danny Baker 1981. LONG TIME GONE by David Crosby & Carl Gottlieb (Doubleday 1982). © David Crosby & Carl Gottlieb 1988. Used by permission of Doubleday, a division of Bantam Doubleday Dell Publishing Group, Inc. SIMON LEBON: THE FACE INTERVIEW by Fiona Russell Powell first published by *The Face* in February 1984. © Fiona Russell Powell 1984. THE STRANGE AND MYSTERIOUS DEATH OF MRS JERRY LEE LEWIS by Richard Ben Cramer first appeared in *Rolling Stone* on March 1, 1984. © Straight Arrow Publishers, Inc 1984. All rights reserved. Reprinted by permission. TROUBLE MAN by David Ritz first appeared in *Arena* in March 1994. © David Ritz 1994. FRONTLINES: ANNIE LENNOX by Julie Burchill first appeared in *Time Out* on January 23, 1985. © Julie Burchill 1985. HOME THOUGHTS FROM ABROAD by Frank Owen first appeared in *The Melody Maker* on September 27, 1986. © Frank Owen 1986. POOR BOY, RICH BOY GEORGE by Mick Brown first appeared in *The Sunday Times Magazine* on April 12, 1987. © Times Newspapers Limited 1987. MADONNA: THE PROS & CONS first appeared in *The Tatler* in September 1987. © The Tatler, Conde Nast Publications Ltd 1987. THE SUN AND THE STAR by John Sweeney first appeared in *The Independent Magazine* on February 11, 1989. © John Sweeney 1989. WHAT MAKES

MALCOLM RUN by Alix Sharkey first appeared in *20/20* in June 1989. © Alix Sharkey 1989. AGEING SMOOTHIE by Tony Parsons first appeared in *Arena* in September 1989. © Tony Parsons 1989. AXL GRINDING by Georgina Howell first appeared in *The Sunday Times Magazine* in 1992. © Georgina Howell 1992. WHO THE HELL DOES RINGO STARR THINK HE IS? By Tom Hibbert first appeared in *Q* in June 1992. © Tom Hibbert 1992. SEX AND DRUGS AND ROCK 'N' ROLL, ESPECIALLY SEX by Mike Sager first appeared in *Spy* in February 1993. © Spy Magazine 1993. Reprinted with permission from Spy Magazine. THE MAN WHO FELL TO EARTH? by Charles Shaar Murray first appeared in *Arena* in May 1993. © Charles Shaar Murray 1993. THE DEVIL IN U2 by Sean O'Hagan first appeared in *Arena* in December 1993. © Sean O'Hagan 1993. A CRISIS OF FAITH by Robert Sandall first appeared in *The Sunday Times Magazine* on December 5, 1993. © Robert Sandall 1993. A DEATH IN THE FAMILY by Steve Dougherty, Johnny Dodd, Bill Donahue and Craig Tomashoff first appeared in *People* on April 25, 1994. © Time Inc 1994. DON'T DO THAT ON STAGE ANYMORE by Ian Penman first appeared in *The Wire* in 1995. © Ian Penman 1995. CHARMED ROBBERY by James Brown first appeared in *Loaded* in June 1995. © James Brown 1995. TOP BREEDERS RECOMMEND IT by Adrian Deevoy first appeared in *Q* in July 1995. © Adrian Deevoy 1995. HE GETS ALL THESE SEX STARVED YOUNG GIRLS WITH BIG BREASTS by Miranda Sawyer first appeared in *The Observer Life Magazine* on September 17, 1995. © Miranda Sawyer 1995. WHITE, SOUTHERN & MIDDLE CLASS by Jessica Berens first appeared in British *GQ* in October 1995. © Jessica Berens, GQ, The Conde Nast Publications Ltd 1995. WHAT'S LOVE GO TO DO WITH IT? by Robert Chalmers first appeared in *The Observer Life Magazine* on October 1, 1995. © Robert Chalmers 1995.